D1625301

Ancient Syrian Copper Cross at the Syrian Catholic Church,
Muttuchira, Kerala, India

CHRISTIANITY IN INDIA

A History in Ecumenical Perspective

Edited by

H. C. PERUMALIL, C.M.I., & E. R. HAMBYE, S.J.

Published by

Prakasam Publications
Alleppey, S. India.

Printed at St Paul Press Training School, Dasarahalli,
Bangalore 560022

FOREWORD

The story of the birth and growth of Christianity in India is profoundly interesting. It is as old as Christianity itself. Even before the first century A.D. there were extensive trade connections between the Malabar Coast and the Western World. There were many in Europe and the Middle East who had a fairly good knowledge of the geography of the West Coast of India and the customs and habits of the people inhabiting there. Perhaps it was this fact that induced St. Thomas to start for India to carry out his mission at the very commencement of the Christian Era.

Apostle St. Thomas, it is believed, arrived in Kodungallur, which was then known as Mouziris, and began his work of delivering the message of his Master. That is how this place became the cradle of Christianity in India. Places like Parur, Kokkamangalam, Niranam and Palayur (Chowghat) give ample evidence of the pioneering work of early Christians and their connection with Hindu worship in early days. The Christian Church at Palayur (Chowghat), for instance, is situated in a locality where remnants of Hindu worship are seen even today. Proofs are not wanting to believe that many converts to Christianity came from some of the Orthodox Hindus of this place. There were Jews, Brahmins and other caste Hindus among the converts made by St. Thomas. He succeeded in getting some ardent followers who worked with faith and devotion in response to the call of their leader. To give the religion a firm footing, St. Thomas consecrated bishops and priests from his first followers and set up seven churches in seven different places in Kerala. There are some families existing today who feel proud of the fact that their ancestors were priests first consecrated by St. Thomas himself. The Thomas Christians are those who claim their origin from the Apostle. Among them there are different ethnical groups similar to the Hindu castes of the place in which they dwell. Traces of Hindu culture are noticeable in some of their customs even today. For example, "a new-born babe was fed with powdered gold mixed with honey or ghee after its birth. When it was eleven months old it was given boiled rice to eat in the midst of family celebrations. Leopard's toes and mangoose teeth formed part of the ornaments of children. A child beginning to learn the alphabet was made to write the first letter with its finger in raw husked rice. All these are distinctive of the high caste non-Christians of the country from among whom, according to tradition, was formed the first nucleus of the Thomas Christians." (The Thomas Christians—P.J. Podipara, C.M.I.,p.80).

After satisfying himself of the progress of his mission in the West Coast, the Apostle proceeded to the Coromandel Coast to continue his work of evangelisation. While engaged in that he was assassinated by his enemies in Mylapore near Madras in 72 A.D. His body lies buried in a place near Mylapore which ever since is known as St. Thomas Mount.

The domination of the Portuguese in the 16th century made the position of the Thomas Christians rather unhappy. The Portuguese had two ends in view—the conquest of the land and the conquest of the Thomas Christians. They thought that the conquest of the land would be easy if they were able to bring the people to their side. With this objective they tried their level best by coaxing and coercing the people to accept their view but they did not succeed. The Portuguese then adopted more stringent measures against the Thomas Christians. They burnt the historical and liturgical books of the Thomas Christians and compelled them to renounce all Hindu practices and customs. Thus they made all possible attempts to Latinize Thomas Christians and succeeded to a very large extent. It is said that Christianity in India till then was "Hindu in culture, Christian in religion and oriental in worship". The Portuguese put an end to all this. The Kerala Thomas Christian community has yet to regain its former status, especially in the changing circumstances of this country.

The story of the growth and development of Christianity in India is a thrilling one. At first the work of its followers was confined to the preaching of the Gospel and spreading the Message of the Master. Gradually the pioneers began to pay attention to the needs and requirements of the people for a better and happier life. The contribution of the Christian Missionaries in the field of education is substantial and beneficial. For a very long time Christian Missionaries have been trying to spread primary and even higher education in India. They regarded educational institutions not only as means of combating ignorance, but also as centres for building up character and instilling high ideals. Educationalists like Dr. Miller, Dr. Larsen and Dr. Skinner of Madras and Father Heras of Bombay have left behind them a record of unselfish service, the memory of which will ever remain green and fresh in the minds of the people of India.

The Christian Missionaries have also made valuable contribution for the development of the language and literature of the places in which they lived and worked. Their contribution in interpreting the wisdom and culture of India to westerners by translating books from Sanskrit and other Indian languages into European languages, is unique. There is no denying the fact that Christianity has enriched the composite culture of India by adding its own share.

They did praiseworthy work in their fight against ignorance, dirt and disease. The Y.M.C.A. Re-construction Centres, the Agricultural Farm at Katpadi, the Medical College and Hospital at Vellore, and London Missionary Hospital at Neyyoor bear ample testimony to their welfare work in general.

There are over 500 hospitals and dispensaries scattered throughout India and Pakistan under the auspices of Christian organisations, doing excellent service to the suffering people. It is difficult to exaggerate the good work that is being done by the Christian Missions in mitigating the sufferings of the disabled and physically handicaped, like the blind, the deaf and lepers. Their work in reforming and rehabilitating Criminal Tribes is equally praiseworthy.

There is now noticeable a growing tendency among the Christians in India to cast off their foreign embellishments and to Indianise themselves in their customs and practices.

It is the 1900th Anniversary of the martyrdom of St. Thomas that is being celebrated in 1972. It is a unique occasion which will be celebrated in a fitting manner.

The Prakasam Publications have to be congratulated for bringing out this Volume, which contains informative articles from eminent scholars and historians, which I have no doubt will be read with interest and profit by Christians and Non-Christians alike.

K.P. Kesava Menon

'Mathrubhumi'
Calicut, April 18, 1972.

INTRODUCTION

The celebration of the nineteenth hundredth year since the death of St. Thomas the Apostle gave us the idea of preparing *this History of Christianity in India.*

There have been in recent years several attempts both in this country and abroad at publishing on Christian history in India. This includes those sections on India which are found in various general historical works. Will it be too much to say that some of those contributions fall short of our expectations? Without trying to dismiss them unjustly they have been often either Jejune, or sometimes even one-sided.

There is however no lack of special studies, also very modern ones, on the many local Churches, regions, missionary societies, various works and associations, and personalities. All these have composed in course of time the variegated picture of Christianity in India as known today to its citizens. It was thought that the writing of such a *History* was not only a fitting tribute to the apostolic origins of the Church in this country but met also a common and long felt need.

Yet the least acquaintance with Christianity and Christians in India shows how vast is the area to be covered, how numerous and varied the details to be enlisted, how intricated the problems to be reviewed, how challenging the manysided developments to be explained. These difficulties are not lessened by the minority character of the Christian communities in this country. For, as it is well-known, minorities tend to protect, if not enhance, their prestige by making doubtful claims concerning their ancestry and origin.

It was soon found out that the only possible solution within the frame-work of a medium-size *History* would be the ecumenical one. Not only can this approach lead to an honest evaluation of the Christian past in India, but it also corresponds to the inner urge of the Churches, both at the national and international levels. India indeed has been one of the most active workshops of the ecumenical movement for the last hundred years at least. Her Christian sons and daughters are today engaged in a crucial re-appraisal of their identity within the nation and the world.

Our *History* does not claim to have succeeded in covering each and every fact, and in describing every personality of some importance. It was not meant to do it either. It was our common understanding that whatever Christianity in India stands for today should be given its proper historical background. As far as possible unnecessary duplications have been avoided. It cannot be denied however that our treatment suffers from some omissions, and quite consciously at that. In more than one case the methods through which the Christians in India dealt with their contemporaries have not been sufficently expected; problems of language and culture have not been always given due emphasis; the contribution of christianity to the developme*nt* of fine arts and scientific investigation has on the whole been left out. However in a short appendix a summary of the Armenian presence in India has been provided on account of its historical importance.

From the start we became convinced that such a complex history, seen in an ecumenical perspective, needed a team of competent scholars. One of our first collaborators came from the Church of Mar-Thoma, the Reverend Dr. T.V. Philip. His years of training were spent both in India and in the U.S.A. (Hartford). Not only is he today the professor and head of the Department of Church History at the United Theological College, Bangalore, but he has enjoyed much ecumenical experience, e.g., as the secretary of the World Student Federation at Geneva. Miss M.E. Gibbs, who is an Oxford and Manchester scholar, was for many decades an active member of the Anglican Church in India. Until her retirement in 1962, she was professor of history at St. John's College, Agra, for thirty years; since 1952 she was also the head of the Department of History there. She has to her credit several learned articles, and two books, the more recent one being a history of the Anglican Church in India (1972). The Syrian Orthodox Church in India gave us one of its ablest young scholars, the Reverend Dr. N. J. Thomas, Principal of St. Stephen's College, Pathanapuram (Kerala). His doctoral thesis in German on the History, Liturgy and Customs of his Church prepared him well for his present task.

The other contributions belong to the Catholic Church. Dr. G. M. Moraes, besides the books and many articles that go to his credit was well-known until recently as professor of history at the University of Bombay; today he is in charge of the post-graduate students at the Panaji Bombay University Extension and Research Centre. Since the First Order of the Carmelites has in India nearly 350 years of unbroken tradition, one of its members, Rev. Father Dominic of St. Theresa, O.C.D., also came forward to participate in this work. While being the rector of the Pontifical Seminary at Alwaye, he is also the professor of Church history and missiology. He has published books and articles on historical, missiological and spiritual subjects. One of the best specialists today concerning Christian origins in India is Father A. M. Mundadan, C.M.I., who recently became one of the three provincial superiors of the Syrian Carmelites of Mary Immaculate, though he still keeps his professorship in Church History at Dharmaram College, Bangalore. His two books on the Thomas Christians and his articles are of the best critical type. Though a resident in Rome for many years, Father Joseph Wicki is a Swiss Jesuit, member of his Order's Historical Institute, and editor of St. Francis Xavier's Letters and of the *Documenta Indica,* the most complete collection of Jesuit documents on India for the 16th century; he is also one of the directors of the post-graduate studies at the Gregorian University. Nobody can ignore today the lasting influence of the Franciscan Order on the Indian Catholics thanks to the many books and articles that have come from the learned pen of Father Achilles Meersman, O.F.M., who has been on Indian soil since 1934; he is a *lector generalis* of his Order, and teaches Church History to many students in Bangalore.

A word must aslo be said about Father Hormice C. Peru-malil, C.M.I., who is the chief editor of this publication. Like his *confrere* A. M. Mundadan and Dr. T.V. Philip, he hails from an ancient Thomas Christian family of Kerala. After having enjoyed a vast experience in many fields, he is today the General Editor and General Manager of Prakasam publications, Alleppey (Kerala), a Christian publication firm which have already left its mark on the world of Malayalam literature. It is entirely due to his initiative and perseverance that the present volume could be prepared and completed. It was due to consideration for him that I undertook to help him in this task, my only qualifications, besides the debt I must acknowledge here towards my History Professors both in the Society of Jesus and at Louvain University, are those of a professor of Church History at the Jesuit Theologates of Delhi (Formerly at Kurseong) and Poona, and my abiding interest in Early Christian and Jesuit history in India.

Each contributor was given full freedom within the limits set to his respective subject. Owing to their personal and scholarly approach, this historical survey of the Indian Church has considerably gained in the quality of its information and the worth of its interpretation. May they be all thanked most sincerely for their unflinching collaboration and their selfless work.

The very character of this volume as a symposium obliged us to print the bibliography for each character at the end of the text. It has to be noticed that this bibliographical account varies a good deal according to each author's wishes.

This *History* could not have been completely usable, if at all, without adding a list of chronological events, a general index of names and places, and some maps. We are indebted for the latter to the skill of Br. Matthew Elamkunnapuzha, C.M.I.

Our work could not have been completed without the co-operation, sometimes entailing heavy services, of some of the C.M.I. students of Dharmaram College, Bangalore, and others of the Jesuit De Nobili College, Poona. We thank them all very cordially.

E. R. Hambye, S.J.,
Asst. Editor.

PREFACE

In the context of the proliferation of profane, obscene and frequently anti-God literature, the Prakasam Publications were started as a modest attempt to counteract the evil by providing sound reading material of cultural as well as religious value. Over 30 books and two souvenirs have already been brought out, and they have all been well received by the reading public of Kerala. To mark the 19th Century of the Martyrdom of St. Thomas, the Apostle of India, we are bringing out this Volume as well as another one in Malayalam entitled *Kristu Mathavum Barathavum*.

We have been singularly fortunate in bringing together in this Volume a galaxy of eminent scholars, specialists in their respective fields: Rev. Dr. T.V.Philip, Miss M.E.Gibbs, Rev. Dr. N.J.Thomas, Dr. G.M.Moraes, Father Dominic of St Theresa, O.C.D., Father A.M.Mundadan, C.M.I. Father Joseph Wicki, S.J., and Father Achilles Meersman, O.F.M. Our sincere thanks are due to these learned contributors. We are particularly obliged to Father E.R.Hambye, S.J. who condescended to become the associate editor of the volume. But for his encouragement and guidance this volume would not have seen the light of day.

A lot of other people have been of assistance to us in this noble endeavour. Special mention must be made of the Scholastics of Dharmaram College, Bangalore, and those of De Nobili College, Poona, Mr.C.A.Sheppard and Fr.Sebastian Poonolly of Devagiri College, Calicut. It is to the skill of Rev.Mathew Elamkunnapuzha, C.M.I., that we owe the maps in this volume. We are grateful to St. Paul's Press, Dasarahalli, Bangalore, and its Manager Rev. Vincent Joseph Njarackatt for bringing out the volume so neatly and in so short a time.

We are very much obliged to Mr. K.P.Kesava Menon who, inspite of his advanced age and numerous preoccupations, could find time to grace the volume with a learned 'Foreword'.

It is our hope and prayer that this little volume may lead to a better understanding of the Church among non-Christians and to a greater co-operation among the Christian Churches in India.

H.C.Perumalil C.M.I.,
for P.B.S., the Publishers

CONTENTS

CHAPTER I

ORIGINS OF CHRISTIANITY IN INDIA
(1st—6th CENTURY)

A. M. Mundadan C.M.I.

There are two views among scholars about the origins of Christianity in India. According to one, the foundations of the Church in India were laid by St. Thomas, the Apostle, or even by two Apostles, St.Thomas and St.Bartholomew. The other view would ascribe the arrival of Christianity in India to the enterprise of Christian merchants and missionaries of the East Syrian or Persian Church. Those who propound the apostolic origin do not deny the role of the East Syrian Church in reinforcing Indian Christianity. In this chapter we will first examine the apostolic claim, and then deal with the early contacts of India with the Church of Persia.

I

APOSTOLIC ORIGINS

St. Thomas in India

The most ancient record about the apostolate of St.Thomas is the New Testament apocryphal: *Acts of Apostle Thomas,* written in Syriac in the Edassan circle about the turn of the third century A.D. Even though this work has been acknowledged as apocryphal, Gnostic in origin, and romantic in style, several scholars admit in it a historical nucleus which represents the second century tradition about the apostolate of St. Thomas in India.[1] Besides, a number of fragmentary passages in other writings of the third, fourth and the following centuries speak in unambiguous terms about the Indian apostolate of St. Thomas. From the fourth century onwards the major Churches are unanimous in their witnessing to the tradition.[2]

In spite of this constant tradition in the West, a small group of authors do not hesitate to deny outright that St. Thomas ever went to India or to any countries of East Asia. A larger group would restrict his apostolate to north-west India. The majority of scholars, however, support a South Indian apostolate of St. Thomas. Several of the last group assign greater importance to a South Indian apostolate in view of the living tradition of the community of the St. Thomas Christians (or Syrian Christians) of Malabar, and the tomb of Mylapore.[3]

The possibility of one or two Apostles of Christ having preached the Gospel in India, and even in China, no serious-minded scholar would object to. At the dawn of Christianity there were trade routes connecting the Near East and the East, routes very much frequented. The land routes reached parts of North India, while the sea routes reached the coasts of Malabar and other parts of South India.[4] The tradition as it is found in the *Acts* and in the witnesses of various authors and Churches make this possibility a probability. Add to this the living testimony of the community of Thomas Christians and the witness of the tomb of Mylapore, the Little Mount and the St. Thomas Mount in the vicinity of Mylapore, together with the traditions connected with these monuments. In such a combination of the various traditions scholars are inclined to find an argument of convergence in favour of a certitude of the apostolate of St. Thomas in India.

The contents of western tradition may be summarised here. St. Thomas, following the well-established trade routes, reached India some time in the middle of the first century of the Christian era. He preached the Gospel in Parthia and India, converted many, including members of royal families, suffered martyrdom in India, and was buried there; later his mortal remains were transferred to the West (to Edessa) where they were honourably deposited and venerated. The *Acts* describes the journey and activities of the Apostle in a romantic manner, and much of it is the fruit of fertile imagination. Still the following points have attracted the comments of serious students of history. His apostolate in India is supposed to have begun in the kingdom of Gudnaphar. The ruler asks his guest Thomas to build him a palace. But the Apostle spends the alloted sum on the poor, and the angry king puts him in prison. Thereupon, Gad, Gudnaphar's brother, dies and when brought to life narrates the beauty of the palace Thomas has built in heaven. The King receives baptism together with his brother, and the Apostle preaches faith all through the country. He then passes on to another kingdom at the invitation of its king, Mazdai. Here too he converts many. At last he is stabbed to death by the King's order on the top of a hill, half a mile from town. Long afterwards a son of the ruler falls sick. Mazdai had the tomb of the martyr opened up for the relics to give his son a healing touch. But, to his dismay, the bones were found missing, "for one of the brethren had taken them away secretly and conveyed them to the West."

Many attempts have been made to identify the kings mentioned in the *Acts* and to locate their respective kingdoms. It is suggested by several scholars that Gudnaphar might be a king of North India (probably the writer of the *Acts* had in mind Gondophares, who reigned in North-West India some time in the first century B.C.), and Mazdai a South Indian king ,who ruled some time in the first century A.D. in Kerala, or in Coromandel, or even in the present-day Mysore. Attempts were also made to identify even Gudnaphar with a South Indian King, e.g. Kandappa (or Kutnappar) Raja.5 The description of the place of St. Thomas' martyrdom would easily suggest Mylapore as the town of king Mazdai.

What we have exposed above is conveniently called western tradition as it originated outside India. This tradition is generally taken as based on the *Acts of Thomas*. Therefore those authors who deny any kind of historic value to this work, deny absolutely the Indian apostolate of St. Thomas; while those who assert the North Indian apostolate attribute some historic value to the *Acts*. However, Farquhar, and after him a few other scholars, take the view that the Acts alone cannot be the source of western tradition, which is constant and universal from the beginning of the fourth century, particularly since the *Acts* were acknowledged by certain Fathers already in the fourth century as apocryphal. There must have existed already before the composition of the *Acts* some element in the oral tradition about the apostolate of St.Thomas, which probably formed the nucleus or the point of departure for the romantic *Acts.* These authors argue that the western tradition is not a single tradition, but the combination of two traditions, of which one originated in Edessa and the other in Alexandria.[6]

Indian Tradition

As against the western tradition there is the Indian tradition, handed from generation to generation by word of mouth among the Christians of St. Thomas and to some extent among their non-Christian neighbours. This tradition might be considered to consist of elements of the traditions of Malabar, Mylapore or Coromandel, and the Chaldean Church. Some details of this combined tradition may be found in a few songs (e.g. the *Rabban Pattu,* the *Veeradyan Pattu,* the *Margam Kali Pattu* and others), and some historical accounts both of which now exist in written records.[7] But these written accounts in their present form cannot be traced farther back than the 18th and the 17th centuries. Nevertheless, the people of Malabar undoubtedly possessed a rich oral tradition, which were reflected fully or partially in their folk songs and even in written annals. And all these various vehicles of tradition were available in the 16th century to the inquisitive Portuguese, who made ample use of these sources and wrote down their accounts in the form of letters, reports, depositions, and well-composed histories. Such accounts went on accumulating during the whole of the 16th century and well into the 17th century. They are today the richest, and perhaps, the earliest written sources of the Indian tradition on the apostolate and tomb of St. Thomas.[8]

According to the Indian tradition, St. Thomas came by sea, and first landed at Cranganore about the year 52 A.D.; converted high caste Hindu families in Cranganore, Palayur, Quilon and some other places; visited the Coromandel coast, making conversions; crossed over to China and preached the Gospel; returned to India and organized the Christians of Malabar under some guides (priests) from among the leading families he had converted, and erected few public places of worship. Then he moved to the Coromandel, and suffered martyrdom on or near the Little Mount. His body was brought to the town of Mylapore and was buried in a holy shrine he had built. Christians, goes the tradition, from Malabar, the Near East and even from China used to go on pilgrimage to Mylapore and venerate the tomb.[9]

In the 16th century the Portuguese were told of this burial place by the natives and others, and were taken there by Armenian merchants on a pilgrimage. This was in the year 1517. From that year onwards the Portuguese began to visit the place and even settled down in Mylapore. In a few years they discovered many other places and monuments in the vicinity of Mylapore, such as the Big Mount and the Little Mount. In the year 1523 they excavated the tomb and found a few relics therein.[10]

The Indian tradition, in which elements of the traditions of Malabar, Coromandel and the Persian Church intermingled, firmly held: Thomas the Apostle died near the ancient town of Mylapore; his mortal remains were buried in the town; it was his burial place situated in the right-hand chapel of the church or 'house' known after his name, that the Portuguese excavated in 1523. In spite of this firm belief of the Christians in India, objections have been raised against the authenticity of the tomb. A number of scholars appear to share the view expressed by L.W. Brown: "It is clear that the identification of the Mylapore tomb as the burial place of St. Thomas the Apostle and the ascription of special sanctity to various places in the locality—St. Thomas Mount and the Little Mount—were entirely the work of the Portuguese, whose known attitude towards the saints, and eager desire to find apostolic relics do not induce confidence in their historical judgment or critical examination of the facts."[11]

This categorical statement that the identification of the tomb was the work of the Portuguese may not hold water when one makes even a casual examination of the records which refer to the tomb of St. Thomas before the "unreliable" Portuguese appear on the scene. Beginning with the *Acts of Ap. Thomas* (c. 200), almost in every century we have one or more testimonies to the existence of the tomb in India. From the 7th century starts the specification of the place name: "Calamina" or "Qali-maya" in India (7th and the following centuries), Myluph or Meilan (12th—14th centuries). From the end of the 14th century onwards there are many references to the tomb, and all these references are, beyond any doubt, to the church and tomb of the Apostle Thomas in Mylapore. It is remarkable that once the identity of the place is established we find that it is no other than Mylapore, and that no other place has put forward any serious claim of possessing the grave of the Apostle.

What we have indicated above should be a convincing proof against the contention that the identification of the tomb was the work of the Portuguese in the 16th century. We are quite justified in saying with Figredo that the Portuguese did not discover the tomb. No, it was known to exist and they were informed about it by European travellers, 'Armenian' merchants and the Christians of Malabar. Barros is right when he says: "When the Portuguese reached India in 1498 the Christians of that country were unanimous on the point that the Apostle St. Thomas suffered martyrdom at Mylapore.[12]

To resume the points so far discussed, about the turn of the third century we have the testimony of the apocryphal *Acts of Thomas* concerning the Indian apostolate of St. Thomas. This romantic account is probably based on a historical nucleus, representing the first and second century oral tradition. From the fourth century on there is unanimity in the Churches about the tradition. It is likely that this tradition has a double, independent origin.

Now the question is what part of India the tradition assigns as the field of St. Thomas' apostolic activity. The *Acts* seem to point to North India as well as South India. A distinction may be found in the case of the other sources of the western tradition. The ante-Nicean writers generally mention Parthia (eastern Persia and north-west India), while the post-Nicean references prefer the general term, India. From this it may be concluded that in the western tradition the apostolic field of St. Thomas can be North India and / or South India.

For the early christianization of North India we do not possess any actual vestiges as we have for that of South India. The South Indian claim to the apostolate of St. Thomas is supported by two monuments: the community of St. Thomas Christians with their living tradition; and the tomb of Mylapore, which is definitely identified as the burial place of St. Thomas at least from the 14th century onwards. The conclusion seems to be inevitable. St. Thomas the Apostle preached the Gospel in South India. The origin of Indian Christians is to be ascribed to this preaching.

St. Bartholomew the Apostle and India

Two ancient testimonies about the alleged apostolate of
St. Bartholomew in India are those of Eusebius of Caesarea
(early 4th century) and of St. Jerome (late 4th century).[13]
Both of these writers refer to this tradition while speaking about
the reported visit of Pantaenus to India in the second century.
According to Eusebius, Pantaenus, "is said to have gone among
the Indians, where a report is that he discovered the Gospel according to Matthew among some there who knew Christ, which
had anticipated his arrival; Bartholomew, one of the Apostles,
had preached to them and had left them the writings of Matthew in Hebrew letters, which writing they preserved until the
afore-said time..." St. Jerome would have that Demetrius, Bishop
of Alexandria, sent to him India, at the request of legates of
that nation. In India Pantaenus "found that Bartholomew, one
of the twelve Apostles, had preached the advent of Lord Jesus
according to the Gospel of Matthew, and on his return to Alexandria he brought this with him written in Hebrew charact-
ers..." Eusebius appears to be not quite sure of the reported
fact; Jerome is more forthright.[14]

Previously the consensus of opinion among scholars was
against the apostolate of St.Bartholomew in India. Beginning
with the Bollandist; Fr Stiltingus, S.J., a few have supported
his Indian apostolate. But the large majority are still sceptical
about it.[15] Their main argument is that the India of Eusebius
and Jerome should be in fact Ethiopia or Arabia Felix. Two recent studies, one by Fr.Perumalil and the other by Dr.Moraes,[16]
have attempted to show that this argument is untenable. They
hold that the Bombay region on the Konkan coast, a region which
just have been known after the ancient town Kalyan, was the
field of Bartholomew's missionary activities, and his martyrdom.
The town of Kalyan, situated as it is at the north-east end of the
Thana Greek, was an ancient port and it is supposed to be the
"Kalliana", the traveller Cosmas Indicopleustes visited in the
6th century as he reports in his Christian Typography.[17]

According to Pseudo-Sophronius (7th century) St. Bartholomew preached to the "Indians who are called Happy", and
according to the Greek tradition the Apostle went to "India

Felix". The word *Kalyan* means "felix" or "happy", and it is argued that the Kalyan region came to be known to the foreign writers "India Felix" and its inhabitants, Indians "called the happy". Fr. Perumalil interprets the "India Citerior" of *Hieronymian Martyrology* as western India, and the "India" of the *Passio Bartholmei* as the Maratha country.

Now for the Indian apostolate of St.Bartholomew there is no Indian tradition as we have one for St.Thomas. This absence, Dr.Moraes would explain, is due to the fact that the history of the Christians of Bartholomew got intermingled with that of the Thomas Christians who came under the control of the Persian Church. And in the tradition of this Church Bartholomew was associated with Armenia and not with India. Fr. Perumalil, however, thinks that the Bartholomew Christians continued as a separate community till the coming of the Portuguese and then got merged with the Christians of Bombay.

II

HISTORY OF CHRISTIANITY AFTER THE APOSTOLIC TIMES

From the discussion on the Indian apostolate of St.Thomas, it is obvious that, to assess the origins of the Christianity in India, there is no other way than to have recourse to tradition. This is generally true also with regard to their history till the end of the 15th century. A few records do exist both in the West and in the East, which refer to the existence of Christians in India in the ancient and mediaeval times, but they are few and far-between. The western records contain very jejune references to occasional visitors from Europe who came to India and saw scattered communities of Christians. Almost all of them testify to the existence of the Church and community of Mylapore. As far as the first six centuries are concerned we have first a reference to a certain Theophilus, apparently a native of the Maldives, who was sent in 354 to his native Island and to India by Emperor Constantine. Again in the 6th century we hear of a monk, Theodore by name, of having visited India and reported to Gregory of Tours about the house or monastery of St.Thomas in India.[18]

The records of the East, particularly those of the Church of Persia, are richer when compared to those of the West. They give us an inkling of the relation of the Church of India with that of Persia. The contents of the records may be examined after we have drawn the picture one gets from tradition.

Where are we to search for the tradition? The living memory of a community is a depository of tradition. Several attempts have been made to tap this source and put into writing the oral tradition. Fr.Bernard's Malayalam history of the Thomas Christians contains a good deal of this; the works of L.W.Brown and E. Tisserant give some of it.[19] The earliest source of the tradition seems to be the same as those indicated in connection with the Indian tradition on St. Thomas: a few folk songs, oral tradition contained in one or two narratives. The Portuguese documents of the 16th and the 17th century are richest of all. The value and importance of these accounts can be gauged from the following considerations. They are from the pens of those Portuguese who penetrated rather deeply into the life, customs and traditions of the community. They drew freely on the oral tradition, folk songs, written accounts and Syriac books which the then community possessed. It should be borne in mind that the oral tradition and folk songs must later have shed much of its 16th and 17th century richness and liveliness in course of time; and that almost all the local accounts, especially the Syriac books, perished in the *auto-da-fe* programme entered upon by the Portuguese before, during and after the Synod of Diamper. This loss is compensated in some measure by the extent Portuguese records on the 16th century tradition of the community of the Thomas Christians.[20]

About the origins of the Thomas Christians as a community, varying versions were available to the Portuguese in the 16th century. According to one version, the origin is entirely the fruit of the apostolate of St.Thomas on the Malabar coast. According to another, the community originated from those people who were converted to the Christian faith by the Apostle on the Coromandel coast, and who migrated into Malabar and settled down at various places. Other versions would combine these opinions and say that the community of the Christians of the Malabar coast consists of Christians converted by the Apostle Thomas in Malabar and of those who emigrated from Mylapore. Almost all the Portuguese reports on the tradition agree that there had been once a flourishing community of Christians on the Coromandel coast and they at one time or another had migrated to Malabar. As to the cause of the migration, there are different views: some speak of natural disasters like floods, earthquakes; others would have man-made disasters like war, persecution and so on.21

The Church of India and the Church of Persia

The original community, whether it consisted of Malabar elements alone or Mylapore elements only, or of both, is alleged to have undergone, in course of time, a decline. But it was reconstituted and reinvigorated by groups of Christians who came from Persia (Chaldaea or Babylon). It is beyond doubt that some kind of relation between the Christians of India and the Church of Persia existed from very early centuries. The tradition of the Christians of St. Thomas is rich in stories regarding these relations. Two events are especially told of how the Church, founded by Apostle Thomas, came into contact with the Chaldaean Church in the middle of the 4th century, and how these relations were further reinforced in 8th or in the 9th century. The first is the arrival of a group of Chaldaean Christians in the company of Thomas of Cana, and the second, the arrival of another such group together with Mar Sapor and Mar Peroz (or Prot). We shall meet them again in the next chapter.

Here a word about the Church of Persia or Chaldaea is called for. It is the Church which exists and existed in those regions which were once the Persian Empire, the great rival of the Roman Empire; i.e., the Church more or less of the present Iran and Iraq. As this part of the world was successively ruled over by the Babylonians, the Assyrians, the Chaldaeans, and the Persians, it has been known in history by these various names. Assyria, Babylon, Chaldaea, and Persia. Also the Church in this part has been called by all these names, and some others in addition, e.g., Church of Mesopotamia (Euphrates-Tigris valley).

The civilization which was built up in this region by each successive people was predominantly a commercial one. This is only natural because it lay at the cross-roads of the ancient east-west and north-south trade routes. These trade routes were greatly helpful to the activities of the missionaries of the Chald-aean Church. The commercial language continued to be Chald-aean or Aramaic (East Syrian) even after the Persians took over the reins of the Empire in the 6th century B.C. And the people (merchants and missionaries) hailing from these parts were generally known in Malabar as "Arameans", and their country as "Aramea"— terms which the Portuguese confused with "Armenians" and "Armenia".

The beginnings of Christianity in Persia are shrouded in legends. Though the name of the Apostle Thomas is intimately connected with the Church, two early missionaries, Agai and Mari, are reputed as the founders. The lot of the Church was much affected by the changing politics of the country. When the Roman Empire became Christian in the 4th century, the Christ-ians of the Persian Empire were suspected by their rulers of divided loyalty. The persecution which followed fostered in the Christians a tendency towards what is called centrifugalism—the desire for forming a national Church more or less independent of the Antiochian Church, which was situated within the Roman Empire, and to which it was juridically subject. The Christolo-gical controversies of the 5th century contributed their share to this spirit of independence. The Synod of Markabta Tayyayye (424 A.D.) took the first steps, and the Synod of Seleucia-Ctesi-phon (486 A.D.) made the final step towards independence. These two events are looked upon by many authors as schism and as the acceptance of Nestorian heresy respectively. But there are others who refuse to subscribe to such a view.

In any case the Church of Chaldaea, now beyond any sus-picion of disloyalty to the fatherland, and enjoying more or less permanent peace under the Sassanid rulers of Persia, developed from the end of the 5th century onwards its own theology, canon law, liturgy and so on. The first repercussions of the Moham-medan occupation of Persia (from 642 A.D.) were not too dis-astrous for the Church. But in course of time the Christians were reduced to the status of second rate citizens, and many were also forced to abandon their faith.[22]

Regarding the relations of the Chaldaean Church with India, two events stand out in tradition to which reference has already been made. Thomas of Cana is reported in slightly different names and appears variously as a merchant, traveller and pilgrim. He and the Chaldaean Christians who came with him allegedly played a great role in the organization and building up of the Church and community of Cranganore. Many interesting stories are told about this man. Cranganore, wh'ch was previously a waste land, is said to have been transformed into a Christian city by him.

It is significant that tradition puts the arrival of this colony of Persian Christians in the 4th century when a state of persecution against the Christians prevailed in their homeland.

The Northist-Southist endogamous division among the Christians of St.Thomas is attributed to the arrival of Thomas of Cana and his men. The Portuguese, who witnessed many quarrels between these two rival groups during the 16th century, came across several versions about the cause of the division. They derived their own conclusions from the stories they heard and put forward a number of plausible explanations for the origin of the division. The theory that one group (the Northists) originated from the missionary activities of St. Thomas the Apostle and the other from Thomas of Cana, appeared to the majority of the Portuguese as most acceptable.23

One of the local sources of tradition, the account of Fr. Matthew, puts these events more or less in the following manner. After the death of Thomas the Apostle, the Malabar Church was left without a preacher and leader, and after 93 years there were no priests at all. At that time a pagan magician called Manikkabashar (Manikkavachakar) appeared. He went to Mylapore and worked wonders by his magic, seducing many Christians from the true faith. Those who remained faithful took refuge in Malabar and were kindly received by the believing brethren there. After that the 160 Christian families were for several long periods left without priests and leaders. Divisions also sprang up among them at different times for various reasons. Some of them left the orthodox faith, but others persevered.

In a vision at night the Metropolitan of Edessa saw the sad plight of the Malabar Christians and the next day narrated his vision to the Catholicos of the East. The latter, on hearing the dream, sent messengers to all the Churches, monasteries and towns under his jurisdiction and summoned all the Christians before him. Great multitudes, with their respective bishops and merchants, gathered before the Catholicos who addressed them and told of the vision. One of the faithful, a certain Thomas of Jerusalem, said that they had heard about Malabar and India from strangers. The Catholicos ordered him to visit Malabar and report back. Thomas, accordingly, set sail and arrived in Maliamkara, where he met the Christians of St. Thomas, who narrated him everything. After consoling them, he returned to the Catholicos, who thereupon showed his readiness even to sacrifice his own life for the Christians of Malabar. Thomas came back to Malabar with the Bishop, who had the vision at night, priests and deacons, men, women and children from Jerusalem, Bagdad and Niniveh. They landed at Maliamkara in 345 A. D.

The native Christians gladly received them. After much thought and consultation, all proceeded together to "Sharkun" the King of all Malabar. The latter complied with all their wishes, gave them as much land as they wanted; conferred upon them royal honours and inscribed the grant and the honours on copper plates. These plates were preserved among the Christians when this account was written (1730). Then they returned and built a church and a town. The Church was erected on the land of Kuramakulur (Cranganore), which was given to them by the King. The newly built town stretched from the East to West, and 472 families dwelt in it with authority.

From that time onwards Syrian Fathers used to come to the town by order of the Catholicos of the East, because it was he who sent the Syrians to other parts of the world until they were superseded. These Syrian Fathers governed the diocese of India and Malabar.

Thus in tradition, Thomas of Cana already appears as the link which brought the Chaldean Church into such direct and intimate communication with the Christians of India. This intimacy the Portuguese came to know on their arrival. The Jesuit Dionysio, after having narrated the Thomas Cana and Sapor-Peroz stories, concluded: It is why this Christianity has such an affection and respect for the Bishops who came from Babylon and Syria. Monserrate, another Jesuit priest, also tells us that it was consequent on the arrival of Thomas of Cana that the Christians of Malabar accepted the rites and ceremonies of the Syrian Church, because Thomas always managed to get Syrian bishops for Malabar where they were held in great esteem.24

Documentary evidence, as it has been pointed out earlier, not only corroborates a number of points stated by tradition, but also sheds clearer light on certain others which are rather obscure in tradition. The few records found in Eastern sources, mainly in Syriac and Arabic literature, are particularly precious from this point of view.25

References, earlier than the 6th century, are casual, and all of them are not of indubitable authenticity. The following instances, however, may be mentioned. In the list of the Bishops, who attended the Nicean Council of 325 is mentioned one "John, the Persian", who according to the history of Gelasius, written in the second half of the 5th century, was bishop of the whole of Persia and Greater India. This statement may be an indication of the situation, obtaining not necessarily in the beginning of the 4th century, but at the time of Gelasius' writing.26

A few other cases found in the *Chronicle of Seert* are of greater historical value.27 The Chronicle speaks of Bishop David of Basrah, who sometimes between 250 and 300 A.D. left his episcopal see and journeyed to India where he did conversion work. Many are supposed to have accepted his leadership and submitted to his preaching. David was considered by the chronicler as one of the eminent doctors of the Persian Church.

Mana, a writer of the last quarter of the 5th century, is said to have sent his translations of Diodorus to different countries including India. He was the Metropolitan of Re-Ardashir between 485 and 497. The same chronicle gives yet another instance which happened at the close of the 6th century. A certain Bishop Maruta (also called Parwa) was ambassador of the Byzantine Emperor Maurice (582-602) to the Sassanid Emperor Khosrau II (590-628). In Seleucia-Ctesiphon, the capital, he met the Eastern Patriarch Sabrisho I (596-604), and received as presents from him perfumes and gifts, which used to be sent to the Patriarch from India and China.

To this list may be added the name of a certain Bod about whom J.S. Assemani speaks. At the end of the 6th century he bore the title of *periodeutes* (Syriac: *periodiota*). The title meant a delegate of a bishop entrusted with teaching and visiting Christian communities, generally in country-side or in regions situated away from centres. This Bod is supposed to have been conversant with Sanskrit, according to the source used by Assemani.[28] How authentic the text is, it is difficult to say.

The *Christian Topography* of the traveller Cosmas Indicopleustes, belonging to the 6th century, is by far the most important testimony of this early period. The author who visited India between 520 and 525 speaks of Christians in Socotra and their clergy, who were ordained in Persia; in Ceylon there was a Church of Persian settlers with a priest ordained in Persia, a deacon and minor clergy; both at Male (Malabar coast) and Kalliana (Kalyan near Bombay) a bishop ordained in Persia, and a Christian community lived.[29] This text is a definite indication of the hierarchical connection of the Christians of India with the Persian Church. A clearer and more precise picture of the hierarchical relations can be gathered from the letters of two Chaldean Patriarchs, Mar Ishoyahb III and Mar Timothy I. This will be dealt with in the next chapter.

CHAPTER II

MEDIEVAL CHRISTIANITY IN INDIA

Part 1. THE EASTERN CHURCH by E. R. Hambye s.j.

Introduction

We now take up the thread left by Fr. A.M. Mundadan CMI, and proceed with the medieval history of Christianity. We first treat of the Eastern Church from the 6th/7th century down to the eve of the Portuguese landing in Calicut. In the following section Dr.G.M.Moraes covers the history of the Latin presence in India during the same period.

By and large medieval Christianity in India belonged to the Eastern Church, more precisely to one of its branches generally known as the East Syrian Church, though its traditional title was the Church of the East. Its supreme head was called the Catholicos-Patriarch of the East, and during the period under review he generally resided either in Irak or in western Iran.

Relations between India and the Middle East

Under Catholicos Ezechiel (557-81) a priest, called Bodh[1] seems to have come to Iran and India as a *periodeutes,* i.e. a delegate entrusted with teaching and visiting scattered communities of his Church. This mission is said to have been prompted by some heretical threat, perhaps even by Manichaeism. This story, which is not absolutely reliable[2], makes also the priest conversant with Sanskrit, even to the extent of having translated into Syriac the Book of Kalibagh and Damnagh. A few years later we learn that Catholicos Sabrisho I (596-604) used to receive presents of perfumes and other wares from India, presumably from his faithful there[3].

At the time of Catholicos Ishoyahb II (628-46) priests, mostly belonging to the monastic order, and bishops from his Church were sent to India; this indicates likely the strengthening of the existing bonds between the Indian Christians and the East-Syrian Church. The custom of sending Middle-East clergy to India lasted with ups and downs beyond the middle of the 16th century.[4]

Following on the remarkable expansion of the East-Syrian Church in Asia, metropolitan and episcopal sees were established accordingly. It appears that the Christians in India first depended on the metropolitan of Perat d'Maisan (Basrah), and on that of Rew-Ardasir in south-west Iran since the 5th century.[5] However the Church in India obtained its own metropolitan see sometime in the 7th or 8th century,[6] presumably in Kerala.

The scanty indications we have about the increasing relations with the East-Syrian catholicate are fortunately supplemented by the Malabar tradition and its few documents.

Thus on two occasions Christian immigrants from the Persian empire, be from Irak or from Iran, landed in Kerala and joined the already existing communities. The first group reached about A.D. 774/795. It was led by a bishop, called Thomas, perhaps the monk Thomas consecrated by Catholicos Timothy I.[7] The second party of immigrants reached likely Quilon either in A.D. 813/825 or a century later in A.D. 910. They were led by two bishops, called Proth and Sabor,[8] and by the merchant Sabrisho.[9] As a later result of this we find the two copper plates or *Sasanam* of c.A.D. 880 making a grant of King Ayyan of Venad over to the Tarisa (=Orthodox) church of Quilon.[10] It is also possible that the Persian cross at the Great Mount at Mylapore and the oldest of two such crosses at the Valiapalli church at Kottayam (Kerala) belongs to the same period. It may well be also that by the time the St. Thomas' shrine at Mylapore was either built or rebuilt, though this surmise cannot be proved so far. In Kerala the two bishops were attributed with the building of several churches, still existing in the 16th century, and bearing their names. This means that they had been locally 'canonized', and that those churches were either actually built under their care or erected later on in their honour. At least one church was built by them at Quilon, and they were buried there.

The hierarchical relations between the Indian Church and the catholicate were kept alive through the rest of the centuries, though rather irregular at that.[11]   According to the only preserved Syriac manuscript written in Kerala during the medieval period the metropolitan of India under Catholicos Yahballaha III (1281—1317) was in 1301 Bishop Jacob.[12]

About the same time unexpected circumstances provided for a while the Indian Church with western contacts. These are discussed in the second section of this chapter.   Two of those visitors stand out as particularly important from the view-point of inter-Christian relations. The first was the Dominican friar, Jordan Catalani of Severac (d.c. 1336), who after a first stay in India prompted Pope John XXII (1316—44) to establish at Quilon the first Latin-rite diocese in the sub-continent.   It was however a very short-lived attempt. The second was the Franciscan and papal envoy, John de Marignolli, who stayed in Quilon for sixteen months in 1348—49.[13]

Expansion

Their reports as well as those of other such casual visitors help us somehow to get at a clearer picture of Eastern Christianity in India in these centuries.

The majority of its faithful was concentrated in Kerala, more precisely between Cranganore in the north and Quilon in the south.[14] Syrian Christian communities were also found scattered along the west coast, in Goa, Saimur (Chaul), Thana, Sopara, Gujerat and Sind. On the east coast Mylapore had also such a Christian community close to the St. Thomas' shrine.[15] It should also be noted that scores of stones marked with a cross have been found on the southern slopes of the Nilgiris.[16] This relatively wide, though sparse, diffusion extended up to Kashmir where near Tankse, on the eastern side of Leh, rock inscriptions still bear witness today to a settlement of Syrian Christians, which existed there around A.D. 800.[17]

The shrine of St. Thomas at Mylapore may have been known already to the Frankish monk Theodore about A.D. 590, but during the 13th—15th century its reputation was much enhanced, as proved by the fact that both Mussulman devotees and western Christian pilgrims frequented it. It led to the spread of some attractive, though completely legendary, stories concerning fantastic miracles performed by the Saint's hand.[18]

Organisation

We mentioned already that the medieval church in India had its own metropolitan, likely always a man from Irak-Iran. Its official title was 'Metropolitan and Door of (all) India'; in the above mentioned Vatican Mss of 1301 he is named 'Metropolitan and Director of the Holy Church in India'. His see was already then at Kodungallur (known since Portuguese time under the corrupt form of Cranganore), and it was still the case at the beginning of the 16th century.

Had this metropolitan any suffragan bishops? It is not certain, though at least at Quilon and at Mylapore there may have been bishops at times. It is also possible that those bishops known through East-Syrian sources as those of Ceylon, the Maldives and Socotra[19] depended on the Indian metropolitan. It also appears that at times that territory called Beth-Qataraya i.e. the islands of the Persian Gulf on the one hand,[20] and the scattered communities of Malaysia—Indonesia[21] on the other hand fell under the authority of the metropolitan.

All through those medieval centuries the succession of the metropolitans was fraught with difficulty. This uncertain situation but increased during the last two centuries before the 16th when both the decadence of the East-Syrian Church and the hampering of communications brought the coming of such bishops to a near stand-still.

Owing to its early presence in many parts of Asia the Church of the East paid special importance to the rank held by each metropolitan see. In the 8th century i.e. the starting-point of its history, the Indian see held the 10th place before that of China[22]; later on its rank was lowered, e.g. the 13th between those of China and Fars according to 'Amr, the 14th according to the great Syrian canonist 'Abdisho d'Soba and only the 15th if we have to accept Seliba's testimony.[23]

The metropolitan's authority was extensive both in spiritual and temporal matters. He obviously stood as the living intermediary between the Catholicos and the Indian communities.

To the former he was expected to send taxes and free gifts towards the support of the Catholicos' house.[24]   Though he could have been elected with the Catholicos' advice, he was mostly appointed, and always ordained, by the Catholicos.[25] Since he belonged to the category of 'exterior metropolitans', the Indian prelate had no right to share in the election of the Catholicos.[26]

His right-hand man was the Archdeacon. In spite of the name he was a local priest, likely unmarried; the office in India, presumably in Kerala, goes back to Catholicos Timothy I (d.823)[27] Known as the 'Prince of the head of the Faithful', the 'Lord of the Nation', 'Archdeacon of all India and its Confines', he enjoyed a considerable influence, all the more so since he often headed the Church during the prolonged vacancies of the metropolitan see. Besides the privileges such Archdeacons enjoyed in the East-Syrian Church, he was entitled in India to grant dispensations of all kind, to appoint clerics to Churches and to prefer candidates to Holy Orders. Not only could he administer church properties, but he was also regarded by the local rulers as the secular superior of the Christians. This gave him the first place among the chieftains, known generally as *raja,* owing allegiance to the king of Cochin.

By the 16th century the office had become somewhat hereditary in the Pakalomattom clan of Kuravilangad.[28]

At the local church level the parish-council looked after the properties and also the whole religious life of the community. When needed a larger type of assembly, gathering representatives either of a group of churches or even of all the Thomas Christian churches, was called into being.[29]

Some Striking Customs[30]

The Christians of St.Thomas were mostly hard-working farmers, though quite a few were also merchants; they were especially busy with cultivating, selling and exporting pepper and other such spices. John de Marignolli, already mentioned on account of his prolonged stay at Quilon, says that at his time the pepper-trade there was handled by the Thomas Christians. As such they were also the masters of the public weighing- office.

Military tradition prevailed also among them. Thanks also to their spirit of independence and self-reliance, they enjoyed besides a kind of autonomy under the petty *rajas* of Kerala. This status combined with their military prowess may have been the origin of their special relation with a royal family, called *Villarvattam,* at Udayamperur (Diamper), which was entrusted with protecting the Thomas Christians.[31] After it had become extinct, its responsibility towards them passed over to the king of Cochin.[32]

It is not unlikely that the Christian soldiers serving the Vijayanagar emperors in the 15th and 16th centuries had also come from Kerala, and belonged therefore to the Thomas Christian community.[33]

Thanks to having their roots deep in the Indian soil those Christians were regarded as equal to the higher Hindu castes, if not always to the Brahmins, at least to the Nairs. They were also regarded as superior to the local Jews and Moslems.[34] This social status was also due to privileges granted at times by the local rulers, as seen already in the previous chapter and as we mentioned above while speaking of the Quilon copper-plates.

Owing to their position they were often called *Mapilas* (=great sons), *Perumals* (chieftains), etc. It explains also why they had become the acknowledged protectors of some eighteen artisan-castes among the Hindus. Their religious outlook was so highly regarded that they were not unfrequently called to live near a Hindu temple so that when occasion arose they could be asked to come and purify by their touch the sacred vessels.

Needless to insist here once more on their social division into two endogamous groups, the Nordists and the Suddists. There is little doubt that it remained enforced throughout.

As can be expected from their socio-cultural integration, the Thomas Christians had many Hindu customs, more or less adapted to their own way of life. Most of them were attached to the main events of human life. Religious meals were held on festive occasions, on the day of burial and death-anniversary. They were originally held inside the Church. Offerings given before the Eucharistic service used to be—still are—auctioned after it was over, and the proceedings were given to the poor, used for parish work, etc. *Prasad* or edible as token of communion with God, with a saint, was distributed to benefactors, devotees on important feast-days.

The church-building combined a basic East-Syrian plan, generally of the simplest form possible, with an architecture and decoration inspired by local Hindu craftsmen, particularly by the local Kerala temples, so typical of that region. A flag-staff always stood close to the western entrance of the church, and instead of bells, the *simantron* of the Greeks, called *nagosia* in Syriac, i.e. a heavy wooden plank struck by a hammer was used to call the faithful to the services.

Outside these marks of cultural integration, the Thomas Christians well deserved their name 'Syrian' since they did practise the ways of worship known as the East-Syrian, Chaldaean rite.[35] They regarded it as an apostolic legacy, and all their baptismal names were limited to some O. T. and N. T. patron-saints. For the elements of the Eucharist, they used fermented bread, and wine made from dry-grapes. It is not impossible however that when wheat and grapes could not be obtained they used rice-cake and palm-wine.[36]

Liturgical participation was remarkable at a time when apparently no vernacular was used. The faithful knew enough the liturgical language so as to enjoy a measure of participation not only in the Eucharist but also in the canonical prayers. Their devotion to the church-building, as symbol of the church itself, and to the cross was outstanding. Processions were popular with those gorgeous red, green, white and gold umbrellas still in use today (one of them was a royal emblem carried as a shining proof of the old privileges), with the priests carrying hand-crosses, and on great festivals with an especially bound and much revered copy of the Bible. The latter was found in every church, and its binding decorated by silver plaques and precious stones must have resembled those which have come down to us in the west.

Pilgrimages were also well frequented, e.g. at Maliankara, 10 kms from Cranganore, where each year on Nov. 21 huge crowds celebrated the anniversary-day of the landing of St. Thomas there.

The clergy was generally married. They received a basic training in Scriptures, Liturgy and some Canon Law under the guidance of a priest, the *malpan* or teacher of some repute. Candidates to Orders were generally presented by their own parish and recommended to the bishop by the Archdeacon. The priests were locally and officially called *kathanar*. They often came from the same families, and some of these at least could trace back a sacerdotal genealogy to St. Thomas himself. Their living came mostly from the income of church properties, from the faithful's offerings and from the funerals, without speaking of the usual church fees for sacramental rites.

From the little that can be known from the local tradition, from the Indian background, and from the East-Syrian influences, it is difficult to believe that there was no Christian monasticism in India at any time during the middle ages.[37] Yet, the local testimonies are very vague indeed, and mention only in general terms houses for religious men and religious women. It is certain, however, that there was a monastery around the shrine of St. Thomas at Mylapore.[38]

For centuries the Thomas Christians expanded, thanks to their own zeal, though inspired also by the apostolic spirit of their East-Syrian brethren. We know that some monks from India went to the Far East, if not to China and central Asia.[39] Thomas Christians during the 10th—11th c. tried to spread their faith in the Maldive Islands,[40] and as late as the 15th century Nairs in Kerala were still joining their ranks.[41]

There even existed among those Christians four prominent families of very ancient origin, whose own duty was to foster the integration of new members into the community.

However, by the end of the 15th century a combination of factors, above all the spread of Islam, had somewhat diminished the inherent dynamism of those Eastern Christians. Though still fairly well-established, they had suffered drawbacks, including the near total destruction of their communities outside Kerala.

LATIN CHURCH

George M. Moraes

The Latin Christianity came to India only in the thirteenth century despite the fact that Christianity had been in India from first centuries and had flourished to some extent in the South and the North West. The beginnings of the Latin Missions were due to the tense and frightening situation in Europe in the thirteenth century. The invading Mongols threatened to ransack the whole of Christian Europe. Alarmed and appalled by the havoc, massacres, and excesses committed by the marauding Mongols, Pope Gregory IX (1227-41) in 1241 called upon the Cistercians, Dominicans, and Franciscans to preach a crusade against the Mongols. But Gregory died that very year and Innocent IV who succeeded him during a lull in the activities of the Mongols, went a step further. He conceived and initiated the bold project of sending missionaries to convert them. By this he also proposed to out-manoeuvre the forces of Islam as well.[1]

This decision proved to be providential for the Church in India. Once the project was initiated it meant that sooner or later missionaries would come to India and would not rest content with contacting only the Mongols in Persia and elsewhere in Asia; they would even succeed in opening a flourishing mission in China itself. Those days there were three ways to reach Peking or Khan Balik from Europe. Two were by road through enemy infested regions, across turbulent flooded rivers, over high, rugged mountain passes, and across deserts. The third one was by sea. If anybody chose this route, India would become a strategic point

---

With the kind permission of the publishers, this section is an abridged version of Chapter III of the author's work entitled *A History of Christianity in India from early times to St. Francis Xavier: A.D. 52—1542*, Bombay, Manaktalas, 1964. Since no new sources on the subject of Latin Missions in India in the Middle Ages have been discovered for the last ten years, it was found that such an abridged text would meet the requirements of this volume.

on the route to China. The Arab merchants embarked at Hormuz and headed for one of the many Arab port-colonies that dotted the coast of India. They then crossed over to the Bay of Bengal and skirting Malaya and Indo-China headed for China. On account of this strategic importance, India "almost immediately drew the attention of these (China bound) missionaries to its own religious needs, and it was not long before that missions were started in the country itself."[2]

Despite initial set-backs, mission work was being done in Persia and its environs long before the first missionaries even arrived in Peking. Surprisingly the efforts to establish contact at Peking seem to have at times been mutual. When Kublai was Grand Khan he invited representatives of all the world's religions to his court in China. He was amiable, tolerant and broadminded. In 1263 he sent two Venetians, Nicolo and Maffei Polo, on a mission to the Pope with a request to send a hundred Christians, proficient in the Christian arts, who would prove the superiority of the Christian religion. Pope Gregory X (1271-76) could only send two Friar-Preachers both of whom succumbed to the rigours of the journey. The two Polos returned with the famed Marco Polo without the Friar-Preachers.[3] It was only many years later that a missionary did reach the court at Khan Balik.

John of Monte Corvino Passes through India in 1291-92

John of Monte Corvino, a Franciscan, was the first Catholic missioner to present himself at the court of the Grand Khan at Khan Balik (Peking). Accompanied by the Dominican Nicolas of Pistoia he set out in 1291 after receiving the Papal blessing and with the power and title of a papal legate. They decided to take the sea route. This route was to prove equally taxing in its own way as the over land routes. John himself testifies to this effect.[4] Part of the reason for this was that they braved the journey in a single masted dhow of the Arabs.

The two wearied missionaries landed at Mylapore, a city made famous by the martyrdom of St. Thomas, the apostle. For some unaccountable reason they were detained there for thirteen months. But this time was not wasted. Noting that Mylapore was equidistant from their headquarters in Tabriz and China, the new mission field, John decided to make it a midway stop for the China-bound missionaries and gradually, if possible, a centre of apostolate. He himself set about observing the character and customs of the people. His observations and conclusions are at times weird.[5] But then he lacked the knowledge of the native language and did not have discussions with the intellectual classes. He was impressed by the simplicity and friendliness of the people and the peace that reigned in the land. In places in and about Mylapore he himself baptised more than one hundred people.[6] These successes urged him to decide to leave behind his Dominican companion. However, just before he set sail he was bereft by the rather sudden death of his dear friend. It was with a heavy heart that he left his neophytes in 1292 for the still distant land of China, whither he had been specifically ordered to go.

In China his mission was blessed with great success despite bad relations with the Nestorian Christians. By 1308 he was an archbishop having a patriarchal status with two suffragan bishops, five others having died on the way. Among them they had more than 30,000 people to care for.[7] Despite his arduous labours he had not forgotten the brethren at Mylapore. In 1306 he appealed to his brethren in Persia to attend to the mission in India. He wrote: "I have seen the greater part of India and made inquiries about the rest, and can say that it would be most profitable to preach to them the Faith of Christ, if the brethren would but come".[8] But as the Church in China was going from strength to strength no one could be spared for India. It was left to the Friar-Preacher, Jordan of Severac, to establish the Latin Church in India. In 1318 Pope John XXII divided the missionary territory, assigning the Far East to the Franciscans, and entrusted to the Dominicans the whole of the Middle East which included the whole of West Asia, Turkestan as far as Arabia and Ethiopia, and the Indies.[9]

Jordan Catalani of Severac, Founder of the Latin Mission in India:

Jordan Catalani of Severac is the real founder of the Latin Missions in India. He was also the first Latin bishop in India. He was a Frenchman born at Severac-le-Chateau in the district of Rouergue in the present department of Aveyron, some ninety miles to the north-east of Toulouse.[10] For many years he worked in the Middle East while residing in his Order's monastery at Tabriz. His heart was aflame with zeal and he was eager to bring people to Christ. It is possible that he either read the appeals made by John of Monte Corvino or that he learned of the possibilities and the dire need for missionaries in India from the brethren who passed through Tabriz on their way to Europe. Moreover, one of his own confreres had died at Mylapore. He, therefore, decided to leave for India as soon as he was allowed to do so. An opportunity presented itself in 1320. Four Friars Minor were on their way to China. Jordan volunteered to fill the place left vacant by the death of Nicolas of Pistoia. His generous offer was accepted.[11]

Towards the end of 1320 these five men left Tabriz for Hormuz. Two months later they embarked for Quilon. After a laborious journey the ship called at Thana (a suburb of present day Bombay) which had replaced Kalyan as the principal port. Thana though populated predominantly by Hindus was in the hands of the Mohammedans under the Delhi Sultanate. The few European merchants and the much reduced 'Nestorian' community of Thana extended a warm welcome to these servants of God who were unable to proceed to Quilon as the monsoon was about to break.[12]

The news of the arrival of the missionaries spread quickly. Very soon they were invited to Broach in Gujarat two hundred and fifty kilometers from Thana. There a number of catechumens are waiting to be instructed and baptized.[13] Jordan responded to their need and undertook the journey with two 'Nestorians' to act as interpreters. They stopped at Sopara on the way where there was a church and a small christian community. Jordan instructed the people and baptized about ninety people and administered the Eucharist to them. After about fifteen days he hired a boat for Broach. But as the boat suddenly and unexpectedly sprang a leak he interpreted this to be a sign from God not to proceed to Broach. He immediately sent back the two interpreters to Thana to inquire after the welfare of his Franciscan companions while he himself retired to the Church to pray for them.[14] Next night the christians came to him and requested him to flee in order to save his life as the others had been arrested. But he decided to return to Thana and see whether his better knowledge of Persian could help his companions in distress[15] little knowing that the four of them had been martyred. Many things had happened during his short absence.

All the trouble began when three of the Franciscans were summoned to a court as witnesses to testify for the mistress of the house where they had been staying. They were required to confirm whether her allegations of brutal treatment by her husband were true or not. As the case was being heard it occurred to an Alexandrian Muslim to suggest to the Qadi (judge) that he should arrange a religious disputation for them. In their discussions with the Qadi, the Malick, and others, the relative superiority of the Bible and the Koran became the bone of contention. Friar Thomas defended the Christian truth with consummate skill. But when asked what he thought of Mohammed, he replied rather brazenly and in the spirit of the age, that Mohammed was the son of perdition. This roused the people and immediately the Friars were stripped naked, rubbed with oil and exposed to the burning sun. To the surprise of the crowd they were unaffected.[15] The Qadi therefore decided that in order to test the truth of what they taught they ought to be made to undertake the test by fire. The fire too did not affect them and the crowd now leaned to their side and began to chant that they were saints. Fearing that now the Friars would all the more easily spread the christian faith the Qadi and the Qotwal (inspector) arranged to have them murdered. Before beheading them the executioners prayed their forgiveness saying: "You must know that we have orders from the Qadi and the Malick (Qotwal) to slay you; and we are reluctant to do it, for ye are good and holy men. But we cannot do otherwise. For if we do not their behest we and all our children and wives shall die!.[18] The friars died confessing their joy to die for the Lord. The next morning when friar Peter of Sienna refused to acknowledge Muhammad as the Prophet they hanged him from the nearest tree. At night when they found that he had not died they cut him in two.[19]

When Jordan returned to Thana he obtained the help of a young Genoese and had the bodies of the martyrs removed for burial in the church of St.Thomas at Sopara.[20] Later the relics were taken by Friar Odoric to Zaytun in China.[21] The relics were finally taken to Europe by way of Tibet.

Jordan himself had no difficulty in moving about and doing his work. The reason for this is that when the news of the slaying reached Delhi, the Sultan called for the Qotwal or inspector whose duty was to maintain order, and had him put to death. On hearing of the execution the Qadi took to his heels and fled from the dominions of the Sultan.[22] Unhampered in his work Jordan went about it with success. Within six months he baptized a hundred and fifteen persons in Broach alone and thirty five between Thana and Sopara. Sensing the field to be fertile he wrote to the headquarters in Persia for more personnel so as to develop Sopara, Broach and Quilon.[23] He intimated his superiors in 1318 that he himself felt drawn to work in Ethiopia where tradition had it that St. Matthew the apostle had preached.[24] But this was not to be, and very soon Jordan was to suffer for the Lord in the persecutions that broke out about 1324. He was badly tortured and treated like a criminal.[25] Despite these atrocities he was able to continue to bring people to Christ. During this period more than a hundred and fifteen persons were baptized by him. He felt sure that many more could be brought to Christ if more workers would come to the harvest field.[26] This time five Dominicans were sent and they were dispatched to the stations in Kanara, Mysore, Malabar and Travancore. Jordan was right in what he did for by 1328 there were more than 10,000 conversions.[27] This was accomplished despite the persecutions that took place from time to time. Quite a number of the sons of St. Dominic were called upon to shed their blood for the faith.

After the martyrdom of the last of his Dominican companions Jordan proceeded to the Papal court then at Avignon to convince the Pope of the need of establishing regular ecclesiastical government in the new mission field as well as of sending more missionaries to the area which held out high promises for the future. Pope John XXII (1316-34) appointed Jordan himself as the first Bishop of Quilon.[28] Jordan was also successful in obtaining many more missionaries. He returned to India some time in 1330.

A series of papal letters were issued after the consecration of the new bishop in order to facilitate his apostolate. They were addressed not only to the Emperor at Delhi and the king of Quilon but also to the many groups of Christians, such as the christian converts in North India, the christians of Quilon and of the Mountains of Albors and the christians of Melephata (probably) in Tinnevelly district). Many of the letters to the dissident christians contained moving appeals for christian unity.

Bishop Jordan founded many houses of his Order in India.29 Many more people too were brought into the Church. This proved to be too much for the Muslims to stomach and they stoned Jordan to death at Thana. The exact year of his martyrdom is not known but it most probably was 1336.30

The Missions Languish:

Already during the time of Jordan the Church suffered greatly at the hands of the Muslims who had the support of the state behind them. In fact Jordan had even wished that the Pope could build a couple of gallies to give a chase to the Sultan of Alexandria on the high seas.31 Soon, because of the political and religious turmoils both in Europe and the Mission fields, disaster struck the missions. No new personnel were forthcoming to replace the missionaries that had laid down their lives for the faith. The first blow to the missions was dealt in China when the Ming Dynasty came to power in 1368 by overthrowing the Mongols under whom the Church enjoyed freedom of action and protection. Soon the turn of Tartary, Persia and India came. By the fifteenth century the Turks were the masters of the whole of West-Asia. Coinciding with these political upheavals in the missions was the loss of vitality in the Western Church itself as a result of the outbreak of the Black Death and the Great Schism. Missionaries who were to return to these areas in the sixteenth and seventeenth centuries were to find but traces of what once upon a time had been flourishing missions.32

The Last of the Missionaries of the Middle Ages to visit India:

John de Marignolli, Franciscan, was the last known missionary of the Latin Church to visit India. He was Papal legate in China but left China some time in 1347. On his way back he stopped over in India spending some sixteen months in the land. It is probable that he arrived in Quilon about Easter 1348. This was to be the base from which he worked.   From his recollections written in Europe in 1354 or 55 he provides us with an interesting description of his stay in these southern regions.

Marignolli was treated well as befitted his status as Papal legate by the St. Thomas Christians as well as the Latins. He noted that the St. Thomas Christians were far better off than the Latins.[33] He saw in the city the Latin church of St. George which may have been Jordan's Cathedral.

During his stay at Quilon he paid a visit to St. Thomas' tomb at Mylapore and collected the stories about that place. On the shores of Cape Comorin he erected a marble pillar on which was engraved the papal coat-of-arms as well as his own. During the ceremony he invoked a blessing over India and Ceylon in the presence of multitude of people. Though he laboured for some time in Quilon it is rather strange that he has reported only of one conversion which turned out to be a very remarkable one. It is the curious story of a Hindu priest who one day came to him from a far off island saying that his idol had told him that as he was not on the path of salvation he ought to seek the holy man that would show him the way. As soon as the Hindu saw John he recognised him to be the envoy of heaven.   This institution of his was confirmed by the fact that he found his long lost son in the company of John. His son acted as interpreter for his instruction. After his reception into the Church he set out with his son promising that he would preach the faith to his countrymen.[34]

Thus came to an end for the time being the efforts of the Latin missionaries. Stupendous were these efforts when one considers the material and moral difficulties that they encountered. Though their achievements were short-lived they were to serve as an example for the centuries to come.

CHAPTER III

THE PORTUGUESE PADROADO IN INDIA IN THE 16th CENTURY & ST. FRANCIS XAVIER

by Wicki, s.j.

The following survey of the 'Padroado' in India is limited to the period from 1500 to 1580, that is, from the establishment of the Portuguese power in India to the extinction of the rule of the House of Avis in Portugal. We will mention only briefly the earlier history of the Padroado during the fifteenth century, when its foundations were laid.

Early History

With the Portuguese Padroado a completely new element was introduced into the religious history of India. It would later become a power to be reckoned with, when its influence was extended to the "Thomas Christians" in Malabar, to the interior of India, the Molucass, China and Japan. For all practical purposes it would cease to exist in India only 1961 with the occupation of the tiny settlements in Goa, Damao, and Diu; it still survives in the diocese of Macao.[1]

When, after centuries of warfare, the Portuguese had driven the last of the Mohammedan overlords from their homeland, they turned to the offensive. This became completely apparent with the conquest of Ceuta in North Africa in 1415. For decades after the Portuguese ships systematically explored the western coast of that continent, until Vasco da Gama finally discovered the sea route to India in 1498, when he landed in the harbour of Calicut. In contrast to the Spaniards in America, and later those in the Philippines, and the Portuguese themselves in Brazil, they never tried to conquer India. They were content to occupy by force or by treaty, a number of strongholds (mostly islands or peninsulas). Only decades later did they strike out to expand the territories they already held; for example, the annexation of

Salcete and Bardez to Goa, and that of the island of Salsette and the area around it up to Bassein.

For the rest, the only basis of Portugal's power was its fleet and its predominance on the sea. In the first half of the sixteenth century they had a naval monopoly that was seriously threatened only by the repeated incursions against them by the Turkish Empire. In the second half of the same century, they were hard pressed on land and sea by the Malabar pirates, the Achinese and other Mohammedan powers that in 1570-1571 tried to drive them out of India—an enterprise which shattered on the heroic valour of the Portuguese.

Every year hundreds and even thousands of the Portuguese came to India in warships. They were predominantly merchants or soldiers who went there for a longer or a shorter stay and then, after having bought spices or fulfilled several years of military service, would return to their homeland. As many of them were not married or were forced by circumstances to live separated from their wives, new relationships were established with the native women. Alfonso de Albuquerque, the conqueror of Goa (1510) was the most zealous promotor of marriages between the Portuguese and the native women. Thus originated the half-breeds called Eurasians. For a long time very few Portuguese women came to India.

The Regent Catharine of Austria (1557-1562) sent a number of orphan girls to India so that they could find husbands there. Furthermore, many Indians were won over to Christianity, but only in 1535-1537 do we find the caste of the Paravas on the Fisher Coast prepared to become Christians as a group in order to protect themselves against the threat of the Mohammedans.[2] They were followed in 1544 by the Mukkuvas in Travancore who were also fishermen.[3] Further apostolic successes occurred: in the 1540's in Bassein and its surroundings through the ministry of the Franciscans; from 1557 to 1560 on the island of Goa under the Governor Francisco Barnete and especially under the Missionary-Viceroy Don Constantino de Bragabca; also under Viceroy Don Antao de Noronha (1564-1568) on the peninsulas of Bardez (Franciscans) and Salcete (Jesuits). Then it came more or less to a standstill. It was especially continuous wars, sieges of the Portuguese fortressed cities, deceptions, orders given by the Indian rulers against conversion, attackes, upon mission stations and repeated burning down of churches, that impeded or made completely impossible any peaceful development. Again and again European and native christians fled to the territories of Mohammedan neighbours (Bijapur, Gujerat, Bengal etc) often to avoid the just retribution of their crimes. All these various aspects should be kept in mind as we discuss the structure of the Padroado or the then organization of the Latin Church in India.

The Portuguese colony in India was officially established in 1505, but Goa was conquered only in 1510. Two decades later, in 1530, it became the capital of Portuguese in India. Until that date Cochin, the seat of a Hindu King, had served that function. The *Imperio* was governed by a governor, or viceroy, according to the guidelines established by the king of Portugal. Captains, some named by the King and others by his representative in India, governed the settlements. They united military and civil authority in themselves and often ruled quite despotically.[4] The most important centre of Portuguese India was Goa. Next came Cochin and then Bassein, in the "Northern Province". Other important places were: Diu (Gujerat), Chaul, Quilon, Colombo in Ceylon, Tuticorin, Nagapatanam, S. Thome-Mylapore, etc. The most official appointments were for a term of three years.

The ecclesiastical organization developed much more slowly in Brazil, Africa and Asia than it did in Spanish America. There were various reasons for this. The voyage to America was incomparably shorter than that to India. Thus even for Brazil the voyage lasted normally three months, whereas for India (with the circumnavigation of Africa) the journey lasted twice as long even under favourable conditions. Furthermore, Portugal, with a much smaller population than that of Spain, was much less able to master satisfactorily the enormous problems of governing colonies in three continents, especially since many of the emigrants were poor. Let us now describe in detail the development of the Latin Church in India during the sixteenth century.

Origins of the Padroado i.e. Portuguese Patronage

During the course of the fifteenth century, the bulls concerning the Padroado were promulgated. They gave Portugal and Spain the sole right to sail the sea, to conquer the new lands that had been, or would be, discovered, and to take possession of their riches under the condition that they would be christianized and that full responsibility would be taken for the financing of all phases of cultic life. But neither Iberian kings nor the popes were then conscious of the immense extension and importance of these documents. Thus we read in Pope Nicholas V's bull, *Romanus, Pontifex,* of January 8, 1455 which stands as the foundation of the Padroado, this weighty sentence: "All lands and seas that have been discovered or will be discovered belong forever to the king of Portugal".5 Another buttress of the Padroado was the 1494 line of demarcation, called "of Tordesillas" (Spain). It was intended to apply primarily to the West; but it later became of great importance also in the East, where it passed through southern Japan and the eastern part of Molucass. In the sixteenth century, however, geographical knowledge was not sufficient to fix it exactly, with the result that Spanish considered China to be "their" territory and would doubtless have conquered it if circumstances had permitted.

Once the sea route to India had been discovered and Latin Christians had begun to live there, according to the law of the time, a diocese had to be erected there. There was long delay before one was finally founded. To begin with, Alexander VI, in the brief *Cum sicut majestas,* of March 26, 1500, which he granted at the request of the Cardinal of Lisbon, Jorge da Costa, gave King Manuel I the right to name an Apostolic Commissioner for the region from the Cape of Good Hope to India and to send him into that region in order to attract the population to the Catholic Faith and to instruct them in it.6 For financial reasons the King delayed naming such a commissioner until 1514.

With Leo X's bull *Dum fidei constantiam* of June 7, 1514, the new territories in India and all houses of worship already erected there or which would be erected were placed under the jurisdiction of the Vicar of Tomar and all churches and ecclesiastical benefices were reserved to the king of Portugal.7 As the administration of the office of Grand Master of the Order of Christ

4

(the seat of which was Tomar) was a prerogative of the king, who could appoint ministers of the churches, the extension of the papal document is manifest. A few days later, on June 12, 1514, the same Pope in the bull *Pro Excellenti Praeeminentia,* erected the diocese of Funchal on the island of Madeira as a suffragan see of the archdiocese of Lisbon. The rights of the vicariate of Tomar *(Diocesis nullius)* were thereby extinguished in the territory from Cape Bojapor to India since these were assigned to the new diocese, which also belonged to the Padroado.[8] The newly named bishop of Funchal, Don Diogo Pinheiro (1514-1526), who had previously been Vicar of Tomar never visited his new bishopric during his whole time in office and sought to fulfil his pastoral duty by sending the so-called 'ring bishops'. These had received episcopal consecration; yet they had no jurisdiction and were to visit the various communities, bless the holy oils and confirm the baptized. The first was the well known Don Duarte Nunes, O.P., who exercised his office from 1519 to 1524.[9] Then there followed a Don Martinho, about whom almost nothing is known.[10] Another one, whose name even is unknown, was appointed in 1529, under Costa's successor. Finally in 1532, there was Friar Fernando Vaqueiro, O.F.M., Bishop of Aureopolis, who died in Ormus (Southern Persia) in 1535 on his journey home.[11]

A general vicar exercised jurisdiction in India. He was appointed by the king and could be either from the secular or the regular clergy. Some of them were Master Diogo Pereira (1505-1510), Joao Fernandez (1510-1513), Friar Domingos de Sousa, O.P., who was Albuquerque's chaplain (1513-1532), and from 1532 to 1547 Miguel Vas,[12] the most important of all.

Indian Dioceses

During Miguel Vaz's term in office, a new phase in the development of the Church in India began. The power of Portugal had ground and the number of Christians had increased, so that it was time for the establishment of an independent diocese. Pope Clement VII did so in 1533, but he died before the decree had been put into execution. Thus it was Paul III who, in the bull *Aequum reputamus* of November 3. 1534, separated the territory of India, taken in the widest sense of the term, from the diocese of Funchal and named Goa the seat of the new bishopric.[13] Funchal now became an archbishopric and Goa its suffragan see.

Don Francisco de Melo was chosen the first bishop of the new Padroado diocese; but he died in 1536 before he could begin the journey to India. So the Spanish Franciscan Juan de Albuquerque, the confessor of king John III, was proposed by the king for the office and the choice was ratified by Pope Paul III. Albuquerque set out for India in 1538 and in June 1539 solemnly took possession of the cathedral in Goa. His task was to build up a diocese which included Eastern Africa, Malacca, the Molucass, China and Japan the last of which had been 'discovered' in 1543. So he established a cathedral chapter, which was organized according to the medieval European model (with cantor, treasurer, etc); founded several parishes, confirmed the faithful, made visitations to Cochin, and once accompanied a viceroy to Ceylon. There is no evidence that he ever visited the East Coast. His income and expenses were, for the most part, provided for by the king in his function as master of the Padroado. His most capable assistants were his general vicar, Miguel Vaz, several Franciscans, and after 1542 also Jesuits, especially Francis Xavier. After several years he felt old and exhausted, and would have preferred to return to Europe, but he remained in the East and died in Goa toward the end of February 1553.[14] The see remained vacant for a long time, during which period the ecclesiastical organization of Portuguese Asia was remodelled. On February 4, 1558, the new archbishopric of Goa was established, with the suffragan sees of Cochin and Malacca. The diocese of Cochin included the Dravidian South and Bengal, whereas the Molucass, China and Japan were placed under Malacca.

The new archbishop of Goa, Don Gaspar de Leao Pereira, had had a close relationship for years with Cardinal Henrique, the brother of King John III, as his chaplain and preacher. Don Gaspar, as he is referred to in contemporary documents, finally arrived in Goa on December 1, 1560. In the meantime, since 1559, the bishop of Malacca, Don Jorge de Santa Luzia, O.P., had governed the diocese. Don Gaspar already held the title of Primate of India (for the Latin Church), which the Patriarch of Mesopotamia, Abd-Isho, who was in union with Rome, had already claimed in 1562. Don Gaspar resigned his office in 1567 during the First Council of Goa, and in 1569 he founded the Congregation of the Reformed Franciscans with its headquarters at the friary of Madre de Deus near Goa. His successor as archbishop was Don Jorge Temudo, who governed from 1567 to 1571. He presided over the conclusion of the Council of Goa in 1567 and, in 1568, had the Constitutions of the archdiocese of Goa printed. They, together with the decrees of the Council, established the direction which the whole Latin East was to follow.

After Temudo's premature death, the see again remained vacant; but this difficulty was got over by the recall of Don Gaspar. Yet this prelate also died in 1576.[17] Meanwhile, in 1572, a brief had been issued in Rome, according to which the bishop of Cochin was to come to Goa as administrator of the archdiocese and was to name a substitute for his own diocese.[16] The bishop of Cochin at that time, Don Henrique de Tavora, seems to have had little inclination to transfer himself to Goa since he was found still in his see in the years 1577 and 1578.[17] As he had meanwhile been appointed archbishop of Goa, he finally moved to the capital in the autumn of 1578.[18] His solemn enthronement took place on November 1, 1579. His manner of governing was stern, he visited his archdiocese and was poisoned at Chaul in 1581.[19]

From the above we see that from the time of the erection of the diocese, later archdiocese, of Goa, the prelates named to the see actually governed only in the year 1538-1553, 1560-1572, 1574-1576 and 1578-1581. They were all presented to the Pope by the king of Portugal and their appointments were ratified by the Pope. It seems that these appointments proceeded smoothly, as relations between the Crown and Rome were generally quite good and all the prelates named were distinguished by a worthy manner of life and conscientious performance of their duties.

Further Developments

When bishop Juan de Albuquerque landed in 1538, there were only thirteen parishes in his diocese. Of these only those of Goa, Cochin, Diu, Chaul, Cannanore, Quilon and San Tome were on the Indian soil.[20] What progress the new archdiocese (without Cochin) had made in 1576 is evident from the schedule of regular contributions made by the king for the State and the Church. The archbishop of Goa had received 5,000 cruzados a year, of which 1,000 were a donation to the archdiocese and 4,000 were a royal grant. In the service of the cathedral were the following: a dean and four dignitaries (Cantor, Archdeacon, Treasurer and School Master), twelve chaplains, six choir boys, a music master, two janitors, seven singers, an organist, a Latin teacher, the pastor, a bell ringer, an usher, and a jailer. The king was responsible for the expenses for the mass wine, the flour for the hosts, oil for the lamps, wood, water and other supplies for the sacristy, as also for the maintenance of the cathedral. Besides these there was a special allowance owed by the cathedral chapter for the Vespers and for the procession on the feast of St. Martin to celebrate the victory at Diu (1546). There follow entries for the many parishes, with their clergy, that existed in the city and on the island of Goa, in Bardez and on Salcete (Goa) and for the hospital for the natives. These included not only the expenses for the persons, but also those for sacristies, mass wine, hosts, oil etc. Sometimes there was a policeman for the protection of the native Christians, as also disbursements for the catechumens (for their support during the time of preparation for baptism and for their baptismal garments), for several confessors for the local Christians, for four soldiers for the protection of Margao (site of the mission), and for the tax collector on Salcete and his scribe.[21]

The rest of the parishes of the archdiocese of Goa had to be cared for in a similar fashion. Thus, for example, there is extent schedule for the year 1565 according to which a vicar for the fortress of Damaun, four prebendaries, two choir boys, a treasurer for the church (a total of eight persons) were to receive their income from the patron, who also had to provide for the ordinary expenses (mass wine etc), for the sacristy, the *Misericordia,* and the royal hospital.[22]

The second Latin diocese of the Padroado in India was that of Cochin, which was separated from that of Goa as a suffragan see in 1558. In the bull of foundation mention is made of the importance of the place as the seat of a king (Hindu) and as a harbour of great importance, as well as of the large number of new Christians and the great distance from Goa, with the consequent difficulty for pastoral visitation.[23] The patron had to provide for the bishop, a vicar for the parish, and six prebendaries: the vicar was to receive sixty ducats a year, the prebendaries thirty ducats each. Including these six, there were to be twelve prebendaries for the cathedral. There would be provision for twelve canons, the cathedral chapter.24 There were only a few other parishes in the diocese, for example those at Quilon and San Tome. In 1576 the Bishop sent two Jesuits to Bengal, and shortly after a diocesan priest also, to visit there briefly in order to remind the Portuguese, who traded there and who lived rather freely of their christian duties. About 1577 there were vicars of the bishop of Cochin on the island of Mannar and in Tuticorin. Ceylon with the city of Colombo also came under his jurisdiction.

The first bishop of Cochin came to India in 1559. He was Don Jorge Temudo, O.P., who governed his see until 1567 and then, as already stated, became archbishop of Goa. In 1566-67 he undertook a long journey of pastoral visitation, which took him through Quilon down to the Fishery Coast and San Tome. In many places he was the first to confer the sacrament of confirmation. His successor was Don Henrique de Tavora, O.P., who had taken part in the last session of the Council of Trent and worked according to its spirit. He also did not hesitate to use the weapon of excommunication. At the death of Don Gaspar in 1576 he became first the vicar for, and later the actual archbishop of, Goa. As bishop of Cochin he visited his diocese, going as far as Quilon and the Fishery Coast. The third bishop was Friar Mateus de Medina of the order of Christ; he came to Goa in 1579 and then went on to Cochin. In 1588 he also became archbishop of Goa.25

Under the Portuguese kings two provincial councils were held in Goa. The first was called and presided over by Don Gaspar in 1567; Tavora continued and concluded it. At the request of the council, the then Viceroy Don Antao de Noronha published a rather long list of decrees in the name of king Sebastian. The fathers of the council had requested it so that several of their decisions would have more effect through the aid of the secular arm.26 The second council took place in 1575, again under the presidency of Don Gaspar. It was supposed to have been held in 1571; but the prelates found that, instead of arriving for the opening of the council, they had come for the burial of the archbishop.27 Both councils had the purpose of implementing the reform of the Council of Trent,28 which had been accepted by the Portuguese crown, and was therefore carried out in Portuguese India with the support of the civil authorities.

In 1579 the question arose in Goa as to whether the invitation of the Emperor Akbar to send Jesuits to his court should be accepted or not. Viceroy Ataide had the question decided by a mixed commission of prelates and civil delegates. It was able to overcome his distrust of the invitation.[29] Such cases, in which civil and ecclesiastical delegates dealt with matters that touched both spheres were of frequent occurrence; for example, whether or not to tolerate non-Christian rites. Thus in 1571, the *Mesa da Conciencia* was established also in Goa for the solution of such matters.

Religious, Missions and Education

In addition to the development of the hierarchy and the support of prelates, pastors and prebendaries, and the construction and maintenance of churches, hospitals etc., the Padroado was also responsible for sending religious, for their support while they were overseas, and for the foundation of cloisters with their churches and missions. The popes repeatedly exhorted the Portuguese kings as to their duty in regard to missions. Thus the fleets usually carried a greater or smaller number of secular and religious priests to India, either as chaplains or as future apostles. Among the religious were first of all Franciscans and Dominicans. The former began their activity by building monasteries in Goa (1518-1527) and Cochin (1519-1522). The Dominicans, however, did not have enough confidence in their future in Goa to start building a monastery until 1548. The first Jesuit to arrive was Francis Xavier in 1542. The Augustinians came in 1572. In the course of time these four orders built large cloisters in Goa, Cochin etc., and had a leading role in the spread of the Faith. Especially numerous were the Franciscans and Jesuits; the number of Dominicans was much smaller. Whereas there exist lists of the Jesuits and Augustinians who came to India,[30] such lists are lacking for the other Orders; especially for the latter very little source material is extant in any case. In 1574 the king usually paid 100 ducats for the voyage of each missionary from Portugal to India. Besides the outfitting and maintenance of the missionary clergy, books were an important item of expense in as much as the first religious printing press was established in India by the Jesuits in 1556. Johannes Von Endem soon founded another, but they were far from fulfilling the demand. The king showed himself to be especially generous when he provided a printing press for the Patriarch of Ethiopia, Nunes Barreto, in 1556.

In India itself the king had to provide for the maintenance of a large number of religious, for example, for the Franciscans in Goa, Cochin, Quilon, Bassein, etc. The first complete list of their establishments and members that we possess is from the year 1585. It gives impressive testimony in regard to their diffusion and labours.[32] Some of the Jesuit establishments were royal foundations, such as the Colleges in Goa, Bassein, Cochin and Salcete; others received income from the treasury, such as the hospital for the local population in Goa or the small college in Quilon (which was almost always on the verge of starvation). The Fathers on the Fishery Coast were supported by the local population, beginning about 1567-68 perhaps a unique situation in that time.[33] As the Dominicans and Augustinians possessed few cloisters in India before 1580, the king's outlay for them was much smaller than that for the other orders. The royal money expended for the individual orders and works are recorded with exactitude in regard to place and amount in the *Regimentos,* as are also the disbursements for the hierarchy and for the diocesan clergy. In the cases where the administration of the funds depended on the viceroys or the local captains, the clergy was very dependent on their good will. As the cost of maintenance and support increased continuously because of the growth in number of religious, the frequent wars, and the recurring illnesses and epidemics, complaints regarding the lack of sufficient subsidies became ever more frequent. Yet it would be quite erroneous to believe that it was the king who provided everything necessary for building, for outfitting the missionaries, the 'sacristy' etc. The extant documents often speak of the benefactors whose voluntary gifts contributed much toward the adornment of the churches and the social apostolate.

Let us here take special note of the educational situation. Where the Portuguese established themselves, schools also arose, in the shadows of the cathedrals and even in humbler cities and villages. They were predominantly elementary schools, where instruction was being given in reading, writing, and arithmetic (because of the trade). Frequently the schools that had been founded before 1542 were later taken over by the Jesuits, who also directed humanistic secondary schools in Goa, Cochin, and Bassein and who taught philosophy and theology in Goa to outsiders as well as to their fellow Jesuits. Furthermore, the Franciscans had schools for local boys at Reis Magos (Bardez), Cranganore, and in the northern province. They and the Dominicans educated candidates for the order in their own friaries. Since at that time there existed neither taxes in the modern sense nor compulsory education, the schools were supported by the king, who sometimes met the expenses for their foundation.[34] There were paid sacristans and catechists in the villages. Another item of expense was the printing of *Cartilhas,* or Catechisms.[35]

Thus we see that the patron (the king) had a number of duties. These included not only the maintenance of the clergy and the construction of churches, but also the spread of the Faith, in as much as according to the ideas of the time, baptism was a necessary condition for salvation. This is also a partial explanation of the great missionary zeal and the almost unbelievable optimism of those days, especially since the successes in Spanish America made a great impression on the missionaries in the Portuguese East. By 1580, however, considerable disillusionment had arisen in the East. After Philip II's having taken possession of the throne of Portugal, hopes were placed in the military occupation of large areas and in energetic support from the viceroys.

It has often been noted how little mention there is of missionary activity in the reports of the Portuguese chroniclers who wrote about India and the surrounding areas, Correa, Gastanheda, Barros, Couto, etc. Yet they give detailed and self-satisfied reports on the numerous wars and their consequent destructions and conflagrations. Even Joao dos Santos, O.P., is no better than the rest. In his listing of the viceroys and governors he remarks only that Pedro Mascarenhas had partitioned the island of Goa among the three orders and that Antao de Noronha had greatly furthered Christendom.[36] Sebastiao Gonsalves provides much more details in his description of the missions (1614), but only the section upto 1570 is extant. For most of the viceroys he reports what they did for the spread of the Faith and for the Church, in which connection Constantino de Braganca and Antao de Noronha take the pride of place. The patronage of kings John III (1521-1557) and Sebastian (1557-1578) occupies a large space in his account, primarily in regard to the Jesuits.[37]

From Paulo de Trindade, O.F.M. (about 1635), we learn the attitude of each viceroy and governor toward the Franciscans. As especially friendly to them are named Francisco de Almeida (1505-1509), who is said to have built them a small monastery at Quilon; and Diogo Loues de Sequeira (1518-1522), who brought a number of Franciscans to India and saw the beginnings of their foundations in Goa and Cochin. Vasco da Gama, who died in Cochin in 1524, was buried in the Franciscan church. Gracia de Sa, who was assisted by the Franciscans on his deathbed, was laid to rest in their church at his own request (1540).[38] In contrast to Santos, Trindade treats of the Padroado (fifteenth century) in a separate chapter.[39] In it he also discusses the ticklish question as to whether the Franciscans and the other orders administered the parishes as vicars of the bishops or with apostolic authority through mandate of the king of Portugal.[40] This matter had already given rise to difficulties with the Jesuits under Don Gaspar de Leao (1561);[41] and it was not soon laid to rest since the question of exemption from the bishops also played a part in it.

Legislation and Tithes

An area that must be touched upon in any consideration of the Padroado is that of the Portuguese mission legislation. It goes back especially to 1559, under the Regent Catharine of Austria, and had lasting consequences; but it had already been instituted under John III. Let us take special note of certain points. When slaves of Mohammedans or Hindus became Christians, they had to be sold to Christians for a suitable sum. Official positions in India were to be given to Christians, definitely not to Brahmins. The law of inheritance was changed in favour of daughters in cases where there was no male heir. Non-Christian orphans were to be educated in Christian schools and were later to make a personal decision as to which religion they desired to belong (this law in particular was forcibly attacked by the Hindus and often evaded). Converted Christians in Goa were to have the same privileges as the Portuguese there. The inheritance of Christian orphans was not to be administered by Brahmins or other non-Christians. The construction of Pagodas (temples), the worship of idols, and the practice of non-Christian ceremonies were forbidden under the pain of punishment. Many decrees had their origin during the time of Braganca (1558-1561): thus, for example, daughters who became christians received a right to inherit; one regulation was directed against those who tried to hinder the conversion of others; another banished from Goa a limited number of Brahmins who were considered to be harmful; finally, the viceroy forbade the *sati*.[42]

Most of the royal and viceregal decrees concerning conversions were gathered together by the so-called *Pai dos Cristaos* and preserved in a hand-written manual. This *Pai* is first mentioned in 1537 and the last reference to its existence is from 1842 or 1843. This was a personage.

In the earlier decades, when there were few native christians and there were as yet no resident bishops, little mention is made of tithes. But from about 1539 references to them become more frequent. According to the testimony of Miguel Vaz, no tithes were demanded from non-Christians (although, for example, it is well known that the Mohammedans levied a tax on Christians); but, as soon as one became a christian, the Collectors were already knocking at the door. They extracted the tithes from the poor neophytes with much importunity and harassment. The general vicar was for the abolishing of their payment. John III had information gathered as to whether in Goa the tithes could be included in the ordinary tribute whereas in the other places they would be abolished.[48] Father Lancillotto, who worked in Quilon and Travancore, suggested in 1550 that, because of the poverty of the Christians there, the tithes might be replaced by some other method of expressing obedience.[49] In 1566 Nunes Barreto also stated the opinion that tithes should not be demanded from neophytes for many years, especially when these lived in the territories of non-Christian rulers; the king could demand them from Portuguese Christians, but not from the Indian ones.[50] Henrique Henriques was also against the exaction of tithes; he found it especially scandalous that the money was collected by the captains.[51] Queen Catharine had already shown the way in this matter in 1561; no tithes were to be required during the first ten years after conversion.[52] Later, in 1571, 1580 and 1581 this period was increased to fifteen years.[53] On the Fishery Coast the agreement was made that the Christians were to pay no tithes since they supported the missionaries in any case (which was not to be considered as a substitute for the tithes, however).[54]

The Padroado: A Tentative Estimation

If we now wish to evaluate the institution of the Padroado, the first thing we must note is that at that time there existed no other means of spreading the Faith. One knows of no pope or cardinal who would have given a single penny for the missions in India, while the assessments for the briefs and bulls amounted to noteworthy sums. In 1580 the first Indian Jesuit Pedro Luis criticized the "rich Roman Cardinals", who constructed showy palaces, but had nothing to give to the missions. The Portuguese kings were all truly devout Catholics and, especially from the time of John III, genuinely solicitous for the spread of the Faith in the new territories. They made great financial sacrifices for that purpose. They wished to be kept constantly informed about what progress was being made in spreading the faith and established a personal relationship with the missionaries (farewell before departure, welcome on returning, instructions for the viceroys, legislation favouring the missions, construction and maintenance of churches, cloisters, hospitals, and schools). They understood the importance of worthy and zealous priests and missionaries. If the reality did not always correspond to their expectations, it was certainly not due to them. On the other hand, the intimate alliance of Christianity with Portugal had several serious drawbacks. The name "Franguis" (Franks)*, loaded with overtones from the time of the crusades and applied to the Portuguese and the neophytes, is enough to demonstrate this. Together with zealous (and sometimes imprudent) missionaries, many soldiers and merchants voyaged across the sea to India.

---

* which in India became either *Firanguis* or *Paranguis*

Unfortunately the soldiers, whose courage was often undeniable, also fell prey to frenzies of destruction and cruelty. Chaplains rushing forward into battle with cross in hand might not have been much of a recommendation for the religion of love. The ideas on "just war" current at the time could hardly be acceptable today. The activities of the Inquisition after 1560 certainly had a crippling effect on the population. At the time there were many complaints about excessively authoritarian viceroys and governors and about numerous captains whose greed during their three years in office seemed to know no bounds or moral restraints. Moreover, the dependence of the Church on the civil authorities was great, especially since the latter were to disburse money to the missionaries—or in certain circumstances delayed or even refused to pay them. Yet it must be stated that generally speaking during the period when the Portuguese kings held sway in India the relations between Church and state were quite good. It was precisely during those years that the foundations of the Latin Church in India were laid.

St. Francis Xavier and India[55]

When Francis Xavier came to Goa in the beginning of May 1542, he was 32 years old, and 5 years a priest. He was born in Navarra. In Paris, where he spent eleven years in all, he joined Ignatius of Loyola. He then moved on to Italy sometime in 1536-37, with the intention of travelling to, and working in, the Holy Land. However, as no pilgrim-ship sailed then from Venice to the Near East, Ignatius and his companions placed themselves at the disposal of Pope Paul III.

The principal of St. Barbara's College in Paris had already by then asked one of Ignatius' companions, the Portuguese Simon Rodrigues, whether they would be ready to go as missionaries to the East India in order to work among the newly converted people of Malabar, i.e. of the Fishery Coast. Through Pedro Mascarenhas, his envoy in Rome, the Portuguese king John III obtained two fathers for that purpose. Ignatius chose the above mentioned Simon Rodrigues and the Spaniard Nicolas Bobadilla for that task. The latter, however, was so ill on his arrival in Rome from Naples, the Ignatius had to look for a substitute. He chose Francis Xavier.

Xavier and Rodrigues, fully empowered by the Pope as his Envoys (Nuntii), in the broad sense of the term, were sent to all the Christians of the Portuguese East. This explains the many journeys the Saint was to undertake later. In 1541-42 while Xavier was on his way to India from Lisbon round Cape of Good Hope, Rodrigues had remained in Portugal where he founded the Mission College in Coimbra and thereby looked after the necessary supply of personnel.

In Goa Xavier met Master Diogo, the founder of St. Paul's College. This College had just been established as a mission-seminary, but it required a rector. Xavier accepted the post reluctantly, for he still had then in mind the newly founded Society of Jesus as a body of men constantly on the move. He however left Micer Paulo to support Diogo in Goa. He himself, together with some Indian clerics went as soon as possible to the Paravas of the Fishery Coast who had become Christians in 1535-37. For one year he laboured there untiringly, trying to convey to them in their own mother-tongue the most important truths of the faith and baptizing children etc. After a brief stay in Goa and Cochin (December 1543—January 1544) he returned to his field of work.

His numerous letters in 1544 to his colleague Mansilhas have been preserved, and they convey to us a vivid description of his activities. At the end of 1544 Xavier went to Travancore, where, with the permission of the local authorities, he baptised within a month over 10,000 Mukkuvar fisherfolk, and thereby laid the foundation of Latin Christianity in Travancore. He then moved on to Quilon and from there to Cochin, Goa and then back to Cochin in order to mail his yearly letters (ships left for Portugal in January and February). Passing through Nagapatanam he went further on to S. Tome, Mylapore. There, at the grave of the Apostle, whom he very highly venerated and whose name he, already in 1542, introduced into the Confiteor of the Mass—he prayed earnestly for counsel.

Better enlightened and encouraged he decided to travel on to Malacca, in order from there to go to Macassar. In fact, however, since a priest was already working in Macassar, he went on to the Christians of Moluccaa. Since mid-January 1548, the Saint was once more in India, where he worked in Cochin, Bassein, Goa and for a short while, also on the Fishery Coast. During

1545, 1546 and 1548 new fellow-Jesuits came from Europe. By then candidates were being accepted into the Order in India. Thus new establishments were made possible.

During the year 1548-49 new Jesuit houses mushroomed in Cochin, Bassein, Quilon and S. Tome (Mylapore). These houses were all very modest and could be maintained without stable financial backing. Nevertheless a number of zealous and selfless fellow-Jesuits stood by Xavier, e.g. Lancilotto, the first Superior of Quilon, where a modest seminary sprang up. It was meant for the training of local youth as catechists for Travancore and the Fishery Coast. Other examples of outstanding missionaries on the Fishery Coast were Antonio Criminale and Henrique Henriques.

A matter of great concern for Xavier was the strengthening of all that was newly undertaken, specially the supply of missionaries and the training of local catechists. As he could not be present personally in all places, he wrote in the light of his rich life-experiences and with great skill instructions for the missionaries and their helpers, as well as different catechisms and an explanation of the Faith (credo). Some of these writings were translated already then into Tamil. During 1548-49 Xavier became quite interested in the Thomas Christians and their bishop.

After a long absence in Japan (1549-51), Xavier returned to Cochin at the end of January 1552, then went back to Goa in February, stayed there for a very short while, and finally left India for good by the middle of April of the same year. In the meantime, from the status of a "Mission" India had become the overseas Province of the Jesuit Order, and Xavier was appointed its first Provincial. During those weeks he controlled the affairs of the Order in India, appointed the industrious Gaspar Berze Vice-Provincial in his absence and dismissed from the Order the imprudent Antonio Gomes who had brought to ruin St. Paul's College which was meant for the local boys. Finally he bid farewell to his fellow-Jesuits in Goa, in order, in vain however, to launch out for China.

Xavier is justifiably called the pioneer of the more recent missions in Asia, of which India had a share. His sanctity, which was already well known and acknowledged by his contemporaries, is uncontested. He was certainly very exacting and dismissed without much ceremony those who did not measure up to the ideal. His standard could not be maintained however as asserted by the Jesuit historian Sebastian Gonsalves in 1614. By founding various schools at important places Xavier contributed also to the spread of education in India. The fact that he took a special interest in the poor people (fisherfolk, the sick etc) redounded to his popularity. His concern for the growth of a native clergy and an increase of catechists indicated his wide vision. The fact that he communicated the Christian teaching in the native languages of the East (Tamil, Malayalam, Japanese) and prepared many copies of his writings shows that he made an earnest effort to have Christianity understood from within.

Yet it must be admitted that he knew very little about the genius and wealth of the Indian culture. Actually his contacts with India were only through the coastal regions of the South-West and South-East, and with its less educated people. Besides he lacked the peace and leisure that would be enjoyed by many future missionaries; after the first three years (May 1542—May 1545) he was in India only from January 1548 until April 1549 and then from January until April 1553. These circumstances probably contributed to the fact that he regarded the character of the Indians under less favourable light than that of the Japanese. However, while in Japan Christianity nearly died out on account of persecution, it was developed uninterruptedly in India in spite of all difficulties, and proved right Fr. Henrique Henriques who was more optimistic than his superior. The great shrines in Goa and Kottar, the many churches, colleges and institutions spread all over India, that are named after Xavier prove that the country remained faithful and grateful to the Saint.

CHAPTER IV

DEVELOPMENT OF THE CHURCH UNDER THE PADROADO

From the death of St. Francis Xavier to the Eclipse of the Portuguese in the 17th century, 1552-1665.

A. Meersman, o.f.m.

The expansion of the Church under the Portuguese Royal Patronage (Padroado) followed closely but not exclusively on the pattern set up by its secular counterpart. First there were the enclaves ruled by the Portuguese *Estado da India* such as Goa, Bassein and its neighbouring districts (Thana, Bombay, etc), Damao and the lesser possessions such as the forts and factories in Diu, Chaul, Cochin, Quilon, Nagapatanam, and San Tome. In the second place the Apostles of the Gospel fanned out in territories where the Portuguese influence was still felt to some extent, e.g. the Fishery Coast and Malabar (Kerala). Thirdly, they still penetrated further wherever circumstances favoured their coming, e.g. in S. India with Madurai and later on Mysore, and in N. India with Mogul Empire and Bengal. Finally faithful from already christianized areas migrated and gave rise to new centres. In describing the expansion of Christianity under the Padroado after the death of St. Francis Xavier it is this order we shall follow.

The Portuguese Enclaves and their Forts and Settlements

Goa.

By 1552 the Portuguese possessions in India had almost reached their greatest extent. In all these and also in those they would still acquire during the period under review, chiefly during the first decades, the Portuguese established the Church. In the Goan enclave, in that part which was to become the Province of Ilhas, a number of converts were made in and around the city of Goa, and some churches were erected. But in the rest of Ilhas and in Bardez and Salsette, incorporated as recently as 1543, relatively little had been accomplished. It was only in

5

1555 that the mission work was properly organized. In that year the Viceroy entrusted Salsette to the Jesuits and Bardez to the Franciscans. Ilhas was parcelled out between the Dominicans and the Jesuits. In course of time the bulk of the population accepted Christianity and soon these Provinces were covered with veritable network of parishes. The boundaries of each parish in general coincided with the limits fixed in pre-Portuguese times to determine the extent of each agricultural community. By about 1630, besides the eight parishes in the city of Goa, there were 30 in Ilhas, 25 in Salsette and 28 Bardez. The number of Christians attached to each was the highest in Salsette and the lowest in Bardez. The percentage of Catholics c. 1670 may have been around 85% of the population. However, this had not been achieved in a day. It took decades before certain villages or sections thereof accepted Christianity. Thus the Brahmins of Moira only about 1620 decided as a group to join the Church.

In the meantime, on 4 February, 1557, Pope Paul IV raised Goa to the dignity of an archdiocese with Cochin and Malacca (Malay) as suffragans. Originally the diocese of Goa, under the patronage of the Portuguese kings, extended from the Cape of Good Hope to China. All Catholics, including the St. Thomas Christians, so it was presumed, resorted under its jurisdiction. Hence the archdiocese of Angamali or Serra of the Syro-Malabarians was considered as depending on Goa. This claim was finally fully acknowledged by the Holy See when Pope Clement VIII on 4 August, 1600, reduced it to the status of a diocese and a suffragan of Goa and officially subjected it to the patronage of the Portuguese kings. Before this on 5 November 1599, in the person of Francisco Roz, S.J. it had been given its first Latin Bishop. Later Pope V, on 22 December 1608 restored Angamali to the rank of an archbishopric. Shortly afterwards, on 3 December 1609, its see was transferred to Cranganore, since there was a Portuguese fort there which offered more security.

In the meantime, on 9 January 1606, Pope Paul V erected the diocese of S. Tome—Mylapore, as a suffragan of Goa. As there was some disagreement concerning the boundaries of Angamali (Cranganore), Cochin and Mylapore, on 22 December

1610, the Archbishop of Goa, Dom Aleixo de Menezes, deputed thereto by the Holy See, fixed the boundaries of these three bishoprics. Later, on 6 February 1616, Paul V ordered the decisions regarding the limits between Cranganore and Cochin to be implemented. The rest of India covering more than half its extent continued to resort directly under the Archdiocese of Goa.

However, Goa continued as the chief ecclesiastical centre not only of India, but of the whole Portuguese East as well. Hence it was there too that the religious—Franciscans (1510), Jesuits (1542), Dominicans (1548), Augustinians (1572), Carmelites (1614), Theatines (1640)—established their principal residences or provincialates and their houses of formation, and from there they dispatched their men as missionaries not only to various parts of India, but also to other regions such as Ceylon, Burma, Malay, Indonesia, Vietnam, China, Japan.

Bassein, Bombay and Neighbourhood

After Goa, the most valuable and extensive enclave the Portuguese possessed was the one called Bassein, ceded to them in 1535 and comprising besides the Island of the same name, Salsette, Bandra, Karanja, Bombay and a number of lesser islands. A formidable fort was erected on Bassein as well as a string of fortifications at strategic points of this island-group. The whole area was subsequently divided up according to some kind of feudal system and alloted in fief to various families. Within the walled town where both the civil and ecclesiastical governments functioned, various religious bodies, such as the Franciscans, Jesuits, Augustinians and Dominicans founded important residences. There too the Jesuits maintained a college, originally a Franciscan foundation ceded to the Jesuits when the Friars opened another at Borivli (Mt Poinsur). Slowly the majority of the population, chiefly due to the efforts of the Jesuits and Franciscans, accepted Christianity. To give an example, the Island of Salsette consisting of 114 villages was divided into 21 parishes around 1630. Of these the diocesan clergy administered three, the Augustinians one, the Franciscans eleven and the Jesuits six. In all of them there were then 28,379 Catholics.

Bombay, destined to receive the first Indian Cardinal at the time it was ceded to the Portuguese, was not considered of any great importance. Originally it consisted of seven islands which had to a large extent coalesced. The mission in this island was entrusted to the Franciscans. Though there may very well have been some kind of chapel attached to the manor house belonging to the one to whom Bombay-island proper had been granted in fief, the earliest church. N.S. da Esperanca, situated where the Victoria Terminus now stands, can hardly have been founded before 1565. In course of time four parishes were established: besides N.S. da Esperanca, St. Michael's (Mahim), Salvacao (Dadar), and Gloria (Mazagaon). The last mentioned was ceded to the diocesan priests by the Franciscans about the year 1610. When Bombay was surrendered to the English, the population numbered some 15,000, the vast majority of whom were Catholics.

It was to provide a greater measure of security for this Bassein enclave that 1559 the Portuguese seized Damaun. After its conquest not only did they strengthen the defences of the harbour itself, but they also erected a number of forts or strongholds, such as Mahim, Kelva, Mazagaon, Tarapur, Asheri, Dahanu along the coast and in the interior between this territory and that of Bassein. The mission work was taken in hand not only in the town itself but in the rest of the enclave as well. Diocesan priests were placed in charge of the principal parish churches. The religious—Augustinians, Dominicans, Franciscans, Jesuits—at an early or later date settled either in the city itself or in one or other of its dependencies. By 1635 the number of Catholics in the Damaun enclave is estimated as having been around 30,000.

Cochin and S. India

Besides these three enclaves, the Portuguese established a number of forts and settlements along Indian coast, the first and foremost of them all being Cochin. By 1552 it had ceased to be the capital of Portuguese India. Notwithstanding it continued to serve as a base for their fleet and as a busy trade-emporium. It was well protected by fortifications. Ecclesiastically too it was important. As we have seen in 1557 it became a diocese. When the Portuguese first arrived in Cochin, its king welcomed them. With their aid he hoped at least to neutralize the preponderance of Calicut in Malabar affairs and at the same time enrich his kingdom through trade. However, as far as the spreading of the Gospel in his realm was concerned, he was not enthusiastic and he forbade the missionaries to approach the members of certain castes for the sake of conversion. They were permitted to seek catechumens from other castes or sections of the population, which they did. A large portion of these people accepted Christianity, and in course of time a number of parishes were erected within the walled town, which were entrusted to the diocesan clergy, and in what we may call its suburbs and on the neighbouring islands. Thus before 1560 the Franciscans built a church on Vypeen Island and a second one in 1606.

The religious, who from the beginning had shared in the work of conversion, founded residences, centres whence they controlled the work of their members in the South. The College, the Jesuits founded in course of time became the Provincialate of their Malabar Province (1602) under which the famous Madurai and other missions resorted. The Franciscans for many years maintained a house of studies, which in 1633 became the head of a custody or vice-province to which the Friars in the South and on Ceylon belonged. The Augustinians and the Dominicans too had residences there, the latter maintaining a novitiate at their priory. Finally Cochin could boast of a seminary, at least during the incumbency of Don Andre de S. Maria O.F.M. (1588-1615) as bishop of the diocese.

The relations between the Portuguese and the rulers of Calicut can be described as anything but cordial. Though for a short period they possessed a fort there, owing to constant opposition they withdrew and instead, to control the shipping they constructed one at neighbouring Chaliyam (Challe) where they maintained themselves upto 1571. It is understandable that even though the Jesuits settled there for a short while and the Dominicans and Franciscans maintained each their residence, very little missionary work could be performed. It is only later about the year 1597 that the Jesuits were able to return to the area. In Calicut and two neighbouring places they built churches.

The fort the Portuguese constructed at Cannanore dates

back to the very first years after their coming to India. Diocesan priests were placed in charge of the chief church and the Franciscans founded a priory. Prospects, as far as conversion of the people is concerned, seemed good, but the initial promise was never realized. Moreover they were forbidden to move into the interior. By 1658, in the whole area, there was only one clergyman, a Franciscan, who resided in Cannanore itself.

Cranganore, where the Portuguese erected a fort, was as a matter of fact a centre of the Syrian Christians. It was for them that in 1540 the Franciscans erected a seminary. Though in the beginning some of the priests trained there worked among the St. Thomas Christians, slowly on owing to the fact that the education they received was modelled on similar institutions in Portugal and that no Syriac was taught and more and more of the Portuguese or sons of the Portuguese were enrolled, it became predominantly an establishment for the Latins. Later in 1577 the Jesuits opened a residence in the neighbourhood and shortly afterwards founded a seminary where Syriac was taught. However, the Franciscans continued operating their College and caring for the Christians, obviously Latins, at the church attached to their seminary. Though the Dutch seized Cranganore in 1662, they allowed the Franciscans to remain for a few years until they were expelled.

At Quilon the Portuguese maintained a strong fort and a bust trading-post, as the area was rich in pepper. It was also a centre of the Syrian Christians. Diocesan priests were in charge of the chief church, and the Jesuits and Franciscans maintained residences within the fortified area. It was from here that the Franciscans founded a mission in the neighbourhood, which will be dealt with further down.

On the Coromandel Coast the Portuguese settled in two places chiefly for trade purposes. They were Mylapore and Nagapatanam. Eventually at both places forts were erected. Both too attracted people among whom Christianity was propagated. In both places a number of parishes, generally placed incharge of the diocesan clergy, were erected. In both places the Augustinians, Dominicans, Franciscans and the Jesuits established themselves. Both too suffered from the same disability, viz., the missionaries were forbidden to use these places as bases for extending Christianity into the interior. A few chapels were founded in the immediate neighbourhood, such as Velanganni near Nagapatanam, which later on became the foremost Marian Shrine in India. Originally meant for a small group of fishermen the Franciscans had converted before 1630, it developed into a place of pilgrimage only during latter part of the 18th century.

Eventually the Portuguese in both places were eliminated or eclipsed. Nagapatanam was captured in 1658 by the Dutch. All clergy-men were expelled and all church property confiscated. Many Christians fled. However, after a few years the Dutch allowed one Franciscan to officiate at one church and care for the 8 to 10 thousand Catholics living there. During the greatest part of the period during which they were the masters, the Dutch also permitted one friar to remain at Velanganni.

At S. Tome Mylapore which, as we have noted became a diocese in 1606, the changes were more gradual, but in the end they proved to be almost as radical. In 1639 the English erected fort St. George in neighbouring Madras. They had by then already monopolized a great part of the trade, thus impoverishing Mylapore. Many Christians began moving thither for the sake of employment. To look after them, in 1642 they constrained the Capuchin, Ephrem de Nevers, to found a residence, thus introducing the first Propaganda-missionary in the area. In 1662 Mylapore was besieged and taken by the forces of Golconda. Most of the Christians fled, as did the clergy and religious. Eventually, after many vicissitudes and changes of masters the diocesan clergy and various religious orders returned, but Mylapore, which remained under the Padroado, never regained its ascendancy.

From the beginning the Portuguese controlled the shipping along the Kanara Coast and set up trading posts at various points. They needed them for their commerce and for procuring the rice they needed for the ever-increasing population of Goa. However, the Malabarian pirates preyed on their shipping. Hence they decided to seize a number of ports and fortify them. In 1558 they took Mangalore and the following year occupied Hanowar and from there hurried on to Barcelor (Lower Barcelor, Kundapur). Later when the entrance to this harbour shifted, they built a fort at Gangolly.

In all these places they established churches. In Mangalore

a Dominican built the first church. Later the Franciscans settled there and at Gangolly. The chief church in Mangalore and those built in the other places were entrusted to diocesan priests. In all these towns and their neighbourhood unsuccessful attempts were made to convert the local population.

In the year 1563-7 the Nayak of Ikkeri seized all the Portuguese forts. But though he eliminated them as a power, he did allow them to continue at some of their trading posts. The clergy abandoned these places, for it is reported that in 1568 there was not a single priest in Kanara.

Chaul, Diu and Sindh

Besides the forts so far mentioned, the Portuguese had two lonely strongholds further North, one at Chaul, south of Bombay, the other at Diu on the gulf of Cambay. Originally both had been chosen for their strategical positions, since from there the shipping lanes along which the Red Sea and Persian Gulf trade flowed, could be controlled. Chaul was an important harbour and its population large. It was among them that the diocesan priests, Dominicans, Franciscans and Jesuits laboured. However they were not permitted to move into the interior. In course of time people from areas already Christianized migrated to nearby places, from time to time they were visited by missionaries, but proselytization was out of the question. At Diu, a formidable bastion at that, conditions were similar. It was also an important trading-centre and people flocked thither for employment. Among these the diocesan clergy and the religious—Dominicans and Franciscans—worked. At one time there were over 5,000 Catholics. But towards the middle of the 17th century, due to the fact that the Dutch and English had entered the field and the Mogul authorities were diverting trade to their own ports, Diu had lost much of its importance. Unlike at Chaul, we do not hear of any Christians settling in the interior and being visited by priests from Diu.

During this period on the west coast there were three places, where the Portuguese had trading posts and where the Propaganda missionaries settled. Sooner or later conflicts were bound to erupt. The one was Surat, a harbour with a population of over two lakhs. The Jesuits settled there for a while, but they abandoned it, according to Godinho, who visited the town in 1663, because the Mogul emperors, each time a conflict arose with the Portuguese, held the Jesuits responsible. It was only after their departure that the French Capuchins under Propaganda in 1639-40 installed themselves in Surat and built a church. They remained the sole clergy working there during the period under review.

The other two were in the Indus valley, at the ports of Lahri Bandar and Tatta. Already before 1600 the Portuguese had opened trading posts. Their ships regularly overwintered there. In 1618 the Carmelites established themselves in Tatta. They had come from Persia without leave from the Padroado and the Propaganda was as yet to be founded. When founded in 1622 they had recourse to it but they were considered intruders. Hence in 1624 the Archbishop of Goa sent there Augustinians who challenged the jurisdiction of the Carmelites. They established themselves in Lahri Bandar. In 1632 Shah Jahan ordered all churches to be destroyed in his empire including those on the Indus. It was only in 1641 that permission was granted to rebuild them. Around 1650, when the Portuguese prestige and commerce had declined, the Augustinians withdrew. A few decades later, when the Christian community had dwindled to almost nothing, the Carmelites did the same.

In territories under the Indian Princes

The Portuguese did not restrict themselves to founding the church in their enclaves or at their forts and settlements. Under the patronage of the kings they also extended it to territories under the sovereignty of Indian rulers. The first such extension was the one in the Fishery Coast. Though the Portuguese had a small settlement and trading post at Tuticorin and for many years offered protection to the Paravas, it never became a Portuguese enclave not a restricted area around a fort or settlement. It included the whole of the Fishery Coast. The Jesuits maintained this mission, bequeathed to them by St. Francis Xavier. They divided the coast and founded five or six central residences, whence they served a number of subsidiary chapels and churches. In 1658 the Dutch seized Tuticorin and confiscated all church property including the hospice and the church the Franciscans had founded there to house the friars travelling to and from their mission in Ceylon.

On the Travancore coast from Quilon to Cape Comorin where the Fishery Coast began, St. Francis Xavier founded a mission which his confreres inherited and developed. Eventually they organized the whole area into ten parishes and from central residences served some 50 to 60 additional churches and chapels.

The Jesuits had extended their mission beyond Quilon, but in a limited sense. The Franciscans, however, had begun a mission with headquarters at Quilon and there was a possibility that a controversy might ensue. Hence in 1601 the Viceroy of Goa divided the territory between the two orders. Henceforth the Jesuits would restrict themselves to the area lying to the South of Quilon, their Travancore mission just described, whereas the Franciscans would develop their mission to the North. Eventually the latter founded four or five central parishes and residences whence they served a dozen or more chapels or churches.

Ironically it was under the aegis of the Portuguese Padroado that the controversial and at the same time the most famous mission in India was established. It was inaugurated by the Jesuit, Robert de Nobili (1577-1656), at Madurai, one of the ancient centres of Tamil culture. The episode is so well known that we need not go into many details.

De Nobili and Madurai Mission

Robert de Nobili arrived in 1606 in Madurai. There he met his confrere Concalo Fernandez, who was caring for a small group of Paravas on the Fishery Coast and making vain attempts to introduce Christianity among its citizens. The reason for this lack of success was that in the mind of the people, the missionary was to much associated with things foreign. They wore an alien garb, they followed certain customs which in their eyes were repugnant, they made use of incomprehensible signs and symbols. The doctrine they proclaimed was formulated too much in accordance with the genius of the West and overstressed those aspects of the eternal truths which appealed only to the occidental. A break with the past, a discarding of the current approach was required and the introduction of a new one or perhaps a returning to one of an earlier age. It was De Nobili who did just this. Externally he severed all connections with his confreres and took up his abode in a simple house of his own. Henceforth he addressed and comported himself as a member of the Rajah caste, wearing the thread, the kudumi and other marks of this caste. After all he too was a noble man, albeit a Roman, and these Indian marks did not necessarily carry a religious significance. They could also be considered as signs to denote a person's lineage. As a matter of fact this interpretation had already been accepted in the case of the Raja of Tanur, but it was not so much for the sake of adaptation that it was adopted, but to allow him to remain a crypto-Catholic. In a letter of 20 October 1549, Dom Joao de Albuquerque O.F.M., the first bishop of Goa, wrote: "He (the Tanur Raja) became a catholic secretly and wears the Brahmin thread and the other external signs, the same as before he became a christian, but he wears a metal cross in his bosom, which Fr. Vincente gave him. He says he will continue doing so until the chief Nairs are converted..." Later on De Nobili discarded some of these when he adopted the life of a sanyasi.

Once installed in his ashram, De Nobili set to work studying Tamil, later also Telugu, and Sanskrit, India's cultural language. Only then was he able to steep himself in the ancient wisdom of the land and to begin explaining, perhaps reformulating Christianity in terms and thought-patterns more in accordance with the genius of the country. He also uncovered what the spirit, who enlightens every person who comes into the world, had revealed to some Rishis and sanyasis in the distant past which was later codified perhaps under layers of subsequent ponderings.

That he and his method met with opposition is understandable. But he had the support of his Provincial and the Archbishop of Cranganore in whose territory Madurai was located. The case was hotly disputed, especially in Goa. From there it was transferred to Rome, but no decision was taken. Once again it was discussed in Goa, but no agreement could be reached, and they were forced to submit it once again to the Holy See. Finally in 1623 Gregory XV approved the method, although with certain cautions. Thus was De Nobili vindicated. Later on it was again questioned, but this belongs to another period.

That he was right in adopting new approach is borne out by the results. He himself baptized several caste people. And once they had joined, members of the lower castes and of the non-castes asked to be received as well. He himself, being obliged to observe the caste barriers, was not able to accept them. Others called Pandaraswamis, were deputed to do so. Like St. Paul who did not attempt to abolish slavery, so also did De Nobili not insist on breaking down the catse distinctions. This would only come about with a deepening of christianity and a change in society.

In course of time the Madurai mission spread over a wide area in Trichinopoly, Dindigul, Tanjore, the Marava country. By 1660, 11,198 baptisms had been administered, a tremendous success, especially when one considers that before this the doors had been closed.

Others who were inspired to imitate De Nobili, reaped also a measure of success. This was the case of Lo. Cinnami, a Jesuit of the Goa province, the founder of the Mysore mission. Originally he worked on the Kanara Coast but seeing he was unable to make any converts there, he discarded his cassock, adopted the sanyasi-robe and De Nobili's approach and penetrated into Mysore. The first convert he made was at Srirangapattanam. This was in 1648. In course of time this became also a flourishing mission, but its further history does not belong to the period under review.

Bengal

Though Dominicans, Franciscans and Jesuits worked in Bengal, chiefly in periods and places when and where the Portuguese had forts or factories, the Augustinians inaugurated the first permanent mission. This was in 1599, when Andre de S. Maria, O.F.M. was the bishop of Cochin, under which Bengal resorted up to the establishment of the diocese of Mylapore. The first two friars founded their first house at Hugli, where the Portuguese were settled. This place developed into the most important centre of their missionary venture. It is reported that by 1620 there were some 14,000 Christians in Bengal, half of whom were concentrated in Hugli. Between 1599 and 1612 they developed three additional mission stations and by 1632 four more, among them Dacca and Chittagong, then the most important harbour in Bengal. In 1632 Shah Jahan incensed with the Portuguese at Hugli and with the Christians at large seized Hugli and led some five thousand Christians and two Augustinians captive to Delhi and ordered all churches in his realm to be demolished. It was only in 1641 that they were released and permission was granted for churches to be erected. During the period under review the number of Augustinians working in Bengal never seems to have been higher than fifteen.

The Mogul Mission

The inland missions under the Padroado so far described, had to do with the Hindus. However, there was another group, large and influential, whose approach could hardly be contemplated. They were the Mohammedans, the religious enemies and the commercial rivals of the Portuguese. As a matter of fact the initiative to come into contact with the Moslems did not originate with the Jesuits who would undertake this mission but with Akbar, the greatest of the Mogul emperors (1556-1605). Besides being a foremost administrator, he was intelligent and interested in scholarly pursuits. He was fond of discussions, especially on subjects pertaining to religion. It has frequently been stated that he was not a convinced Moslem. Be as it may, his vision belonged to different religions. To unify them he hit upon the idea of instituting a religion of his own *Din Illahi* which would combine, according to his opinion, the best elements of each one. To acquaint himself better with Christianity he invited Fr. Julian Pereira from Satgaon, who arrived at his court in Fathepur Sikri in March 1578. After several discussions Fr. Pereira felt he was not sufficiently grounded in theology and suggested to him to summon Jesuits from Goa. In 1579 three Jesuits under the leadership of Rudolf Aquaviva, travelled to Akbar's court. They were well received and they held several discussions with the Emperor. After three years when they understood they would not be able as yet to accomplish anything, they withdrew.

A few years later when he maintained his court in Lahore, Akbar once again dispatched a messenger to Goa with request for Jesuits. Frs. Durate Leitao and Christobal de Vega were sent. Their stay lasted less than a year, when of their own accord they departed. From discussions it became apparent that Akbar was bent on developing and propagating his own religion, and they did not want to have any part in it.

In 1594 for a third time Akbar sent an ambassador to the Viceroy in Goa to ask for priests. The Jesuits were none too keen to accept the request, but the Viceroy insisted some should go as these missions and the good relationships they engendered were politically advantageous. Consequently Jerome Xavier, a grand-nephew of St. Francis Xavier, with Manoel Pinheiro and Br. Benedict de Goes travelled to Lahore. This was the beginning of the permanent mission to the Mogul Empire. Was there still hope that Akbar or some of the notables could be won over? Xavier behaves as if there was. He studied Persian, the language of the Mogul Court, and produced a number of works in this language. At the same time the Jesuits founded a number of churches, at Agra, Delhi, Lahore, Patna and some other places. They kept the faith alive in those Christians who flocked to the Mogul Court or its important centres on business or in search of a livelihood. During the reign of Akbar they would pursue their tasks without disturbance, but after Shah Jahan had been on the throne for some years, he began a persecution. In 1632 he ordered all churches to be demolished. It was only in 1641 that permission was granted to rebuild them.

The Jesuits had so far concentrated on Mohammedans, chiefly with the leaders on the hope of effecting a mass-movement. Since so far they had not been successful, Fr. Roth thought of turning towards the Hindus. After all they were still in the majority. It was for this reason that in the years 1658-60, he devoted himself to the study of Sanskrit and in 1660-62 composed a Sanskrit grammar which was the first one written by a European.

The relations of the Jesuits with the Emperor Aurengazeb were good and he did show some interest in Christianity, but when in 1667 Fr. Busi (Uwens, Buys), a native of Nymegen in Holland, died, he ceased to do so. This brings us up to the end of our period.

Expansion through Migration

The Indians who had accepted Christianity in the missions under the Padroado, did not necessarily remain in the areas where they were converted or baptized, but migrated elsewhere. Thus we have seen that christians settled in various places of the Mogul Empire and were cared for by the Jesuits. This occurred in other regions as well and gave rise to new christian centres. Thus from Goa many settled not only in the kingdom of Sundem and in areas under Bijapur, contiguous to Goa, but also on the Kanara coast. Frequently these people were neglected and this gave the Propaganda-missionaries an opportunity and reason to come in. The country which attracted christians, chiefly from Bardez, was Kanara. In the 16th century already many had left their native land and migrated thither in search of betterment or escape, and this trend continued during the following centuries. They were even enticed to come, as there was a dearth of agriculturists in that kingdom. As long as there were priests in Mangalore and at other Portuguese forts, the people in the neighbourhood were cared for and those living farther away could be periodically visited, but after the Nayak of Ikkeri seized these places, conditions worsened. Thus the Carmelite, Vincent of St. Catharine, reported in 1658 that there were 6000 catholics in the area, but not a single priest. Later on things improved, but this change for the better occurred after the period to which we have restricted ourselves.

From the Fishery coast christians migrated to the neighbouring places. Thus the church in Tranquebar owes its origin to them. Before 1597 already they had built a church and invited a Jesuit from Nagapatanam to officiate there. Later, before 1620, he settled there. When the Dutch expelled the clergy from Nagapatanam in 1659, the Jesuit, who was dependent on the Rector there, withdrew and henceforth the Catholics were cared for by the priests deputed by the Bishop of Mylapore.

Though missionaries were forbidden to enter Tanjore, christians on a whole were not. Thus Caesar Frederick, who visited the town c. 1570, reported that he found many "Portugals and Christians" there. They must have come from Nagapatanam, from the Fishery coast, perhaps from Goa: merchants, adventurers attracted to the court, those willing to serve in the army (artillery-men trained by the Portuguese were everywhere welcome), the unemployed, slaves who had fled their masters. These were the categories who migrated to other regions as well. So when De Nobili extended his mission to Tanjore he found a number of catholics there already. Henceforth the Jesuits, besides increasing the faithful there and in the neighbourhood, would also care for them.

In 1652 the Augustinians established a hospice at Masulipatanam. This served their missionaries as a stop-over on their way to and from Bengal, but it was also meant as a residence for the Fathers caring for the Catholics who had settled there. They also erected a church in this town and in others in the neighbourhood, one of them being in Vizagapatanam. Two churches were also founded by them deeper into the interior, one at the court of the king of Golconda and another at a distance of two leagues. It was the Augustinians who introduced the first Theatine Father into these areas.

Undoubtedly christians moved to areas other than the ones we have described and more would do so in the future. However, what has been indicated is sufficient to show how the Gospel was spread through the migration of christians.

The Eclipse of the Portuguese

We have seen the extent of the Portuguese power in India. However by the year 1665 their prestige had declined and their possessions diminished. The Dutch, besides the forts and factories they had founded in Ceylon, seized those along the coasts, from Cannanore on the west to Nagapatanam on the east coast. The Portuguese settlement in Mylapore had been eclipsed by the proximity of the English at fort St. George in Madras and the Dutch in Pulicat. Their forts on the Kanara coast had been taken by the Nayak of Ikkeri. Bombay was ceded to the English in the year 1661-5. What was left of their former possessions were their enclaves of Goa, Bassein and Damaun and the two isolated forts in Chaul and Diu. But these were impoverished and sections of the population had migrated elsewhere. Most of their former trade was now in the hands of the Dutch and English. Less and less ships were frequenting their ports as they were being attracted elsewhere, including the harbours of Indian rulers. On land they were surrounded by enemies. Still they survived only because the Indians were not united and the Portuguese were able to play one party against the other.

It is understandable that in these circumstances the church under the Padroado suffered. The authorities were unable to offer the same support as they were used to. The number of missionaries from abroad had long ago past its peak. Portugal, a nation of one to two million, was depleted. The missionary zeal had waned, but even if there had been more volunteers, they would have been able to transport and support them as in their heyday. In their own enclaves there was still a sufficiently large body of clergy. There was even a surplus, especially in Goa. Many of these volunteered for the missions, but not all. They felt that theirs was not a missionary vocation. It is remarkable, however, that in the circumstances the missions in the interior were being maintained and even new ones were being established.

CHAPTER V

THE EASTERN CHURCH 16th-17th CENTURIES

By Rev. Dr. A.M. Mundadan CMI.

On the 21st of May, 1498 Vasco da Gama cast anchor in the road-stead of Calicut. For the Europeans of the time the exploit was the conversion into fact of long-drawn dream, the fruition of the sustained sea-faring efforts of a century. For the Christians of St. Thomas in India it was sudden and unexpected and the beginning of a new epoch of tremendous impact, the entering into a new world of existence. One might rightly say that till the arrival of the Portuguese the Thomas Christians were living as if in two worlds: the geographical, political and social world of the Malabar coast; and the ecclesiastical world which was more or less Chaldaean in character, for the Chaldaean prelates governed them in spiritual matters; they shared the theological, juridical and liturgical traditions of the Chaldaean Church. This dependence was both an advantage and a disadvantage to the Indian Christians. Perhaps the community of the Thomas Christians was able to keep up a strong Christian tradition on account of this dependence. At the same time it is true that the varying fortunes of the Chaldaean Church could not but affect the Indian Church too. The dependence further prevented the Church of India from developing an Indian Christian culture, especially an Indian theology and an Indian liturgy.

Nonetheless, in the social set up the Christians of India lived a life not much different from that of their high-caste Hindu neighbours. Though they were spread over various kingdoms and principalities of Malabar, they had the Chief of the Villarvattam dynasty as their special protector-king. Their socio-ecclesiastical life was organized under the combined leadership of the Metropolitan, who was always a foreigner, and the Archdeacon, who invariably was a national leader.[1]

Thus at the arrival of the Portuguese the Thomas Christians were leading a life full of reminiscences of their past, and enjoying a very high status in society, but adhering, as they were, to their peculiar ecclesiastical and social customs and practices. It is this particular mode of life which somehow or other came into conflict with the particular Christian way of life of the Portuguese. The struggle began very early in the 16th century and grew towards its end. The crisis of the mid-17th century, and all the troubles of the 18th and 19th centuries are expressions of this conflict.

If the Thomas Christians were living in two worlds prior to the arrival of the Portuguese, with the coming of the Portuguese a new third world, the world of Western Christendom, was also opened up before them. It exercised, in course of time, such influence over them as they would find it difficult to shed its traces even if they desired to.

The 16th century opens with a bright outlook. The Portuguese feel satisfied that their centuries-old dream of discovering India and Eastern Christians has been fulfilled; that through their instrumentality, Western and Eastern Christendoms have been somewhat united. They set great hopes on the Christians of India. The Thomas Christians, on their part, experience a spontaneous relief and joy at the arrival of powerful Christians from the West and expect the new-comers to help strengthen their own privileged existence. It is in such an atmosphere of euphoria that a life-contact begins between the Portuguese and the Thomas Christians. This contact, after many a vicissitude, culminated in a moment of tension created by the circumstance in which the Synod of Diamper was convened at the close of the 16th century. With the Synod the long-standing relations of the Church of India with that of Chaldaean was artificially terminated, and the Thomas Christians were brought under the Latin jurisdiction of the Portuguese *Padroado*.

During the whole of the 16th century these Christians were ruled over by bishops from Chaldaea. The first half under Mar Jacob (1503-1552) was rather peaceful, though much of the initial enthusiasm and expectations soon died out. The second half under Mar Joseph (1558-1569) and Mar Abraham (1569-1597) witnessed a more tumultous situation, but even this did not yet take the proportions of the tense years of the 17th century which burst out into what is known as the "Koonen Kurisu Oath" of 1653.

Thomas Christians under Mar Jacob[2]

The dependence of India on the Church of Chaldaea for bishops left her, it seems, without prelates for long intervals, especially since the final decline of the Chaldaean Church, established in the 13th century. One such interval occurred in the second half of the 15th century. At the end of it in 1490 two bishops were brought to Malabar by a delegation of the Thomas Christians. More bishops came in at the beginning of the 16th century. Thus there must have been four or five bishops in Malabar when the Portuguese began their first contacts with the Thomas Christians. However, in the twenties one hears only of two bishops: Mar Jacob and a younger bishop. Others might have died or left Malabar earlier. Mar Jacob lived till the middle of the 16th century and ruled the Indian Church. His simplicity, virtue, zeal and disinterestedness in the service of God and his faithful are well borne out by his letters. There is also ample testimony by the Portuguese, both lay and clerical, to support this. He was loved and esteemed by all. St. Francis Xavier is all praise for him. It was providential that this virtuous prelate guided the Christians of St. Thomas during the first stage of their new era.

Vasco da Gama, who came to India in 1498 on his first voyage, returned home with a false satisfaction that he had met Christians at Calicut. It would appear that he and his men mistook the caste Hindus for Christians and their temples for Christian churches. Pedro Alvares Cabral followed Gama in 1500 and met real Christians at Cochin and even took two of them to Portugal with him.

When Vasco da Gama arrived at Cochin (1502 A.D.) on his second voyage, a delegation of Thomas Christians went to meet him. They presented him a 'rod of justice' and swore allegiance to the Portuguese king and implored Portuguese protection. The Admiral received them very kindly and promised all help and protection. The significance of this event is variously interpreted by historians. One thing is certain that with this a very cordial and intimate relation was established between the native Christians and the new-comers. The following year Alfonso d'Albuquerque's visit to Quilon further strengthened this relation.

During the first twenty years or so it so more with Portuguese navigators and traders that the Thomas Christians came into contact. Only from the year 1516/17 the influence of the Portuguese missionaries appear to have impact on the life of the Christians of St. Thomas. By the time the churchmen become active, the initial enthusiasm suffered minor setbacks. Tension began to mount as more and more missionaries started to deal with the community.

Before proceeding to the survey of the contacts of the Thomas Christians with the Portuguese missionaries and churchmen it will be quite in place to make an observation or two on the fundamental attitudes of the Portuguese and the Thomas Christians in their approach to each other. The official attitude of the Portuguese towards the Christians of St. Thomas, towards all other Christians in the East for that matter, was one of sympathy and understanding but always motivated by a sense of superiority, whether such a sense was explicit or not, about their form of Christianity which was, according to them, the true form, and to which all Christians should conform in order to be perfect Christians. The local customs and the particular usages of the different rites were adulterations and abuses which should be some way or other eradicated. In short the Christians should conform to the Portuguese in everything. Ample evidence is provided for this basic attitude by the events that ensued after the initial period. They would ask the Christians bluntly to conform to the Portuguese in all matters. They put it this way: The Mohammedans, wherever they lived in the world, had uniform customs. So too the Jews. The Christians should have the like uniformity. And since the customs of the Portuguese were perfectly Christian customs, the Christians of Malabar too were to conform to the Portuguese customs.

The attitude of the priests and the missionaries who appeared on the scene was not at all different; on the contrary they were naturally more sensitive to the differences. Their aim generally was to make the Christians of India conform to the Portuguese ways and usages which were Roman by derivation. This some did as bluntly as Fr. Penteado; others attempted doing it more tactfully, though they had more or less the same mentality.

The Christians of India, on the other hand, although more or less conscious of their imperfections especially in the matter of doctrine, never had the idea that only the Latin or Western form of Christianity was true Christianity. They could very well appreciate the Latin usages and liturgical and canonical disciplines. But they were not for them just as their own particular customs and practices in these matters were not for the Portuguese. Their notion could be analysed thus: both the Portuguese and they were Christians and both belonged to the universal Church. But each local community had their customs and usages including church discipline, these customs and usages probably going back to the times of the Apostles themselves. In this sense one could speak of the 'Law of Peter' the 'Law of Thomas' and so on. They could never entertain the idea of giving up their customs and practices both social and ecclesiastical which had been sacred to them for centuries. They were ready to accept from the Latin missionaries what they lacked: instruction, a better discipline; but would not accept those missionaries in the position of their prelates and the priests.

Another factor was that the Thomas Christians considered the Portuguese as their own people in friendly recognition as Christians and brethren, but this recognition did not mean that the Christians were prepared to admit the Portuguese into the set up of their communal life, which was a closed one, to which all strangers, whether Christians or not (in this sense the high caste people of Malabar were less strangers to them than the Portuguese), were prohibited entrance and assimilation. They conceived the Portuguese in this exclusive spirit and thought of them as strangers and outsiders.

This uncompromising attitude of the Christians of St. Thomas is amply illustrated by many documents. Just an example may be quoted here. Fr. Penteado writing to the Portuguese King in 1516 or 1517 says: "The Christians of St. Thomas do not care for the communication with the Portuguese, not because they were not happy that they are Christians as we are, but because we are among them as the English and the Germans are among us. As regards their national customs, their will is corrupted by their priests who say that just as there were twelve Apostles, even so, they founded twelve customs."

Thus we see the approach of the Portuguese and that of the Christians of St. Thomas are from different and almost opposite angles. The Christians wanted the communities to remain unimpaired in any way, each independent of the other, but with full cooperation for the good of both. To use a modern term they wanted coexistence and not absorption of one community in the other. The Portuguese were unable to grasp this idea of coexistence. What they wanted was absorption, and that too of native Christians into that of the Portuguese. To what extent they wanted this absorption is difficult to state precisely. They put no limit to it going as far as to assimilate even food, clothes and even names.

It is easy, therefore, to understand the conflicts in opinions and methods from the beginning of the mission work of the Latin priests among the Thomas Christians. At last the stronger party (the Portuguese) would win for the moment (the Synod of Diamper) but the solution thus brought about would lead to violence and the whole problem would become crucial and lead to an explosion in its own time (the events from 1653). After this, a real and lasting solution would have to be sought in partial retreat to the old ways and in a new approach (from the end of 19th century on). We see seeds sown in the twenties, thirties and forties of the fifteenth century for the later dramatic harvesting.

The first note of open discord with the Thomas Christians was struck with the rather imprudent activities of Fr. Penteado, a Portuguese diocesan priest, who came to India on his initiative and took up work among the Thomas Christians some time in 1517, this without leave from the authorities of Thomas Christians. Mar Jacob's letter of 1524 which he wrote to the King of Portugal, echoes the resentment of the Christians against Fr. Penteado as well as some other causes of misunderstanding and misgiving on their part. It is at this time a Dominican priest, John Caro by name, appears in Malabar and offers to help Mar Jacob. His sympathetic approach did in fact make up for much of the harm done by Fr. Penteado. But the latter's interference for a second time caused a much greater breach of peace; the good offices of the Franciscans somehow cleared the atmosphere though it seems there emerged a small hard core who refused to have anything to do with the Portuguese.

In the last years of Mar Jacob's rule the Portuguese made a more radical and systematic attempt to latinize the Christians of St. Thomas by establishing a seminary or college at Crangan- ore. The seminary was founded by a Franciscan friar, Vicente de Lagos, with a view to training the children of Thomas Christ- ians to priesthood. The friar was a good educationist and dis- ciplinarian and the Portuguese writers have not minced words in praising his work. His only drawback was that he failed to understand and appreciate the particular pattern of the religious culture of the boys committed to his care and to pay any regard for their maternal rite. All those who came out of the seminary had been formed on the Latin and Western lines. They differed little from the Portuguese Latin missionaries. The Thomas Christian parents though in the beginning were enthusiastic about the good training their sons received at the seminary later only felt sorry to find them being estranged from the community way of life. These latinised priests were never assimilated into the community, but were kept out treated just as the other Latin priests.

While these activities were going on in Cranganore Mar Jacob who was already advanced in years, and who realized that matters had gone beyond his control, prudently retired from active life. He had tried his best to keep a healthy middle course between the extreme groups both among the Portuguese and his own Christians. But he refused to be a party to disrupting the integrity of the oriental character of the community. The Portuguese systematic attempts to latinise the community made his position most difficult. He retired to the Franciscan monas- tery of Cochin and spent his last years in its peaceful atmosphere and died there around 1552.

The death of Mar Jacob, was in the eyes of the Portuguese, the breaking of the last link which connected the Church of India with that of Chaldaea. Mar Jacob was good, and meek, and to some extent had given in to the Portuguese and retired. Still his presence was a symbol of the relation of the Church of India with the East-Syrian Church—a symbol of the whole ecclesiastical life of the Thomas Christians. By the death of Mar Jacob that symbol was broken, the Portuguese thought. With his death the last obstacle to their plans of latinizing the community was removed. But the Thomas Christians were determined to continue their relations with the Church of the East and secretly negotiated to get prelates from there to rule over them. Bishops did come in spite of all the vigilance of the Portuguese authorities and ruled the Church of India for another half a century more.

Mar Joseph and Mar Abraham[3]

In 1552 Simon Sulaqua was approved by Pope Julius III as Patriarch of the Chaldaeans, consequent upon this event there emerged in the mid-16th century two lines of East Syrian Patriarchs, one in union with Rome and the other outside such a union. For the sake of clarity the first we may call the Catholic line and the second, the Nestorian line. Accordingly the community was also divided. The Christians of India do not seem to have been much affected by these developments in Mesopotamia immediately. They, in all probability, looked on that Church still as one and undivided. After the death of Mar Jacob they allegedly sent a message to 'Babylon' requesting bishops to rule over them. And bishops came to India from both parties.

The first to reach Malabar was, most likely, the one sent by the Nestorian Patriarch. It now seems certain that Mar Abraham was sent to India by Mar Simon VIII (1551-58) of the Nestorian line. He arrived in Malabar sometime before 1557 and it seems he claimed for himself the approval of the Pope to rule the Indian Church. In any case, in order to avoid trouble from the Portuguese, he kept himself out of reach of their influence and ruled the Christians of St. Thomas for an year or two. The Portuguese were very much annoyed at his presence, for they considered him an intruder who entered the sheepfold through the backdoor. They tried all means at their disposal to get him ousted but their attempts were successfully foiled by him.

Here we have to resume the story of Simon Sulaqua. After having been confirmed by Pope Julius III he returned to Mesopotamia in the company of two Maltese Dominicans, deputed by the Pope himself, Bishop Ambrose Buttigeg and Fr. Antonius Zahara. Sulaqua governed the Church only for a short time as he soon died a martyr at the instigation of the rival party. Abd'sho succeeded him in 1555, and he also went to Rome and was confirmed Patriarch by Pope Pius IV. On returning to Mosul, he sent two bishops Mar Joseph, the brother of the martyred Patriarch Sulaqua, and Mar Elias together with the two Dominicans mentioned above, to look after the affairs of the Church of Malabar. The mission arrived in Goa by the end of 1555; but they were stopped at Goa by the Portuguese authorities and prevented from proceeding to Malabar. The two Chaldaean bishops were taken to Mozambique whence, after some time, they were shifted to a Franciscan monastery at Bessein in Salsette. Here they were confined for more than a year. Meanwhile, the two Dominicans remained in their monastery in Goa trying by every means to get their own liberty and that of the two detained Chaldeans. Finally in 1557 they were all set free and proceeded to Malabar. It is not unlikely that such a course was decided upon by the Portuguese authorities because that was the only way, they thought, to get rid of Mar Abraham who was working in Malabar as described earlier. The Jesuit Fr. Dionysio wrote in 1578: "...while he (Mar Abraham) was governing, there came three bishops through Ormuz, namely bishop Ambrose, an Italian (actually Maltese) and Mar Joseph and Mar Elias, both Syrians. Between Mar Abraham and these three prelates there arose a dispute. The issue raised was whether Mar Abraham was legitimately instituted or not. Later he was deposed." There is no doubt that Mar Abraham was finally persuaded or forced to quit the country.

One of the bishops of the Chaldean mission, Mar Elias, soon left India. Mar Joseph worked for a few years in Malabar in the company of the Dominicans. Bishop Buttigeg died not long after at Cochin, leaving Antonius Zahara alone to assist Mar Joseph. They worked together and reformed much the Church of Malabar. After sometime Mar Joseph was accused of heresy and deported to Goa. More or less at the same time

Antonius was also called back to Rome. The charge of heresy against Mar Joseph seems to have been only a very handy means of getting rid of someone who gave embarassment to the Portuguese authorities. For, not only was Mar Joseph finally acquitted, when he was subsequently taken to Lisbon, but we have in his favour a letter written at this time by the Prior of the Dominican monastery in Goa, whose hospitality Mar Joseph had accepted before being taken to Lisbon. The Prior, in the letter, speaks of him as a person deserving all honour and approbation. Well, Mar Joseph was taken to Lisbon, which he might have reached at least by the beginning of 1564. As we have said above he was forthwith acquitted and through the influence of Antonius Zahara was the recipient of an apostolic brief authorising him to go back to India and take care of the Christians of St. Thomas. So Mar Joseph did not go to Rome as he had first desired, but returned to Malabar with the recommendation of Cardinal Henry who was at that time both Regent and Grand Inquisitor. Mar Joseph might have reached India some time in 1565.

While Mar Joseph was absent in Europe the Portuguese made a concerted attempt to bring the Christians of St. Thomas to the subjection of Padroado bishop of Cochin, Don Temudo. Perhaps the Christians would have succumbed to the pressure and persuasion in their despair to get a prelate from Mesopotamia. But they would not give in easily; they sent a secret message to Patriarch Abdisho asking for a bishop. It was quite likely in answer to this request that the Patriarch sent Mar Abraham to India.

We have seen earlier how Mar Abraham, consequent upon the arrival of Mar Joseph in Malabar, departed from India some time after 1557. When exactly he left India and when he reached Mesopotamia are points difficult to establish with precision. It is quite probable that he was converted to Catholicism before he left Malabar; so too it is probable that he on his return to Mesopotamia approached the Patriarch Abdisho, of the Catholic line, and not patriarch Elias VI (1558-76) of the Nestorian line, who had succeeded Mar Simon VIII. Mar Abdisho seems to have received him kindly and was perhaps ever since waiting for opportunity to sent him back to India.

The opportunity arrived when the request for a bishop came from the Christians of St. Thomas sometimes after 1565. It is not unlikely that Mar Abraham was till that time a simple priest and had not received episcopal consecration, though in India he had pretended the contrary. Abdisho consecrated him bishop and directed him to go to Rome and to represent his case before Pope Pius IV. This was a precautionary measure against the possible objection the Portuguese might raise against him in India, as they did even against Mar Joseph. Mar Abraham must have reached Rome by the beginning of 1565, where the Pope received him benevolently. He made his profession, and, if we are to believe Fr. Dionysio, at his own request, he was ordained anew and consecrated, because he had his own scruples about his earlier consecration. The Pope gave him letters of recommendation, to Patriarch Abdisho, to the Archbishop of Goa, to the bishop of Cochin. He returned to Mesopotamia where he received further letters of recommendation from the Patriarch. Armed with all these letters of recommendations he proceeded to India and landed in Goa in the beginning of 1568. The Portuguese authorities were least prepared to accept the recommendation letters at their face value; and Mar Abraham was detained. But the shrewd prelate escaped the vigilance, and travelling overland reached his Christians in Malabar by April 1568.

At this time Mar Joseph was not in Malabar; he had again gone to Europe. As said above he might have reached India after his first journey to Europe some time in 1565. But he was soon accused of heresy by the Portuguese for a second time and was taken to Europe. This time he proceeded to Rome and pleaded his cause so well that he was acquitted by the Roman authorities. Unfortunately he could not go back to India, as he died in Rome in the year 1569. Cardinal Tisserant has this entry in his book: "The Roman judges, however, like the Franciscan guardian of Bassein previously, felt obliged to give way before the piety of Mar Joseph, and to recognize his orthodoxy. Yet the measure of suffering was full, and Mar Joseph received near the tomb of the Apostles, the crown which he had merited, through his long and slow martyrdom which was perhaps more painful one than that of his heroic brother. Eighteen Syriac manuscripts, and one Arabic and one Persian manuscript, which he had always carried with him on his travels, were incorporated in the Apostolic Library of the Vatican by right of spoil."[4]

With the death of Mar Joseph Mar Abraham's adventures had an end and now he was left alone in Malabar as the Metropolitan of All India. The bitter experiences he had undergone on previous occasions taught him to keep clear of the Portuguese circles of influence. He chose Angamaly his residence, instead of Cranganore which had by this time developed into a Portuguese stronghold. Mar Abraham refused to attend the second Provincial Council of Goa held in 1575, though he was formally invited to it by the Archbishop of Goa.

Mar Abraham's relations with the Portuguese missionaries (now mainly Jesuits) frequently alternated between discord and reconciliation. The Jesuits had then been in Malabar for over 25 years, but their contacts with the Thomas Christians had been so far sporadic and occasional. At this time a certain Mar Simeon from Mesopotamia, pretending to be a bishop sent by the Pope, had come to Malabar and had set up his camp at Kaduthuruthy. He had the following of a few churches and priests. Mar Abraham had tried his best to get this rival bishop out of Malabar; but to no avail. The Jesuits offered the Archbishop all their help to oust Mar Simeon. From Mar Abraham they obtained permission to establish themselves at Vaipicotta (Chennamangalam) and to go and preach and administer sacraments regularly in the churches of the St. Thomas Christians. Mar Simeon was finally forced to withdraw from India. The Jesuits, with the full approbation of Mar Abraham and his Archdeacon George of Christ, visited the Christians and succeeded in introducing many "reforms" such as priestly celibacy, confession before communion, burying the dead near the churches, some feasts of the Latin Calendar and so on—most of these "reforms" were merely Latin customs. A diocesan synod held at Angamaly in 1583 was the finale of these reformatory attempts.

In that synod probably a decision was made to start a new seminary for the clerics of the St. Thomas Christians. The Jesuits thought that such a seminary under their auspices would bring to full fruition the reforming activities already begun and approved by the synod. The seminary began to function at Vaipicotta probably in 1584 with the full approval of the Archbishop and his Archdeacon. Soon it became a centre of ecclesiastical learning, to which students flocked from all over Malabar. Even priests were desirous of going to the seminary to profit by the course of Moral theology and *casus conscientiae* conducted there. Knowing from experience how ineffective the seminary at Cranganore had turn out to be to minister to the needs of the Thomas Christians, care was taken at Vaipicotta to teach Syriac along with Latin, although this policy suffered some reverses later on. Courses in Malayalam were given for foreign Jesuits, and Syriac, Latin and Portuguese for native seminarians.

So far so good; but it was not too long before troubles began to brew. The Jesuits were not one in their minds about the policy they were to adopt with regard to the Thomas Christians. While one group wanted total and quick reduction of these Christians to the Latin rite and the Portuguese jurisdiction, another group would do it tactfully through a slow process without offending the feelings, keeping even the Syriac language for liturgical purposes. Still others counselled that their Rite be kept intact, and that their subjection to the Catholic Patriarch of the Chaldeans be not disturbed. At the same time they would insist that the Latin Jesuits should have a decisive role in educating them and disciplining them. In that way, they hoped, they would be able to purge them of what they thought were abuses and errors.

Even the mildest of their attitudes was provocative in the eyes of the Archbishop, his Archdeacon and the people. The events which followed only helped the situation to get worse. In 1585 there took place the Third Provincial Council of Goa. Mar Abraham was invited, and he attended it as the Pope had desired. The third session of the Council enacted ten decrees concerning the Church of Malabar. The main ones dealt with the training of the students in the seminary at Vaipicotta, the translation of the Pontifical and sacramentary from Latin to Syriac for use in the churches of Malabar, the entrance into Malabar of a few Chaldean bishops who were obliged to show their letters patent to the Archbishop of Goa before proceeding to Malabar, and so on. Francis Ros, a Catalan (Spanish) Jesuit, who had arrived in India in 1584, and who accompanied Mar

Abraham to Goa for the Council, was commissioned to implement the decisions taken in the Council.

Probably Mar Abraham's rift with the Jesuits began to widen once Ros progressed in his work of correcting the books. In any case soon news began to reach Rome that Mar Abraham had decidedly heretical tendencies. Pope Clement VIII issued a brief on January 27, 1595, authorising Archbishop Alexis de Menezes of Goa to inquire into the case of Mar Abraham. Some time later, on January 21, 1597, another brief was directed by the same Pope to the Archbishop of Goa, in which he was given faculties to appoint an administrator for the archbishopric of Angamali, in the event of the death of Mar Abraham.

But it seems that by the end of 1594 there was again raproachment between Mar Abraham and the Jesuits. He wrote to the Jesuit General at the close of 1594 that his days on earth were numbered and soon he would be called to give his account before God. He fell seriously ill in the beginning of 1595. He had hoped that he could provide for his succession and die in peace. Already in the 80s he had sought the help of the Jesuits and the King of Cochin to get his previous Archdeacon, George of Christ, consecrated co-adjutor. In that he did not succeed because the Archdeacon, it is said, out of humility declined the nomination. George of Christ died in 1593 without receiving episcopal consecration. Now Mar Abraham sought the help of the Jesuits again to plead for the current Archdeacon, George of the Cross. But he was denied this consolation; he never received any reply from the Pope, or the King of Portugal or even from the Jesuits General to all of whom he had written with the request that provision be made for his Archdeacon to succeed him. Ros wrote to the Jesuit General in 1597: "It is four years since Fr. Mannuel de Vega went to Rome with letters requesting His Holiness to appoint as his successor the Archdeacon, his Vicar General. I do not think His Holiness will have difficulty in making out the contents of the letters written in Chaldean, as they are accompanied by a Latin translation. But such was the will of the Lord that the Archbishop never received any reply..."

On his death-bed Mar Abraham solicited the concurrence of the Jesuits to appoint the Archdeacon his successor in virtue of the faculties he had from the Chaldean Patriarch. They refused to oblige him, either because the position was not quite clear to them, or because they were already committed to the idea that a Latin bishop should succeed him in order to smoothen the complete subjection of the Thomas Christians to the *Padroado* jurisdiction. This attitude of the Jesuits pained the Metropolitan; this likely made him defy the attempts of the Jesuits Fathers to administer to him the last sacraments according to the Latin rite. The Jesuit letters about his death allude to this defiant attitude towards them. He breathed his last in early January, 1597.

The Synod of Diamper[5]

News of the illness of Mar Abraham had already reached Rome but not of his death, when Pope Clement VIII by a brief of 1597 authorised Archbishop Menezes to appoint a Vicar Apostolic for Angamali, in the event of the death of Mar Abraham. As soon as Mar Abraham died, the Archdeacon George of the Cross, took up the reins of the Church in his own hands, as was the custom before. When Menezes arrived in Malabar he had reluctantly to confirm the Archdeacon as Administrator. But the Archbishop, who probably read more than intended into the brief of Clement VIII, made a visitation of Malabar, ordained many to priesthood and made all arrangements to convoke a synod. All these measures were stoutly opposed by the Archdeacon but the Archbishop brought pressure on the Archdeacon who finally gave in.

The Synod was held in the church of Diamper (Udayamperur) from June 20 to 26, 1599. Various views have been expressed about the validity and propriety of the synod. Dr. Jonas Thaliath, whose study is the latest on the subject, considers the synod invalid on the grounds that it was convoked without authority, conducted not according to the sacred canons, and was never approved by Rome. Despite the invalidity, the event has furnished us with a document which throw much light on the situation of the Church of India during and before the Portuguese period. It ratified and consolidated the latinising efforts of the Portuguese which had begun early in the 16th century.

Even a superficial glance at the acts and decrees of the synod would suffice to convince one what a radical change of the life pattern of the Christians was envisaged by it. "Many people nowadays are shocked by the tendency to reduce everything to the standard of Roman and Portuguese customs. Was not this tendency the leading principle of Archbishop de Menezes and his collaborators?" asks Card. Tisserant. The Cardinal after having delineated the various changes decreed by the synod says: "...what was foremost in the mind of the Archbishop of Goa was to remove for good all Mesopotamian and Nestorian influence in matters of faith and Church organization, and in liturgical formulas. This was a somewhat delicate procedure, since it endangered that Christian edifice to which, in spite of all its imperfections, these people had been accustomed for centuries. Moreover, were they not well worth some sympathy for their ignorance and simplicity? Alexis de Menezes, born and brought up in the atmosphere of the Counter-Reformation in Europe, was not the man however to yield even an inch when he thought something to to be his duty."

Some of the decrees insist that there was to be only one law, that of Christ; there were not to be two different laws, one of St. Thomas and the other of St. Peter, as some apparently thought. The obvious purpose was to inculcate in the Christians of St. Thomas that they should sever all ties with the East-Syrian Patriarch and accept only bishops appointed by Rome. Thus the long-standing hierarchical subjection of the Church of India on the East-Syrian Church was arbitrarily terminated. C. de Clerq remarks: "All the causes of the subsequent dissension... are provoked by Menezes' excessive reforms and also by doing away with the hierarchy of the rite." Menezes sought to destroy at one blow what he considered the root-cause of all the shortcomings that he found in the Church of Malabar. By means of threats, bribes and force he succeeded in severing the long-standing connection of the Malabar Church with the Patriarchate of Chaldaea, even though the Patriarch in question (Simon Denha) was fully in communion with Rome. The next step was to entrust that Church to a Latin prelate and to bring it under the patronage of the Portuguese crown. Several of the ceremonies and rites in the celebration of holy mass and the administration of the sacraments, were hastily and unnecessarily changed in order to bring them more in line with Latin usages. All this invariably provoked an amount of discontent. In several of the decrees ground was cleared for the radical substitution of most of the East-Syrian and Indian customs and disciplinary laws which were prevalent in India, by the western disciplinary laws especially of those of the Council of Trent. This produced an unhappy admixture of Latin customs and Eastern customs, and the identity of the Indian Syrian Church became very much blurred for a long time.

Perhaps the most radical action taken to sever the Syrian Church of India from the East Syrian Church was the prescription of the 14th decree of Act III which condemned by name literary works which were branded as dangerous, and were subjected to the *auto-da-fe* programme that continued even after the synod was over.

The synod concluded on June 26. All the rectors of the churches were enjoined to keep in their archives at least one copy of the Malayalam translation of the acts of the synod. This translation was to be the official one, signed by Archdeacon George and by the Superior of the College of Vaipicotta. In order that all the faithful might be taught the prescriptions of the synod, its acts were to be read by sections whenever there was no sermon at the services on Sundays and Feast days. Two authentic copies, signed by the Archbishop, were to be kept, the first at Vaipicotta, the second one at Angamali.

Most of these instructions were put into practices under the supervision of archbishop Menezes himself during his post-synodal visitation from July to November of the same year.

Jesuit Bishops under the Padroado[6]

There can be no doubt about the fact that the tone of the 16th century is set by the Synod of Diamper, which in practice was the denial of the age-long particular pattern of the life of the Christians of St. Thomas. The initial calm is belied by the ensuing violent reactions. At the surface everything seems to have been set in good order but at bottom their lurked dissatisfaction and resentment, which manifested themselves not in one single violent eruption, but in a series of events apparently insignificant among themselves. The synod had arbitrarily severed all the ties of the Indian Church with the Chaldean Patriarch. Bishops under the Padroado jurisdiction were appointed to rule the St.Thomas Christians. The first choice was Francis Ros who ruled them from 1600 to 1624. The other two who followed him were also Jesuits: Stephen de Britto (1624-41), and Francis Garcia (1641-1659). The respective Archdeacons who assisted these prelates were: George of the Cross (d.1637) and Thomas Parampil (Thomas de Campo) who rebelled against Garcia in 1653 and later became Thomas I, Bishop of those who broke communion with Rome. The residence of the Metropolitan was Angamali during the reign of Mar Abraham. Ros made Cranganore again his residence.

Both under Ros and Britto the story of Mar Abraham seems to be repeated in the person of the Archdeacon—quarrel and reconciliation with the Portuguese prelate alternate. The difference is in the fact that now the Portuguese Jesuits are the superiors and the native Archdeacons subordinates. This made the situation even more unbearable. The community witnessed helplessly to some of the high handed actions of the Archbishops, who, it may be true, did everything with the best of intentions. One such occasion was when Ros denied the Archdeacon many of his prestine privileges and rights and even dared to substitute him with a foreign Jesuit priest. Things came to a head under Archbishop Garcia. The arrival of an Eastern bishop, Aiatallah, provided the occasion for the final outbreak.

The Revolt of 1553[7]

It seems now proved that Aiatallah who came to India in the middle of the 17th century originally hailed from the Jacobite Church of Syria; later he was converted to Catholicism. He came to India at the request of the Coptic Patriarch while he was staying in Cairo. Till his death he seems to have remained faithful to the Catholic allegiance.

But in India the Syrian Christians (except perhaps a leader or two among them) took him as a Patriarch or Metropolitan sent from the East Syrian bishop with the approbation of the Pope of Rome. The Portuguese thought that he was a 'Nestorian' or East Syrian intruder. The rift, his presence and his forced removal from India caused in the community, is to be understood *in the light of the attachment the Indian Christians still cherished* for the East-Syrian Church. That St. Thomas Christians always remained very attached to the bishops of their own rite and merely tolerated the government of the Latin bishops, is clear from the many petitions that they wrote from time to time to the various authorities, in which they pleaded for Syrian bishops. Garcia himself noted this with utter disappointment. He gloomily wrote in the last month of 1652: "It is astonishing to see how attached these Cattanars and Christians are to the bishops from Babylon. Some young men who went on a pilgrimage to the tomb of St. Thomas, in spite of the fact that they are at present studying in the College of Vaipicotta and are treated with so much tenderness by the Jesuit Fathers, no sooner they see this schismatic (Aiatallah) at the tomb of St. Thomas, than they run back post-haste to announce the news to the Archdeacon, narrating also the many 'miracles' performed by the schismatic."

It seems most likely that it was during the years 1648 and 1649 that the Archdeacon Thomas Parampil took the fatal step of writing secretly to the Coptic Patriarch of Alexandria, to the Jacobite Patriarch of Antioch and the Nestorian Patriarch of Babylon, giving the exaggerated reports of the state of abandonment in which the St. Thomas Christians found themselves because of the alleged absence of a bishop, and asking them to be so kind as to remedy the situation. In the previous year (1647) he had sent his complaints and petitions to Rome through the good offices of certain Carmelite priests. On the same occasion and also two years later he appointed these same priests his procurators in Rome, Lisbon and Goa. In spite of all this, it would seem that he did not have much hope of any prompt action on the part of Rome. Past experience showed him that his adversaries were far too powerful for him in Rome and still more in Portugal. It must have been, then, the feeling that there was no way out of the situation, that drove the Archdeacon to write secretly to the Eastern Patriarchs not in communion with Rome.

When the letter of the Archdeacon reached the Coptic Patriarch, in all likelihood Aiatallah was in Cairo, where he was waiting for some letters of appointment from Rome. He was once the Metropolitan of Damascus of which See he was dispossessed by the intrigues of his rivals. Then he had charge of the Jacobites in Persia, who at his instigation, had given allegiance to Rome. In Cairo he was expecting to receive appointment as administrator of these Syrian Catholics in Persia. He was there at least from 1646. In Cairo it was well known that he was wishing to have a Church to govern. So when the letter of the Archdeacon reached the Alexandrian Patriarch, the Patriarch invited Aiatallah to proceed to Malabar to help the Christians there.

Aiatallah accepted the invitation and set out for India at once. He landed in Surat in March 1652 and in August of the same year he reached Mylapore. There he was able to meet and talk to three seminarians and a layman from Kerala, who had gone to Mylapore on a pilgrimage in July of the same year. It is through them he managed to send a letter to the Archdeacon. In the letter he declared himself to be "Ignatius, Patriarch of the whole of India and China", who had received all powers from the Pope. The rest of the story which led to what is known as the "Coonen Cross Oath" and ended in the split of the community of St. Thomas Christians is well known which I need not narrate here nor it is pertinent to our point. It is enough to remember that consequent upon the rift caused by this event, one group accepted the allegiance of Rome definitely and the other group eventually accepted the allegiance to the Antiochene Jacobite (West Syrian) Patriarch. But it took a long time before the latter gave up most of the customs and practices of the East-Syrian Church and even East-Syrian language.

CHAPTER VI

THE LATIN MISSIONS UNDER THE JURISDICTION OF PROPAGANDA
(1637 - 1838)

by Dominic, O.C.D., Alwaye.

The history of the 17th century shows undoubtedly the intention of the Popes to direct the evangelizing work of the Church, and to carry out this mission by sending directly, if necessary, missionaries even to those areas, which, in the previous century, had been entrusted to the jurisdiction of the Padroado.

A decisive step in this direction was taken by Pope Gregory XIV on January 22, 1622—the foundation of the Congregation for the Propagation of Faith, more commonly known as Propaganda. In the mind of those who planned it—among others the Belgian Jean de Vendeville, the Spanish Carmelites Thomas of Jesus and Dominic of Jesus Mary, and the Capuchin Jerome of Narni—the aims of the Congregation were to organize and unify the work of evangelization, and to promote the adequate formation of future missionaries. In connection with this last named aim, special mention must be made of the foundation of the Urban College as a seminary of the Missions in 1627. In the wake of this Roman College, a few others also were founded in different places. Most of the missionaries sent out by the Propaganda in the following centuries had come out of these institutions.

The idea of a Central Body immediately responsible to the Pope for directing mission work was all the more necessary at this point of mission history when more particularly the Portuguese Patronage was more increasingly unable to carry out the missionary commitments which it had undertaken in previous centuries. This brings us to the central issue of this chapter.

Religious and Political Conditions of the areas under the Padroado in India

The symptoms of this fact were many. Some should be mentioned here. The ideal of the "Propagation of the Faith and the empire" of the Lusiadas had not in the 17th century the same lustre and attraction as previously. The financial situation in Portugal, which had been under Spanish rule for the last sixty years did not permit her to support generously the existing missions, let alone to embark on new ventures as of old. In some of the Portuguese possessions in India as Goa, there were quite a good number of priests, though many among them felt no attraction for mission work. Thus, by the time Propaganda was founded, Rome had formally realized that the evangelization of these vast eastern regions was in danger, were the Holy See to take into account only the rights of the Padroado.

The situation regarding the possibility of evangelization by the Padroado personnel went from bad to worse as other European powers appeared on the scene—Holland, England and Denmark. These were Protestant nations, and, with the mentality of the time, they would not allow Padroado clergy to work in areas under their control. Of particularly bad consequences for the Padroado was the ever-growing presence of the Dutch, who, with their fresh memories of the recent war against Spain, brought to Asia the political and religious rivalries of Europe.

Thus, by the second half of the 17th century, two things had become clear: first, the Padroado extended over immense regions over which the Portuguese power had no hold; secondly, the Padroado clergy, especially the Portuguese nationals, were looked upon by the other contending European powers as unwanted, if not dangerous, elements. Rome was thus faced with such problems as: how to look after the existing Christian communities, which were left without pastors, how to provide for the evangelization of those territories.

To these limitations and problems of the Padroado missionary activity one must add the political situation among the Indian States which had also its own repercussions on Padroado and Propaganda. This was the case of the wars waged by the Marathas against the Moghul Empire; again, further down in the South, the Mysore wars (1766-99) conducted by Hayder Ali and his son Tippu Sultan affected badly the Christian communities of Canara and Malabar. All these wars not only sent the Portuguese back to their own small enclaves, but also at times made work in the hinterland next to impossible.

There was, however, another factor which sapped, as it were, the vitality of those who were in charge of evangelization. I refer to the religious crisis through which the European countries were passing, especially in the 18th century. One of the results was the suppression of the Jesuits in 1759 which crippled many a mission field. The French Revolution, and later on the suppression of Religious Orders struck at the very source of missionary reinforcements.

Propaganda and the Apostolic Vicariates in the Missions

The first step taken by Propaganda for reinforcing the missionary personnel in India was to send missionaries directly from Rome without passing through the Lisbon-Goa route as was the practice till then. This was not easy. When missionaries were sent by Rome, the Portuguese authorities did not always welcome them, rather looked with suspicion on them, and were slow in giving them embarking facilities. Truly enough there was the land-route. The Apostolic Constitution Sedis Apostolicae (June 1608) had allowed the Mendicant Orders to go to India by the route they found more convenient; the Constitution Ex Debito Pastoralis Officii (1633) had extended it to all Orders and Missionary Congregations. But the land-route was perilous, and in fact between 1622 to 1635 only three missionaries were able to come that way. Moreover, even if they reached their destination by this route, they fell at once under the Ordinaries of the Padroado, who could not but treat them with some suspicion.

Thus it happened that in the first years of the foundation of Propaganda, the Holy See not only did not allow further extension of the Padroado but thought of establishing an hierarchy that would depend directly on the Pope. After some hesitation Rome finally decided to nominate directly Bishops in those regions like Japan, where the Royal Patronage was not allowed (1636), and Vicars Apostolic, with episcopal character, in the territories where the Padroado had still jurisdiction.

The idea of Vicars Apostolic in the missions was a fresh solution to the new situation, though rather a compromise than a perfect solution. In India, as well as in South East Asia, the Vicars Apostolic directly appointed by Rome took full charge of the pastoral and missionary work in regions, which, at that time, were juridically under the care of the Padroado. The Portuguese authorities would dub them "intruders". For short and temporary tasks Propaganda would appoint Apostolic Commissaries or Apostolic Visitors. But the Vicars Apostolic who were always titular bishops had a permanent mission within the provisional character proper to all Apostolic Vicariates.

Such was the measure, since the relations between Rome and Lisbon were somewhat tense, and also because the new colonizing powers were opposed to missionaries of Portuguese origin, Propaganda used to send apostolic missionaries and Vicars belonging to other nationalities. The Religious Orders of recent origin which had not been very much connected with the Padroado, such as the Capuchins, the Discalced Carmelites, the Theatines, and later on the Foreign Missionary Society of Paris were being particularly utilized by Rome for a work, which was intended only to complement the labours of the Padroado. Lack of agreement between Rome and Portugal regarding the erection of Vicariates, their provisional character, lack of clarity concerning the powers the Vicars enjoyed, the interference of other powers in some cases, all these contributed much to turn this complementary intervention of Propaganda into a kind of permanent conflict with the Padroado.

The First Apostolic Vicariate: Idalcan or of the Great Moghul

In 1637 the first Apostolic Vicariate in Asia was born. Its origin is closely connected with its first head, Dom Matthew de Castro, a Goan Brahmin ordained priest in Rome in 1630. In 1636 Rome was giving the finishing touch to its plan to send Bishops appointed by Propaganda to Japan. Father de Castro was in Rome at the time and he spoke to the authorities concerning a small kingdom in the neighbourhood of Goa, called Idalcan or Bijapur, which was outside the political influence of Portugal, and was badly in need of priests. This was in fact one of the three Muslim kingdoms in India at that time. Its population was about a million, comprising Muslims as well as Hindus. There were also Christians, who had migrated or run away from Goa to avoid Portuguese taxes. A certain Jesuit Father who visited the place in 1637 speaks of a few thousand christians there. As time went on, the original Vicariate of Idalcan was to be enlarged beyond measure as it were: it would include the kingdom of Golconda, and finally the whole of the Moghul Empire; for some time, even the kingdom of Pegu (Burma) was made part of it. That is why from 1697 the official documents refer to it under different names: Vicariate of Bijapur, Golconda and of the Great Moghul. The title of the Great Moghul or simply Moghul would become common in the 18th century till 1832 when its territory was curtailed and was renamed the Vicariate of Bombay.

Appointed Vicar Apostolic in 1637, Dom Matthew de Castro encountered great opposition from the Archbishop of Goa, who was not prepared to accept an hierarchy independent of the Padroado. Yet, he succeeded in obtaining permission from the Sultan to build a church and planned to ordain priests some young men hailing from Goa, even if they carried no letters dimissory from the Archbishop. His somewhat belligerent temperament and his precipitate action in ordaining priests without such letters, besides the jurisdictional conflict which was there already, only added to the friction with the Archbishop and alienated him from many others, who, otherwise, could have supported him. This compelled him to seek refuge outside Goa, and to return to Rome first in 1643, and then for good in 1655. The difficulties concerning Vicariates in the territories under the Padroado, and the idiosyncrasy of Matthew de Castro did not prevent Propaganda from seeing the advantages of its policy; it was clear that it made possible for priests to build churches, to attend to the spiritual needs of the faithful and eventually to carry evangelization in places where this was not possible under the Padroado system. Promotion to priesthood of young local clerics —a principle very much in favour with Propaganda—was also a distinct possibility in these Vicariates. Even the founding of Seminaries was to be a settled policy of all Vicariates.

That the Padroado authorities would not brook such an hierarchy was beyond doubt from the very beginning. The fact that the relations between the Holy See and Portugal were not friendly since 1640, when Portugal shook off the Spanish yoke, till 1660 was an additional difficulty in the way of an agreed solution of the missionary problem in the region. In 1642 the Portuguese king forbade the entry of non-Portuguese mission-aries and in fact in 1649 Father Ephrem O.F.M. Cap. was sub-jected to trial of the inquisition for having exercised aposto-late in Madras, independently of Goa. In 1652 the Portuguese Cortes banned the acceptance of papal documents unless offici-ally recognized by the realm. This meant in practice that papal letters appointing Vicars Apostolic were not be acknowledged. In 1672 the same Cortes would order the Viceroy of Goa to sent to Goa all the missionaries or bishops who had not passed through Lisbon. Later on, a vow of fidelity to the Royal Patron would be demanded from all missionaries.

Following the vicissitudes of our Vicariate, we find that in 1669 a new Vicar Apostolic was appointed, Dom Custodio de Pinho. He followed the policy of Matthew de Castro concern-ing the building of churches and ordination of priests. He even thought of founding a seminary. He did not have as many diffi-culties as his predecessor had with the Archbishop of Goa, part-ly thanks to the moderation and prudence with which he acted. In fact, in this Vicariate, conflicts were never very intense, for there was hardly any Padroado representative to be found in its territory. Another Vicar was appointed in 1696, Dom Vis-conti, but he could not take charge since he died in the same year. Then there appeared on the scene Fr. Peter Paul of St. Francis, a Discalced Carmelite missionary in Malabar. With him the Discalced Carmelites entered the Vicariate and continued at its head till 1850.

Fr Peter Paul was a nephew of Pope Innocent XII. Be-fore taking charge, he approached the Dutch Government in Amsterdam with the help of Leopold I of Austria for permiss-ion for the Carmelite missionaries of Propaganda to reside in places controlled by the Dutch. Arriving in his Vicariate, he made his headquarters at Surat, still then an important harbour. He lived in a hospice run by the Capuchin Friars. By this time, i.e. 1697, the small Vicariate of Idalcan had already been extended to Golconda and to the Great Moghul Empire.

The 18th Century: Conflicts and Problems

During the tenure of office of the third Vicar, Mauritius of St. Teresa, two events took place which showed the influence of the colonial powers in the history of this Vicariate, and the gravity of the conflicts which arose between Propaganda and the Padroado. The scene of the first event was Goa, that of the second Bombay. In the beginning of the 18th century, the Carmelites of the Monastery of Goa, all non-Portuguese nationals, faced the alternative of taking the vow of fidelity to the Royal Patron or quitting Goa. As they refused the oath, the Carmelites had to leave Goa and their monastery was handed over to the Fathers of the Oratory of St. Philip Neri (1709); the same happened to the Carmelite Residence in Diu (1710). The missionaries made for the town of Karwar, or Sunkery, in north Kanara. The Vicar Apostolic resided in this town from 1712 to 1717, when he moved to Bombay as we shall see later. With their headquarters in Karwar, the missionaries carried on mostly pastoral activity on behalf of the faithful scattered in these parts. Evangelization, however, was not entirely neglected. It was at this time that, in view of the refusal of the Archbishop of Goa to recognize the vicar Apostolic, Rome had to declare that Mgr. Mauritius was the true Bishop and Vicar Apostolic of the Great Moghul (1717) and that all had to recognize him as such.

The relations between the Archbishop and the Vicar became worse when the latter was put in charge of the administration of the churches of Bombay island. Already in 1716 negotiations between Rome and London had begun with a view to change the jurisdiction over Bombay churches from the Archbishop of Goa to the Vicar Apostolic. The final decision was taken in May 1720: the Portuguese priests were expelled from the city by the British Governor, Charles Boone, and the existing four churches of Bombay were entrusted to the Vicar Apostolic and the five

Carmelite missionaries who arrived soon on the spot. The Goan priests were allowed to remain, but had to come under the jurisdiction of Vicar. This change-over was against the hierarchical conception of the Padroado and was accepted neither by the Archbishop nor by the king who invoked the principle of not accepting papal documents and nominations unless they had been officially acknowledged. The reply from Rome to the Portuguese objections was that the existing political situation impeded the jurisdiction of the Padroado and that the Vicar Apostolic would exercise jurisdiction only so long as the Archbishop was prevented from doing so.

In spite of the explanation given by Rome, a good number of the laity and even of the priests could not reconcile themselves with breaking off contacts with the Padroado. This was one of the basic causes of some of the difficulties and conflicts, which now and then we see plaguing the history of this Vicariate, and of the strange decisions of the end of the 18th century when Churches passed from one jurisdiction to another, and finally of the origin of the so called "double jurisdiction" in the area. In fact, in 1789, the churches were transferred again to the Archbishop of Goa, but this lasted only for one year. For realizing that the change did not please many of the faithful, the Governor decided that the churches return to the Vicar Apostolic. Obviously, this situation was not to the liking of the party favouring Padroado, and this led to the decision of 1794, when on the advice of the British authorities the double jurisdiction was established: two important churches (Nossa Senhora de Esperanca and St. Michael's, upper Mahim) would be under the Vicar Apostolic (Propaganda) and the other two (Salvacaon, lower Mahim and Nossa Senhora de Gloria, Mazagaon) under the Archbishop (Padroado). The solution pleased no one, and did not do away with the cause of unholy rivalries; on the contrary, it helped to make the meddling of the laity in ecclesiastical affairs more frequent and more troublesome.

The personal relations between the Archbishop of Goa and the Vicar, however, improved towards the end of the century when the more equanimous Dom Emmanuel de Santo Galdino succeeded in Goa to Dom Emmanuel de Santa Catarina, a zealous but little flexible man, and Fr. Peter de Alcantara was appointed

Vicar Apostolic. He was admittedly, a man of great qualities and prudence; he ruled the Vicariate from 1796 to 1840. By this date (1849) the Holy See had taken radical measures with regard to the Padroado and the Vicariates.

The size of the Vicariate of the Great Moghul was enormous. It marked the territory where the Propaganda could send workers to look after the Catholic communities of varying strength, which sprang up in the wake of new trade settlements. There was however not much possibility of expanding further afield. This would require more personnel and finance and the Propaganda did not have either. The Carmelites never counted more than five men; to these one must add the local Priests and a few Capuchins. The suppression of the Society of Jesus did not improve the already bad situation. In other words, there were not enough priests even to cater to the pastoral needs of the Catholic communities themselves. It was in view of this situation that the Vicar Apostolic, Charles of St. Conrad, obtained faculties from Rome to delegate two missionaries for the administration of Confirmation—one in Idalcan, the other in Hindustan. In 1781, the two missionaries left Bombay—Gregory of the Presentation and Angelo of St. Joseph. The former made his headquarters in Delhi, where he died in 1806, before that he had succeeded in 1790 in baptizing Begum Johana Sumroo of Sardhana who founded a christian community in her small kingdom and in 1826 built a beautiful church.

There could be no improvement except with the help of a well-trained and sufficiently numerous local clergy. On more than one occasion the Vicars tried to organize the training of candidates to the priesthood. Around 1770 a Seminary was founded attached to the residence of the Vicar but the candidates were a few; in 1784 the students numbered four priests, one subdeacon, two students in philosophy and a few in Grammar.

The 19th Century: Dawn of a New Era

The report of the first years of 1800 gives us some idea of the scarcity of personnel and of the consequent impossibility of doing much work. The Vicar Apostolic, Peter de Alcantara, had four Carmelites to help him: one in Delhi, one in Karwar, one in Surat and the fourth one living in Bombay with the Vicar; there were also two Capuchins and eleven diocesan priests. This meant 17 priests to look after the spiritual needs of the scattered Christians. In some places however there were larger communities: 10,000 in Bombay (excluding those under the Padroado), 4,000 in Golconda, 500 in Surat, 285 in Karwar, 50 in Poona and some smaller groups in Gujerat. In addition to these needs, there were other obligations enjoined on the same clergy for lack of personnel. Thus, we may recall that Mgr. de Alcantara was appointed Visitor of Coorg and of the Carmelite Mission of Malabar; later on he had to look after this mission also. In 1834-35 he was also Visitor of the Capuchins of Madras.

All these facts suggest that little could be done in the field of evangelization. It is true, on several occasions mention is made of new Christians, sometimes even in sizable numbers as in Karwar. The Padroado also was unable to do much for further expansion. Perhaps those difficulties could have been tided over had the Padroado and Propaganda come together and organized jointly the training of the local missionary vocations most of whom could be obtained in the area of actual Padroado influence.

The missionary activity proper would dawn again in the second half of the 19th century, thanks to the zeal and vision of Pope Gregory XVI, who, previous to his election, had been the Prefect of Propaganda. He saw the need of territorial re-distribution, and called in Orders and Congregations to shoulder the responsibility of evangelization in territories assigned to them. Thus in 1832 he erected the Vicariate of Madras which took over a great part of Golconda, in 1834 the Vicariate of Bengal which was given a part of the Great Moghul, and that of Ceylon, and in 1836 the Vicariate of Coromandel comprising Pondicherry and and Madras. As said above, from 1832 the central, northern and western parts of the former Great Moghul were called the Vicariate of Bombay. In 1854, part of it was taken out to form another Vicariate, that of Poona. Four years earlier, the Carmelites, weakened by dissensions, and asked to choose between Verapoly and Bombay, had left the latter to make room to Bishop Hartman O.F.M. Cap, who initiated the modern organization of the Church in Bombay. We should not pass over an important date for these

Vicariates, April 24, 1838, when the same Gregory XVI issued the Brief, *Multa Praeclare,* limiting the jurisdiction of the Padroado only to the territory of Goa, and giving elsewhere exclusive jurisdiction to Vicars Apostolic. Though the measure had to be modified and corrected later on, it turned out to be the policy that succeeded in the end.

The Vicariate of Malabar, later on of Verapoly

As we shall see in Chapter V the relations between the Discalced Carmelites (O.C.D) and Malabar (Kerala) were provoked by the revolt of St. Thomas Christians against the Padroado missionaries, i.e. the Jesuits. Despite difficulties of all kinds Fr. Matthew of St. Joseph O.C.D. succeeded in starting a house for his Order at Chatiath in 1673 and later on at Vazhpura, more often known as Verapoly.

Thanks to the better dispositions of the Dutch East India Company, more such Carmelite priests could come and settle in Malabar since 1676 onwards. By 1698 it was agreed upon that twelve such priests, Belgian, German, Austrian or Italian, could stay there.

Though the main task of these apostles was to look after the Catholic St. Thomas Christians, they soon dealt with the Latin Catholics and did not hesitate to attract other people to the Church. Already by about 1680 Verapoly had a catechumenate for prospective christians. When the new Carmelite Vicar Apostolic, Fr. Angelus Francis of St. Theresa was nominated by Rome in February 1700, his duty reached out also to those Latin parishes, which were juridically under the Padroado diocese of Cochin, but which could not be attended by its clergy, owing to the Dutch forbidding any Portuguese to stay there.

Verapoly became also the official residence of the Vicar Apostolic and his successors. Its catechumenate was formally organized in 1719; another one of the same type was opened at Mattancherry by the third quarter of the XVIII century. Some time earlier the Carmelite priest, Fra Dominic of the Holy Cross started working at Mahe—then a French enclave—where after some decades a sizeable Christian community could be found.

In 1764, the Propaganda decided that a Seminary common

to both Syrian and Latin clerics be opend in the Vicariate of Malabar. Two years later, the institution started, though for a while the Syrians and Latins were kept separately in two diffe-rent localities, Alengad and Verapoly respectively In 1774, both the Clerics were brought together to Verapoly according to the wishes of Propaganda. In 1866, this institution was transferred to Puthenpally, and in 1932 to Alwaye.

The first decades of the 19th century were still a period of decline. To the existing causes of conflicts we must add new sources of confusion as for example the entry into politics of the East India Company and the arrival of a British and Ameri-can Missionaries with the ensuing frictions. On the other hand, due to the French Revolution, the coming of new hands became more difficult, which made the few missionaries that the Vicari-ate had still fewer. Add to this the insufficient and inept rule of the first three Vicars of the 19th century, namely, Mgr. Ray-mond Revigla, Mgr. Milesius Prendergast and Mgr. Mauritius Stabilini. Better times dawned with the arrival of Mgr. Francis Xavier (1831-1844), a man of outstanding moral qualities and great common sense, who had been working in Sunkey (Karwar) since 1801 and had succeeded in reorganizing there the Christ-ian community which had suffered much from the invasion of Tippu Sultan in 1784. In Malabar, he reorganized the seminary of Verapoly which had been in trouble on account of the admis-sion of candidates from the Latin fisher-folk community, and began also to set in order the local churches.

Mgr. Francis Xavier gave his wholehearted cooperation to Pope Gregory XVI (1831-1846) in his plan for the reorganiza-tion of the mission. Thus the Vicariate of Malabar, with its centre at Verapoly, was extended to the whole coast of Malabar, from Cape Comorin to Canara. In the same year, the 30,000 christians of Canara with their centre at Mangalore asked to be received under its jurisdiction. Thus, in all this area the problem of double jurisdiction was solved, at least for the time being. But it gave rise to painful and sad conflicts in several churches which were not willing to accept the transfer—conflicts related to the so called "Goan Schism".

As a result of this ecclesiastical reorganization, the area of

8

the Vicariate of Malabar or Verapoly became very vast—it is enough to recall that today there are 18 dioceses in the same territory, nine Latin and nine Oriental. The number of these well organized units suggests, on the other hand, that the pastoral work carried out by the Vicariate in the last century was successful to a remarkable degree. For a more efficient rule, the following Vicar Apostolic, Mgr. Ludovicus Martin (1844-1852) divided the area into three regions: Quilon in the South, with Bernardine Bacinelli as Apostolic Pro-Vicar, Canara in the North with Mangalore as its centre under Bernardine Pontanova as Pro-Vicar and Bishop Coadjutor, and the central region with its headquarters at Verapoly.

Taking charge of his post in Mangalore in 1845, Mgr. Bernardine Pontanova opened at once a seminary, transferred to Jeppu in 1858. During the time of the first Vicar of Mangalore alone, Mgr. Michael Anthony (1853-1870), this Seminary gave 36 priests. With a view to promoting education, primary schools were founded, and the Brothers of the Christian Schools were brought in. Education received a further push with the arrival of the Carmelite Tertiary Sisters (Apostolic Carmel) from France during the time of the second Vicar, Mgr. Ephrem. In 1872, the Jesuits took over this Vicariate, thus enabling the Carmelites to concentrate on pastoral and missionary work in the southern parts of the Vicariate of Verapoly. A new Vicariate—Quilon had been erected in 1847, with Mgr. Bernardine Bacinelli as its first Vicar. By 1860 it had its own Seminary. A man of a wide vision, Mgr. Bernardine was soon transferred to Verapoly as its Vicar (1853-1868), where he organized the training of priestly candidates, encouraged religious life, promoted catechetical instruction and popular missions in parishes. Before long, the Vicariate of Malabar, later called Verapoly, would vanish through its normal transformation into other permanent ecclesiastical units of the Church in this area.

The Vicariate of Canara (1674)

The third Vicariate Apostolic erected by Propaganda covered the region of Canara, where in 1657 the Nayak of Ikkery had seized the Portuguese forts, and the clergy had abandoned the place. In 1657 and 1660 when Mgr. Sebastiani passed through Canara on his way, to and from, Malabar he reported that there were about 6000 Christians in the region but no priests, and he informed Rome of the situation. In the following years the situation did not improve much inspite of the efforts of the Padroado who had entered into treaties with the Ikkery rulers. At the same time the Dutch appeared on the coast of Bednore, exposing thus the weakness of the Portuguese defence.

These conditions moved Rome to sent a Vicar Apostolic to these regions also. The choice fell on Dom Thomas de Castro, a Konkani Brahmin from Goa and a nephew of Dom Matthew de Castro whom we already met as Vicar Apostolic of Idalcan. He was nominated on December 17, 1674 but could arrive in the place only in 1677 after overcoming the resistance of Portugal. He set up his central residence in Bangalore. He had joined the Congregation of the Theatines, but his confreres in Goa did not like him much as they feared that the Padroado would not approve of him. The years of his Vicariate which ended with his death in 1685 are marked with serious conflicts between the Padroado and Propaganda. He ordained 20 priests to work under him, but several of them returned to Goa from where they hailed. From Bangalore as well as Calicut where he had also a residence, he tried to send priests to Canara. Both he and the Prelates of Goa at the time lacked sufficient flexibility and vision, which might have helped in easing the tensions involved in such double jurisdiction. The presence of Mgr. de Castro and his priests perhaps spurred the Goan leaders to send their clergy. Mgr. de Castro on the one hand and Mgr. Brandao and Mgr. Manuel de Sousa Meneses on the other hand did not rise to the occasion and did not find ways of working in collaboration under the circumstances. But there was a noble exception. One of the Goan priests sent by the Cathedral Chapter that was at the helm in Goa before the appointment of Mgr. Meneses gave proofs not only of heroic missionary spirit but also of humility and detachment with which the thorny problem had to be approached and tackled. His behaviour before Mgr. de Castro revealed his delicate and well-formed conscience and evangelical spirit. He helped to rejuvenate the Christian life which had been languishing for lack of priestly ministry. His stay among the Christians proved very beneficial to them. The priest was none other than the Venerable Jose Vaz, known as the "Apostle of Ceylon" for his later work.

After the death of Dom de Castro, in spite of his having nominated a Vicar General, his own nephew, Jose de Castro, the Vicariate was not resumed. Thus after the death of the Vicar General in 1700, the region passed again to Goa, being ruled by a Vicar from Goa. Later, in the wake of a Maratha invasion of Goa, many Christians from Bardes (Goa) migrated to Mangalore, where they would have to face in the 18th century not a few serious crises.

The Missions and the Prefectures of Surat, Madras & Pondicherry

The different enclaves in India where the European powers competed with each another in establishing their trade settlements became also centres of activity for missionaries sent directly from Rome. e.g. Madras, Surat, Pondicherry and to a lesser degree Mahe and Chandernagore. The workers of the vineyard in these places were the members of the Capuchin Order.

Surat Mission

We noted above how the Capuchins arrived in Surat in 1639. It was as it were an extension of the missions they had in Persia and Mesopotamia. In fact it was their Guardian residing in Alleppo who sent the first three French Missionaries: two of them Fr. Zenon and Fr. Peter stayed on in Surat and the third, Fr. Ephrem, was to go to Madras as we shall see below.

In Surat their work consisted in ministering to the spiritual needs of the European merchants in the city. But they did pay visits to the neighbouring villages where they discovered a group of Christian families.

The Capuchins continued their silent work for many years. We have seen previously that the Carmelite Vicar Apostolic of the Great Moghul resided for some time in Surat as a guest of the Capuchins. In the 18th century the political events that shook up the great Moghul Empire after the death of Aurengazeb, resulted also in the decline of the prosperous Surat. In 1747, a great fire broke in the city which destroyed among other things the Capuchin house also. Later on the British set their foot in Surat and established there their trade. A Carmelite missionary under the jurisdiction of the Vicar Apostolic of the Great Moghul used to live there in order to attend to the spiritual needs of the English Catholics. As time went on, the importance of Surat decreased in favour of Bombay. In 1825 the last Capuchin Father died and thus there came to an end a mission that had lasted for nearly two hundred years.

The Apostolic Prefecture of Madras

One of the three priests who arrived in Surat in 1639 was Fr.Ephrem, a man of many parts. Leaving his two companions in Surat, he proceeded further through Indian territories with his eyes set on the kingdom of Pegu, the modern Burma. 1642 he reached Madras, a small town at the time. From 1639 the East India Company had settled there with a view to having a firm footing on the coast of Coromandel. They had built a small fort, the Fort of St.George. Fr.Ephrem had to spend a few days in Madras in order to find a conveyance that would take him to Burma. First the Christians who lived there, and then the head of the British settlement requested Fr.Ephrem to stay on in Madras to look after their spiritual needs. The Padroado See of Mylapore was close but these christians preferred a priest independent of the Padroado jurisdiction. Though at first he refused, he later acquiesced to their request after getting the necessary permission from his Roman superiors. This was the beginning of the Capuchin Mission in Madras area.

In view of the vicinity of the Padroado See, trouble could be foreseen and indeed it did not take long before it started. In 1643 Fr. Ephrem fell into the hands of the Padroado agents, and was transferred to Goa where he was detained in the inquisitorial jail for 22 months. However this incident did not spell the end of the mission. Fr. Zenon of Surat came down to replace him, and stayed on in Madras until Fr. Eprehm, released by the Goan authorities under the pressure of the French king, could return there. Soon a church was built. In 1661, the British Factory was raised to Residence and thus the importance of this British enclave began to grow. In 1693 there were about 800 catholics, with three priests to attend to their needs. By the beginning of the 18th century the Capuchins were well settled down and in 1707 the mission was raised to the status of the Apostolic Prefecture. Their pastoral and missionary activity was not restricted to Fort St. George, but was extended to the towns which came gradually under the British control. At times they also catered to the needs of the Armenian christians who were without their clergy. From Madras, which was the headquarters of the Prefecture, the Capuchins went to Pondicherry as we shall see below, and also to Chandernagore, which had been ceded by the Great Moghul to the French Company in India. The residence of the Capuchins in these places was meant mostly to minister to the French catholics. Moreover Chandernagore was the springboard for the mission of Tibet and Nepal. Similarly at times Fathers went from Madras to minister to the people of the Mahe enclave on the Malabar coast.

During the Anglo-French wars which affected also the Indian scene, the Capuchins met with difficult times. In 1756 they had to leave Madras, where, however, they could return three years later. The end of the 18th century was marked as elsewhere by lack of new personnel and also by conflicts with the Bishop or Vicar General of San Tome who wanted to exercise jurisdiction over these territories under the British control. These conflicts were aggravated by internal dissensions among the missionaries themselves. This state of affairs necessitated an apostolic visit, which was duly carried out in 1819 by Mgr. Peter de Alcantara, O.C.D., Vicar Apostolic of the Great Moghul. The visit did not bear much fruit. At this time there were two churches in Madras and others in the three neighbouring towns. From 1811 onwards the Capuchins came from Italy since France was unable to send any more priests. Yet this solution did not result in remedying the situation so much so that the number of missionaries went on decreasing. So a reorganisation of the missions in the territories under the East India Company was badly needed, and as seen already it was carried out by Pope Gregory XVI. First he issued a Brief in 1832, which did not have the desired result. Then in 1834 he established the Apostolic Vicariate of Madras with Daniel O'Connor of Ireland as its first Vicar Apostolic. This Vicariate was to take over the responsibility of the Capuchin mission and inherit the House where for nearly two hundred years the Capuchins had been working.

The Mission of Pondicherry

The first attempt in this region is connected with the arrival of the French Company of the East Indies in 1671. It was not for the first time that the French had reached the coast of Coromandel nor the first time that the Capuchins had come to the spiritual aid of the French Catholics. But now the arrival of the Company at Pondicherry seemed to indicate that their stay would be permanent. As the French Catholics of the Company knew that there were French Capuchins working in Madras, they invited them to come to their Pondicherry enclave. In 1674, Fr. Cosmas came from Madras and a small church was built. He joined the Company as chaplain and became the parish priest of the local catholics who settled down there—catholics known as "Malabara". As parish priest he was under the jurisdiction of the Bishop of San Tome (Mylapore) but in his apostolic missions he did not recognize the Padroado. As the activities of the Company extended in India, so did the activity of the French Capuchins. In 1686, when another Capuchin Father joined Fr. Cosmas, the church building was extended and in 1690 we find them working also in the neighbouring villages. From 1689, there were other missionaries in Pondicherry. That year, some Jesuits arrived—they had been expelled from the mission of Siam in 1687. They were welcomed and given residence in the House of the Capuchin Fathers. In 1691 the Jesuits also built a church and began to carry out a fruitful apostolate. Their success was taken note of by the authorities concerned so that in 1695, thanks to the representations made by St. John de Britto, Louis XIV entrusted Jesuits the task of evangelizing the French territories in India. The Jesuits however could not remain satisfied with these territories alone, so they tried to extend their activities right into the interior of the country, which was canonically under the jurisdiction of San Tome. This gave rise to what is known as the Carnatic Mission which included the coast of Coromandel, the north of the river. Ponneyar and from Madurai right up to the borders of the Great Moghul. This resulted in restricting Capuchin Mission to the French Catholics and their servants in the Colony.

From 1699, after an interval of three years when they were compelled to leave due to the fact that Pondicherry had fallen to the Dutch, the Capuchins did organise better their mission in Pondicherry under the leadership of Father James, their Vicar General. Pondicherry became the base for all the Capuchins in the Indian Missions, their Guardian residing there.

In 1709 Mgr. Maillard de Tornon, Titular Latin Patriarch of Antioch and Legate of Clement XI spent some time at the residence of the Capuchins in Pondicherry. He had been sent to study the question of the "Malabar Rites". Some time later, in 1738, they tried and in fact succeeded in bringing European Sisters to the colony, i.e. the Ursulines. But this venture did not last long since local circumstances were not favourable, and since some of the missionaries including Father Norbert, their Director, did not promote it well enough. So the Sisters returned to France; and it was only in 1827 that European Sisters came again to Indian Missions, this time the help and encouragement of the foreign Mission Society of Paris. Better success was met by the Jesuits who planned a local Congregation (Carmelites) in 1748, which was put in charge of an orphanage. They were Carmelite Tertiary Sisters.

The second half of the 18th century began with much trouble for the mission owing to the Anglo-French wars (1744-1761). The situation improved with the treaty of Paris (1763), but after a brief spell of time war broke out again; in 1776 the Capuchin House was nearly destroyed.

The year 1776 is also important for another reason. It was in this year that the Missions of Coromandel which had been so far under the care of the Jesuits, were transferred to the Foreign Missions Society of Paris owing to the suppression of the Society of Jesus (1773). The first superior of this Mission was Father Pierre Brigot, who resided in Pondicherry itself. As there was already in Pondicherry the Prefect Apostolic of the Capuchin Mission, since the Bishop of San Tome claimed also jurisdiction in these areas, the knotty problem of mutual relations did not take long to raise its head. It was solved by Rome which decreed that the Prefect of the Capuchin Mission would have authority only over the Europeans and their servants, while the Superior of the Foreign Missions would take care of the Indian and *mestizo* Christians. Chandernagore which was under the Jesuits passed under the Prefect. In 1793, the local ecclesiastical authorities came to an amicable settlement among themselves, giving each other the necessary faculties. This was certainly a wise decision.

Be that as it may, times did not allow wastage of energies over unnecessary internal disputes. The terrible loss that was caused by the suppression of the Jesuits, was aggravated by the wars in Mysore, the war between France and England and the repercussions of the French Revolutions in Pondicherry. The crisis in France did not allow new missionaries from that country to come to India, and therefore the last French missionary, Father Arnoldine, died in 1811. Italian Capuchins were sent to Pondicherry to make good the losses. In 1820 they recorded that there were 2000 catholics under them. The French who took back the control of Pondicherry in 1815, preferred to have missionaries from their own country. After much correspondence between the authorities concerned the Capuchin Mission of Pondicherry was handed over to the Congregation of the Holy Spirit in 1828 with Mgr. Calmel as it first prefect. In 1829 they took charge, and in 1836 all the properties of the Capuchins passed over to them. But one Capuchin or another continued to work till 1845 when the last Capuchin Fr. Michael died closing thus a history of nearly two hundred years of Capuchin activity in Pondicherry. We may note that the Prefecture of Pondicherry had jurisdiction over Chandernagore, and this in spite of the erection of the Apostolic Vicariate of Coromandel, and of Pondicherry later on. The final integration took place only in 1887 when one single authority was established in the area.

The Missions of Coromandel under the Foreign Missionary Society of Paris

We have already met the name of the Foreign Missions Society of Paris while treating of Pondicherry. In fact, this missionary institute, that launched in the 17th century the movement of Foreign Mission Societies (many others have been established since then) was from 1776 onwards in charge of the mission of the coast of Coromandel, or Carnatic Mission, called also the Mission of Malabar. The occasion, as already mentioned, was the suppression of the Society of Jesus.

The Fathers of the Paris Society were not entirely unknown in Pondicherry. Their very founders Pallu and La Motte Lambert as well as Mgr. Cotolendi had passed through India, and maintained relations with the French Company, in India. Mgr. Cotolendi died in Mazulipatanam. Moreover, the same revolution in Siam that had landed the Jesuits in Pondicherry, was instrumental in exiling the Procurator of the Foreign Missions from the Siamese capital Ayithia. He came first to Bengal and finally settled in Pondicherry, where his office functioned till 1795. In 1771, even the General College, which the Society had in Siam since 1664 for the training of local candidates to the priesthood was shifted to Virampatanam, near Pondicherry.

The Carnatic Mission had at this moment about 30,000 catholics. Ten thousand of these were in the area of Pondicherry and two thousand in that of Karikal. In 1788, the jurisdiction of the superior of the Mission of Malabar was extended to the Mission of Madurai, Marava and Tanjore which counted about 150,000 catholics. Yet, for lack of personnel and to avoid direct confrontation with the Padroado, the Superior could hardly render any help there. The situation in the matter of jurisdiction was not quite happy. In Pondicherry itself as we saw above, the Capuchins took care of the European catholics, and in the remaining area the Bishop of San Tome was supposed to look after the faithful. An apparent way out of this tangle was found in calling the first head of the Mission, Mgr. Brigot, simply *Superior* of the Mission while the Capuchins kept the office of Prefect Apostolic. As noted above they reached an agreement on exchanging their faculties. A similar accord obtained also, but not permanently with regard to the priests who were under the Bishop of San Tome.

As personnel Mgr. Brigot had in 1776 only five priests of the Paris Society, who were joined by about fifteen ex-Jesuits To the scarcity of men one had to add the problems and ruins caused by the political situation. The wars between France and England affected these regions also, Pondicherry being occupied by the British for a number of years. The Mysore region was afflicted by the wars of Tippu Sultan. Besides disturbing things in Pondicherry, the French Revolution could but stop new arrivals from France. Hence the period down to 1816 proved very hard for the first superior and his two immediate successors. In 1816 the situation began improving in several places. The successors of Mgr. Brigot were Mgr. Champenois (1791-1810) and Mgr. Herbert (1810-1836).

To meet the scarcity of clergy and in compliance of the policy of the Paris Society, its Superiors thought of founding a College on the same lines as the one at Virampatanam which was training clergy for Siam, and was actually closed down in 1791. As a first step, use was made of the College which Father Busson, S.J. had built in Oulgaret. In 1788, the first priest was ordained, Father Thomas, and the second one year later. Some time after a new Seminary was founded near the Cathedral of Pondicherry, but the results of the institution hardly commensurated with the efforts made, and were quite unequal to the actual needs; upto 1811 only nine priests came out of this Seminary.

The Missionaries tried their best to attend to the spiritual needs of the faithful entrusted to them, and their task was all the more difficult as the catholics were scattered over a vast area. In the course of their difficult apostolate the missionaries followed different roads. Thus one of them passed into history as a keen observer of the local customs. I refer to Abbe Dubois, who, after the fall of Tippu Sultan visited the christian communities of Mysore, Coimbatore and Salem, and wrote his classical work: *Hindu Customs and Manners.*

The problem of personnel found already some solution when the Society was restored in France in 1815. From 1819 new missionaries began to arrive. Up to 1823, already 23 new hands had joined the field. This enabled the Superior to reorganise the existing christian communities and to open new ones. The transfer of the Apostolic Prefecture from the Capuchins to the Congregation of the Holy Spirit raised again the problem of jurisdiction as the new Prefect Apostolic Mgr. Calmel wanted to extend his jurisdiction to all the faithful living within the French possessions.

In the southern region (Madurai) the situation was rather precarious. There were some priests from Goa and Malabar, but never enough for the pastoral needs of the faithful. In 1830 a delegation from the Christian community of Trichinopoly approached Mgr. Herbert and requested him to send European missionaries to their place. Only five years later, in 1835, could he send three priests, who however could not do much work because of the conflict with the Padroado. For Cochin and Cranganore had jurisdiction in that region. All this made an ecclesiastical reorganization urgent. In 1836, the Vicariate of the coast of Coromandel with its headquarters in Pondicherry was established. The first Vicar, Mgr. Bonnard (1836-1847) started with only nine priests, three of them Indian. But reinforcements were not long in coming; within the first ten years twentynine priests arrived. The erection of the Vicariate did not solve the jurisdiction wholly and the Prefecture of Pondicherry continued ruling over the European catholics and their servants up to 1887. In 1836 again Pope Gregory XVI entrusted the Southern region, corresponding to the former mission of Madurai, to the French Jesuits. In 1838, the first four arrived; they were welcomed by Mgr. Bonnard with open arms. In 1846, the territory was raised to the status of an Apostolic Vicariate with Madurai as its headquarters, and Mgr. Canoz became its first Apostolic Vicar. In spite of the difficulties that arose on account of the so-called "Goan Schism", ecclesiastical reorganization, the better selection of missionary vocations, and the continued and intense help from the Catholic world were to be the foundations of the modern church in those regions. The Fathers of the Paris Society could concentrate in the North, and the Jesuits in the south.

Tibet-Nepal (1707-1769)

It was in 1703 that the Congregation of Propaganda Fide decided to establish a mission in Tibet, entrusting it to the Capuchins. The idea was due to a great extent to a Capuchin priest, Francis of Jours, a veteran missionary in Surat and Pondicherry. One of the reasons he gave Propaganda to launch the mission was the idea shared by many of his contemporaries, that there was a christian community without priests in the Himalayas. Though it is well known that Jesuit missionaries had visited western Tibet earlier, the existence of a christian Community in the region was merely a legend.

The Capuchin Order set out immediately to organize the mission. On May 6, 1704 the first batch of six missionaries started for their destination, Tibet. Two died on the way, and to replace them more were assigned in 1706. In fact sickness and death were the frequent toll that the long journey to Tibet and the not always comfortable stay there exacted from the Capuchin missionaries. The Order endeavoured to replace the missionaries dying prematurely in the field or those who were obliged to return, even before they were back home. This proves the great spirit of sacrifice and the zeal with which the Order and its members were actuated.

The first batch made their way to Tibet passing through different places in India: Pondicherry, Madras and Chandernagore, where they arrived on April 18, 1706. One of them stayed on in Chandernagore, and gradually this enclave became the base of communication for the missionaries of Tibet. They built in Chandernagore an hospice in 1709, to which later on, in 1715 was added a church, where the Procurator of the Missions used to reside. When the Society of Jesus was suppressed, the Capuchins took up the care of the christians of Chandernagore till then under the Jesuits.

Let us follow our first Tibet missionaries: Two missionaries arrived at Patna on November 8, 1706. Patna was to become a base in India for the Tibet Mission. Therefore in 1715, the Capuchins founded an hospice there, which proved important for the future. When the missionaries left Tibet for good in 1745, this hospice together with that of Kathmandu, was to serve as centres for the mission in Nepal. From 1769, after the mission of Nepal also had been closed, it became the headquarters of the Mission of North India.

Finally on the last lap of their journey, Father Joseph of Asocoli, the Prefect of the Mission, and Father Francis Mary of Tours left Patna on January 17, 1707 and arrived in Lhasa on June 12 of the same year. The two missionaries were well received there and even appreciated as physicians as they were known, but they soon faced serious financial difficulties in spite of the help they received from an American chirstian. These difficulties obliged them to leave Lhasa in 1711 and thus ended the first unsuccessful phase of the mission. Wiser by the experience, the Superiors sent a second expedition in 1716, which was better equipped, though not as much as was necessary. Arriving in Lhasa, the missionaries found Father Hyppolitus Desideri, S.J., who had come the same year with the same intentions. One of the new Capuchin missionaries was Father Francis Orazio della Penna, a man of Vision and tenacity, who succeeded in acquiring a remarkable mastery over the Tibetan language. This time the mission was better organized, besides a small hospice in Dvags-po-k'yer, a house and a small church were built in Lhasa (1725). With regard to conversions, only a few persons of Nepali origin (Newar) became christians there.

In this connection it may be recalled that in 1715, while passing through Kathmandu, the mission of Napal had been somewhat organized: a first hospice was put up in Kathmandu in that year, which was followed by two others in Batgaon and Patan. Little by little, however, the resources in finance and Personnel dried out and the mission again had to be abandoned with the departure of the last missionary in 1733. In Rome, however, especially after hearing Father della Penna about the situation of the mission and the need of manning it at least with twelve Fathers and providing it with sufficient economic help, the authorities decided to reopen the mission. So in 1738 eleven missionaries set out for Tibet, seven of whom arrived in Lhasa at the beginning of 1741. Better prepared than their predecessors, and with Father Francis Orazio as their Prefect, this time the missionaries pursued more direct evangelization than earlier expeditions had done, both at the royal court and among the people. The result was the baptism of about twenty persons, men and women, which indeed was the first real missionary fruit in the locality. But at same time this success turned out to be the beginning of the end. It aroused first suspicions among the Lamas, soon followed by open hostility; the Buddhist monks succeeded in fanning the feelings of a section of the people against the tiny newly formed christian community. In 1742 they were denounced and some of them flogged publicly. Moreover the missionaries were given to understand that their evangelization work was not acceptable to the country. They tried to defend themselves but in vain. Thus we see them leaving Lhasa for good on April 20, 1745. Later on attempts were made to return but to no purpose. The little community of the Christians left to themselves continued faithfully hoping that some priests may come back. Gradually they died out, leaving no trace.

On their way out from Tibet, the missionaries had been well received in Nepal, and their arrival thus reinforced the personnel already working there. This helped for some time the communities of Kathmandu Batgaon and Patan. It looked as if the mission of Nepal had a great future. But soon the tide turned against the christians. Towards this time, Prithvi Narayan, king of the Gurkhas, conquered the Kathmandu valley. He showed himself quite ill-disposed towards the christians, who finally had to migrate from Nepal to Bettiah, in India. The migration ended in 1769 with the last missionaries leaving Nepal. In the following years, the missionaries tried to return there, and in fact Father Joseph of Marcellys O.F.M. Cap. succeeded in doing so. He spent some years in the kingdom as a physician. But the mission as such could not be reopened. What continued to be called the Mission of Tibet actually consisted of territories in India.

The Vicariate of Tibet-Hindustan

Out of Tibet and Nepal, the Capuchins could now concentrate on India, especially around Patna and Battiah in 1787; they were asked to take over what was called the Vicariate of Hindustan which was being left unmanned by the dying ex-Jesuits. But the Capuchins too were not in a position to supply a sufficient number of priests needed in this vast area. So the closing years of 18th and the first years of the 19th centuries are characterized by mediocrity. To this bleak situation there must be added serious tensions among the missionaries. They necessitated an apostolic visitation which was entrusted to Mgr. Champenois of Pondicherry. He fulfilled this task by delegating Father Rene Louis Foulon.

In 1820, the mission was reorganized radically, with the erection of a new Vicariate, called the Vicariate of Tibet-Hindustan. The first vicar was Mgr. Zenobio Benucci, who established his see in Agra. The territory was immense and it was useless, nay impossible, to plan anything on some scale. So a further reorganization was necessary, which was done in 1845 with the erection of two Vicariates, Agra and Patna. In the last named Vicariate, there worked the saintly Swiss Capuchin, Anastasius Hartman, one of the most remarkable missionaries in India in modern times.

CHAPTER VII

THE CATHOLIC CHURCH UNDER THE PORTUGUESE PATRONAGE

By Dr. George M. Moraes

Part I

In modern times the Archdiocese of Goa has had the good fortune to be served by some of the ablest men that Portugal could spare. Archbishop Dom Antonio Sebastao Valente, the first Metropolitan to bear the title of Patriarch *ad honorem* of the East Indies, reigned for twenty-eight years from 1881 to 1909. The title was conferred on the Archbishop by the immortal Leo XIII on the establishment of the Indian hierarchy in 1886. And the gesture was only a token of recognition by the Holy See of the memorable services the Goan clergy had rendered in bearing the burden of the day and its scorching heat at the task of keeping Catholicism alive and extending its bounds, alone and unassisted, 'from Com'rin Point to Everest Peak' for two hundred years. It was also a recognition of the intrinsic importance of the historic Primatial and Metropolitan See of Goa—the *alma mater* of Catholic India.[1]

D. Valente signalized his reign by a series of decrees which ensured cleanliness in the churches and regulated divine service, investing it with a new splendour. He reformed sacred music in the Archdiocese, and his circular which was considered a classic statement on the subject was translated into more than one European language. This was in 1892, long before Pope Pius X issued his *motu proprio* laying down the norms for church music. Two synods were held during his regime, which virtually transformed the social and religious life of Goa.[2]

For years the niveau of ecclesiastical studies in Goa had been maintained at a high level. Commenting on the culture and learning of our priests in 1827, the French priests, Cottineau de Klougen, who had opportunities of close contact with them both in

Bombay and Goa, observed that they were well-versed in philosophy and theology and could preach in Konkani and Portuguese as well, and hold forth in Latin. This was an accomplishment which, writing at about the same time Dr. John Wilson, the famous Protestant missionary and educationist of Bombay, had found in one of the priests he casually encountered in Goa to his own discomfiture.[3] Cottineau compares the Goan clergy to the mass of the French priests who on account of their unquestioned learning have alone among the continental clergy been spared the imputation of ignorance even by their enemies.[4]

Dom Valente who had graced the chair of theology at the University of Coimbra before his appointment as Archbishop was not satisfied with this standard, sufficiently high though it admittedly was. He wanted his priests to have the benefit of the best ecclesiastical, training available anywhere in the world. And so he re-organized ecclesiastical studies leading to the priesthood to such good effect at the Diocesan Seminary of Rachol that in 1887 Pope Leo XIII could not refuse a model institution the request that it should be granted the faculty of conferring the B.D. degree.[5] This was a unique privilege which until it lasted was enjoyed in the country alone by Rachol. Soon the seminary rose to the highest expectations of the Pontiff, being regarded by discriminating visitors as comparable to the best of its kind in Europe.

The Seminary came to be increasingly sought after by students, lay no less than clerical, when on the establishment of the Republic in 1910 which revived the obsolete law of 1834, making it impossible for Religious Orders to run their educational establishments, the task of educating Christian youth devolved on the diocesan clergy. With its well rounded courses in the humanities, mathematics and natural sciences, the Seminary, which was opened to all and sundry up to the last year of philosophy, acquired the character of a highly prized and most popular public school, the Goan Eton as it were, reckoning among its alumni some of the Goan celebrities of the modern times. The preliminary studies leading to theology, from which however students who had no intention of taking holy orders were naturally excluded, were deemed equivalent, in regard to the quantum of the subjects taught, to the final year of the Lycee, the more expensive higher secondary school maintained by Government at Panjim, the capital. They were certainly distinctly superior to the Matriculation of the University of Bombay which was the best among similar school-leaving certificate courses offered by any university of S.S.C. Board in other parts of British India, running, as the Bombay Matriculation did, neck to neck with Senior Cambridge. And the present writer has it on the authority of his Jesuit friends who joined the Society after or shortly before taking holy orders from Rachol that they were admired by their Jesuit masters for their sheer knowledge of the Latin classics, while the Jesuit seminaries where they were required to revise their philosophy had nothing new to teach them. So thorough had been the training they had received at the hands of the competent *corpus docens* of Rachol, made up of the pick of the diocesan clergy, giving of their best to their pupils.

The results of the extreme self-sacrifice of the professoriate of Rachol were patent in the brilliant galaxy of eminent clergymen which was its product, a galaxy which included a long roll of preachers, missioners, philosophers, theologians, canonists, scriptural scholars, bishops, councillors, parliamentarians, university professors and journalists. In his *Clero de Goa,* published in 1927, Fr. Casimiro Cristovao de Nazareth has named 166 from this galaxy who distinguished themselves as writers and scholars, and the writer in the *Memoria Historico-Eclesiastica da Arquidiocese de Goa,* applying a more rigorous test, has selected seventy of their number for special mention on the occasion of the fourth centenary of the Archdiocese in 1933. This is admittedly still a large number for the clergy turned out by a single institution. At all events, it is a singular good fortune to have had glimpses of the men of the stature of Fr. Nazareth whose immortal work, *Mitras Lusitana no Oriente* is brilliant record of the golden deeds of our missioners; Canon Francis Xavier Vaz, noted historical scholar and master of Konkani whose translation of the *Book of Psalms* is said to rival the beauty of the original; Mgr. Francisco Xavier de loyola, a man of varied intellectual culture and renowned founder-editor of *O. Crente,* the diocesan organ; Mgr. Dr. Sebastiao Rogolfo Dalgado, Vicar Vara of Honawar, North Kanara, who rose to be the Professor of Sanskrit at the University of Lisbon and whose well-known *Glossario Luso-Asiatico,* having long replaced the competent work of Yule and Burnell, *Hobson-Jobson,* is now the standard work on the subject; Fr. G.M. Saldanha who wrote the *History of Goa* which is still useful; Mgr. Francis Xavier Barreto who produced biographical sketches of the illustrious Goan priests in two volumes; Canon Joao Francisco Lobo who effectively answered the attacks on Christianity by he high-placed author of *Em Boa Paz* in his *Balanco Critico,* Fr. Manuel de Sa who attempted a pioneer work on the history of Christianity in India; Mgr. Castillo Noronha who was the editor of *A voz de S. Francisco Xavier,* the successor of *O Crente;*[6] and Mgr. Gregorio Magno Antao, the noted canonist and author of a consummate work on the Synod of Diamper which was crowned with *magna laude* at the Gregorian University.

It is a tribute to the prevailing spirit of ecumenism in India that the United Theological College, Bangalore, has been collecting material for a monumental work on Indian Christian theology, and a recent interesting book published in this series *Pioneers of Indian Christianity* by Prof. Kaj Baago—gives a foretaste of this projected work in that it discusses the contributions to this science by Indian Christian thinkers, both Catholic and Evangelical. But this monumental undertaking will be incomplete if account is not taken of the sizeable work of the Goan theologians. Even before D. Valente gave a new impetus to studies at the Seminary of Rachol by his reforms, theology had been studied in depth with reference to all its aspects. Thus to speak of the publications of only the last hundred years that nearly come to mind, Fr Antonio Jose Nicolau Barreto (1802-1878) who was for some time a professor at Rachol wrote his *Elementos de Filosofia Racional e Moral* (1860), Dr. Antonio Filipe Lourenco (d.1869) produced his *Cursus Theologiae,* Fr Constatino Barreto (d.1874), some time Professor and Rector of the Seminary published a book on Moral Theology, Fr Domingo Salvador Marinho de Silva (1825-1897) wrote three volumes on the same subject, while Fr. Guilerme Pinto a professor of Philosophy at Mapuca, produced a work entitled *Additamento ao Compendio de Filosofia Nacional de Joao A. de Souza* (1885).

And after the studies were reorganized by D. Valente and Rachol was seized with the burning problems of the new age into which the world was entering, the Seminary rose equal to the challenge of the times with Canon Antonio Jose de Heredia bringing out his lectures on Apologetics in book form in 1932, and Canon Castilio Serpa de Noronha examining Indian Philosophy in the light of the *Philosophia Perennis* and bringing out his two important works on Indian philosophical thought, *O Budismo em confronto com o Cristianismo* (1925) and *Bramanismo philosophico*. Lastly the chronic irritant to the smooth functioning of the Church endemic of Latin peoples of which Goa could not but have its share. The authority of the Church was sought to be met by Mgr. Ganganeli Piedade Rebello (1854-1927), Rector and Professor of the Seminary by his publication *Sobrenatural, Moral Independente e authoridade da Santa Igreja*.[7]

In the galaxy of priests who were inspired by the spirit of service to the sick and the disabled are priests like Fr Manuel Francisco do Rosario e Almeida who opened a home in Macau some time in the second half of the 19th century for unwanted children, treating them with maternal care and going about his work with imperturbable serenity. He supervised a hospital when an epidemic broke out in the city and was responsible for saving countless lives—a testimonial for which he was known among the Chinese as the father of the poor.

No less spectacular is the work of Fr. Antonio Miranda who with his own money built the Hospice of the Sacred Heart of Mary at Margao, Goa, which is now one of the best hospitals in Western India. But service to the poor is a concomitant of the priestly vocation, and there have been among our priests those who, having taken a voluntary vow of poverty, have given their all to the St. Anthony's Bread, an institution in every parish devoted to the relief of the poor. An early instance of this is Fr. Vicente de Souza who made it a rule to distribute among the poor part of his income once a week on Mondays, a practice which in the wake of his example has been kept up in all parishes. We have also instances of priests making a united effort with whatever money they could spare to construct works of public welfare on a humbler scale like the Asilio de N.S. des Milagres, ow-

ing its origin to the benevolence of Frs. Antonio Rejinaldo de
Mendonca, Joao Baptista de Mendonca, Azarias de Souza Menezes and Pedro Damiao Augustinho dos Santos.[8]

One of the most notable events of the episcopate of Dom
Valente was the Second National Eucharistic Congress which he
convoked in Goa and which was attended by eighteen archbishops and bishops of the Indian hierarchy, an assembly which
was beyond the most sanguine expectations of any Portuguese
prelate before him to have succeeded in calling in Goa.[9] These
prelates were so impressed by the strong leadership provided
by the Patriarch, apart from the splendour of the liturgy which
Goa alone could have supplied in the Indian sub-continent, that
returning to their dioceses, filled with admiration and wonder,
they unanimously decided to appeal to His Holiness to raise the
Patriarch to the cardinalate so that the Indian hierarchy may
have a Cardinal at its head. But to their utter disappointment
they were informed that a Portuguese prelate cannot ascend to
the purple except through the usual diplomatic channels.[10] Nor
was the Government keen to promote the cause of a prelate who
had shown in his dealings that he was a bishop first and a Portuguese afterwards. And thus it was that, through the lukewarm-
ness of the Portuguese authorities who would not take the opportunity by the forelock, Goa was baulked of richly deserved
honour of its archbishop being appointed the first Cardinal of
India.

Ironically enough, the honour when it actually came to
India went to an archdiocese—Bombay—whose birth in 1720
Goa agreed to legitimatize only as late as 1857 by the Concordat of that year, and which had done nothing to deserve the
title by way of Church extension. In fact while a flourishing
Christian community was being built up by the Irish Presbyterians in Gujarat and Kathiawar, entering the field a hundred
years after the same territory had been taken by the Archdiocese
of Bombay, the latter was struggling in this vast area, now an
entire state, with a couple of badly maintained mission stations,
having sqaundered its energies in a dispute over a few furlongs
territory with the Padroado in Bombay and fomenting quarrels
among Catholics whom it succeeded in dividing into two hostile
camps. The result was the sad spectacle of the stunted growth

of the local Catholics who were like a house divided against itself in striking contrast to the non-Catholic communities working their way up under their wise leaders and making the best of the opportunities afforded by a benign government, determined to make of Bombay *urbs prima in Indis*. It cost fifty years of solid labour on the part of the German Jesuits who put a stop to this wasteful quarrel by refusing to be a party to it to earn respectability to the Catholic Church in the streets of the city.

During the patriarchate of Dom Matheus de Oliveira Xavier the archdiocese met with a setback, his regime being conterminous with the early years of the Republic which was hostile to the Church. His last days were also clouded by the reversion to Hinduism of a section of the Christian community incensed against the parish priests, because these latter would not bless child marriages which were almost a rule among these Christians, a remnant following the customs of their non-Christian caste-men.

His successor, Dom Teotoni Vieira de Castro, was a veritable missionary apostle who infused his missionary spirit into the priests and people of Goa. As the Bishop of Mylapore, he had helped to make his diocese a model diocese in India. The diocese possessed a first grade college, the Loyola College, already famous, eight high schools, seven middle schools, three training schools, three industrial schools, one deaf, dumb and mute institute, and a private school with a total school-going population of 14,000, of whom 8,000 were boys and 6,000 were girls. Helping the diocesan clergy of 80 priests were two religious orders of men—Jesuits and the Missionary Brothers of St. Francis of Assissi—and thirteen congregations of nuns: Good Shepherd Sisters of Angers, the Sisters of the Presentation Order, Augustinian nuns, Catechist Missionaries of Mary Immaculate, Sisters of St. Anne and Divine Providence. Hospitallers of St. Francis of Assissi, Sisters of Apostolic Carmel, Franciscans of Notre Dame de Bon Secours, Congregation of the Immaculate Heart of Mary, Madras Congregation of St. Anne, and the Trichinopoly Congregation of St. Anne.[11] Before his appointment as Patriarch he had headed a missionary movement in Portugal which was calculated to revive the declining interest in religion and missions among his countrymen. Even though advanced in years at the time of his new appointment, he brought to bear on his work in Goa the energy of his earlier years. He built chapels in the eastern parts of the Goa territory, the so-called New Conquests, where the Christians had gone without priestly ministration. These were regarded as mission centres, and the priests who were appointed to these centres were expressly apprised of what was expected of them in the dual capacity of parish priest and missioner. In the former capacity they had to minister to the Christians, and as missioner they were expected to evangelise the non-Christians, carrying the message of Christ through schools and institutions of charity. At Birondem, one of these mission stations, the Patriarch opened a catechetical training school for the training of missionary personnel in the methods of effective approach to non-Christians. And in the more promising mission fields, he opened at Dadra and Nagar Haveli, the determined effort of the humble but efficient Franciscan Brothers of Mount Poinsur resulted in thousands of conversions.

In the educational field the damage caused by the retrograde policy of the Republic was repaired by the invitation to the Jesuit Fathers to open their institutions in Goa. The Jesuits readily responded by opening two first rate schools at two populous Catholic centres—Margao in Salsette and Mapuca in Bardes. At about the same time the Franciscans (Capuchins) entered Goa and sought to revive their high traditions by the establishment of their present highly reputed Secondary school on the hill-top at Monte Guirim. The education of girls was made over to the various congregations of Sisters who have a reputation for efficiency in this field.12

One of the far-sighted acts of D. Valente was the foundation by him of the Society of St. Francis Xavier. Its members had so far busied themselves with preaching missions in the diocese, and it reckoned among its early members Fr. Agnelo de Souza, a man of heroic virtue, the cause of whose beatification, having been introduced recently, is being watched with increasing interest by the whole of Catholic India. The Society which had for its model similar societies founded at Braga and Oporto in Portugal was now reorganized on the basis of the Portuguese Society of Missions Overseas. But before it could enlarge the sphere of its activities in accordance with the aims and objects under its new constitution, D. Teotonio died, and it was left to his successor, Dom Jose Costa Nunes to make his *debut* as Patriarch by giving it a new stamp, and in time infuse it with his own Dynamism and burning ardour.

Dom Jose who was a missionary bishop *'par excellence'* made the Society of St. Francis Xavier a missionary Society by diverting its energies to the missions instead of merely preaching. He planned and carried into execution a new Seminary of the Missions for a complement of 120 students; and before long twenty priests of the society had taken their place in the mission of Dadra and Nagar Haveli, which was in dire need of increased number of workers, and where they proved quite efficient. The Fathers also turned to the apostolate of the press, and their weekly magazine in the Goan Vernacular, Konkanim, is today one of the most popular newspapers among the Konkani-speaking people. In a short time the Fathers penetrated other fields of activities, suited to their talent, above all industrial education, and are today running a well-established technical school at Bandra, Bombay, an institute with a diploma in industrial management, and several high schools both in Goa and elsewhere in the Indian Union. What distinguishes the Pilar Fathers as they are affectionately known, from other similar congregations is their popular appeal in that supporting their activities there are no fewer than 80,000 Xaverian Cooperators. The ably edited English weekly *India* keeps the clergy and laity throughout the country regularly informed of the activities of this Congregation, the greatest missionary endeavour of the Archdiocese of Goa in modern times. With the abatement of the Jesuit activities in Goa as a result of the merger of its Goa Mission in Poona and the depletion of its best personnel from Goa into Maharashtra, the Casa de Reteriros,[13] maintained by the Pilar Fathers has succeeded to the Jesuit Retreat House, built through the exertions of the late Fr. Le Tellier, as the spiritual power-house of the Archdiocese. It is a sad commentary on the new Jesuit policy, which also deprived Goa of the benefit of University education at the hands of the Jesuit experts, that the building of the Jesuit Retreat House at a fashionable seaside resort, Baga having long ceased to serve its original purpose, is now occupied by a restaurant and a Happy Sanctuary, nature here as elsewhere not tolerating a vacuum.

Dom Costa Nunes elevation to the patriarchate had come about at an appropriate moment both for himself and the archdiocese. He had the rich experience gathered as the dynamic bishop of a diocese like Macau, teeming with problems with which he had successfully grappled. And there were schemes and projects, started or thought of by his predecessor, awaiting to be carried to their logical development. One of these was the crying need for a diocesan congregation of Sisters, a female counterpart of the Society of St. Francis Xavier. Not that there was a dearth of religious orders or congregations of women in Goa. But they had not struck root in the soil. Their activity was mostly limited to the secondary schools which they ran efficiently. It therefore touched only the higher echelons of the community. The sisters generally proferred excuses when asked to open a school at a poor place or to work for the poor or at a mission station. They also did a bit of recruitment in Goa for their establishments in British India, recruiting novices from among their pupils, belonging to rich families where vocations were most numerous. D. Jose Costa Nunes founded two diocesan congregations of sisters who were expected to go out into the villages, and be valued auxiliaries to the parish priests in seconding their efforts for the spiritual uplift of the people. He got their constitutions approved by the Holy See, and he had the satisfaction to see these congregations flourishing and being of incalculable service to the Church in the matter of evangelisation, their apostolate affecting classes beyond the reach of the ordinary apostolic worker.[14]

Dom Teotonio wanted a minor seminary in Bardes, another part of Goa, to relieve the congestion at the Seminary of Rachol where a thousand students lived in separate houses like a medieval university away from the Seminary for want of accommodation in the main building. The system was allegedly not conducive to the sound sacerdotal formation, though the system had produced men like Fr. Agnelo. It was of course contrary to the legislation of the Church in the matter. But D. Teotonio could only lay the foundation of the future seminary at Saligao, Pilerne, leaving to his successor the task of completing the edifice. War and want of resources impeded the work. But Dom Costa Nunes rose equal to the occasion, and raised the present stately establishment at a cost of Rs. 8 lakhs, collected from public subscription and government subsidy. Nothing escaped his attention: proper adornment of the building, laying out of the garden, appointment of the administrative and the teaching staff. As to the major Seminary at Rachol he revised the courses there as in the minor Seminary so that the clerical products of these institutions may match the laymen of their times in their intellectual makeup. He very much wanted to develop the natural aptitude of the Goans for music, and not succeeding in his efforts to import a great maestro for the purpose from Europe, he sent a couple of talented priests to Rome that music may be cultivated to perfection in the seminaries.[15]

It is interesting that at his invitation the Salesian Fathers came to Goa and opened their useful institutions, a Boys Town at the capital and a high school possibly the largest, in the Goa territory at the same place.[16] And the social action of the Patriarch included the introduction of the Conference of St. Vincent de Paul, and the Home of St. Theresa at Margao and the Maternity Home and Creche at Birondem—both part of the Work for the protection of Woman, and a much needed students' Home at the capital.

The last but not the least of his acts was the Diocesan Synod which he convoked, and which deliberated from 31 August to 31 September 1953. The constitution of the Archdiocese drawn up in the regime of D. Valente of cherished memory had clearly become antiquated; a new Code of Canon Law had come into existence in the meanwhile, and the First Plenary Council of India had passed resolutions which were being extended to Portuguese India. Furthermore, the archdiocesan decrees, expressed in the ecclesiastical legislation of the archd'ocese had to be consolidated. Under the direction of the Patriarch the Synod passed the new constitution[18] which indeed constitutes a spiritual testimonial to a church leader who, while welcoming people who daily come to seek him, could find time to write his admirable letters to the priests, the youth and the faithful. He was actually contemplating the foundation of a Clergy Home for aged priests, and had made provision for a small monthly sum to be paid to priests, becoming disabled before attaining pensionable age, when he had to relinquish charge of the archdiocese, being appointed Cardinal Camerlengo at the Vatican.[19]

Costa Nunes bade an affectionate but sad farewell to Goa. It was a wrench for him to be forced to leave a land he loved so much and where his total devotion to the cause for which he had vowed to live and die was already bearing a rich reward and was being gratefully appreciated. It was the wages for our near apostacy during the early years of the Republic, la trhison des clercs; more sufferings were ahead. Besides, D. Costa Nunes was cut up, because he had failed in one of his ambitions: admission of the Goan clergy to the rank of episcopacy. The present writer had no personal dealings with the Patriarch at any time, having but caught a glimpse of him on two occasions. But the news had percolated that he was aiming at converting the Vicariate of the Ghats into a diocese with the bishop at Belgaum, selected from among our priests. The proposal, however, clashed with the main tenet of the *theologia moral Salazariana* (to borrow the apt expression of one of our priests, a bold and far-sighted thinker, used in some other connection), and was still born. When later in 1945 Fr. Valerian Gracias, now Cardinal, was appointed Auxiliary Bishop, the appointment was hailed as a stroke of statesmanship on the part of Mgr. T.D. Roberts, Archbishop of Bombay, an Englishman scoring a march over a Portuguese. In fact, however, it was nothing of the kind. The Holy See had only helped the Archbishop to pull out from an untenable position he had created for himself, and it was a prelude to his own unceremonious departure. In a recent publication on Archbishop Roberts by D. A. Hurn (London, 1966) the Archbishop is reported as making a virtue of this necessity, even accusing Valerian Cardinal Gracias of ingratitude because he was not taken to any of the functions on the occasion of the Eucharistic Congress which he attended as the guest of the Cardinal. Nor was he introduced to His Holiness. But those who have followed the spiritual odyssey of the Archbishop since his resignation from the archdiocese must have their sympathies with the Cardinal. It is pertinent to note here that in a representation to the Goan Union which came at the time into the hands of the present writer the late Rev. Fr. Meneino Rodrigues actually complained that he had been demoted from his position as the parish priest of the Victoria Church, Mahim, only because in the course of a sermon on vocations, preached in his church, he had observed that the time was not far distant when bishops and archbishops will be chosen from among our own priests, and requested the Goan Union to take up his case before the Archbishop, as was being done by other communities under similar circumstances.[20] This was more than three years before the elevation of Cardinal Gracias as the auxiliary bishop, which was in May 1946. It is a travesty of facts that the very persons who having fought a determined rear-guard action against Indianisation were compelled to surrender, should now be described as apostles of Indianisation in two recent publications.[21]

The appointment of an Indian auxiliary bishop for Goa had been recommended by Dom Teotonio as early as 1939. For in his reply dated 21 May of that year to the inquiry of Mgr. Peter Kierkels, the then Delegate Apostolic, regarding the suitability of Mgr. Ferreira da Silva, auxiliary bishop of Goa, for appointment as the superior general of the Portuguese Society of the Overseas Catholic Missions, the Patriarch stated, recommending him for the appointment, that in the event of the latter's departure to fill the new post he would not be able to carry on, at his advanced age of 80 and given the extent of the archdiocese and its increasing load of work, without an auxiliary bishop. He added that it was his considered opinion that it would be opportune *salvo meliori judicio* if the auxiliary bishop would be selected from among the priests of the archdiocese for the reason that in other Indian dioceses there were actually several Indian bishops and the archdiocese of Goa, the mother of all dioceses of India, possesses priests, as Your Excellency knows who are in no way inferior in education, culture, and sacerdotal deportment to the clergy of the other dioceses, e.g., among others one whom your Excellency knows—Mgr. Rebello, secretary of the patriarchate, who is pious, humble, intelligent, prudent, and knows very well the affairs of the archdiocese.[22] The proposal, however, must have foundered on the same rock as did the later proposal of D.Costa Nunes.

It was long since that Goans were admitted to the rank of episcopacy under the Padroado. The earliest instance of such appointment was that of Fr Andre Gomes (d.1657), Vicar Vara of Kanara, who on the recommendation of King Joao IV was appointed Vicar Apostolic of Kanara. But he was already dead when the Bull of his nomination, of which one Fr. Borges was the bearer, reached India. In 1701 the indefatigable missionary, Dom Fr. Manuel de Santa Antonio was nominated by Pope Clement XI bishop of Solor and Timor at the instance of King Pedro II and was consecrated at Macau. In 1748 Dom Manuel de Jesus Maria Jose, an Augustinian and doctor of philosophy and theology, was consecrated Bishop of Mylapore and was for long at the head of the diocese. Finally, in 1841 Dom Frei Joao Xavier de Souza Trindade who was a prior of the monastery of St. Dominic, doctor of theology and deputy to the portuguese parliament in 1839 was elected bishop of Malacca in 1841 and the episcopal governor of Mozambique in 1856, but died in Lisbon. In more recent times we have instance of at least four of our priests who were offered bishoprics in Angola and Brazil where they had worked with distinction, but asked to be excused. And mirabile dictu: we have the instance nearer home of Fr. Antonio Pereira (1817-1876), some time professor of philosophy at the seminary of Rachol, doctor of the Gregorian, and the first Indian Jesuit after reconstitution of the Society who founded a novitiate of the Order in Madura, and in Bombay served as parish priests of Mahim and Mazagon who being proposed for the vicariate of Bombay (Propaganda) rejected it,23 surely not being worth the candle.

Before he left for Rome, Dom Jose Costa Nunes had the consolation of receiving from Pope Pius XII a concrete proof of how high the Archdiocese of Goa stood in his estimation. The Holy Father must have been struck with remorse when he realized how in yielding to the exigencies of the moment he had permitted the just claim of Goa for the cardinalate to go by default. The great pontiff made ample amends for the slight to the historic archdiocese, the *alma mater* of Catholic India, which was still wearing itself in the fulfilment of a task which in its very nature is impossible of reaching completion. Before the departure of the distinguished churchman, he conferred on the archdiocese the greatest honour which was within his power to bestow and which a diocese with only a heroic record of service

can merit—THE GOLDEN ROSE.24 This was act of statesmanship which for ever bound the Goan faithful to the Holy See
by ties of filial affection and to himself by their sense of eternal
gratitude.

Dom Jose Costa Nunes had a worthy successor in Archbishop Jose Vieira Alvernaz of the Padroado diocese of Cochin
where by a strenuous effort he had succeeded in keeping his
flock, as of old, 'the same good, pious and patriotic Christians.
Its fifty parishes which were largely self-supporting and whose
population except in towns is entirely Catholic, were served by
priests almost all of whom were from the place. There were besides two religious orders of men—the Jesuits and the Carmelites of the Discalsed. Third Order—and seven Congregations of
women—Canosian Sisters, Franciscan Missionaries of Mary,
Augustinian Nuns, Sisters of Charity, Sisters of the Holy Cross,
Carmelite Nuns belonging to the Third Order, and Sisters of
the Visitation Order—working in schools, hospitals, orphanages
and industrial schools run by the diocese.25 He had been a victim
of the suppression of the Padroado in the Indian territory on
pressure being brought to bear on the Holy See by the Government and having been compelled to relinquish his diocese in 1951
he was appointed Coadjutor to the Patriarch. It must be said
in the light of the ugly turn that the events took later that who-
ever advised Pandit Jawaharlal Nehru to take this step did a
disservice to every one concerned in this crisis, to Nehru himself, India, Goa and the Church. The suppression of the Padroado in Cochin and Mylapore, it would seem, drove the Portuguese Government into an intransigent attitude towards the question of their peaceful withdrawal from their Indian possessions.
It was gratuitous provocation to have asked the Portuguese bis-
shops to quit the territories in which they served, territories
where no anti-Indian activities were reported and where the
people were appreciative of the work done for their benefit.
This discrimination was felt all the more because missionaries of
every other nationality were left untouched. The result was that
in Madras it was comic to see a French bishop succeeding the
Portuguese. Nor did the events that followed bring us much
credit. Nehru who had been forced into taking the police action
against his conviction could not survive it long enough, and

India has since lost the proud position she had built for itself as the moral mistress of the world. Goa, which could have entered the Indian Union under a treaty on its own terms and choosing the status it wished to enjoy, lost the opportunity of doing so, and the Church was deprived of the devoted service of an institution dedicated to its cause.

After the annexation of Goa, Daman and Diu, D. Alvernaz could not continue in Goa. But before he left in 1962 he had arranged to open a first grade college—St. Xavier's—now crowning an eminence at Mapuca and bidding fair to become a beacon of light to the Union Territory.

Educational activity has shot up in Goa under the auspices of the Archdiocese which is now headed by an apostolic Administrator. The archdiocese has thirty-five high schools for boys and girls, besides primary schools whose name is legion. This is in addition to the high schools run by the various religious orders, some of which deserve to be ranked among the best anywhere in India. The medium of instruction in the schools, be the management Catholic or non-Catholic, being English and with this gigantic educational activity that has gone on for two generations or more, Goa is the only place in the Indian Union where English is spoken with distinction. Mgr. Rebello went all out to promote this activity when under the new political set up the archdiocese was required to refashion its educational institutions from the seminaries downwards to suit the needs of the new era into which Goa had been suddenly ushered. Under his able guidance the Christians achieved a near miracle when compelled to withdraw their children from the Government Primary Schools as a result of the policy of the Government in changing the medium from Portuguese to Marathi, instead of Konkani—the mother-tongue of the Goans, as a means to step up the merger of Goa in Maharashtra, they were required to find alternative institutions for the education of the children. Put on its mettle, each parish raised buildings, some of them magnificent structures, for the type of school suited for its needs; high, middle or primary, almost overnight without so much as a rupee being subscribed by outsiders. It is also to the credit of Mgr. Rebello that the sisters of Nirmala Niketan agreed to open a College of

Education at Panjim and they have since been doing excellent work in a field where they have few rivals.

Recently Mgr. Rebello has been succeeded by the auxiliary bishop, Mgr. Raul Gonsalves, as the Apostolic Administrator. It is very precious inheritance to which the latter is succeeding, and we wish him all success. The present writer believes that it was a special providence that took him to Goa where he was able in the course of a two years' stay to study the situation and estimate the effects of the change of government on the community and the Church. Two of our hospitals have been taken over by the government for no reason whatsoever. And the priceless monuments in Old Goa changed hands overnight by a government order, being declared national monuments, which include the Basilica where the body of St. Francis Xavier lies in a mausolum, the gift of his spiritual childrens gratitude, and the Cathedral. These are instances of injustice perpetrated at a lower administrative level with which the late Pandit Jawaharlal Nehru and his successors have had nothing to do, and representation at the right quarters should be able to get the grievances redressed.

Again, the *esprit de corps* which was so much in evidence among our priests under the old regime has suffered after the withdrawal of the Patriarch. To give only one instance, realising the presence of high talent in Goa, both among the clergy and the laity, D. Jose Costa Nunes had ventured to convert *A voz de S. Francis Xavier,* the organ of the Archdiocese, comparable to our *Examiner,* into a learned monthly, calling it *Boletim Eclesiastico da Arcediocese de Goa.* This journal which was definitely superior to anything we have been able to produce this side of the Indian sub-continent, including the *Clergy Monthly,* went on regularly from 1941 to 1963 or so, then started becoming irregular, and has not been appearing for the last two years. The reason for this is not far to seek; two of its prominent collaborators having defected, the editor tried to pull on by filling the pages with Biblical exegesis, his special study, and was forced to stop through sheer exhaustion. The present writer offered his services to the Apostolic Administrator to bring out the *Boletim* regularly and was told that efforts would be made and the Journal would be started again whereas consulting the zealous younger priests in Panjim, they were able to give names of fifteen learned priests and as many laymen who could be depended upon for regular contributions, provided that the old team spirit was restored.

This is not the place to speak of the ills from which the archdiocese is suffering, ills which are due to the lack of strong leadership and not to anything intrinsically wrong with its structure or body politic. These ills are rightly blamed on the make-shift arrangements which the Vatican could not help making during the past few years. But now that the situation is clear, it is expected that better counsel would prevail and that no problems are created where none exists. The Archdiocese of Goa, even though it is now restricted practically to the Union Territory and has not in recent times embarked on spectacular missions, as it did under its former Primate, Dom Aleixo de Menezes, is even in our day thanks to its intense Catholic life, its learned and edifying clergy, and enlightened and devoted laity a model to the whole of India. As well, thanks to divine grace and the protection of St. Francis Xavier there has been no dearth of vocations to priesthood or religious life in the archdiocese. In fact with its population of 350,000 Christians Goa can easily supply 500 priests[26] on condition that its resources are properly deployed under able leadership.

Inspired by the example of their patron who made the whole of the East his parish, the Goan clergy has regarded the whole world as the proper field of their mission. Thus when Ceylon fell to the Dutch in 1656 and Catholicism was threatened with extinction, the Goan Oratorians rushed to its rescue headed by the saintly Fr. Jose Vaz. Emulating the latter's example, his nephew Fr. Carvalho went all out, when the epidemic of small pox broke out at Kandy, assisting the stricken population with spiritual ministration and temporal aid, carrying on his shoulders baskets of food, curing their wounds, disposing of their excrements, and burying their fetid corpses. Sharing his hardships in the spiritual conquest of the island, Fr. Jose de Menezes, the successor of Fr. Jose Vaz, died there in the odour of sanctity. Starting from Goa in 1705 and traversing the island bare-footed, Fr. Miguel de Mello made during the seven months of life left to him such an impression of his sanctity that when he died the Christians were went to carry handfuls of dust from his grave: while Fr. Jacome Gonsalves wrote forty volumes of edifying literature for the use of his neophytes and laid the foundations of a Christian literature in Sinhalese.

Again, when Bassein and Salsette fell to the Marathas in 1739, and the European clergy could not continue at their posts, the Goan clergy boldly stepped into the breech and repaired the damage done to the Christians by the Maratha soldiery. And finally when the Portuguese laws of 1758 and 1833 deprived the missions of the services respectively of the Jesuits and other Religious Orders, it again fell to the lot of the Goan priests to save the situation and prevent Christianity planted with the blood, tears and sweat of the missionaries of the past from disappearing from the Orient.

In more recent times in the roll of the more prominent names are Fr. Benjamin Amarante (1812-1879), missionary and later Governor of the diocese of Mylapore who at a critical time founded the English High School, and with a large sum of money collected in Goa established the present Seminary of the Diocese; he edited the *St. Thomas Catholic Chronicle*, a weekly, from 1853 to 1863; published a Tamil grammar, and wrote in the same language a prayer book entitled *Atma Pariksha;* Fr. Christovao Nazareth (1830-1928), Vicar General of the diocese of Cochin, who re-opened the Seminary of Alleppey, providing funds for its efficient management, established a number of primary schools throughout the diocese, and the Ornella's High School at Tuticorin; Canon Reginaldo Salvador Santana Pinto who as Vicar of Karwar rendered valuable service to his flock helping them not to swerve from the right path at a trying time; Fr. Joaquim Milagres Pimenta who showed extra-ordinary zeal and courage when plague broke out in Bombay, in tending the sick irrespective of their creed; Fr. Jose Udalrico da Lapa Rodrigues who, having been ordained in Goa in 1878, entered the Society of Jesus in Portugal and for thirty years held the chair of Philosophy at the Scholasticate of the Society, counting among his students Mgr. Joaquim Rodrigues Lima who became the Archbishop of Bombay; Mgr. Herculano Damasceno Gonsalves, Vicar General of the Ghats,

who while in Bombay opened the Little Flower of Jesus School;
Fr. Damiao Fernandes, religious of the diocese of Nagpur who
distinguished himself as an educationist, having started the Holy
Cross Girls' School with subscription collected in Goa; Fr. Vincent Lobo (1886-1922) who in order to impart religious
instruction to his countrymen, knowing no other language than
Konkani, founded at Karachi *The Messenger of the Sacred Heart*
in that language; Fr. Antonio Ludovico Pereira who not only took
up the editorship of this periodical when it fell vacant, but lived
to write a number of books on religious subjects; Fr. Antonio
Ciriaco Fernandes who after graduating in theology from the
Seminary of Rachol, proceeded to Portugal where he entered the
Society of Jesus, and at Recife in Brazil founded the Marian
Congregation, an institution offering facilities for sports, study
circles, religious meetings and library; and Fr. Lucina de Sa
(1889-1929), an alumnus of Rachol, who entering the Congregation of the Holy Spirit in France was appointed Superior of
the Mission of the Congregation at Zanzibar. He so devoted
himself to the welfare of the refugees flocking to the islands of
Pemba and Zanzibar that he won the admiration of the Bishop
who is said to have exclaimed that descended as he was from
the converts of St. Francis Xavier, the spirit of the Saint had
become incarnate in him.27

True to this spiritual heritage one hundred of our priests
are serving in different dioceses of India (according to statistics
of the terms of Cardinal Costa Nune). In West Africa too there
are a number who are serving under their own bishops as elsewhere in the dioceses of Beira, Sa de Badeira and Cabo Verde.
Shortage of priests in South America, Brazil, has taken our Priests
to these regions also. This is indeed a glorious record. It is
also a heavy burden which our priests have been carrying for
the last two hundred and fifty years or more, the magnitude of
which can be realized only when it is known that in India alone,
according to the 8th schedule of our Constitution, there are no
fewer than fifteen major languages and there are besides two
hundred minor ones. And if a thorough mastery of language
of a people among the lot of a priest is cast is a *sine qua non* of
the success of his mission, it may truly be maintained that the

incessant demand for our priests on the part of the outside world is a measure of the efficiency with which they have been fulfilling their mission.

On the historic occasion of the presentation of the GOLDEN ROSE the following Prophetic words were uttered by the Papal Legate in regard to what the future holds for our primatial and patriarchal archdiocese:

> The gesture of the Holy Father does not
> merely signify an acknowledgement of a
> glorious past and of a present which
> does honour to the Episcopate, the clergy
> and the faithful of the Archdiocese of
> Goa but is a prediction of a much greater
> future in the unity of faith of Our Lord
> Jesus Christ.[28]

This prediction of a much greater future for the Archdiocese of Goa, interpreted in the light of an inspired message of a saintly missionary editor in his editorial on the fourth centenary of the Archdiocese, exactly twenty years before, is to be once again the source of a Christian renaissance in India as momentous as that of the 16th century.[29]

THE CATHOLIC CHURCH UNDER THE PORTUGUESE PATRONAGE IN THE 19TH AND THE 20TH CENTURIES

By Dr. George M. Moraes.

During the early years of the Portuguese supremacy in the East-Asia Portuguese depended for its ecclesiastical organisation on the episcopal see of Funchal in Medeira. This diocese had been established by Pope Leo X on 10 June 1514. Goa was naturally the first diocese to be carved out of the limitless expanse of this bishopric, thus becoming the mother of all the dioceses of the East. The bull *Aequm Reputamus* of 3 November 1534 which founded the diocese of Goa brought within its limits the whole hemisphere to the east of the Cape of Good Hope, comprising East Africa, South East Asia and the Far East.[1]

This demarcation, naturally enough, could only be provisional, and the multiplication of Christian settlements, in the wake of the progress of Portuguese political and Commercial influence in the East, soon called for further splitting of the territory. Accordingly, the Apostolic Constitution *Esti Sancta et immaculata* of 4 February 1557 raised Goa to the rank of a metropolitan see with jurisdiction over two dioceses which were then established, Cochin and Malacca. The archdiocese continued to belong in *perpetuum* to Portuguese Patronage, and yielded to the two new dioceses the territories from the Malabar coast and beyond, Cochin comprising the present Kerala and the entire coast of the Bay of Bengal as far as Burma, and leaving the rest of the eastern world to be lorded over by the diocese of Malacca. The diocese of Cochin was soon found to be too unwieldy, and had to cede a large part of its territory to a new diocese that came to be formed on 9 January 1606, Mylapore, consisting of the Coromandel Coast, Orissa, Bengal and Pegu. In the meanwhile the ancient archdiocese of Angamaly which had come within the ambit of the *Catholic* (Latin) Church was converted with the death of archbishop Mar Abraham into a diocese by a Brief of Clement VIII, dated 20 December 1599, and was confided to the patronage of the Portuguese Crown, but was restored to its former archepiscopal status in 1608.[2]

When the Apostolic Constitution *Esti Sancta et immaculata* placed the archdiocese of Goa with its suffragans perpetually under the Portuguese Patronage (Padroado), the Holy See was not going out of its way to mete out favoured treatment to Portugal. In Christendom it was the common practice to place the dioceses under royal Patronage in recognition of the services to the Holy See by the royal patron. This royal Patronage was compounded of privileges and obligations: the privileges being to present candidates, in the event of there being a vacancy of bishop, for selection by the Holy See to fill the vacancy from among them (the Holy See reserving the right to fill it independently), to administer the funds made over to the diocese by the patron, and in general be in possession of the diocese, all of which privileges the patron enjoyed in return for obligation to maintain the personnel of the diocese and propagate the faith. It was therefore an onerous privilege, a bilateral contract which could not be rescinded except with the consent of both the parties. It was thus a right or *jus*, and not a gracious privilege which could be abridged or abolished at will.[3]

On its part the Portuguese Crown undertook to carry out its obligation to the letter. It sent missioners in sufficient numbers, built churches, founded benefices, and endowed them generously.[4] The result of this endeavour is seen not only in the flourishing Christian settlements on the Indian seaboard but in the crowning glory of the Padroado, the Jesuit Mission of Madura, immortalized by the names of De Nobili, Beschi and De Britto, an achievement without parallel in the Christian annals anywhere in the world. By presenting Christianity in terms of Hindu wisdom, the Jesuits brought to the Christian fold within a little over a hundred years a large number of Hindus of high castes so that at the closure of the mission consequent on the suppression of the Jesuits in Portugal in 1758 the Christian population in Madura reckoned 150,000 souls.

But the Padroado was a human institution, and it was not long before frailties to which human nature is heir manifested themselves in the exercise of the royal patronage.   This was specially noticeable in the reluctance of the European missioners to take into partnership the Indian priests who were being produced in increasing numbers by the educational institutions in the hands of the religious orders in Portuguese India-universities, colleges and secondary schools—thanks to the clerical turn education had taken in these institutions.[5] But it is not true, as is alleged by the critics of the Padroado, that missionary effort during the period of the Portuguese monopoly hardly touched the interior of the subcontinent due to the 'tendency of the Portuguese clergy to stay in the villages of the coast, fortified places, and trading factories.'[6] In actual fact the Jesuits had built up a fruitful connection with the Mughal Court, a connection which they maintained unbroken for two centuries and which enabled them to open out stations in the heart of the Empire and even to breach the impenetrable barriers, isolating the Himalayan kingdoms of Nepal and Tibet.

It is, however, a just criticism that the Church under the Padroado appeared very much like the spiritual appendage of the Portuguese Empire, and the missionary personnel depending for its appointment in the Council of India as much as did the captain and viceroys, ran the danger of being considered as functionaries of the colonial state. They were automatically excluded from the territories of powers hostile to the Portuguese as much as they were welcome in friendly states.[7] But the balance of advantage lay with the Padroado; for it is a matter of common historical knowledge that during the period of Muslim domination, before the Portuguese could establish their hold on the country, the missioners had come to India only to die as martyrs.

By his bull *Inscrutabile* of 22 July 1622 Gregory XV established the Congregation of the *Propaganda Fide,* after having sought information and counsel from various sources, a congregation which was intended by this pontiff to centralize the organization, direction and control of the propagation of faith in non-Catholic countries. Studies were submitted to the Propaganda on the ways and means of spreading the faith in these countries and the removal of obstacles, and accordingly, in regard to India Francisco Ingoli, the

Secretary, produced a report in which he blamed the tardy progress of the faith squarely on the Padroado.[8]

The head and the front of the charges against the Padroado being the alleged failure of its missioners to venture into the interior of India, the Congregation thought itself competent unilaterally to appoint in 1637 Matthew de Castro, a Goan of Brahmin extraction, Vicar Apostolic of the Kingdom of Idalcan, meaning Bijapur, with powers equivalent to those of a diocesan bishop.[9] Matthew left for India some time in March-April 1638.[10] He followed the Land route, and embarking at Venice for Aleppo, and passing through Syria and Iraq, he reached Basra, whence coursing through the Persian Gulf and crossing the Arabian Sea, he disembarked at Surat, the Bombay of those days. From Surat Matthew naturally wanted to go to Goa. This was only a matter of a hop, skip, and a jump, and he was there in a few days.[11]

In Goa one of the first visits, he paid, was to the archbishop, D. Francisco dos Martyres (1636-42). The latter was taken aback when Matthew revealed to him the true nature of his mission. He told Matthew that the whole of India was the patrimony of his sovereign, and it was, therefore, not possible to accord recognition for the exercise of his ministry to a bishop who had not been nominated by him. Matthew answered that the permission of the Portuguese crown appeared superfluous to him, considering that Bijapur like Japan lay outside his dominions. The argument made no impression on the archbishop who dismissed Matthew, remarking that it was bootless to insist.[12]

Now that it was not possible to set up his diocese with the help of the archbishop, Matthew decided to establish it without him. But lacking as he did labourers to work in the diocese, he approached the archbishop for permission to ordain the young men who had gathered round him in Goa, but receiving an evasive reply, he proceeded with the aspirants to Bijapur where he ordained them priests. His action was understandable, and opinion was divided in Goa as to the legality of the ordination, so much so that even the viceroy and the government refused to take sides in the dispute.[13] But when it was learnt that his political intrigues aimed at the total destruction of the Portuguese power, and that he was manoeuvring to deliver a couple of Goan islands to Adil Shah whom he was instigating to invade the Goa territory, and was negotiating with the Hallanders to assist him, Matthew lost all popular sympathy for him.[14]

Matthew left for Rome in 1643 having accomplished little. Charges against him had in the meanwhile poured into the Propaganda from all quarters. But thanks to the support of his patron, Ingoli, he was exculpated. Ingoli even contrived to have him sent back to his vicariate, and Matthew was about to depart for India when the death of another vicar apostolic destined for Ethiopia made the Propaganda change its decision and ask him to proceed to the latter country instead.[15] Matthew, however, met with difficulties which appeared insurmountable, and he made his way to India where he is found, from the Portuguese official sources, about the year 1652-53.[16]

Matthew had been strictly warned by the Propaganda to avoid implicating himself in political activities. But that was his sound nature, and he could not help doing so. He sought and obtained an audience with the Mughal Emperor before whom he denounced the Jesuits, who were at the court as Portuguese spies. The result was a complete cessation of missionary activities in the Empire, while in some of the princely states the missioners were even thrown into prison.[17] No wonder then that when Matthew returned to Rome in 1658 the Congregation of the Propaganda decided that for the sake of peace he should not return to his vicariate.[18]

Notwithstanding this initial failure, the Propaganda proceeded with its programme of creating fresh vicariates. In 1657 it had entrusted the Carmelites with the vicariate of Malabar. In 1676 it appointed a vicar apostolic in Mangalore; while earlier in 1642 it had appointed the French Capuchin Father Ephrem prefect apostolic for Madras which three years before had passed into the hands of the English.

The principle behind the creation of the vicariates, it must be admitted, was sound. India is too vast to have been evangelized with the scanty resources of a small country like Portugal. The vicariates were therefore a much needed innovation, if they were to be created in parts of India quite remote from the old and well established dioceses of the Padroado. This was in actual fact their *raison d'etre*. But they were carved out of territories where the missioners, working under the Padroado, were still active. For it will be appreciated that Madras is situated almost at a stone's throw from Mylapore, and there is only a river dividing Cochin from Verapoly (Ernakulam), the seat of the vicariate of Malabar, both of which towns today constitute a single municipal corporation. And if neglect on the part of the Padroado clergy was the reason for taking over the Padroado territory, Mangalore was ministered to by a pastor like the Ven. Fr. Joseph Vaz than whom the Propaganda could not appoint a better pastor. It is therefore ignorance of geography alone that can account for their creation in such close proximity, nay in the very territory of the Padroado dioceses. For after all the Vatican officials could not have been better informed than the members of the British Foreign Office, who despite the close connections with India of over half a century established by the East India Company, believed, while they were negotiating with Portugal at this time the treaty of 1661 which brought the island of Bombay to Charles II as part of the dowry of Catherine of Braganza, that it was some where off-shore of Brazil. Matthew de Castro could have enlightened the authorities on the correct geographical position. But he was the *tertius gaudens*, and so preferred to keep the knowledge for himself.

As expected by Matthew, the contiguity of the dioceses, apart from the unilateral apportionment of territory, sparked off a regular civil war between the two parties in the same Church, or rather two systems of ecclesiastical colonialism—the Portuguese Padroado and the Italian intrusion backed by the Propaganda—a civil war which starting with the appointment of Matthew in 1637 ended only in our own day in 1953. The nineteenth century with which this chapter is concerned saw this contest in one of its worst phases. And by a cruel irony it was the Goan clergy which had succeeded the European missioners in the Padroado missions that became the target of attacks of the adversaries of the Padroado. Much energy was wasted on both sides, a waste which was prejudicial to the growth of the Church in India and the progress of the Indian Christian community, hopelessly compromising both the parties.

The Goan priests had rushed to the missions actuated by the best of motives. In the nineteenth century, interest in the missions was dwindling in Portugal, this declining interest being the result of a political situation which had suddenly turned viciously antireligious. The lamentable neglect of the missions which followed was threatening to leave little of the splendid work of the early missioners of the Padroado. In 1833 Portugal broke her relations with the Holy See, and what little activity there was in the missions came to a halt thanks to the decree of 30 May 1834 which suppressed the Religious Orders throughout the Portuguese Empire.[19] This was the work of the Portuguese minister of justice, Joaquim Antonio de Aguiar who, obsessed as he was with an implacable hatred of the Religious Orders, demolished by one stroke of his pen what his country had taken three hundred years to achieve. From now on the educational decline of Goa began, because neither the state nor the diocesan clergy could assume control of the schools and colleges which the religious had been forced to close.

Naturally enough, in Rome the thought of the Holy See was concentrated all this while on how to stop the rot. But unhappily for India, the reform was undertaken in a partisan spirit. For the state of the missions under the Propaganda was in no way better, the same disease that had taken its toll in Portugal-enlightenment-having wrought a like havoc in other countries of Catholic Europe. Nor should it be forgotten that this was the time when Europe had not yet recovered from the disastrous effects of the Revolutionary and Napoleonic Wars when men's minds were rivetted on military affairs to the total neglect of everything else. It is also worthy of note that during the two centuries or more (1637 to 1834) that the Propaganda missioners were with us, the gains that accrued to the Church from their presence were negligible. Consequently, when the Cardinal Prefect of the Propaganda of the times warned the Portuguese

Crown that it should either carry out the obligations of the Patron or relinquish its rights of patronage,[20] he was like a man living in a glass house and throwing stones. Nor would Pope Gregory XVI wait till normal relations with Portugal were resumed, but in high dudgeon, on his own initiative, unilaterally, and precipitately, created two vicariates apostolic in territories since long under the Padroado—Calcutta and Madras (1834). They were followed in 1836 by two others—Ceylon and Pondicherry.[21]

This action of the Holy See was as resolutely opposed by the people and the clergy serving under the Padroado, as it was supported by the vicars apostolic, now urging the total abolition of the Padroado outside the Portuguese territories. Pope Gregory was beside himself, and in his anxiety to be absolved of the responsibility for the dissensions his indiscretion had caused in these peaceful Christian settlements, he appointed a commission of three theologians of his own choosing to go into the question whether it was lawful for the Holy See to abolish the Padroado.

The reply of the Commission was in the affirmative, and the Pontiff proceeded to act on the decision by publishing on 24 April 1838 his ill-advised Brief *Multa Praeclare*. According to this brief the Portuguese patronage was to be exercised in all the territories of the archdiocese of Goa and in all the territory of the diocese of Macau. In the non-Portuguese territory, the territory of the diocese of Mylapore would go to the Vicariate apostolic of Madras, the territory of the diocese of Cochin would go to the vicariate apostolic of Verapoly, and lastly, that of Malacca would be annexed to the vicariate apostolic of Ava and Pegu. It may here be noted that the authors of the *Multa Praeclare* were ignorant of the fact that the archbishop of Goa exercised jurisdiction outside the Portuguese territory, an important geographical lapse which later gave rise to serious trouble.[22]

The publication of the brief was like throwing fat on fire. The Padroado authorities rejected it as spurious. They argued that it was not the practice of the Roman Curia to settle such serious questions by means of simple Briefs. Moreover, no papal documents were valid before they received the royal beneplacet.

Still worse, the brief treated the Padroado as a privilege, whereas the ancient bulls were quite explicit and recognized it as a right, *jus patronatus*. The battle was thus joined between the Propaganda and the Padroado. The Propaganda dubbed the followers of the Padroado as dissidents and schismatics, while these latter remained firm in their opinion and treated the Propaganda agents as insolent intruders. Henceforward the age-long activity in which Propaganda missioners had indulged, not in effecting conversions to the faith but bringing about change of jurisdiction among the faithful, assumed a sacrosanct character. It was in their eyes a meritorious act which was tantamount to reducing dissidents to Rome, though in their heart of hearts they must have known that they were only wasting their energy in trying to convert Catholics into Catholics.

This was the situation when after normal relations were restored between the Holy See and Portugal, José Maria da Silva Torres was appointed archbishop of Goa. But knowing as the Pope did that the changes effected by *Multa Praeclare* in the authority of the metropolitan over the dioceses of Cochin, Cranganore, Mylapore, and Malacca would not be accepted by Portugal, he did not mention *Multa Praeclare* in the bull of appointment of Silva Torres. To all intents and purposes, therefore, it conferred on him the same jurisdiction as on his predecessors. The result of this equivocality was that when Silva Torres landed in Bombay and was received by the Vicar General, Padre Antonio Mariano Soares, and was fêted by the Catholic Union of Bombay, an honour which was his due as the rightful prelate, since Bombay then belonged to Goa, he met with the determined opposition of the Vicar apostolic of Grand Mogor, Frey Luis de Santa Teresa, who had taken his residence in Bombay as its vicar apostolic. The stand of the archbishop was consistent. He maintained that he was not bound to take cognizance of a document which was not mentioned in the bull of his appointment, the terms of which he had sworn to observe, and that it should be sacrilegious to impute to the Pope an ignoble comedy that he (archbishop) should be required to swear at one and the same time to observe the terms of the bull and the terms of *Multa Praeclare*.

The position of Gregory XVI was admittedly untenable.

But instead of retrieving his fault, issued a warning to Silva Torres. The archbishop answered the papal warning with a pastoral letter of 29 January 1846 in which he maintained that he did not deserve such a warning from the Holy Father. The latter was being misinformed, as the Propaganda always sided with the vicars apostolic, and firmly rejected the description of him as a 'schismatic' by the vicar apostolic of Bombay.

Gregory XVI died soon after, and was succeeded by Pius IX who, under the persuasion of the Propaganda, sent a new warning to the archbishop, confirming all that had been asserted by his predecessor, and adding new charges. These charges—which were utterly false—were that the archbishop had taken note neither of the death of Gregory XVI nor of his own election, whereas he had performed solemn obsequies on hearing that the former Pontiff had departed this life, and had, on receipt of the news of the latter's election, issued a notification that the event should be worthily celebrated by means of a *Te Deum*. In spite of this, however, instructions were received by the Nuncio in Lisbon for negotiating with the Portuguese government for the recall of the archbishop who had become *persona non grata* with the Holy See.[23]

The Portuguese government yielded to the request of the Nuncio. Silva Torres embarked for Portugal in 1849, and wrote a letter of submission to the Pope at the instance of his government on 8 November 1850. The Pope in his reply added insult to injury in observing that he had taken note of the promise of the archbishop always to obey the directives of the Holy See as behaving on all bishops so that those who have been scandalized by his attitude may in future have better opinion of his behaviour. Not satisfied with this reprimand, the Pope gloated on his victory in the Secret Consistory of 17 February 1851, referring in particular to his insistance, which had been duly obeyed, on the immediate removal of Silva Torres and the latter's submission and offer of profound apology. The Portuguese government lodged a strong protest against this unseemly procedure in a document entitled *Memoir on the allocution of H.H. Pius IX in the Secret Consistory of 17 February 1851*. The document passed in review all the facts relating to the Padroado, making special reference to its onerous character, which had been recognized by a number of Pontiffs, and ending with the hope that outstanding questions, relating to the Padroado, would be speedily settled. This important document paved the way to the Concordat of 1857.[24]

In the meanwhile there were fresh disturbance in Bombay a place of chronic trouble between two rival sections of Catholics. In 1850 Bombay had a new administrator apostolic in the person of Anastasius Hartmann, vicar apostolic of Patna. Ignorant of the true juridical situation, he claimed the whole of Bombay as his fief. But he found the parishes divided.

In the first division which had taken place in 1794 the Propaganda had been given two churches (Our Lady of Hope and St. Michael), and the Padroado the remaining two in the Island (Our Lady of Salvation and Our Lady of Glory).[25] In 1813 the parishioners of Our Lady of Salvation, due to differences with the Curia of Goa, went over to the jurisdiction of the Propaganda, and the vicar apostolic of the times received them with open arms.[26] Years later, in 1850, as a result of another dispute the Salvation Church returned to the Padroado. The Administrator apostolic, Bishop Hartmann, took the case to the court, but the court upheld the decision of the parishioners.[27]

Three years later, in 1853, Bishop Jeronimo da Mata of Macau passed through Bombay on his way to Goa where he had been called to administer the Sacrament of Holy Order to a number of seminarians. Since the time of the recall of Silva Torres to Portugal, these seminarians were waiting to be ordained. In Bombay the bishop was received with great rejoicings by Fr. Antonio Mariano Soares, vicar general of the North, and the Christians of the two Padroado Churches. In the Church the bishop also administered the sacraments of Holy Order and Confirmation.[28]

Bishop Hartmann who gave himself airs of sole pastor of Bombay would not tolerate what he regarded as criminous intrusion on the part of the bishop of Macau.[29] But the situation was further complicated, for the administrator apostolic when a little later the parishioners of the church of St. Michael, having fallen out with the Propaganda, decided, under the instigation of their vicar Jose de Mello and his assistant Gabriel da Silva, to join the Padroado, a question which they were about to resolve by vote. When Hartmann heard of this, he appeared in the church on the day fixed for the ballot—3 March 1853, and he remained in the church a virtual prisoner for fourteen days, being certain that in the event of his leaving the church it would pass to the Padroado. The parishioners took the matter to court, which gave the decision that the church belonged neither to the parishioners nor to the bishop, but to the Confraternity of the Immaculate Conception.[30]

Touched to the quick, Hartmann continued his campaign against the Padroado with all the energy of a quarry driven to bay could muster. He had already despatched his secretary, Fr. Ignatius Persico, to Rome to acquaint the Propaganda with all that had happened in India. He now got his fellow vicars apostolic to join him in the demand that (i) the bishop of Macau be excommunicated or suspended, (ii) that no concordat with Portugal be concluded till it gave up its patronage in the orient, and (iii) that the priests who would refuse obedience to the vicars apostolic be declared schismatics.[31]

Even before this demand reached Rome, Pius IX had already published on 29 June 1853 his Brief *Probe nostis,* finding fault with the bishop of Macau and condemning his procedure in Bombay and in particular with the priests who had spear-headed the resistance to the propaganda in Bombay, 'promoting and propagating dissensions', as the Brief puts it, 'and establishing the schism'. It singled out Fr. Mariano Antonio Soares whom it described as a man who had arrogated to himself the position of vicar general of the prelate of Goa in the territory of Bombay.[32]

This was sheer abuse of authority on the part of the Pope, resulting from a lack of evangelical spirit, to borrow an apt expression used by one of our rising theologians in his review of the English translation of *Le Ministère Sacerdotal,* with reference to such abuse of authority in high places in the Church a lack which renders the exercise of the ministry extremely difficult.[33] The bishop of Macau, who, besides being condemned in

11

the Brief, received two admonitions, was completely innocent and undeserving of the rebuke for the simple reason that the *Multa Praeclare* did not exclude Bombay from the territory of the archdiocese of Goa. For the same reason Fr. Antonio Mariano Soares was the *de jure* vicar general of the archbishop of Goa. It was evident that the secretary of Bishop Hartmann, Fr. Ignatius Persico, had misled the Pope. All the same history cannot condone this *ex parte* proceeding of Pius IX and his victimising of the innocent.

Portuguese government protested officially against the Brief on 28 July 1853, and the Portuguese press was ignorantly critical of the Pope's action, while the Parliament in its session of 20 July 1853 declared the three priests censured in the Brief national heroes, deserving well of the motherland. This is the origin of what is sometimes ignorantly called by the protagonists of the Propaganda Goan Schism.[35]

But considering the case seriously, there is no reason why Fr. Antonio Mariano Soares could be taken to have fallen into schism, because he did not owe obedience to the vicar apostolic of Bombay. He could be charged on some other score, e.g. for fomenting resistance of the priests of the Propaganda against their legitimate superior. As to the other priests mentioned in the brief, however, they stand in an entirely different category, having been ordained by the vicar apostolic. True, they flaunted portuguese names, and may even have been of Goan descent, but by no stretch of imagination could they be considered as having belonged to the Padroado. They were priests of the Propaganda, and by their disobedience to their legitimate superior had incurred canonical penalties and they rightly deserved the censure.[35]

In fact, as Dr. Antonio da Silva Rego whose judicious and balanced studies of the Padroado question have superseded all previous works on the subject including even the remarkably unbiassed and authoritative *Bombay Mission History* of the late Fr. E. R. Hull, has truly observed, the whole *Probe Nostis* is so beset with ignorance that one wonders how Perisco could have managed to extract it from the Pope. For one thing, the *Probe Nostis* refers to four fathers as Goans, whereas only one of them was a Goan. For another, Hartmann thought that *Multa Praeclare* had extinguished the Portuguese jurisdiction outside Portuguese India. In actual fact it was the other way about; the archdiocese of Goa, not having been affected by *Multa Praeclare* Bombay continued to belong, *de jure* to Goa. Then again, the propaganda did not give the right lead, Cardinal Prefect Franzoni, replying on 3 March 1840 to the vicar apostolic of Grand Mogor, wrongly affirming that in virtue of the principles established by *Multa Praeclare* he (the vicar apostolic) was the only ordinary of Bombay. This reply, as has been correctly pointed out by the late Fr. Pierre Charles, S.J., the most outstanding missiologists of our times, is based on non-existing legislations and is a geographical error. *Multa Praeclare* hardly mentions the vicariate apostolic of Grand Mogor, and the Propaganda is unaware or pretends to be unaware of the fact that the archdiocese of Goa was actually in possession of two churches in Bombay, situated in the territory of the same archbishop. And the Pope himself was in error when he in his second admonition to bishop Mata accuses him of having intruded into some other's diocese, whereas the true facts were different.

The *Probe Nostis* refers implicitly to Bombay, and declares it independent of whatever other jurisdiction. But this declaration is based on false supposition, because it may be legitimately asked, to use the argument of Dr. Silva Rego, when was Bombay separated from Goa? The *Multa Praeclare,* as explained above, legislated nothing on the subject. The *Probe Nostis* represents the case as settled and decided, but does not say when and by whom.36

The crass ignorance at the bottom of this brief had baneful consequences. Its direct victim was bishop Jeronimo da Mata. Pius IX, from newspaper reports before Vatican II, is said to be awaiting canonisation, and so does bishop Hartmann. They may have been good men, acting according to their light, and we shall cheerfully accept the verdict of the church since, in these matters, the church is never hasty and is moreover guided from above. But it is at least time that the memory of bishop Mata is cleared of blame and he is vindicated.

The highest authority in the Church having intervened in favour of the Propaganda and vicars apostolic, it appeared as if the days of the Padroado were numbered in the British Empire of India outside the Portuguese possessions. The new Concordat of 1858, therefore, took every one by surprise, because it was a total victory for the Padroado and a complete defeat for the Vicars apostolic. The Concordat confirmed the Portuguese Patronage (Padroado) in the metropolitan and primatial see of Goa and *ad honorem* in the episcopal see of Cranganore, and in the episcopal sees of Cochin, Mylapore and Malacca. Further it gave the right to the creation of a new diocese in any part of the archdiocese of Goa as and when convenience of the faithful in a locality would necessitate such formation, and it explicitly declared once and for all that the Patronage of the Portuguese Crown would be exercised not only in the Portuguese territory but in British India as well.

Thus the Concordat of 1857 was a triumph for the Padroado, the Holy See having recognised the Portuguese Patronage in the very dioceses where the *Multa Praeclare* had decreed its abolition. But in some other respects it went against the Padroado. The archbishop of Goa was now left without metropolitan jurisdiction over the suffragan diocese, and he had to content himself with the extraordinary jurisdiction, delegated to him by the Pope. Again, the Concordat obliged the Portuguese government to recognize tacitly not only *Multa Praeclare* but also *Probe Nostis* in implying that in suppressing the suffragan dioceses the metropolitan jurisdiction of the archbishop had also been suppressed. But despite this detraction, the Concordat was tantamount to a solemn recognition by the Holy See of the right of the Padroado or the Portuguese Patronage.[37]

The Concordat, however, had laid heavy burdens on the Portuguese government both in men and money. At the moment Portugal had neither. Portugal was, therefore, compelled to ask for concessions, i.e. for a new Concordat, which was signed in the Pontificate of the great Leo XIII in 1886.[38]

According to this memorable and statesmanlike document Portuguese Patronage was continued and in the metropolitan and primatial see of Goa the archbishop was vested with the rights of the metropolitan which he was to exercise in the suffragan diocese. He was elevated to the dignity of the Patriarch *ad honorem* of the East Indies with the privilege of presiding over the all-India provincial councils which, it was stipulated, should ordinarily meet in Goa. The Ecclesiastical Province of Goa would consist of Daman, a new diocese whose titular would be archbishop *ad honorem* of Cranganore, Cochin and San Tome of Mylapore,   besides the metropolitan see itself. Lastly, the Portuguese Crown was given the privilege of presenting to the Holy See, in the event of vacancy in any of the four dioceses to be created, viz., Bombay, Mangalore, Quilon, and Madura, a candidate to be selected by him from a list of three names, freely settled by the diocese in question, and submitted to the archbishop of Goa for transmission to His Majesty.[39]

This Concordat was intended to inaugurate an era of religious peace in the four missions, and it did achieve the expected result. But it did not remove what had been the primary cause of the disputes—double jurisdiction. The jurisdiction of the diocese of Mylapore impinged on a part of the city of Calcutta and the newly created diocese of Daman had part of its territory within the limits of the diocese of Bombay. This proximity was eventually prejudicial to the Padroado in that the inconveniences resulting from double jurisdiction were responsible for the Accord of April 1928 under which rather than allow these inconveniences to continue Portugal nobly withdrew from the territories, since its presence in them was for promoting and not hindering progress. This Accord confirmed the Patriarchal dignity of the archbishop of Goa as a title integral with the see of Goa. It enlarged the archdiocese by adding to it the Portuguese possessions of Daman to the north of Bombay and Diu on the Kathiawar Coast, the archbishop receiving the style of Archbishop of Goa and Daman. The rest of the diocese of Daman was to be annexed to the archdiocese of Bombay which was to continue the former's ecclesiastical organization intact. The archbishop of Bombay was alternately to be of Portuguese and British nationality, and the parish-priests of the two Goan parishes of St. Francis Xavier and Our Lady of Glory in Bombay were to have the dignity of Chamberlain of His Holiness *durante munere*. The diocese of Mylapore would be territorically reorganized so as to form a well-knit unit.

The privilege of presenting candidates to the vacant sees was continued, but it was now agreed that, in the event of any vacancy, the Holy See would, after consulting the bishops of the province through the intermediary of the Delegate apostolic, elect a candidate and present him to the President of the Republic through the Portuguese Legation at the Vatican or the Nunciature in Lisbon, and he would within two months present the name to the Holy See.

The Accord was far more favourable to the Propaganda Fide. The Padroado diocese of Daman disappeared, despite the fact, as Dr. Silva Rego observes, that the majority of the Catholics in Bombay are Goans—roughly 80,000. But Mylapore was a gainer, receiving 37,000 Christians from other dioceses in return for 32,789 of its old Christians which it lost. But the gain in Mylapore could not offset what the Padroado lost in Bombay. But this consideration was far from the mind of Portugal who in the exercise of the *Jus Patronatus* did not lose sight of its *raison d'etre*—propagation of the faith. Portugal only insisted that any alteration in the existing conditions should not be executed unilaterally.

The Accord of 1928 was followed a year later by another Accord that of 11 April 1929. It laid down lines on which the reorganization of Mylapore was to proceed so as to achieve a logical and natural expansion of the diocese.[41]

With the execution of the Accord of 1928 Mgr. Joaquim Rodrigues Lima became the archbishop of Bombay. The prelate was affable and efficient, and was assisted by a galaxy of priests, old and experienced and young and learned, some of the latter being today the pride of the Indian hierarchy. Many believed that Bombay had at last entered upon its golden age. Archbishop Lima launched on an educational apostolate with the slogan 'no church without a school'. Very soon new schools made their appearance at Umerkhadi in the city and Papdy in Bassein and several other places, while old schools at Santa Cruz and Bandra saw considerable extensions.[42] The schools yielded quick dividends, and it is to their splendid work in the cause of education of youth that the Catholic community owes the premier place in intellectual life it has occupied in recent years in the city of

Bombay, a benefit to which non-Catholic youth attending these institutions in increasing numbers are likewise admitted.

The untimely death of such a prelate in July 1936 was a catastrophe, especially in view of the fact that his English successor was a man of a different stripe, the appointment being *plus qu'un crime, une faute*. To cut the story short, since it does not concern us here, Archbishop T. D. Roberts soon found it unsafe to continue. But before resigning the archdiocese, he wished to gift it away to a South Indian Jesuit (with a South Indian name, if possible), and acting against the sane advice of his Spanish Vicar general that the archdiocese should rather be made over to the archdiocesan clergy, actually looked for one, though apparently not with a South Indian name, in the absence of one with this qualification, who was also eminent enough to be so selected. In his defence of this strange proceeding of the archbishop, David Abner Hurn, his apologist, has said that the vicar general was opposed to the appointment of the South Indian Jesuit, because of the Jesuit rule which requires that no dignities are to be accepted, nor a bishopric held, by Jesuits.[43] This may have been so; but it must be said to the credit of the vicar general that he must have also felt in his heart of hearts that, given an illustrious clergy like that of the archdiocese, under quite a few of whom he himself could learn a great many things in theology and canon law (his knowledge of these subjects being no more than basic and much more in the difficult art of government, for years, the archbishop was trying the patience of his clergy by putting the hands of the clock back. The fact was that, though our clergy was fully qualified to take over the archdiocese, archbishop Roberts whose mind moved in the imperialist groove of parting with power in stages (corresponding to the steps by which our British rulers had proposed to admit us, their subjects, to a share in the government of our own country, steps which were signalized by the reforms of 1909 giving us legislatures with official majority, of 1919 establishing diarchy, and of 1935 bringing about provincial autonomy, and other reforms not envisaged yet in the long and wearisome journey to dominion status, had not the War forced the pace wanted that there should be a period of transition be-

fore the archdiocese could be consigned to the care of its own
clergy. This was an indefinite period during which the archdiocese
would be left to the mercy of the South Indian Jesuit and his
successors.

The name of the candidate was duly placed before the
Holy See, and was naturally turned down on the ground that
the Accord of 1928 being still in force, it was the turn of a
prelate of Portuguese nationality to succeed, and it would not
be easy to persuade Portugal to renounce its rights.[44] Even a
worm will turn under such a disappointment in being baulked
of a prize which had seemed so close within his reach. In the
event, Fr. Valerian Gracias (now Cardinal), a Goan, to whose
appointment Portugal could not theoretically object, as he
satisfied the protocol, was named, in keeping with the policy
of dalliance of the archbishop, not coadjutor but auxiliary bishop in May 1946. This was not an appointment new to India,
Goa having been given an auxiliary several years before. And
it is elementary courtesy that he should be appointed vicar general and not merely be left with his insignia of office. In the case
of Bishop Gracias, however, the old incumbent continued as
vicar general until he was forced by public opinion to resign.
But archbishop Roberts was not to be beaten. He had recourse
to the familiar expedient of imperialist politics—divide et impera.
He appointed Mgr. Vivian Dyer, an East Indian (another group)
to the post. And so while the auxiliary bishop wore the robes,
Fr. Dyer wielded authority in the archdiocese. There is no explanation of this monstrous anomaly of placing mere priests over
the head of a bishop except that 'the relationship between Bishop
Gracias and Monsignor Dyer was intimate'![45]

The British Parliament conferred dominion status on India
from 14 August 1947, and events soon began to move to a climax.
Fr. Jerome D'Souza, S.J., Principal of the Loyola College, Madras,
functioning in the territory of the Padroado diocese of Mylapore,
managed to get himself elected to the Constituent Assembly, and
after 1949 to the Parliament of India. And it is singular that
the Government of India should decide, while it was actually
negotiating with the Portuguese Government merger of its

Indian possessions, to end the Portuguese Patronage in the dioceses of Cochin and Mylapore in the Indian Union. In consequence, on the representation of Government of India the Holy See called upon the Portuguese government to conclude on 18 July 1950 a new Accord by which the latter ceded the privilege of presentation to the vacancies in the sees of Mangalore, Quilon, Trichinopoly, Cochin, Mylapore and Bombay. The Holy See was released of its obligation to consult the President of the Republic in filling the sees of Cochin and Mylapore, in the event of they being vacant, with Portuguese candidates. The Holy See was also released from the obligation to appoint to the archepiscopal see of Bombay an archbishop alternately of Portuguese and British nationality. What was not altered from the Concordat of 1886 and the Accord of 1928 related to the Metropolitan and Patriarchal dignity of the see of Goa which was to continue in force as also nationality of the priests of the two parishes of Bombay, St. Francis Xavier and Our Lady of Glory, in Bombay, named in the Accord of 1928.[46] The French missions however, were not touched, even though Government of India was carrying on similar negotiations, with the government of France at this time.

By an article VI of the Accord of 1950 the Portuguese had agreed to an eventual dilimitation at a future date of the archdiocese of Goa which embraced a number of Christian settlements in the Indian Union. Accordingly, on 27 September 1953 as a result of the exchange of diplomatic notes between the Holy See and the Portuguese Government the archdiocese of Goa was required to part with its territory extending into the Indian Union. But this was to be a modification in the spirit of the Accord of 1950 and the stipulations in force of whatever other diplomatic instruments, and in particular those that concern the Padroado and the Metropolitan and Patriarchal See of Goa. The Metropolitan and Patriarchal dignity of the archepiscopal see of Goa was, therefore, to remain unaffected.

With this Convention the venerable and glorious archdiocese of Goa, the *alma mater* of the Indian dioceses, confined its jurisdiction to the territory of Portuguese India, i.e., Goa, Daman, Diu.

Throughout its long connection with India, the Padroado had endeavoured to serve the country and, of course, the Church to the best of its ability; whatever were its frailties they were only those from which flesh and blood are rarely exempt.[47] Accordingly, in appreciation of its selfless services through the centuries, the Archbishop of Calcutta moved at the Catholic Bishops' Conference of India, meeting at Bangalore in 1950, after the Portuguese Patronage was ended in the dioceses of Cochin and San Tome of Mylapore, that

The Standing Committee, on behalf of the entire Hierarchy and in the name of the Catholic community of India, place on record the expression of their profound gratitude to the Portuguese nation, which for centuries sent out Prelates, missionary priests and religious to preach the Gospel on the shores of India, and whose generous aid and constant help made it possible to train and form a numerous indigenous clergy, who have instilled in the faithful that splendid loyalty to Christ and to the Church for which they are renowned.

By an article VI of the Accord of 1950 the Portuguese had agreed to an eventual dilimitation at a future date of the archdiocese of Goa which embraced a number of Christian settlements in the Indian Union. Accordingly on 27 September 1953 as a result of the exchange of diplomatic notes between the Holy See and the Portuguese Government, the archdiocese of Goa was required to part with its territory extending into the Indian Union. But this was to be a modification in the spirit of the Accord of 1950 and the stipulations in force of whatever other diplomatic instruments, and in particular those that concern the Padroado and the Metropolitan and Patriarchal See of Goa. The Metropolitan and Patriarchal dignity of the archiepiscopal see of Goa was, therefore, to remain unaffected.

CHAPTER VIII

THE CATHOLIC THOMAS CHRISTIANS
1653 - 1970

E. R. Hambye, s.j., Delhi

It was under Padroado Archbishop of Cranganore, Francis Garcia s.j. (1641-59) that the St. Thomas Christians[1] took the law in their own hands. Since Dr. N. J. Thomas deals with the further history of the Syrian orthodox, we shall focus here on the vicissitudes of their catholic brethren. For brevity's sake, we shall mostly review the key events of the last three hundred years.

Deep Troubles

The revolt was prompted by the arrival in India, more precisely first at Mylapore and then at Cochin, of Bishop Aithallah, a former Syrian Orthodox (Jacobite) metropolitan of Damascus and failed candidate to the patriarchal see of his own church.[2] Though he managed to contact Thomas Christians through intermediaries, he was never allowed to land in Cochin, but was shipped first to Goa, then to Lisbon, and he was on his way to Rome where he died in Paris.

The dream of the Christians—to be once more an autonomous Eastern community under a prelate belonging to one of the great patriarchates—was shattered. Hence the sharp turn of events, the anger, the Koonan cross oath,[3] and finally the episcopal ordination four months later conferred on the Archdeacon, Thomas Pazheparampil by twelve priests at the instigation of the priest Ittithomman Anjilimootil of Kallicherry, a Suddist centre.[4]

According to contemporary documents there is no doubt that the Thomas Christians had no intention to leave the Roman communion as such.[5] At any rate the few who had stayed outside the conflict,[6] as well as the aged Archbishop Garcia and the Jesuits, backed up by the Padroado system, had informed Rome of those events through their envoy, Fr. Hyacinth de Magistris s.j.

Since 1642 occasional contacts between the Thomas Christians and the Discalced Carmelites of Goa had already taken place. Moreover the Carmelites with their spiritual ancestory going back to Palestine and with their existing missions in the Middle East could be regarded as better fitted for yielding an influence on the Syrian Christians of Kerala.

This is why the Roman Congregation *de Propaganda Fide* under orders of Pope Alexander VII (1655-67)[7] decided to send a Carmelite mission to Malabar. It was led by two Apostolic Commissaries empowered to settle the dispute and to reconcile the opponents. One of those Commissaries was Joseph-Mary Sebastiani (d. 1689), and he soon became the key-figure in this attempt at reconciliation. With the help of his *confreres* he achieved already quite a success during his first stay there (1655-58). At least 32 Syrian churches accepted him, besides four other who returned under the jurisdiction of the Cranganore archbishop. He even obtained from the Archdeacon, then still a pseudo-bishop, a promise of recantation, while assuring him that he would remain as the chief leader of the community. This agreement was never implemented, all the more so that meanwhile a new Archdeacon had been appointed by Archbishop Garcia.

During the two-year absence of Sebastiani, three Carmelites stayed back (one died there and then), and courageously continued the work already achieved. In March 1660 Sebastiani came back as bishop with the titular title of Hierapolis, and the authority of the Apostolic Commissary and Administrator of Cranganore. His enhanced status did a lot not only to confirm those already reconciled but to bring about many more under his influence. He was also considerably backed up by the Portuguese officials and clergy of Cochin. Within less than three years such great churches as Udayamperur, Muttam, Kaduthuruthi, Muttuchira, Edapalli, Alangad, Kuravilangad, Todupuzha, Palai, Kanjur, Malayattur, Pallipuram, Chalakudi, Angamali, Akaparambu, stood firmly on Sebastian's side. Such achievements meant also for him much protracted negotiations with the local rajahs including gifts of money and ceaseless journeys here and there accompanied by glamorous receptions, liturgical ceremonies, conferring of Orders and imparting of Confirmation.

However the capture of Cochin by the Dutch in 1662-63 and the end of the Portuguese influence there created for Sebastiani unexpected problems. On the one hand, the Carmelite prelate was for all practical purpose the bishop of the St. Thomas Christians; on the other hand, the Dutch did not want any Catholic missionary to stay in Kerala, with the exception of the few Franciscans left at Cochin. After much *Pourparlers* Sebastiani had to bow before the Dutch with reluctance and decided within the time-limit allotted to him to choose a local priest and to ordain him a bishop.

At a general meeting of the Thomas Christians who sided with Sebastiani, held at Kaduthuruthi, the unanimous choice of the community fell on the Vicar of Kuravilangad, Alexander (Chandy) Palliveetil-Pazheparambil, a close relative of the revolted Archdeacon. He had even sided for a while with him. Thus on February 1, 1663, at Kaduthuruthi also, Alexander became titular bishop of Megara and vicar apostolic of the St. Thomas Christians. Sebastiani left for good on February 14, leaving only one Carmelite behind, the scholarly Matthew of St. Joseph (d. 1691), who had stayed on there ever since the first Carmelite mission; he became one of the official counsellors of the new Indian bishop. Sebastiani recommended also to the protection and sympathy of the Dutch authorities the catholic fold and its prelate.

Bishop Chandy—Double Jurisdiction

Until his death in 1687 Bishop Chandy, very ably assisted for a while by Alexander Kadavil Kathanar, continued Sebastiani's work of reconciliation. Moreover since 1676 Carmelites had been allowed to come again to Malabar. The Bishop, who did not overlook the juridical status of the Oriental metropolitans also freely used their old title of Metropolitan of all India.[8]

Yet meanwhile, the Jesuits,[9] who always then worked under the Padroado, had succeeded in starting anew at Ambazhakad (since 1665) and at Puthenchira, well outside the reach of the Dutch Power. Ambazhakad became both their house of studies and the seminary for the St. Thomas Christians as well as for Latin clerics. Relations between Bishop Chandy and the Jesuits were happy, and this explained why the St. Thomas Christians living under the Jesuits between the Alwaye and Ponnani rivers kept on the whole faithful to their Catholic past.

The Carmelites also had settled down for good, as explained in Chapter VI.[10] In 1682 they set up at Verapoly a seminary for St. Thomas' clerics and for some others belonging to the Latin rite. It died out soon, however, and was only firmly founded in 1766. Since 1705 two scholarships were provided for Malabar seminarians at the Roman College of Propaganda.

Thanks to the strengthening of both the Jesuit and Carmelite missions in Kerala, the St. Thomas Christians had fallen for years to come under a double jurisdiction: that of the Padroado, and that of the Roman Congregation de Propaganda Fide. This state of affairs was not altered by Bishop Chandy's death. He was unfortunately succeeded in 1687 by his own coadjutor (since 1677), Bishop Raphael Figueredo Salgado, who was of Indo-Portuguese origin, belonged to the Latin rite and had been Vicar General of Cochin. Until his death in 1695 he got into troubles with everybody and almost completely failed in fulfilling his duties. Rome already warned had suspended him from his office in January 1694. Yet some more churches, which had followed the Archdeacon, were won over between 1683 and 1700.

It is to be mentioned here that the Roman authorities would have liked then to see the Catholic Archdeacon, Matthew[11], succeed Figueredo. But it was not to come through. The utter failure of Figueredo combined with the growing influence of the Carmelites led to the appointment of one of the latter, Angelus Francis of St. Theresa. Born in 1650, he had been in India since 1676. He was consecrated in 1701 by a roving Chaldean Bishop, Simon of Ada, since no Latin Bishop in India was willing to make Angelus a bishop. With Angelus Francis, who died in 1712, there began the long series of Carmelite Vicars Apostolic, who ruled over the majority of the Catholic Thomas Christians until 1887. Still 1774 the Roman authorities believed that a bishop taken from among the local clergy would indeed gather all those Eastern Catholics under him, thus ending in practice the double jurisdiction, but such an appointment according to Rome inspired by misleading reports would not favour true faith and union with the Church...'

On the other hand, those Catholic Thomas Christians who had consented to depend on the Padroado received also a new archbishop for Cranganore in 1703, the Jesuit John Ribeiro,[12] whose third and last successor both as Jesuit and bishop died in 1777. With the exception of archbishop Kariattil, who at any rate died before reaching Malabar in the 18th century and two Portuguese bishops between 1819 and 1886, the see of Cranganore was henceforward ruled by *governors,* i.e. local priests who had the responsibilities of an administrator apostolic.

Crossing over from one jurisdiction to another was frequent. Relations between the chief representatives of both sides became less acrimonious since 1733, and rather peaceful after 1750.[13] But the Padroado-Propaganda conflict of 1836-86 revived the old opposition Until it bore the title of Verapoly as late as 1838, the Carmelite Vicariate of Malabar (also "of the Mountain— Serra—of Malabar") was supposed to vanish as soon as the see of Cranganore was reorganized. Since this was done in 1703 the Vicariate would have had to pack up its traps. This could not be done however because a majority of Catholic Thomas christians refused to submit to Cranganore for good, and forced Rome, so to speak, to keep alive a Vicariate which was originally meant only for a few decades.

Both these jurisdiction catered also to some Latin parishes, and this explains why during the 18th century quite a number of St. Thomas priests serve in Latin centres belonging to the two well-known groups among them, the 700's and the 300's.

Attempts of Eastern Prelates

The memory of the past links with the East-Syrian or Chaldean Church could not be entirely blotted out. As could be expected, both Padroado and Propaganda jurisdictions were deadly opposed to resuming such links, though later on some Padroado local leaders used to fan out the anti-Propaganda feelings in order to sell the 'Chaldean Idea'.

In this connection we should not forget that during the
17th and 18th centuries Eastern Christians in the Middle-East
often came under catholic influence, and that many of them,
even whole communities, entered in communion with Rome.
The East Syrians (Nestorians, Chaldeans, Assyrians) were no
exception to those movements. Actually by the end of the 17th
century Diarbekir (Amid) had become the stronghold of the
Catholic East Syrians, later on called Chaldeans. A century later
they had become quite strong at Mosul and in the neighbouring
villages. By 1820 the catholic patriarchate of Babylon of the
Chaldeans had become well established.

Contacts between the Indian people and the Chaldeans were
resumed in 1701 with the arrival of Simon, metropolitan of Ada.
As already noticed he conferred on Angelus Francis of St. Theresa
the episcopal order. Simon was a personality of doubtful worthi-
ness, yet he came to India with Rome's approval and with the avowed purpose of reuniting all the St. Thomas Christians under one
pastor. This he did not succeed in doing, for immediately after
having made the Vicar Apostolic a bishop, he was forced to leave
Kerala and to take refuge to nowhere else than Pondicherry,
where he died in August 1720.

Much more successful however was the short-lived advent-
ure of Gabriel, the East-Syrian metropolitan of Azerbaijan. He
landed in Malabar in 1708[14] and making a clever use of the
tension then prevailing between Jesuits and Carmelites he managed to get a following with as much as 22 churches, including
some belonging to the Archdeacon's party. He died in Kottayam
in 1731.[15]

The last thirty years of the 18th century were not particularly kind to the Carmelites, and the Thomas Christians became
increasingly restive. In 1773 a general assembly of 72 churches
led close to a revolt. In 1776 they wanted to expel nearly all
the friars from their parishes; in 1787 at a common meeting
held at Angamali they asked for full autonomy without any interference of the European missionaries.[16]

The mission to Rome of two priests, Joseph Kariattil (1745-
87), a former alumnus of Propaganda College,[17] and of his
friend Thomas Paramakkel (1740-99), who was working under

the Padroado, is to be linked with that growing unrest among the Catholic Thomas Christians. As it will be mentioned later, it had also an ecumenical character. In Rome they did not obtain much, but in Lisbon Kariattil was elected archbishop of Cranganore (16 December 1872) and duly consecrated according to the Latin ordinal. He came back, but only to die in Goa on 9th September exhausted by the voyage and likely by dysentry. If he had succeeded in reaching Malabar and in governing his archdiocese for some time, it can hardly be doubted that he would have gathered all the catholic Thomas Christians under his leadership.

His companion, Thomas Parammakel, replaced Kariattil as governor of the archdiocese, until his death in 1799. From Angamali, his last residence, he exercised such an influence as to have for a while nearly all the Syrian parishes under him. According to Carmelite sources, some of the Syrian representatives wanted 1786 not only to appoint again an archdeacon— this was asked by the majority—but to obtain an Eastern prelate by all means, even a Chaldean, in case Parammakel did not become bishop. Even the then five Carmelite priests, including the Vicar Apostolic of the time, Aloysius Mary of Jesus (1743-1784-1802) agreed that the Thomas Christians should be ruled by an archbishop of their own rite.

This desire led a Malabar delegation to Mosul in 1796. Propaganda was approached, but the French wars prevented it from sending a reply. Finally Hanna Hormez, the chief catholic Chaldean bishop there, who was acknowledged by Rome as patriarch only in 1830, gave the episcopal order to the Malabar priest Paul Pandari. He was back in Kerala in 1798 with two Chaldean priests. Though received as true bishop in Changanacherry, his success was quite limited; he had some followers in and around the town, and also among those Thomas Christians of the Padroado who opposed certain interferences of the Cochin diocese (Latin).

Catholic Chaldean Success and Failure

In order to provide a better solution than that attempted by Paul Pandari, the Roman Congregation of Propaganda went as far as to nominate the Chaldean metropolitan of Salmas (Iran), Iso'yahb John Guriel, former alumnus of Propaganda College, as visitor or delegate apostolic to Malabar.[18] However he never came to India.

From 1838 the dispute and the rift between the adherents of both the Catholic parties in India, Padroado and Propaganda, created in Kerala a situation which favoured once more the idea of resuming the former bonds with Mesopotamia. By the time the Chaldean catholics, though still few and weak, had become fairly well organized, and their patriarch, Joseph 'Audo (1848-79),[19] was not devoid of leadership and above all of a deep sense of the historical tradition.

What is more, by an irony of circumstances, the movement towards restoring the ancient links with the Middle East came out by and large from among those Thomas Christians who belonged to the Padroado jurisdiction, i.e. the archbishopric of Cranganore. Owing to an almost century-old vacancy of the see, the local clergy was ruling it for all practical purposes. Then there came up the Roman policy of restricting the then Padroado to the existing Portuguese territories. This meant the victory of Propaganda and of its 'foreign' missionaries. Hence there developed an unexpected situation: the Padroado clergy of the Thomas Christians standing on the side of Eastern autonomy! It looks as if among the Padroado adherents a kind of local 'nationalism' set itself against direct Roman interferences.

The first sign of such feelings was given in 1861-62. The Padroado-Propaganda contest and desire for one's own oriental identity were sharpened by the order given by the then Vicar Apostolic, Bernardine of St. Theresa (Joseph Baccinelli, 1853-68) to close down all the malpanates, i.e. the local seminaries run by leading diocesan priests. In spite of Rome's opposition and even prohibition the Chaldean Patriarch Joseph 'Audo consecrated in September 1860 Mar Thomas Rokkos for Malabar with the backing of two Thomas Christians priests. They landed in Kerala in May 1861, and very quickly some 80 parishes completely and 34 other partially followed the Chaldean bishop. Yet under the weight of a strong local opposition led by the newly founded Carmelite Tertiaries (known today as the Carmelites of Mary Immaculate) and supported by the Roman authorities, Rokkos had to leave just one year after his arrival. One of his local supporters, Anthony Thondanat failed to obtain episcopal order from 'Audo, but got it all the same from the other East-Syrian catholicos, Simon XVIII Reuben, who belonged to the 'Nestorian' line of succession. After returning to Kerala, he did not succeed in his endeavour, was reconciled with the catholic church, and became assistant in one of the parishes.

Yet the seeds of further tensions had been sown. In about 1860 the Catholic Thomas Christians were divided as follows: 104 churches under the Vicar Apostolic, 37 under the Padroado, 16 shared by both. Twelve years later the Padroado had only 15 churches left, with 12 shared with the Vicariate apostolic. It is also by the time that Deacon Emmanuel Nidhiry[20] of Kuravilangad had begun playing a conspicuous role in the religious and cultural life of his church. In Rome the authorities bided their time, but refused at any rate to accept any further interference from Mosul, the home of the Chaldean patriarch.

However, still more significant was the arrival to Malabar in October 1874 of another Chaldean bishop, Mar John Elias Mellus (d. 1908). Though like Rokkos, he never ceased being in communion with Rome, he stayed for nearly eight years in the country, though by 1877 he was already loaded with excommunication; he was officially recalled by his patriarch in March 1878. Mellus was followed by some 41 parishes from the start, though their number dwindle quickly to a mere fifteen. The main centre of his influence was Trichur and the syrian catholic church built there at the beginning of the 19th century. He had brought with him another bishop, Philippos 'Yaqub of Gazireh, who was the first to withdraw in August 1877. The opposition to Mellus and his followers got better organized than at the time of Rokkos, and it was led again by the Syrian Carmelite Tertiaries and also by Emmanuel Nidhiry, now a priest of renown, who had refused to accept episcopacy from Mellus. The latter left Kerala in March 1882 without having abandoned his dwindling partisans.

The latter were headed by both the Chaldean Chorepisco-pus, Augustine, and by Anthony Thondanat, who had resumed his episcopal office since Mellus' arrival. After hesitating for a while (he would have liked to come back to unity in 1889-90), he continued directing the new 'Mellusian' community until his death in 1900. After having stayed for a while in Palai, he moved back to Trichur. This town had by then become the only left centre of that community.

Today it owns the church and the house of the Metropolitan diocese of the Church of the East for Kerala and India. From 1908 to 1945 it was again ruled by another 'Assyrian' or 'Nestorian' bishop from the Middle East, Mar Timotheos Abimelech (1878-1945). In 1592, those people received again another Middle-East bishop, Mar Thomas Darmo. More recently they have been governed by an Indian prelate, Mar Aprem Mooken, the present metropolitan. Unfortunately they have been affected by the recent split in the catholicosate of the Church of the East. Mar Aprem with the majority of the community stands on the side of a new catholicosate, founded by Mar Thomas Darmo after his return to Irak. Yet a vocal minority has remained faithful to the official catholicos, who though living in California, U.S.A., has succeeded in being recognized for the first time in forty years by the Iraki Republic. This section of the Indian flock obtained recently a bishop of their own.

Towards Autonomy

Hopes for lasting bonds with the Catholic Chaldeans were still voiced in Kerala until the end of the 19th century. However they could not last since by the time the Catholic Thomas Christians had begun enjoying the positive results of their recently acquired juridical status.

For, thanks to the relative success of the 'Chaldean dreams' and to reports made by official visitors[21] sent by Rome, thanks also to the requests[22] repeatedly made by such leaders as Emmanuel Nidhiry and the most influential Syrian Carmelite Tertiaries. Rome was finally roused to move forward and to take concrete steps towards granting self-government to the Eastern Catholics of India.[23] To those causes there must be added the personal touch of Pope Leo XIII, who by the time favoured a much more positive policy towards the Eastern Christians as a whole.

The first attempt failed. It was a compromise still keeping the Catholic Thomas Christians under Verapoly; it was too redolent of 'latinism' to be satisfactory. Its failure was a sign of time.

In spite of last-ditch resistance from vested interests, Rome granted on May 20, 1887, two Vicariates Apostolic to the Thomas Christians. Their first bishops were still outsiders: Charles Lavigne,[24] a French Jesuit, for Kottayam and Adolphe Medlycott,[25] an Anglo-Indian priest from N. India, for Trichur. Mgr. Lavigne soon shifted his headquarters to Changanacherry. They were also requested to appoint local priests both as vicars general and counsellors; the vicars general, e.g. Emmanuel Nidhiry, were allowed to celebrate the Eucharistic Liturgy as quasi-bishops. This was one of the signs that the new Vicars Apostolic were not meant to last long, but had to pave the way to local leadership. In less than ten years this intention was fulfilled.

After the two Vicars Apostolic had gracefully withdrawn, Indian prelates became their successors in July 1896, with the addition of a new Vicar Apostolic for Ernakulam. Unfortunately the appointment for Changanacherry of Mgr. Matthew Makil, who belonged to the Suddist group, did not please the majority of his flock, the Nordists. This was the only reason why in 1911 Pope Pius X gave to the Suddists a special Vicariate, making Kottayam once more the residence of a Syrian Catholic Bishop.

Eastern Hierarchy Autonomy

Under their own prelates the Catholic Thomas Christians progressed rapidly. It led to their reorganization on December 20, 1923. They obtained then their autonomy under a metropolitan see at Ernakulam, with three suffragan eparchies, Trichur, Kottayam and Changanacherry.

Further progress in many fields, a fairly rapid increase in number, and a steady emigration from south to north brought about a new diocese and a second metropolitan see in the years 1950-56. Thus today the Catholic Thomas Christians are gathered under two metropolitan archbishops, i.e. Ernakulam with Tellicherry, Trichur and Kothamangalam as suffragans, and

Changanacherry with Kottayam and Palai. Not only does this church cover since 1955 the whole territory of Kerala state, but its jurisdiction extends also to quite a few neighbouring districts belonging to Tamilnadu (Madras state) and Mysore State. Only certain unsavoury local oppositions prevent it from having more dioceses where pastoral needs require it.

Moreover between 1962 and 1968 the Catholic Thomas Christians have been granted a cherished, though often frustrated, wish, that of shouldering the planting of the Church in India according to their own tradition. They have now six exarchates covering various districts of Andra-Pradesh, Maharashtra and Madya Pradesh. Four of these are under the care of Oriental Carmelites (C.M.I.), one under the Oriental Vincentians (V.C.) and one under the newly founded society for priests, the Society of St. Thomas the Apostle.

If the Church of the Catholic Thomas Christians has to be faithful to the genuine Eastern tradition, it should normally become a patriarchate in the near future.

Internal Life and Developments

After the fateful years 1653-62 the Catholic Thomas Christians were nicknamed the *Pazhayakuttukar,* i.e. old party.

As we already saw their ecclesiastical organization not only became more and more westernized, but, what is more, suffered from divisions, contradictions and oppositions. Yet the ordinary clergy and people kept all through-out a vivid consciousness of belonging to the same community, the same church.

Their devotional life received an increased dose of the Baroque ethos, i. e. that tendency, so particularly prominent in the Hispani peninsula and above all in Italy, to multiply religious exercises outside the liturgical services. Already under the one single Jesuit rule the Thomas Christians had been imbibed with such a pietistic attitude, but later on the Carmelites did not cease quickening the tempo of such devotional practices as novenas, 'months', statues, scapulars, rosaries, litanies etc.

Was this but the natural reaction of missionaries who came from such surroundings and sincerely, though naively, thought that all those practices were outstanding, if not necessary, expressions, of catholic life? Or was it an attempt at alienating those 'Eastern' Christians from their own ancestoral tradition? Most likely, the reply, based on documentary evidence, includes both. Moreover those missionaries were but fulfilling the wishes expressed once upon a time by the Propaganda authorities. They told Sebastiani that the best thing he could do would be to deflect the Thomas Christians from their rite through teaching Latin to their clerics so as to bring them over to the Latin tradition...26 Though the Thomas Christians are still Oriental indeed, in point of fact their eastern character has become until recently very much turned down. For in course of three hundred years, they had become increasingly alienated from a liturgical and biblical life worth the name, without speaking of that basic and living synthesis of liturgy, and devotion, which is the main stay of any real Eastern Church.

It is remarkable that inspite of that pietistic atmosphere (one of the causes of the dechristianization in the west), often devoid of any substance, the people kept at a remarkable degree the sense of their basic Christian doctrine and commitment.

From the liturgical viewpoint,27 hardly any change occurred since the heavily latinized East-Syrian rite was fixed in the Ros' Euchologion of 1604. The Eucharistic service was considerably maimed but was still recognizable as an eastern service, especially the *Raza,* i.e. the most solemn Eucharist, which preserved better traditions than even among the East-Syrians themselves. However the ritual of sacraments and sacramentals was but a Syriac translation—not always literary—of the Latin forms as known in Portugal and Goa at the end of the 16th century. Yet the office or canonical prayers, was perhaps the least affected by the latinizing pressure. As for the Ordinal, it is a fact that from about 1597 until 1958 all the clerics were ordained in the Latin way.

This liturgical situation, the worst ever in the sad history of relations between East and West in Christianity, was not altered by the Roman edition of the Syro-Malabar missal of 1774-75. The ferial breviary, with variable parts taken almost exclusively from the Great Lent offices, was only printed in the 19th century with the addition of commons for saints, etc.

If the attempts towards linking again the Thomas Christians with the Mesopotamian patriarchate had succeeded, their ways of worship would have certainly been remodelled on the East-Syrian traditions as followed by the Catholic Chaldeans. This is actually what many a priest wanted, from Thomas Parammakel at the end of the 18th cent. until Emmanuel Nidhiry and others a century later. But the failure of such attempts with its trail of bitterness almost created an anti-Oriental reaction amongst those latinized Orientals themselves. Neither the first local vicars apostolic nor their leading counsellors thought that a reform should be introduced. The training in seminaries until yesterday was definitely not oriental at all, actually it was often anti-oriental.

Only since 1955 the yearning of old got fulfilled to some extent. Successively the Ordinal and the Eucharistic service (Anaphora of Adai and Mari) were printed according to a restored text prepared by a Roman commission. In the wake of the liturgical reform of Vatican Council II, the Thomas Christian Hierarchy set up its own liturgical commission. Since 1968 it has published not only a slightly improved missal, with simplified rubrics and changes of ceremonial, but also an impressive series of vernacular booklets with such services as Baptism and Marriage, Funerals and Blessings, Solemn Eucharist, Holy Week, and the first volumes of a complete book of hours.[28]

Educational and Religious Progress

As already noted the autonomy and self-government granted after so much procrastinations to the Catholic Thomas Christians had yielded extraordinary results in the fields of education, vocations to the priesthood and religious life, and all-round zeal. Such results set to naught the prophecies of former days, according to which in those days was closely bound with the English sysetm. could not be made up for by local autonomy.

The Catholics of Kerala came rather late to liberal education, which in those days was closely bound with the English system. Previously, among the more prosperous families, the Syrian boys and to a lesser extent the girls of Malabar followed the local indigenous training, which between the age of 4 until about 25 imparted literary instruction. Many boys were also given a strong physical, some even military training.

Only in 1885 was the first Anglo-Malayalam school opened in Mannanam by the Carmelite Tertiaries. Since 1887 and still more after 1896 a fairly quick and remarkable progress was made towards building up a whole system of education, from the primary school attached to each parish church up to the university college. This progress has been particularly impressive since India won its independence. Today the laity is vocal in asking for greater share in and control of the schools and colleges.

Owing to the late appearance of modern educational institutions of their own, the Catholic Thomas Christians remained, more than their fellows of non-catholic churches, attached to their traditional professions, i.e. farming and trading. Their skill in putting the land under the plough is outstanding. One of the socio-economic results of their attachment to agricultural work has been the migration of thousands of small peasants belonging originally to the region of Palai-Changanacherry to the N. Kerala. To such a hunger for land was due the creation of the new diocese of Tellicherry.

However, for the past fifty years or so, they have jointed in increasing number the State services and the liberal professions. It would not be fair however to regard them as a wealthy community as such. Except for barely 10%, the greater majority of those Catholics belongs to the low middle-class, even in many places they are still fairly poor people.

One of the striking features of this Eastern Church is the number of its priests and religious. In 1790 the Verapoly seminary had only one Carmelite Professor with some 24 students. All the other clerics were still trained by one or the other local *malpan* in about 20 centres. In 1866 the Verapoly institution was transferred to Puthenpalli, and the twenty malpanates were replaced by four centres run by the Carmelite Tertiaries. Finally these were also closed down in 1886 to leave Puthenpalli as the only genuine seminary. It was again transferred to Mangalapuzha, a property originally belonging to the Thomas Christians under the Padroado, near Alwaye. Owing to the extraordinary increase of clerics in recent years a new major seminary was opened in 1962 at Vadavathoor near Kottayam. It caters mostly to the southern diocese, and it is run exclusively by the diocesan clergy, thus forging a link with the bygone days of the *malpanates*. Quite a few Thomas Christian clerics are also trained in Latin seminaries outside Kerala; others have gone abroad, especially to Rome, either to undergo their complete training for the priesthood, or to take higher degrees.

Outside those who joined well-established western Congregations in India, the Syro-Malabar Church owns today three religious congregations, three societies for priests, and one for brothers. There was last century a short-lived attempt to form a monastic house in the East-Syrian tradition. Among the religious the Carmelites of Mary Immaculate (C.M.I.) rank first and foremost because they are the first to have been founded in the 19th century and they have the largest number of any India-based congregation, with more than a 1,000 members. They were founded by FF. Thomas Palakal and Thomas Porukara at Mannanam in 1831 under Mgr. Mauritius of St. Theresa, the Carmelite Vicar Apostolic of the time; in 1855 their superior, Cyriac Elias Chavara with the first ten priests took their vows, under the name of "Servants of the Immaculate Mother of Mt. Carmel". In 1861 they became regular tertiaries of the first order of Carmelite. In 1906 they received from Rome final approval under their own prior general. They are now divided into three provinces, one vice-province and one autonomous (mission) region, have their main study house at Bangalore, and continue their apostolic traditions by carrying on preaching and spiritual work, by having missions, both inside and outside Kerala, by editing and printing news papers and reviews, and by directing schools and colleges. Of late there has been a notable change of outlook among them, with a quest for a greater measure of cultural integration, intellectual achievement and adaptation to modern developments.

The many more sisters of the Catholic Thomas Christians are gathered into thirteen congregations. The Carmelite Tertiaries, founded in 1866, with more than 2,500 members today, and the Clarists sisters with about the same number (founded in 1888) are the largest among these. Two or three 'secular institutes' have been started since about 1962. Only one western-based order has today a Syro-Malabar province, the Medical Missionary sisters (Philadelphia).

It should be noted that there is nothing particularly Oriental in origin among those Syro-Malabar religious of both sexes, except for their ordinary ways of life and the practice of their Eastern liturgy. No genuine monastic foundation, having its local and eastern roots, has come out from that community, though some C.M.I. members thought recently of opening one or two houses for monastic experiments.

Apostolic Endeavour

Already since about 1890 the CMI religious launched missions among the depressed classes of Kerala. These efforts have continued parallel to what could be called inner missions of Christian revival. The rapid progress made in the Tellicherry diocese among migrants is also due to the apostolic enterprise of both diocesan and regular clergy.

This is not entirely new. Already in the 18th and 19th centuries we meet occasionally with Thomas Christian priests serving in Latin parishes as far as Madurai. Admittedly such an unexpected presence was due to the suppression of the Jesuit Order, and the sharp decrease of foreign missionaries at the time. In Kerala today in one or two Latin dioceses one finds a good number of clergy who passed over from their original Eastern Church to make up for the difficulty of finding Latin-rite candidates for the priesthood.

Still more significant is the extraordinary development in the number of candidates to Latin dioceses and religious Orders outside Kerala, even outside India. Such a movement began on a small scale in the early 20's. Already in 1923 a mission-fund existed in each Syro-Malabar diocese. In 1947 the diocese of Changanacherry, which then had 400,000 faithful, could boast of 32,000 lay members of such a fund. Since the 50's concerted efforts made together by local associations and by outsiders, both diocesan and religious, gave a sharp boost to the number of such candidates. It has provided the rest of India with many priests and religious, just when foreign missionaries were not allowed to reach the country in a regular manner.

By 1965 the statistics of such Eastern clergy working in Latin territories had become impressive: there were 427 diocesan priests with 338 seminarians; 458 religious priests with 560 members in training. Nor were the religious sisters lagging behind. Practically there is hardly any religious congregation of some importance which does not have some sisters originally belonging to a Syro-Malabar parish. In 1965 there were outside Kerala 3290 such sisters with 1411 novices and juniors. Of the 517 seminarians of the Papal Athanaeum, Poona, belonging to both dioceses and religious congregations, there were 386 hailing from Kerala. Among these 311 have joined Latin dioceses and 99% of them hailed from the Thomas Christian Church.

Since about 1962 also young Thomas Christian women felt the call to Latin sisterhoods in Europe, mostly in Germany and Italy.

Reunion and Ecumenism, Hope and Frustration

Dr. N.J. Thomas reviews in the next chapter the various trials through which the Orthodox branch of the St. Thomas Christians passed during the last three centuries. We owe to historical truth and the future of ecumenical relations in India to sum up now in a historical perspective[29] the relations between them and those who kept united to Rome.

As a living proof that both sides still regarded themselves as one original, community, quite a few churches were still shared by both at the end of the 18th century and intercommunion among them was still fairly common. Passages from one side to another were still pretty frequent, though never on a large scale, until the end of the 19th century.

For centuries the division of the former united church of Kerala was not fully accepted; neither real religious reasons, nor social and cultural ones, could justify it until the hastily built walls between both sides got so strong and so high as to make a dialogue next to impossible.

About 1690/5 a Syrian Catholic bishop, Mar Athanasios Safar 'Al'Attar passed through Malabar, but his stay there was either too short or unprepared to have any lasting result. Mar Thomas IV (1688-1728) approached Rome for reconciliation, and the arrival of Simon of Ada in 1701, as already noted, was also intended as a means of mending the split. Until mid-18th-century Mar Thomas V (1728-65) wanted at times to effect the reunion of all Thomas Christians and wrote in this vein to Pope Benedict XIV in 1748.

Often on the side of the Orthodox party those efforts were perhaps only rather velleities, or they were prompted by the desire of the Mar Thomases to obtain recognition as the only head of all the existing Thomas Christians. Moreover, without questioning their sincerity, it can be doubted whether the Carmelite missionaries looked favourably on the approaches made by the Orthodox side.

Be as it may, they certainly opposed the mission of Kariattil and Parammakel in 1778, of which we have already spoken. For these men were not only prompted by the desire of promoting the spiritual welfare of the Catholic Thomas Christians but also by the wish of reconciling the Orthodox party, then led by the rightly consecrated Mar Dionysios I (1765-1808, consecrated in 1772), the former Thomas VI.[30] They even brought to Rome the prelate's profession of faith. It was of no avail. It had all started with the willingness shown by Dionysios to take steps towards unity. Moreover he was born in a catholic family. It was supported by a leading catholic layman of the time, Matthew Thachil Tharakan, since on the Carmelite or Vicar Apostolic's side there was not much response, the Padroado authorities, especially bishop Joseph de Soledade OCD of Cochin, were approached and were asked to handle the case. It hardly helped at all. Finally, thanks to Thachil's good office, Mar Dionysios was prevailed upon to make his profession of faith as a catholic at Thathampally in June 1799. After a previous common meeting held at Alleppey, he was received by Bishop Paul Pandari, with the support of the Cranganore governor, the Thomas Christian priest, Abraham Kattakayam.

Mar Dionysios had come over with only a few followers, but his good intentions were finally thwarted by the negative attitude of the official catholic authorities. After all had Pandari any delegation of authority to receive them. After six months, Mar Dionysios had come back to his orthodox flock.

As already mentioned the first contacts of the early 19th century with the catholic chaldean patriarchate helped Rome to decide on sending to Malabar bishop Iso'yahb John Guriel, archbishop of Salmas. If he had come, he could have likely created conditions for the reunification of the whole community of Thomas Christians.

Until the last quarter of the 19th century, both the orthodox and catholic christians of Malabar rather hardened their mutual position. Then there came up the influential Syro-Malabar priest, Emmanuel Nidhiry. He had become friend of and adviser to the orthodox metropolitan, Pulikot Mar Dionysios V (1866-1909), especially on account of his protracted litigations with the Mar Thomite party.

It led to the formation of a Catholic-Orthodox association, the *Jathyaikya Sangham*, best interpreted as the (Syrian) National Union Association. It was intended to foster the educational uplift of all Thomas Christians with a view towards their reunion. The Woodland estate was bought in Kottayam (where today stand the M.D. High School and College and the offices of the influential daily, *Malayala Manorama*) mostly through the efforts of Nidhiry. Mar Dionysios was even ready to do things which were almost unthinkable in those days. He wrote a personal letter to Pope Leo XIII, and visited the Apostolic delegate at Oottacamund. Nidhiry had also contacts with two other orthodox bishops and with several priests. Mgr. Ch. Lavigne, the Ordinary of Nidhiry, did not back up entirely his counsellor and vicar general's endeavour. Yet, within the circumstances of his days, the bishop showed some active sympathy towards the incipient move intended to unite all the Thomas Christians. Even the Suddist orthodox went as far as having a meeting with Lavigne's Indian successor, Bishop Makil.

Actually the first Syro-Malabar Vicars Apostolic did not hesitate to furthering the same cause, especially at Ernakulam and at Changanacherry. Later on the Carmelite Tertiaries obtained several footholds in orthodox centres. Bishop Benziger, the Carmelite bishop of Quilon, fostered also the reunion of several orthodox priests and families, though they were asked to pass over to the Syro-Malabar rite. In point of fact, already under bishop Lavigne, some orthodox priests had been received into communion with Rome, while keeping their own Syro-Antiochean tradition. In 1921, Rome in reply to a request made by the Syro-Malabar bishop inspired by some leaders of the patriarch's party granted the general permission of receiving Orthodox people into their own ritual tradition.

In the catholic diocese of Kottayam for the Suddists, Bishop Alexander Chulaparampil (1914-51) took a personal interest in the ecumenical problem existing among his own people. A couple of thousand orthodox with several clergy were received by him, and in 1946, his new coadjutor, and present successor, Mar Thomas Tharayil, was even given the right of celebrating according to the Syro-Anthiochean tradition. Today the Suddist Orthodox, who have joined the catholic communion and who belonged to the aforesaid diocese of Kottayam, have their own episcopal vicar.

However well-intentioned were those efforts from the side of the old Catholic Thomas Christians, they were conceived on the whole as a 'return' to the ancient unity as existing before 1653.

The Syro-Malankara Catholics

Meanwhile, above all since the end of World War I, one orthodox priest, P.T. Givargis by name,[31] was active in bringing about the spiritual renewal of his church, though mostly the section which was then known as the *metran's* party. This is why he became the founder in 1920, of the first orthodox religious order in India, the Order of the Imitation of Christ, with both a male and a female branch.[32] They became known as the Fathers and Sisters of Bethany after the name of the first monastery of men situated at Perunad. He soon discovered, moreover, that the real future of his people lay in linking them again with one of the major patriarchates, even if it were Rome itself.

In 1926, he became metropolitan of Bethany under the name of Mar Ivanios, with special jurisdiction over his religious houses and the people attached to them. Three years later he obtained that one of his monks be his suffragan under the name of Mar Theophilos. By the time also he had opened correspondence with Rome not without the approval of his own orthodox superiors in Kerala. Rome's reply was cordial, though perhaps not quite as open as could have been expected. The *metran's* party of the Orthodox church in India was then busy fighting its case through the civil courts, and on its success or failure depended to a great extent its leaning towards a reconciliation with the Roman side.

Mar Ivanios, his suffragan and his friends had gone already too far in the direction of Rome to back out. Their conviction and conscience were involved. Without waiting any further Mar Ivanios and his first companions were officially received into communion with Rome on September 20, 1930. Within a year of this event they had been followed by most of the Bethany men, all the Bethany sisters, some 35 diocesan priests and about 4,500 faithful.

Within the next forty years this old and new Catholic Eastern Church became some 140,000 members strong, with more than 200 clergy and some 500 sisters. In 1932 they acquired their own autonomy under the name of Syro-Malankara Church with the metropolitan see at Trivandrum and its suffragan eparchy at Thiruvalla. Two more orthodox bishops came over, in 1937 and 1939 respectively. Developments in the educational, socio-charitable and pastoral fields have grown apace. For instance, a university college was set up at Trivandrum, candidates to orders quickly increased in number, and even a secular institute for women was opened at Tiruvalla. Since 1959 the Syro-Malankara Church was privileged in getting the only genuine monastic house existing so far among the Eastern Catholics of Kerala. It is the Kurisumala Ashram founded by the combined initiative of a Belgian Cistercian and an English Benedictine.

It cannot be denied however in an ecumenical history of Indian Christianity, as this volume is intended to be, that the 'reunion movement' as it was called along the years was and is still an object of much bitterness, misgivings and criticisms from the Orthodox side. Whatever has been the zeal of those who launched this movement, it was not always devoid of exaggerated propaganda and of a certain lack of respect and consideration for the orthodox church. In spite of their own purposefulness, the Syro-Malankara catholics were children of their own days, when anything like authentic ecumenical spirit hardly existed, particularly among the catholics of Kerala.

Moreover a certain latinizing current of thought and practice soon after 1930 began affecting the rich liturgical heritage of the Syro-Malankara catholics. Yet thanks to the use of vernacular, inherited from the combined influence of Protestant revivalist and orthodox sense of pastoral needs, such an heritage was kept us on the whole fairly unscathed though it has suffered on several counts from the influence of the other catholics. Too many of these were too ready to offer to their newly discovered coreligionists certain devotional practices as unmistakable signs of catholic adherence. It was altogether wrong, but too often effective.

Since Vatican Council II the ecumenical atmosphere has considerably progressed in Kerala.[33] The Syro-Malankara Catholics are faced today with the problem of finding out their real identity in the ecumenical world and to search for a more authentic unity than their early leaders could dream of.

CHAPTER IX

THE EASTERN ORTHODOX CHURCH IN
INDIA 1653-1972

by N. J. Thomas, S.S.T.

Towards the close of the 16th and the beginning of the 17th centuries, the political atmosphere of the native states on the Malabar coast was quite aggressive. The different western countries who were doing mercantile business here in the states now turned their attention towards the expansion of their colonies. The result was the conquest of the Malabar trade by the Dutch.[1] Some few years ago Cranganore and Cochin had fallen to them.

A Syrian Orthodox Prelate, Aithallah (Theodore) by name, arrived in Mylapore in August, 1652. While at Mylapore, he was visited by pilgrims from the Malabar Church. Mar Aithallah gave them a letter to Archdeacon Thomas. After this, the Roman authorities rushed this self-styled Patriarch to Goa and on their way called at Cochin. The news of the presence of the Syrian Prelate at Cochin Harbour spread like wild fire. The Syrian community under the leadership of the Archdeacon now ran up to that place and tried their best to get him released through the intercession of the Raja of Cochin. But their attempts could not succeed since some obvious deception was prayed by somebody meanwhile. The Syrian Christians in their fury marched towards the port in order to release the Prelate by force. That was also in vain. According to Cardinal Tisserant: "The Portuguese spread the less palatable news that the unfortunate prelate was accidently drowned."[2]

The Koonan Cross and afterwards

To revenge this humiliation, the Syrian Christians assembled in front of the Koonan Cross at Mattancherry, a suburb of Cochin, and took an oath that they would never tolerate any interference of the Portuguese clergy in the affairs of the Malabar Syrian Christian community. In order to confirm it, they held together a long rope tied to the cross. The oath was taken on the 3rd January (Makaram), 1653. Thus they resolved to make up for the freedom and liberty of the Church. This revolt was not merely local. With the exception of about 400 members, all the St. Thomas Christians shared in the revolt. Not long after, they all assembled at Alangad on 22nd May, 1653 and twelve priests laid their hands on the Archdeacon proclaiming him bishop and metropolitan of India. During the ceremony, the supposed letter of investiture from Aithallah was also laid on his head.

Mar Thoma I

Henceforward Mar Thoma I performed episcopal functions. A kind of Church council was also introduced with four members presided over by the Metropolitan. The elected members were four priests viz., Kadavil Chandy Kathanar, Anjilimoottil Itty Thomman Kathanar, Vengoor Givargeese Kathanar and Palliveettil Chandy Kathanar. Thus they aimed at some kind of ecclesiastical autonomy likely with the idea of some connection with an Eastern patriarchate.

Ten years later the Dutch East India Company, now in possession of the Malabar coast, did practically nothing directly to favour the autonomous section of the Malabar Church. Yet they unwittingly did a great service. To promote their own ends, they ordered all foreign ecclesiastics to leave their newly owned territory. Thus ended the one-and-a-half century of the Portuguese dominion in Malabar.

I

THE JACOBITE PERIOD

The earnest prayer and longing of the Malabar Syrian Church for a rightly consecrated Metropolitan was fulfilled by the arrival of Mar Gregorios, Metropolitan of Jerusalem in 1655. Though the then officiating prelate, Mar Thoma I had not received as yet the authentic episcopal consecration, now it gave him the opportunity to receive the same at the hands of Mar Gregorios. The consecration was thus performed and Mar Gregorios helped Mar Thoma I in the administration of the Church.

Mar Gregorios taught and explained to Mar Thomas' people the differences between the teachings of the East Syrians (Nestorians), the Roman Catholics, and the West Syrians (Orthodox). He succeeded in getting them to anathematize anything contrary to his own Orthodox views. In this respect, that section of the St. Thomas Christians is very much indebted to Mar Gregorios. Not long afterwards, both of them died one after the other, perhaps in 1672. Mar Gregorios was interred in Parur Cheriapalli and Mar Thoma in Angamali Church.

Mar Thoma I was succeeded by his nephew Mar Thoma II, who was perhaps consecrated by Mar Gregorios.[3] Little is known of this native prelate except that he was of amiable nature and that he was struck by lightning which caused his death. He was interred in the Church at Niranam in April, 1686.[4]

It was at this time that two new Syrian orthodox bishops, Mar Basilios and Mar Ivanios (John) visited Malabar. Mar Basilios was a Catholicos (Maphrian). He died soon after he reached Kothamangalam where he was buried in the lower Church. His cult has survived to this day. Mar Ivanios was an able and zealous bishop. During the interim period between Mar Thoma II and Mar Thoma III, he was the real shepherd of the Malabar flock. Actually he seems to have given episcopal orders to Mar Thoma III, who also belonged to the Archdeacon's line, the Pakalomattam family. The new local bishop died soon after, in April 1688; and was buried in Kadampanad Church. [5&6] His successor, Mar Thoma IV, again from the same family got also consecrated by Mar Ivanios who died only in August 1694[7] and was buried in Mulanthuruthy church. Mar Thoma IV's career ended in June, 1728. He was buried in Kandanad church in June, 1728.

Just before his death Mar Thoma IV had consecrated his nephew as his successor under the title Mar Thoma V, in 1728. Some of his people were put out because his consecration was not from a foreign bishop. Hence he entered into an agreement with one Deacon Antonios who had come from the Middle East for mercantile purposes, and a letter was sent through him to the Antiochian Patriarch. At last in 1751, a delegation consisting of a Catholicos (maphrian), Mar Basilios Shukrallah, two bishops, Mar Gregorios and Mar Ivanios and some other clergy arrived in Cochin in a Dutch ship. Fearing a proximate death, Mar Thoma V had already cosecrated his successor, Mar Thoma VI, in 1757.

With regard to the payment of the voyage demanded by the Dutch there arose a difference of opinion between the Dutch and Mar Thoma V. The latter had to sell out some of the belongings and properties of the Niranam church in order to settle the accounts with the Dutch. At last the foreign prelates were released from the ship.

In 1763 Catholicos (Maphrian) Basilios, the foreign prelate, died and was buried in the church at Kandanad. According to G.T. Mackenzie, the intervention of Marthanda Varma, the then Raja of Travancore, allayed a strife which occurred between the foreign prelates and Mar Thoma V. Mar Thoma V breathed his last in 1765 and was buried in Niranam church. At his death Mar Thoma VI, his nephew, succeeded him.8

Mar Thoma VI alias Mar Dionysios I, the Great

Mar Thoma VI was now created Metropolitan at Niranam in 1772 by Mar Gregorios and Mar Ivanios. He was given a new title "Dionysios" and this metropolitan was afterwards known by the name "Dionysios the Great". His episcopate synchronized with a period of political turmoils and upheavals. He lived to see the English taking the place of the Dutch on the Malabar Coast. It was during his tenure of office that Dr. Buchanan visited the Syrian Church and discussed the possibility of a union between the Syrian Church and the Church of England. On his return to Europe in 1811, Dr. Buchanan published his "Christian Researches in Asia", a book which throws light on the history of Christians in Asia. This book helped very much to bring to the knowledge of the British people the existence of the ancient Syrian Church in India. Mar Dionysios I presented Dr. Buchanan with the ancient manuscript copy of the Bible in Estrangela Syriac. This book is now kept in the University Library in Cambridge. Under his supervision, even before the arrival of any missionaries from Western countries, the four gospels were translated into Malayalam. Dr. Buchanan got them printed at Bombay. His visit to Mar Dionysios and his conversation with

him, gave Dr. Buchanan a high opinion of the prelate. Also it
was in his time that Col. Macaulay was appointed as the first
British Resident in Travancore. Dr. Kerr, the Senior British
Chaplain at Madras, visited Mar Dionysios towards the close
of his life.

During his time Thachil Mathoo Tharakan, an influential
Catholic Thomas Christian, turned his attention to the possibility of uniting the Syrian Orthodox Church with their Catholic
brethren. But it was all in vain.

The last but a very important act of Mar Dionysios was
the investment in Government securities of an amount equivalent to Rs. 10,500 for charitable and educational purposes, an
act, the benefit and fruits of which the community still enjoys.

After a long and glorious reign which was not free from
difficulties and persecutions, Mar Dionysios I expired in 1808
and his body was buried in the Puthencavu Syrian church which
was built by him.

II

A STRANGE SPLIT

Mar Gregorios, the last of the three Syrian Orthodox prelates, who had come to India in 1751, had in 1772 consecrated
one Kattumangatt Givargeese Ramban as rival Bishop to Mar
Dionysios, and he was given the name Mar Kurilos (Cyril). Mar
Gregorios died very soon and was interred in the Mulanthuruthy
church. A conflict arose between the old and new Malabar prelates. With the assistance of the Government Mar Dionysios
succeeded in driving away the new bishop. The latter took abode
in Anjur or Thozhiyur in the then British Malabar territory.
There he established an independent church known by the name
'Independent Syrian Church of Malabar'. This new autocephalous church, though very small, still exists today, even enjoying
intercommunion with the Mar Thoma Church. It has played a
critical role at certain stages in the subsequent history of the
Syrian Orthodox Church, as we shall notice later.

Mar Thoma VII

Mar Dionysios I was succeeded by his nephew, one Mathen Ramban in 1808, who had already received episcopal orders in 1796. He took the title Mar Thoma VII. But he died soon in 1810. The dying metropolitan's hands were placed on the head of one of his relatives and thus his successor was consecrated with the same name.

Mar Thoma VIII

There arose a difference of opinion among the people as to the validity of the consecration of the new bishop. The staunchest among the opponents were one Ittoop Ramban of Kunnankulam and another Philipose Ramban of Kayamkulam. An appeal was made to Col. Munro, the then British Resident, and a case was filed against the bishop. It was decided in favour of Ittoop Ramban, the appellant; and he was authorised to receive the interest of Rs. 10,500 invested by his predecessor in the Government securities, on condition that he should establish a school for the education of the Syrians. It was fulfilled in 1813 by the establishment of the Old Seminary at Kottayam.

Mar Thoma VIII lived only till 1816. He appointed his successor Mar Thoma IX.

Mar Thoma IX

Ittoop Ramban of Kunnankulam, however, had in 1815 received consecration at the hands of Kidangan Mar Philoxenos II of Thozhiyur, the head of the Independent Syrian Church, and he assumed the title Mar Dionysios II. Helped as it were by the Government, he forced Mar Thoma IX to abdicate in 1817 in his favour.

Thus the custom of choosing bishops from the Pakalomattam family—the heriditary succession of bishops—died out altogether from the history of the Syrian Orthodox Church of Malabar.

Mar Dionysios II

The Travancore and Cochin Governments issued proclamations to the effect that every Syrian Orthodox Christian should obey Mar Dionysios II. From that time onwards, both those Governments began to interfere in the appointments and removal of bishops of the Syrian Orthodox Church, and became even a law afterwards. Thus it was considered penal for a Syrian Christian to disobey the orders of the bishop.

Mar Dionysios II was in good terms with Col. Munro, the British Resident. His meeting with Rev. Norton, the English priest, was an important event of his time. Although Rev. Norton lived with the bishop in the seminary, the bishop did not allow him to do any work for the social or religious advancement of the Syrian community. Mar Dionysios II died in 1818 and was buried in the Old Seminary chapel which was built by him at Kottayam.

Mar Dionysios III

For an interim period Kidangan Mar Philoxenos looked after the affairs of this church. And in the fulness of time, Archdeacon Punnathra Kathanar was consecrated by him as bishop with the title of Mar Dionysios III.

In 1816 three C.M.S. Missionaries, Benjamin Baily, Joseph Fenn and Henry Baker, came to Kottayam. They began at once to cooperate in the works of the Church, with the intention of educating and reforming the Christians. Through the influence of Col. Munro, many Syrian Christians were now appointed as officers in the Government. When it was felt that the presence of the C.M.S. missionaries was not congenial to the interests of the Church, the metropolitan applied to Antioch for help. Here Rev. Fr. James Hough, author of "History of Christianity in India", (London, 1839) came to the scene. However, the metropolitan continued to be on harmonious terms with the missionaries. He died in 1825 and was buried in Cheriapalli, Kottayam.

Mar Dionysios IV

The election of the successor to Mar Dionysios III was made by casting lots which repeatedly fell in favour of Philipose Ramban of Cheppat. He too was consecrated in 1825 by the same Mar Philoxenos of Thozhiyur Independent Syrian Church.

Mar Dionysios IV gradually became hostile to the Anglican missionaries. The new missionaries, Peet and Woodwock, came at this juncture. Daniel Wilson, the Anglican bishop of Calcutta, visited the Syrian Orthodox in 1835; he suggested to the metropolitan the desirability of introducing certain changes in the worship and liturgy of the Church. In 1836 a synod gathered at Mavelikara drew up a document (Padiyola) which proved to Dr. Wilson and the C.M.S. missionaries that neither union, nor compromise, nor even any innovation of the faith was possible. The remaining years of Mar Dionysios' life were spent in seclusion in his home church at Cheppat where he died in September, 1855.

At the time, a group of Syrian Orthodox had already fallen under the spell of the Evangelical Anglicanism brought by the missionaries. To quote Cardinal Tisserant, "Nevertheless a hard core of Protestant sympathisers remained within the Jacobite community." This party was led by Abraham Malpan of Maramon, one of the Professors at the Old Seminary, Kottayam, and by three other priests. Mar Dionysios felt uneasy about the Malpan's activities and excommunicated him along with his party. Abraham now thought out new ways and means for getting his ideals of reformation realised in his Church. His nephew, Deacon Matthew, was sent over to the Jacobite Patriarch, Ignatius Mar Elias II (1842), at Deiras-Zafaran (Mardin) and got him consecrated with the title Mar Matthew Athanasios. This Mar Athanasios became the leader of the Reform Movement.

Mar Dionysios V and the Mar-Thoma Church

Mar Athanasios had come to power on the strength of the Travancore royal proclamation of 1852, and he began to work in line with the policy of his uncle Abraham Malpan, introducing slowly many reforms and innovations in his Church. But the Orthodox Majority was encouraged to resistance by Mar Kurilos, the patriarch's delegate. It elected one Pulikkot Joseph Kathanar, the nephew of the late Mar Dionysius II. He was sent to the Antiochian Patriarch for consecration. He received consecration from Patriarch Jacob II and returned to India in 1865 as Pulikot Mar Dionysios V, thus succeeding Cheppat Mar Dionysius. Mar Dionysius V tried his best to oust Mar Athanasios from power. For a while he could not succeed in his attempt. Mar Athanasius strengthened his position by consecrating (1868) one of his cousins, Thomas, son of the late Abraham Malpan, as his auxiliary and successor under the name Thomas Mar Athanasius.

Since the situation was growing worse, at the request of Mar Dionysius V, Peter III, the Syrian Orthodox Patriarch of Antioch, arrived in Malabar in 1874. Supported by the royal court of Travancore, the Patriarch excommunicated Mar Athanasios. The schism however continued assuming momentum. In 1877 Mar Matthew Athanasius passed away and his remains lie buried in his parish church at Maramon.

Mar Dionysios V filed a suit against Thomas Mar Athanasios. The law-suit which lasted for ten years from 1879 to 1889 between the Syrian Orthodox Church and the Reformed Party went through successive courts in the Travancore judiciary. Finally Mar Dionysios won the case. "The Reformers were finally obliged to relinquish every church they had previously possessed "⁹ except two or three where they had hundred percent majority. Meanwhile Thomas Mar Athanasius had died in 1887 and was succeeded by his brother Mar Thomas Titus I. Henceforth the Reformed party made great progress. Leaving the old churches, they built new ones and took the name of the 'Mar Thoma Syrian Church'. Thus they became a separate body in the Christian world. Titus II was in 1911 consecrated as successor to Titus I.

In fact, the reformists were all sincere, aiming at a revival in the Church. They wanted to cleanse it from all the blemishes which according to them had crept into it over centuries. And the bishops—all of them—"had sacrificed everything for the sake of Evangelical renewal and the Independence of a "Reformed Malabar Church".10

The Church of Mar Thoma is now a thriving community with some 250,000 faithful under a metropolitan and four bishops, with some 450 parishes and 240 clergy. Its evangelical activities, even extending outside Kerala, are remarkable. Its ecumenical outlook and action make it influential in inter-Christian relations. Many of its lay-leaders have promoted advanced social work. Unfortunately since 1960 it has suffered from a secession. A new body called the St. Thomas Evangelical Church came into being with some initial success. Today it is ridden with inner tensions as well.

To go back to the Syrian Orthodox, the Patriarch's visit helped to reinforce the bond between Antioch and the Malabar Church. Peter III held a synod of the whole community at Mulanthuruthy in 1876. Its members drew up a constitution regarding the relation between Antioch and Malabar. It instituted the Malankara association to look after the temporalities and to elect bishops. Six newly[11] elected bishops were then consecrated by the Patriarch; among them was the saintly prelate, Mar Gregorios of Parumala. The Patriarch consecrated Myron (Chrism) also, and two years later he went home.

Under the influence of Fr. Xavier Alvarez, a former Catholic Goan priest of the Padroado, the Latin parish of Brahmavar, near Mangalore, joined in the 1880's movement aiming at an Indepedent Church of Latin Catholic persuasion. Alvarez himself received episcopal order in 1889 from three Syrian Orthodox bishops with their Patriarch's permission and with the name Mar Julius. Yet without the consent of his new superiors, Alvarez gave the same order to the notorious ex-Catholic priest, Rene Vilatte, in 1892. He was intented for a new parish formed in America. The Brahmavar community still depends today on the Syrian Orthodox Church.[12]

The long-felt need of the Syrian Orthodox community to have a church built in the capital city of Trivandrum was fulfilled in 1900. Mar Dionysios V lived to see the celebration of his Golden Jubliee as the Chief Metropolitan of Malabar Church; he died in 1909. His remains were buried in the Old Seminary Chapel at Kottayam.

Mar Dionysios VI (Mar Givargeese Dionysios Vattasserril).
(1908—1935).

His consecration also took place in the Middle East as in the case of his predecessors. He was formerly the Principal and Malpan (Professor) at the Theological Seminary (Old Seminary) at Kottayam. A colleague of his, Mar Kurilos, was also sent with him for consecration.

Seeds of another split among the Syrian Orthodox of India, which took fifty years of law-suits and litigations to heal, were sown in 1911. The visit of Patriarch Abdullah II Sattul was the origin of the lamentable affair. Soon after his arrival in 1909 he summoned a synod of the Church in the old Seminary, Kottayam. He claimed actual authority in Malabar, spiritual and temporal, for the Antiochian Patriarch, a claim to which canonically Mar Dionysios and majority of the Church could not entirely agree.

In 1911 the Patriarch excommunicated Mar Dionysios and his followers. This rash action was repudiated by Mar Dionysios as *ultra vires*. Mar Dionysios held the port. On the side of the Patriarch Mar Kurilos became the Malankara Metropolitan. Paul Athanasius was consecrated bishop. A special diocese for the Syrian Orthodox Suddist was established. Its first metropolitan Thomas Mar Severios was also consecrated by the Patriarch. In all these events, there was much rivalry and underhand dealing. The Patriarch finally left, but, sadly enough two competing parties of equal strength were formed in the Church, though in faith and worship they basically remained loyal to the mother church. Yet Mar Dionysios and his party aimed at an autocephalous status for their Church without however violating its Canon Law. These two parties became known under such names as the Patriarch's (Kurilos) party and the Metran's (catholicos) party.

III

THE PRESENT PERIOD OR THE SYRIAN ORTHODOX CHURCH

Here really began the orthodox period of the Church. Mar Dionysius was still leading, though he abstained from any episcopal functions until he could be released from the bond of excommunication. When people realized that the unity and welfare of the Church was at stake, some among its most active of lay leaders decided to secure at any cost the autonomy of the Malabar Church. They were inspired by the pattern known among the different autocephalous Churches of the Byzantine tradition.

In 1912, Mar Dionysios and his party invited to Malabar the deposed Patriarch Abdul Massih II who gladly came. His deposition forced upon him by the Turkish Government was regarded as uncanonical by many in India. Hence he could be still regarded as the only legitimate supreme head of their Church. The Syrian orthodox catholicosate (Maphrianate) of Tekrit and then Deir-Mar-Mattai had already lapsed by the time. So it gave Mar Dionysios a golden opportunity to get the Catholicosate reestablished here in India. The first thing Mar Abdul Massih did in Kerala was to release Mar Dionysios from his excommunication.

The first and the second Catholicos

At the request of Mar Dionysios and his party, Abdul Massih II consecrated three Metropolitan bishops. In a Synod he installed Mar Paulos Ivanios of Kollencherry as the 'Catholicos of the East' with the title of Mar Basilius I. This great event in the annals of the history of the Church took place in 1912 at Niranam, one of the churches which is attributed to St. Thomas, the Apostle. Henceforth the Metran's party took the name "The Orthodox Syrian Church of Malabar", and the Catholicos was titled "The Catholicos of India and all the East". Patriarch Abdul Massih left for good in 1913 and died in Mardin in 1914.

The claim of Mar Dionysios for the interest of the trust

fund was decided by the court in his favour in 1928. Mar Kurilos the opponent, and his successor Mar Athanasius lost the case. But the litigation did not end there, and it had far-reaching consequences.

In spite of his old age, Mar Dionysios went to Mardin in 1923 to see the then Patriarch Elias II Shakar, with the intention of effecting a compromise between the two parties in the Church. Unfortunately the peace negotiations failed.

The first Catholicos passed away in 1913 and he was succeeded by the second Catholicos Mar Philoxenos Basilius.13 Since then the Malankara metropolitan still supervised the temporalities of the Church. The Catholicos was only busy with spiritual matters.

Catholicos Basilius Givargeese II

When the second Catholicos died in 1928, the third Catholicose, Basilius Givargeese II, was installed in 1929. At the invitation of Lord Irwin (later Viscount of Halifax) the then Viceroy of India, the Antiochian Patriarch Elias III came to Malabar in 1931 in order to effect a reconciliation in the Church. Unfortunately the attempt failed, mostly because the Patriarch died soon; he was buried in the Manjanikkara Church. Mar Dionysius passed away not long after in 1934; he was interred in the Old Seminary chapel at Kottayam.

Mar Dionysios VI is known as the Malankara *Bhasuran,* a name given to him on account of his achievements. He was likely the greatest of the metropolitans the Syrian Orthodox Church has hitherto produced. In the first place he was a keen theologian. *Mathopadesasarangal,* the dogmatic book written by him, contains the essential doctrines of salvation and life as interpreted and taught by the Orthodox Church.

He was a good educationist also. Grammar and English schools were started by him in many centres. Wisdom and shrewdness, strength and character and vigour of mind were his main qualities. Not only did he succeed in establishing the Catholicosate, by no means a small achievement, but he also wrote a constitution for the well-being of his church (it was revised in 1951).

Another Secession: The Malankara Catholics

Before his death, Mar Dionysios VI got consecrated his disciple Fr. P.T. Givargeese as bishop under the name of Mar Ivanios. In 1928 Mar Ivanios became a metropolitan. Since 1926 he opened a correspondence between the Antiochian. Syrian Catholic Patriarch Mar Ephrem Rahmani, and then directly with Rome. Finally on the 20th of September, 1930, Mar Ivanios together with his suffragan Mar Theophilos signed their profession of adhesion to the Catholic Church. Their followers are now known as the Syro-Malankara Catholics.

Catholicos Mar Basilios II

When Mar Dionysios VI died, the then Catholicos Mar Basilios Givargeese II became the Malankara metropolitan in 1934, by being elected to that post by the Malankara Association. The same year just before assuming these new responsibilities the Catholicos visited the Antiochian Patriarch in Homs (Syria) for peace negotiations. But unfortunately they also failed.

In 1937 the Catholicos represented the Malabar Orthodox Church at the Ecumenical Conference for Faith and Order held at Edinburgh.

In 1938, Paulos Mar Athanasius, the successor of Mar Kurilos who represented the Patriarch's party, failed a suit claiming that he was the lawful metropolitan of Malankara. While it was pending in the court, a Round Table Conference of the Prelates of both parties met at Alwaye on March 24, 1941. Following this event, Mar Timotheos of the Patriarch's party joined the Catholicos. Meanwhile the case went through the courts of Travancore more than once, and, except in the lower court, in all others, it was decided in favour of the plaintiff. At last it went up to the supreme court where once for all it was decided in favour of the defendant, the Catholicos, in September, 1958. Thus the long litigation came to an end after fifty years of struggle and feuds.

The Re-union of the Parties

On the basis of the judgement of the Supreme Court, Mar Ignatius Jacob III, the Antiochian Patriarch, and the Catholicos of this Church mutually recognized each other. Both of them issued official documents to legalise the union of the two parties. In this way the integration officially took place on December 16, 1958 in the Old Seminary chapel, Kottayam, with the mutual recognition of the Ecclesiastical Prelates of both parties. In continuation of it, a meeting of the representatives of all the churches of the new United Orthodox Church of Malabar was held on December 26, 1958, at Puthencavu.

In 1948, 1954 and 1961 the then Catholicos' delegate attended the general assemblies of the World Council of Churches held at Amsterdam, Evanston and New Delhi respectively. After having lived to see the Church free from any party-dissensions, the Malankara Metropolitan, the Third Catholicos, passed away on January 3, 1964, and was buried in the Devalokam Aramana chapel which was built by him. At present Devalokam, near Kottayam, is the official residence of the Catholicos.

Catholicos Basilios Augen I

After the former Catholicos had passed away, the eldest of the metropolitans was voted to the position. For his installation, Patriarch Mar Ignatius Jacob III was invited and the rite was conducted by him in May 1964. However the old age of the new Catholicos made it necessary that a successor as Catholicos-designate be elected. At the general meeting of the Malankara Association, the Supreme elective Body of the Church, held at the M.D. Seminary, Kottayam, in December, 1970, Mar Matthew Athanasius, Metropolitan of the outside-Kerala diocese was unanimously chosen to this post.

Meanwhile the Syrian Orthodox Church of Malabar had also sent her delegates to the IV General Assembly of the World Council of Churches held at Upsala, Sweden, in 1967.

By virtue of his supreme office, the Catholicos is legally the Malankara Metropolitan also. The Church spared no pain in keeping up the necessary number of bishops for the respective dioceses. Besides the Catholicos, there are now ten bishops, all of whom are enjoying the title of Metropolitan.

Theological education has been strengthened and modernised. The clergy are comparatively well-educated, and much effort is deployed to improve their instruction, especially in pastoral matters. It is well known that the Syrian Orthodox is quite progressive in the field of education. Women are not lagging behind in this respect. There are now altogether ten Colleges run by the Church, two being Professional Colleges. 60 High Schools and 440 Upper and Elementary Schools are also run by her, either belonging to the corporate management or to the individual managements. Facilities are also provided in these institutions for religious and moral education.

Monastic life is encouraged by the Church since it is at the very core of the Orthodox life. There are altogether seven monasteries and nine convents directly depending on the Supreme head of the Church. Missionary associations are also at work in the Church; actually some of the monastic institutions are engaged in this field of activities.

No other ecclesiastical institution in the Church has undergone such a vigorous growth as the Sunday School Association. It also owns printing presses for their periodical publications. Besides this, there are other Syrian Orthodox Publications such as weeklies and monthlies published from various centres. Such Associations as The Orthodox Students Movements, The Youth League, The Martha Mariam Samajam (Association of Women), The Syrian Congress, The Association of Knanites are thriving. A fund known as the 'catholicate Fund' is yearly collected from the parishes for the many common works of the Church.

The number of churches and parishes is estimated at about 1200 which are looked after by nearly 960 priests. The number of faithful is not exactly known but it may well reach about 1.2 millions, if we include the family members living scattered in different parts of India.

14

Retrospects and Prospects

The strong attachment of the Syrian Orthodox Church of India to the ancient oriental customs, forms of worship, faith, discipline and order, make her one with the Oriental group of Orthodox churches. She is now an independent Church though she acknowledges the spiritual authority of the Syrian Orthodox Patriarch of Antioch, now staying at Damascus, Syria.

From the apostolic viewpoint, this Church is quite import- ant. Her ritual and forms of worship, which are purely eastern in character, her insistence on self-mortification (fasting, abstin- ence etc.) and the zeal of its members can become quite attractive to the people of India.

The Syrian Orthodox Church aims at creating an atmo- sphere of friendliness and cooperation among the various Christ- ian churches in India. But she is now engaged in establishing also closer links with the Byzantine Churches. Thus any impedi- ment for intercommunion between the Oriental Orthodox Churches and the Byzantine Orthodox can be removed. When this hope is fulfilled, the ecumenical movement all over the world, including India, will have progressed considerably.

ANGLICAN AND PROTESTANT MISSIONS, 1706-1857

by M.E. Gibbs

Early Anglicans

The first Anglican clergy came to India as chaplains on the East India Company's shfps. They were usually engaged for the round voyage, which lasted about three years and spent some time ashore at the English factories of Surat and Bantam. One of these chaplains, Patrick Copeland, seems to have been responsible for the conversion of the first Indian Anglican on record. He was a young man "from the Bay of Bengala" who had been taught by Copeland and who was baptized in London at the church of St. Denis Backchurch in Eenchurch Street on December 22, 1616, King James I, who took a great interest in the affair, suggesting his baptismal name of Peter. He returned with Copeland to the Indies with the idea that he should evangelize his fellow-countrymen, but no more is heard of him.

In 1640 the English acquired the settlement of Fort St. George, Madras, and the era of more permanently settled chaplains began. One of their preoccupations was the education of the children of unions between English soldiers and women of the country, mostly, 'Portugese' or 'mestios' and therefore Roman Catholics, in their father's rather than their mother's faith, a matter which led to constant disputes with the Roman Catholic priests who were also permitted to live in Fort St. George to minister to the 'Portugese' soldiers employed by the Company. The chaplains were encouraged in this matter by Streynsham Masters who became Governor of Madras in 1677. He had previously served in the west of India, where the Company had moved its headquarters from Surat to Bombay, ceded to Charles II of England in 1661. Here the Governor, Sir Gerald Aungier, in 1671 busied himself with the building of a church "inviting the natives and strangers to a reverence and embracing of our wholly (? holy) reformed religion". The church was planned to hold a thousand people, an amazing undertaking considering that there could have been no more than three hundred Anglicans in Bombay at the time; but missionary purpose failed with the death of Augier in 1677 and Streynsham Master's removal to Madras. There he was responsible for building the church of St. Mary on a much smaller scale, as space within the Fort was extremely limited. The care for the education of the children of soldiers and others of mixed blood developed in Madras into a notable system of charity schools and orphanages for both boys and girls; and a similar development took place in Calcutta, founded in 1699. Bombay lagged behind; and the projected great church also remained an unfinished shell till an energetic chaplain, Richard Cobbe, secured its completion in 1718. So large is St. Thomas's church that, with the addition of a Victorian chancel, it serves to-day as a very adequate cathedral for the diocese of Bombay.

Missionary feeling developed in England towards the end of the seventeenth century; and when the Company's charter was renewed in 1698, a clause was added requiring the chaplains to learn Portuguese and the local languages so as to enable them to instruct the local inhabitants in the Protestant religion. In this year the oldest Anglican missionary society was founded, the Society for Promoting Christian knowledge (S.P.C.K.). Three years later, in 1701, the Society for the Propagation of the Gospel in Foreign Parts (S.P.G.) was founded and incorporated by royal charter, but for the first century of its existence its work lay exclusively in the English colonies in America.

Lutherans at Tranquebar and in Tamilnadu

The first impulse to Protestant missions in India came from Denmark. King Frederick IV founded a mission in the Danish settlement of Tranquebar in the extreme south and a mission college in Copenhagen to direct the work. He found his missionaries in the university of Halle in the dominions of the Elector of Brandenburg, which had been founded under the influence of pietism. Official Lutheranism had rather quickly degenerated into a tepid formalism, and pietism had arisen to make good its deficiencies. It was extremely individualistic, stressing above all the personal experience of the believer. Under the influence of the pietist leaders, the two Francks, father and son, Halle became a centre of missionary endeavour. The two first missionaries of the Royal Danish Mission, Ziegenbalg and Plutschau, both Germans, came from Halle and arrived in Tranquebar in 1706. Plutschau returned to Europe in 1711. Ziegenbalg also returned in 1714, but was back in India in 1718 and died there on February 22, 1719 at the age of thirty-six. He was the real founder of the Danish Lutheran Mission. He had to face considerable difficulties, including, in spite of the King's protection, the opposition of the Danish authorities in Tranquebar, and converts were very difficult to make. Still by 1719 he had built the large and beautiful Jerusalem church in Tranquebar and had translated the New Testament into Tamil. His colleague Grundler died a year after he did, and the work was then carried on for some time mainly by Benjamin Schultze. In 1733 a prominent convert of the Sudra caste, later known as Aaron the Priest, received Lutheran ordination. Another capable catechist was Rajanaiken, a Pariah by birth, a sub-officer in the army of Tanjore and a very nominal Roman Catholic.

From the first the group of Anglican churchmen who were responsible for the foundation of S. P. C. K. and S. P. G. had taken a great interest in the Danish Royal Mission. The chief point of contact was M. Boehm, the Lutheran chaplain of Prince George of Denmark, husband of Queen Anne and uncle of Frederick IV; who was on very friendly terms with them; and information about the mission was published from time to time in England. When Schultze at Tranquebar was reinforced by new missionaries with whom he did not get on very well, he moved, in 1728, to Madras and started a new mission there. British power and influence were increasing, and Madras seemed a better centre for a mission than Tranquebar. But Danish support was not available for missionaries working outside the Danish settlement, and so S. P. C. K. undertook responsibility for the new mission. So began the 'English mission', a remarkable example of international and interdenominational co-operation. The missionaries were all Lutherans, mostly Germans, with very few Scandinavians. They were trained at Halle and recommended by Francke and his son and successor; but they crossed to England to take their passage to India, and were received by the Committee of S. P. C. K. with an exchange of speeches in Latin.

S.P.C.K. required reports of their work and accounts of expenses, and were consulted on important points like locations and ordinations; but distances were so great and communications so slow that in practice the missionaries did pretty much as they liked. With Lutheran missionaries and no Anglican bishop in India, the form of the Church was bound to be Lutheran, though S. P. C. K. tried to give it as Anglican a look as possible, having the Book of Common Prayer translated, and trying to insist on its use.

Schultze returned to Germany in 1743 and was succeeded in charge of the mission at Madras by Fabricius who died there in extreme old age in 1791. Fabricius's name is chiefly associated with the translation of the whole Bible into Tamil, the first to be made in any Indian language, a work which attained something of the esteem among Tamil-speaking Christians as the English Authorized Version. It seems probable that the version which finally came to bear the name of Fabricius was the end product of the versions by more than one missionary of Ziegenbalg's pioneer work. Rhenius of the C. M. S. (in India 1823-1838) was dissatisfied with Fabricius's version, and devoted himself to making a new one, but this did not win much favour. When, in the latter part of the nineteenth century, a committee of the Bible Society undertook the revision of the Fabricius version, they were astonished at its scholarly excellence.

The earliest S. P. C. K. missionaries in Madras had their headquarters in Black Town, now Georgetown; but when Madras fell to the French in 1746, Fabricius and his colleagues retired to Pulicat and their buildings were demolished. On their return in 1748, they received, in place of their old property, a chapel and land at Vepery, a village a little outside the town. This had been founded by Coja Petrus Uscan, an Armenian merchant who had become a Roman Catholic, and had become a mission station for French Capuchins during the French occupation. Vepery, now well inside the modern city, is still an important Christian centre.

The most famous of the S. P. C. K. missionaries was Christian Frederick Schwartz. He was born in Brandenburg in 1726 and his thoughts were turned to missionary work at Halle by a meeting with Schultz and the finding there of a Tamil Bible Abstract. He arrived in Tranquebar on July 30th, 1751 and died at Tanjore on February 19th, 1798. He worked at first with the Danish Royal Mission at Tranquebar, but from 1762 he began visiting Tiruche-rapalli and in 1767 was transferred to S. P. C. K. as their missionary there. About the same time he began to pay visits to Tanjore. In 1773 Tanjore was captured by the Nawab of the Carnatic, and when Raja Tulyaji was restored in 1776 it was with a British *resident at court and a British garrison in the Fort. In* 1777 Schwartz came to live permanently at Tanjore where he acted as chaplain to the British garrison and built two churches, one in the Fort for the garrison and the other about a mile away for the Indian congregation. Schwartz was drawn into the political affairs of the day, protecting Serfoji or Saraboji, the adopted son and destined successor of Raja Tulyaji against an usurper and helping to carry out the plan of reform imposed on Tanjore by the Madras government. In 1779 he also went as an envoy of the British Government to Haider Ali of Mysore. Some people criticized Schwartz as more involved in politics than became a missionary; but these political employments were forced on him because of the respect inspired by his Christian character, and he never seems to have let them deflect him from his missionary duties.

Schwartz was a great ascetic and he was almost alone among the Lutheran missionaries of his day in thinking that, for him at least, a missionary life must involve celibacy. But in 1768 he was joined by a boy of sixteen, John Caspar Kohlhoff, the eldest son of John Baltazar Kohlhoff, one of the senior Tranquebar missionaries whom he came to look upon almost as a son. John Caspar Kohlhoff received Lutheran orders in 1787, when he preached a sermon in Tamil "with a graceful ease" which was not surprising, for he had known Tamil all his life. He became Schwartz's successor at Tanjore and died in 1844 at the age of nearly eighty-two, the last of the S. P. C. K. missionaries. He had the faults and merits of a man of the second generation. He was sincere, devoted and kind-hearted to a fault, and thoroughly acquainted with the people of Tamilnad which he never left in his whole life; but his experience was limited, he was a poor judge of character and had no head for accounts, and these defects were responsible for some of the short-comings of the Tanjore mission in years to come.

Distance and difficulty of communication made the finances

of the S. P. C. K. missions very different from later practice. In theory the missionaries were paid very modest salaries. For buying such articles as printing press and books, the remittances from England arrived very irregularly, so that the missionaries sometimes found themselves embarrassingly short of money. At times they were supplied with equally embarrassing large sums too. These they lent to the Government on interest, or, if the Government had no need of a loan, to private borrowers. This was sometimes very profitable, but could be disastrous, as when Fabricius in old age, apparently misled by an untrustworthy catechist, was cast into prison for debt at Madras. A similar catastrophe befell Kiernander in Calcutta. Sahwartz was more fortunate, as was Gericke, who succeeded Fabricius at Vepery in 1788 and died in 1803. Both Schwartz and Gericke had lucrative appointments as chaplains and both used their money for the work of their missions and left considerable funds as endowments after their deaths. But this wealth was by no means spiritually healthy for the churches of Tanjore and Vepery. The Christians tended to think that they had a right to be supported by the mission and quarrels, which were sometimes scandalous, broke out about property.

Another weakness of the South Indian missions was their attitude to cast. Although, as Christians, the missionaries disapproved of caste, they found it necessary to make very considerable concessions in practice, which they justified to themselves by the hope that the leaven of Christianity would gradually loosen it; but even at the beginning of the nineteenth century there was no sign that this was happening. Sudra and Pariah Christians occupied different sides of the church, separated by some feet of space and seated on different mats. At a communion service all the Sudras, men and women, communicated before the Pariahs. At one time in Tranquebar there were two chalices in use, one for Sudras, the other for Pariahs, but Dr. John, the Royal Danish missionary, had them melted down into one. Though there were a few Pariah catechists, only Sudras were ordained, the missionaries rejecting a suggestion from Europe that the Pariah Rajanaiken should be ordained by saying that to be required to receive the sacrament at the hands of a Pariah might lessen the people's reverence for it. These Sudra "country priest" as they were rather oddly called[1] often refused to enter the house of their Pariah parishioners or to allow Pariah Christians to enter their houses. There were separate burial grounds for the two classes.

Towards the end of the eighteenth century, and especially after the death of Schwartz and Gericke, the Lutheran missions in South India began to decline. The younger Francke was dead, and Halle had become a centre of enlightenment rather than of pietism and was then engulfed with the rest of Europe in the Napoleonic Wars. Arrivals of missionaries became rare and those who came were not of the same quality as their predecessors. Holzberg at Cuddalore was a notorious drunkard and was dismissed by S. P. C. K. in 1813, but as they had no means of enforcing his dismissal and no one to send in his place, he continued till his death in 1824. Paezold, at Vepery, was quarrelsome and doubtfully honest and there was scandalous litigation between him and his congregation. When in 1825 S. P. C. K. decided to hand over its South Indian missions to S. P. G. there were only five missionaries, including the veterans Rottler at Vepery and Kohlhoff at Tanjore. By this time there was an Anglican bishop in India and S. P. G. had a strict rule that they would employ no one who had not received episcopal ordination. The old missionaries in Lutheran orders, however, continued in the pay of S. P. C. K. for the remainder of their service, though in fact they served S. P. G. Diocesan Committees of S. P. C. K. and later of S. P. G. were formed, and the missionaries thankfully handed over their mission funds to be administered by them. At Tranquebar, the last Royal Danish missionary Augustus Frederick Caemmerer died in 1837. The sons of Kohlhoff and Caemmerer were educated at Bishop's College in Calcutta, and they took Anglican orders, and had long and useful careers as S. P. G. missionaries. The Anglican Church had absorbed the old Lutheran missions, and when the Leipzig Society began to work as a Lutheran mission in this part of India in 1842, it really represented a new beginning.

---

1 They were, of course, in Lutheran orders and "country" in this connection means "native" or belonging to the country (India). It does not mean rural.

English Societies and Mission

S. P. C. K. had early extended its work to Cuddalore, but when the French took Fort St. David in 1758, the missionary there, Kiernander, a Swede, took refuge in Calcutta, probably at the invitation of Clive who had won the battle of Plassey the year before. He soon collected a congregation of about two hundred, though only a few of these were adult converts from Hinduism or Islam, the rest being Anglo-Indians or Portuguese converted from Roman Catholicism and their families. At one time Kiernander was helped by no fewer than four former Roman Catholic priests most of them being ex-Augustinan frairs. For the 'Portuguese' here and in Madras, the Bible and Book of Common Prayer were translated into that language, and services held in it until, early in the nineteenth century, it was found that they were unnecessary, since English was now better understood than Portuguese. Presently Kiernander married as his second wife a wealthy widow, and though his fortune was probably exaggerated by rumour, it was sufficient for him to build at his own expense the church later known as the Old Church or Old Mission Church, which still stands, though very much altered from its original appearance. But in 1787 Kiernander was declared bankrupt and retired to Chinsurah, whilst the Old Church legally his private property, was put up for sale. It was rescued by three friends, the civilian Charles Grant, his brother-in-law, William Chambers, and the Chaplain David Brown. These three became trustees for the church and David Brown became responsible for it until S. P. C. K. could send out another missionary. Abraham Thomas Clarke, a Cambridge graduate; arrived in 1790, the first Englishman in Anglican orders to come to India as a missionary; but within a year of his arrival he had accepted a chaplaincy and left the mission church. In his place S. P. C. K. sent a German Lutheran, William Toby Ringeltaube in 1797, but he felt himself unsuited to the work and did not stay long. Instead he offered his services to the newly formed London Missionary Society and was sent to open their work in the extreme south of India. After a few years of devoted work under the most austere conditions among Tamil speakers near Nagercoil, he left in 1816 for a voyage to the East Indies and was never heard of again. David

Brown continued to minister to the congregation of the Old Church.

The eighteenth century saw a most remarkable movement of religious revival in England, whose best-known leaders were John and Charles Wesley and George Whitefield. They were Anglicans but, like the German pietists with whom they had some contact, they, stressed strongly personal religious experience and they expected every Christian to undergo what they called conversion which, rather than the baptism which he had received in infancy, was thought of as the real beginning of a Christian life. John Wesley's religious societies were intended by their founder to remain within the Anglican Church, but his own action in authorizing some of his lay preachers to administer Holy Communion made separation inevitable and after his death at the end of the century the Methodist Church became a non-conformist denomination in England. Methodism had its greatest success among a rather lower social class than the three old dissenting denominations—Presbyterians. Congregationalists or Independents and Baptists who were strongest in the urban middle class; and it had also great success in the United States of America. Parallel with Methodism was the Evangelical movement within the Church of England, many of whose supporters, like William Wiberforce, an influential member of Parliament and friend of the Prime Minister, William Pitt the Younger, were prominent and wealthy men.

The influence of the new movement made itself felt in Calcutta, especially on Sir John Shore, afterwards Governor General and later Lord Teignmouth, and on Charles Grant. Grant had been greatly encouraged by the arrival from England of the young chaplain David Brown, the disciple at Cambridge of Charles Simeon, who, as fellow of King's College, had a long life of influence on undergraduates there. David Brown was a very young man—too young to have received more than deacon's orders—who came out originally to take charge of a new military orphanage in Calcutta, a charge which he had to give up when he insisted in carrying on his ministrations at the Old Church, though his appointment as chaplain made the financial sacrifice bearable.

1787, at Brown's suggestion, Grant, Brown and Chambers addressed letters to religious leaders in England, including the

Archbishop of Canterbury, Wilberforce and Simeon, suggesting a Government sponsored mission to Bengal with missionary clergy, catechists and schoolmasters in important centres, though there would be no compulsion on anyone to adopt Christianity. Few of those addressed responded, but Simeon's interest in India was aroused and from that time onward he exerted himself to encourage suitable young clergymen of Evangelical views to apply for chaplaincies under the East India Company. Grant retured to England in 1790 and soon acquired a predominant influence in the Court of Directors which was responsible for these appointments, so that Simeon's nominees were generally accepted. He also became a close friend of Wilberforce and a member of the so-called Clapham sect of Evangelicals. When in 1793 the Charter of the East India Company came before Parliament for renewal, Wilberforce secured the passage of resolutions embodying a plan for the employment of missionary educators very similar to that which Grant, Brown and Chambers had suggested; but as no clauses activating the scheme were included in the Act, nothing was done in the matter. In fact by this time strong opposition to Christian missions had developed among Englishman concerned with the East India Company and the government of India. The S.P.C.K. missions had received patronage and help from the Company; but in those days it was still mainly a commercial concern. Now that the British had acquired large territories in India and were well on the way to ruling the whole country, a fear developed that any active support of Christian missions, even, sometimes any open profession of Christianity, might so alarm Hindus and Moslems as to endanger British rule. The East India Company claimed the right to exclude from their territory any European of whom they disapproved; and they used it to exclude anyone who came with an openly missionary purpose.

They could not, however, exclude the Evangelical chaplains recommended by Simeon. The first of these was Claudius Buchanan who arrived in Calcutta in 1797. He found favour with the Governor General, Lord Wellesley, who appointed him, with David Brown to the superintendance of his ambitious Fort William College, intended principally for the education of young civilians, but which Wellesley hoped to make also a centre for the translation of the Bible and other sacred books. The Directors, however, disapproved of the project and it was reduced to an establishment for giving a one year course in languages and other Indian subjects to the young civilians of Bengal; and when Wellesley left in 1805 Buchanan fell into deep disfavour with the Government for his defence of the Baptist missionaries of Serampore; but before any action could be taken, he had left India for reasons of health. Buchanan produced a somewhat grandiose plan for the establishment of an Anglican episcopate in India; and with Kerr from Madras, he was one of the first Anglican priests to visit Travancore to get in touch with the Jacobite Syrians there and to give an account of them to the English-speaking world.

Just about the time that Buchanan was leaving India, Henry Martyn arrived. One of the most brilliant Cambridge scholars of his day, he had been the first Englishman to offer himself to the newly formed Church Missionary Society, but he later had to withdraw the offer for family reasons. Simeon then suggested that he should apply for an Indian chaplaincy instead. His career in India was very short, from 1807 to 1811, spent partly at Dinapur and partly at Kanpur; but during this time he translated the New Testament into Urdu and at Kanpur was the means of the conversion of a Moslem of good family, Sheikh Salah, who heard Martyn preaching on Sundays to a crowd of beggars gathered before his bungalow and afterwards took employment as a copyist under him. This gave him the opportunity to study the New Testament and when Martyn's health—he was in an advanced stage of tuberculosis—forced him to leave Kanpur, he came forward and asked for baptism. This was not at once granted, but he accompanied Martyn to Calcutta where, after further instruction, he was baptized by David Brown in the Old Church on Whitsunday, May 19th, 1811, taking the Christian name of Abdul Masih. Martyn, meanwhile had left India to travel home overland by Persia, where he hoped to be able to perfect his Persian translation of the New Testament. He spent a year at Shiraz in this work and in debates with Moslem scholars, and then set out for home, but died of exhaustion at Tokhat in Armenia, and was buried by Armenian monks, through whom the news of his death and his papers eventually reached England. Short as Martyn's Indian career was, he left an unforgetable memory.

Martyn had the company during his last days at Kanpur of his friend and fellow-chaplain, Daniel Corrie, who was destined to a much longer Indian career. Ill-health forced Corrie too to return to Calcutta shortly after this; but in 1812, just after David Brown's death, he left for Agra accompanied by Abdul Masih, who was going as a C.M.S. catechist under his supervision. Abdul Masih's work opened in the centre of the city, at a place now known as *Abdul Masih Ka Kattra,* which is still a Christian quarter and where, forty years later, the large church of St. John was built.

Meanwhile in 1808 Thomas Thomason at last arrived to relieve David Brown of the charge of the Old Church. Bishop Heber later described him as "a very good and a very learned man —a child in guilelessness and facility of disposition—the most unsuspicious being in the world—inclined to think well of everybody—and an excellent preacher." He had been in charge of a church near Cambridge, and in his family Simeon, who had renounced marriage for himself because it was incompatible with his position at King's College, had been able to enjoy a taste of family life. Thomason spent the rest of his active life in India, dying in 1829.

Besides the five famous Evangelical Chaplains of Bengal —Brown, Buchanan, Martyn, Corrie and Thomason—there were Evangelical Chaplains at Madras—Richard Hall Kerr Charles Church, Marmaduke Thomason and James Hough, the latter of whom played an important part in the history of the Church in Tirunelvelli.

W'Carey and the Serampore Baptists

William Carey was born on August 17th. 1761 at Paulers Pury in Northamptonshire in the very centre of England, where his father and grandfather had been parish clerks and village schoolmasters. Carey, however, joined the Particular Baptists in 1779 and became a shoe-maker and Baptist preacher. He had a remarkable talent for languages, and taught himself Latin, Greek, Hebrew, French and Dutch. In 1792 Carey preached a sermon to a gathering of Baptist ministers at Nottingham, proving that it was the duty of Christians to fulfil the Lord's command to preach the Gospel to every creature. It seems strange that any one could have doubted this, but the Particular Baptists were strict Calvinists and it had been customary to argue that God Himself would provide for the Gospel to reach all who were predestined to salvation. The result of Carey's sermon was the formation of the Baptist Missionary Society with a subscription of £13.2.6. and Carey's departure to Bengal as their first missionary on June 13th. 1793. Carey and his party had undertaken to provide for themselves by their own earnings in Bengal, and this, and the sustained disapproval of the Government involved them in great hardships in their earlier years. Finally on January 10th. 1800 the Baptist Missionaries settled at Serampore, then still a Danish possession. Carey had been joined in 1799 by John Marshman, a schoolmaster and William Ward, a printer. These three—Carey, Marshman and Ward—were the great Serampore trio who worked together for many years.[2] Marshman and his wife Hannah opened profitable boarding schools for boys and girls and in 1801 Carey was appointed professor of Bengali in Wellesley's Fort William College at a handsome salary, and he later became professor of Sanskrit also. Carey held these appointments for many years. In this way the financial difficulties of Serampore were greatly relieved. About the time of the settlement in Serampore the first noteworthy converts began to be made. The Serampore missionaries also took in hand an ambitious programme of Bible translation as a preparation for missions to the whole of Asia—they included not only Indian languages but even Chinese. These versions were pioneer work which have long since been superseded by more accurate translations. The Serampore missionaries were also pioneers in the printing of Indian scripts and in the production of newspapers in Bengali. In 1818 they produced the Monthly Bengali magazine *Dig Darshan* and at the same time a weekly newspaper *Samachar Darpan*. These were among the very first of their kind ever published. In English journalism Serampore founded *The Friend of India,* which continues in the modern *"Statesman"*.

In 1818 Serampore College was founded and in 1820 it was

---

2. Carey died June 9th, 1834, Ward of cholera in 1823 and Marshman in 1837.

opened to non-Christian as well as Christian pupils. In 1827 a Danish charter was obtained which enabled Serampore College to give divinity degrees. It is still the only institution in India empowered to do so.

Baptist missionaries sent out from Serampore were established in various parts of India such as Monghyr, Benares, Agra and Delhi, though many of these were at first very weak and did not always have a continuous existence. The greatest strength of the Baptist mission continued to be in Bengal.

The Baptist missionaries in Bengal never returned home, and one consequence of this was that they gradually lost touch with the committee which supported them there. So when in 1818 new missionaries arrived who were very critical of the Serampore trio, their complaints were believed and serious trouble followed. Instead of supporting the Lall Badar congregation in Calcutta, the new arrivals founded a new Baptist church at Entally and established their own *Calcutta Missionary Society*. A reconciliation with the schismatics took place in 1820, but it was not till 1830 that the trouble with the home society was settled by the transfer of Serampore to eleven home trustees with right of occupation to the existing missionaries for the rest of their lives.

Carey and his colleagues belonged to the Particular or Calvinistic Baptists, who were predestinarians; but in 1829 there arrived missionaries from the General or Freewill Baptists, a more numerous denomination. Carey directed them to Orissa, where they have worked ever since.

New British Missionary Societies

In 1813 Parliament was due to renew the East India Company's Charter, and Wilberforce and Grant, now also a member of Parliament, prepared a campaign for the insertion of religious clauses in the new Act. A diocese of Calcutta was to be founded with three archdeaconries, for the presidency towns of Calcutta, Madras and Bombay. This was comparatively easy, as it could be represented as a necessary completion of the chaplaincy establishment for the benefit of the Company's European servants. It was more difficult to obtain clauses in the Bill which would open India to the work of missionaries. The position had changed since 1793 through the foundation of some important missionary societies, which made the plan proposed in 1793 obsolete. Of the B.M.S, we have already seen something. In 1795 an inter-denominational society called at first simply the Missionary Society was founded. Later, to distinguish it from other societies it became known as the London Missionary Society (L.M.S.). It has never in theory lost its interdenominational character, but, as the other denominations founded their own societies, it came to be in practice almost entirely a Congregational society. In 1799 a group of Evangelical clergy and laity in the Anglican Church founded the Church Missionary Society for Africa and the East (C. M. S.) which was to become the largest and most influential of all British missionary societies. It differed from S. P. G., now almost a hundred years old, in two important respects. It was a private venture with a large lay element, which included Wilberforce and Grant, whilst none of the clergy concerned held high preferment and most were unbeneficed in 1799. It was not till 1841 that the English archbishops and bishops all became officially associated with the Society. Secondly, whilst S. P. G. did not represent any party in the Church, the principles of C. M. S. were definitely Evangelical; and indeed it became much the Greatest achievement of Evangelicalism in the Church of England. The result was that, as almost all Evangelical support for missions was channelled through C. M. S., S. P. G. came to be thought of as the High Church society. S. P. C. K. which concerned itself mainly with Christian literature and education, remained unpartisan. In 1805 the British and Foreign Bible Society was formed. It was interdenominational and its object was to provide copies of the Christian scriptures in all languages at a low price. In order to avoid disputes about interpretation it was early decided that the Society's scriptures should be "without note or comment".

The clause in the East India Act of 1813 which occasioned most controversy was XXXIII, which declared it to be "the duty of this Country to promote the Interest and Happiness of the Native inhabitants of the British Dominions in India" by introducing "useful Knowledge and religious Improvement" and "to make provision for granting Permission to Persons desirous of going to or residing in India for the above Purposes". One of the greatest speeches of Wilberforce's career ensured the

15

passage of this clause and India was opened to missionary effort. The C. M. S. and L. M. S. had anticipated this permission, but C. M. S. as an Anglican society, could not defy authority in the same way.

The First Anglican Hierarchy in India

The first bishop of the new diocese of Calcutta was Thomas Fanshawe Middleton. who arrived at the end of 1814. He was a high churchman of the old style, a highly respectable and scholarly man who had been much interested in the affairs of S. P. C. K. and S. P. G. He found himself, however, in a very difficult position. Neither the Government nor the Chaplains really wanted a bishop in Calcutta and Middleton did not help matters by an excessively pompous manner. He arrived impressed with the necessity of proceeding with great caution with regard to missions; but experience soon showed him that this was unnecessary, and especially after a visitation tour in South India, he greatly modified his attitude. He continued, however, to be very much puzzled about his legal relation to the C. M. S. missionaries who began to arrive in considerable numbers. In 1818 he received a letter from S. P. G. asking him how the Society could best help him, and he replied suggesting the foundation of a mission college in Calcutta which should be a centre of Christian learning, a place where clergy could be trained and missionaries on their first arrival introduced to the languages and customs of the country and perhaps a centre of general education. The result was the founding of Bishop's College at Howrah, in the buildings now occupied by the engineering college; but this was not ready to be opened till after its founder's death. In its early years it experienced very considerable difficulties; for though its staff included some able and devoted men, it had been planned on too grandiose a scale for the infant Anglican Church of those days, and was also badly placed. Almost all the strength of the Church lay in the south, and it was not convenient for young men from south India to come to Calcutta for their theological education.

Middleton died on July 8, 1822 after an episcopate of eight years. It was not till October 10, 1824 that his successor, Reginald Heber, arrived in Calcutta. Shortly after Middleton's death, the Archdeacon who, according to the Letters Patent, administered the diocese during the vacancy, died; and the Government then placed the administration in the hands of the two presidency Chaplains of whom the senior was Daniel Corrie. When Heber arrived, one of his first acts was to make Corrie Archdeacon. Heber was a man of great ability, charm and devotion, who might have expected high preferment in England if he had not chosen to come to India. He had composed a book of hymns, written by himself and his friends, some of which have become indispensible.[3] He had also had the advantage of being able to talk over some of Middleton's legal perplexities before he left England, and an Act of Parliament had been passed in 1824 making clear his legal right to ordain Indians, which Middleton had refused to do. C. M. S. had wished to have two of their catechists, Abdul Masih and William Bowley, the son of an English soldier by an Indian mother, ordained by Middleton, but they had instead been ordained by Lutheran missionaries in the employ of the Society. Heber began by licensing all the C. M. S. missionaries in Anglican orders, which Middleton had refused to do, and in 1825 he bestowed Anglican orders on Abdul Masih and William Bowley. This was objected to by the Lutheran missionary who had presided at the ordination in 1819, but Heber defended his action by saying that he did not admit ordination by presbyters without a bishop to be valid, although those good men were not to be condemned who, in exceptional cases, resorted to it for the perpetuation of the ministry. Ordination stood on a different footing from baptism. "Though a man can be only once *regenerate,* he may be often *renewed* and *quickened* by the Holy Ghost"; and he pointed out that no formal renunciation of the former orders had been required.

Before these ordinations, from June 6, 1824 to October 1825, Heber had undertaken a remarkable visitation tour, which took him first to Dacca, then through North India to Agra and Delhi, then through Rajastan to Bombay; and from thence to Ceylon which had been added to the diocese of Calcutta, as had

3. The hymn for Trinity Sunday, "Holy, holy, holy, Lord God Almighty", the hymn for St. Stephen's day, "The Son of God goes forth to war" the Epiphany hymn, "Brightest and best of the sons of the morning", and his friend H.H.Milman's Palm Sunday hymn, "Ride on, ride on in majesty."

"New South Wales and its dependencies";4 and finally back by sea to Calcutta. On January 30th 1826 he set out on another visitation, going to Madras and South India; but he died at Trichinapoly on April 3rd. Heber's devotion and attractive character—Corrie wondered whether it came by nature or by grace, but was inclined to think it must be by grace—has made him one of the saints of Anglicanism in India.

Corrie as Archdeacon had for a second time to administer the diocese of Calcutta until the arrival of Heber's successor, John Thomas James, in January 1828; but Bishop James died in the following August, and once again Corrie was in charge till the arrival of the fourth bishop, John Matthias Turner, in December 1829. Turner was able to undertake a visitation to South India, but died in Calcutta on July 7th 1831. Corrie was in charge for the fourth time, and it was understandably difficult to find a successor. Eventually the choice fell on Daniel Wilson, a leading Evangelical already fifty-four years of age. When he arrived in Calcutta in November 1832, he was dissatisfied with the arrangements which had been made for furnishing the episcopal palace. "I thought", my Lord", said Corrie, "that there was enough for eighteen months". Wilson stayed for twenty-five years, dying in Calcutta on January 1st 1858 at the age of nearly eighty.

The Company's charter was due to be renewed in 1833, and Wilson arrived in Calcutta knowing that the new East India Act would provide for the division of the unwieldy diocese of Calcutta which had already worn out four bishops, by establishing dioceses of Madras and Bombay. In 1835, accordingly, Daniel Corrie became the first Bishop of Madras and in 1837 Thomas Carr, another Evangelical chaplain who had been Archdeacon of Bombay, became its first bishop. In 1836 Australia received its first Anglican bishop and in 1845 the diocese of Colombo was established by Letters Patent. It was however considered that, because the first Anglican sees in India had been established by Act of Parliament, a further act would be necessary to establish any new ones in the territory controlled by the East India Company; and this blocked the way for any further development of ecclesiastical organization for some forty years.

4. Australia and New Zealand.

Meanwhile C. M. S. missionaries had begun to arrive in India. In preparation for them Corresponding Committees of C. M. S. supporters were formed in Calcutta and Madras, consisting of Evangelical chaplains and laymen, many of the latter distinguished Government servants. In Calcutta, Thomson was the first Secretary and Corrie, after acting jointly with him for a time, became his successor. In Madras the first Secretary was Marmaduke Thompson. When a similar development took place in Bombay, Carr became the first Secretary. The laymen on these corresponding committees could be very helpful to the mission in such matters as buildings and financial transactions; but there were considerable difficulties about their relations both with the bishop of the diocese and with the Home Committee of the Society which came to head in the thirties, in a complicated three-cornered quarrel between the Home committee, the local Committees in Calcutta and Madras, and Bishop Wilson who, although he had been a strong supporter of C. M. S. long before he arrived in India, was a masterful man with a high idea of a bishop's authority. The differences between Wilson and the Society were settled by an agreement in 1836 which remained unmodified for more than a generation:-

I. The Bishop expresses by granting or withholding his licence on which the sphere of the missionary's labour is mentioned, his approbation or otherwise of that location.

II. He superintends the Missionary afterwards as the other clergy, in the discharge of his ecclesiastical duties.

III. He receives from them (the Committee and the Secretary who still stand to him in the relation of lay patrons) such communications concerning his ecclesiastical duties as may enable him to discharge that paternal supervision.

IV. If the Bishop or Archdeacon fills at the request of the Society the office of Patron, President, Vice-President, Treasurer, Secretary & c. he receives further such confidential information at all times as the Bishop officially neither could wish nor would probably ask.

The difficulties between the Parent Committee at home and

the Correspoding Committees in Calcutta and Madras were resolved about the same time by the resignation of most of the members of the Correspoding Committees and their reconstruction
with smaller numbers and the requirement that the approval of
the Parent Committee must be obtained for all appointments.
In addition, Secretaries for the Committees were sent out from
England. These Secretaries were generally men of distinction
and influence, especially John Tucker, the first missionary Secretary of the Madras Corresponding Committee, who was also
a note-worthy preacher to an English congregation in Tucker's
Chapel in Black Twon.

Church Missionary Society and S.P.G. in Tamilnadu.

The first C. M. S. missionaries to come to India arrived in
1814—two Englishmen, Thomas Norton and William Greenfield
—and two German Lutherans—Rhenius and Schnarre. C. M. S.
had found it exceedingly difficult in its early days to find English
missionaries, and had temporarily solved the difficulty by copy-
ing S. P. C. K. in its employment of German Lutherans. But now
that there was an Anglican bishop in India, and Corresponding
committees exercising an entirely new kind of control, the conditions under which Lutherans could happily serve an Anglican
society had entirely changed.

Of the four first arrivals, Thomas Norton had a long career
at Alleppey in Travancore, where he built up a church and
schools and made converts, mostly of the low Ezhava caste.
Greenfield went to Bengal where his career was chequered and
not entirely satisfactory. Schnarré died quite soon. Rhenius
turned out to be one of the most remarkable of the early C.M.S.
missionaries.

A generation before this a movement towards Christianity
had begun in Tirunelvelli among the Shanars or toddy-drawing
caste.5 They ranked as Pariahs, having priests and deities of
their own, but they considered themselves to be the highest caste
included in this category, and their ownership of the toddy palms

---

5. Now called Nadars, a name originally given to a superior class of
headmen among them.

gave them rare economic independence. Though almost all illiterate at this time, they were shrewd and energetic. Schwadtz visited their country and baptized a great many of them, and the work was afterwards carried on by a S.P.C.K. missionary called Jaenicke and by Sathianaden, the best of the old "country priests". But the health of both failed, and they left the district only to die; and when, in 1816, Hough arrived in Palamcottah as chaplain, the Christians in Tirunelvelli had been almost entirely neglected for more than a decade. Hough trained and supervised catechists for them and opened schools; but as a chaplain he was liable to transfer at any time, and besides his health was failing. When he could not get S.P.C.K. to send a missionary, he turned to C.M.S. Rhenius in Madras had come to be on such bad terms with the Corresponding Committee that his return to Europe was being contemplated, when the suggestion was made that he should be sent to Palamcottah where, in a more independent position, his undoubted talents could be used without friction. He arrived in 1820 and Hough was delighted with him; and as he had to leave Palamcottah and, shortly afterwards India altogether, Rhenius was soon in independent charge of the mission. Hough spent much of the rest of his life in writing a History of Christianity in India, intended originally as a reply to Abbe Dubois's very pessimistic estimate of the prospects of Christianity there, which is an indispensable source for the early history of Protestant missions.

In the next decade Christianity spread rapidly among the Shanars of Tirunelvelli, and Rhenius showed remarkable organizing ability in the arrangements he made for those who came forward in large groups to place themselves under Christian instruction. They were admitted as catechumens and in many cases settled in Christian villages where a strong Church life would be possible. They were generally expected to prove their sincerity by destroying their idol temple and providing a house and salary for a catechist. Rhenius also organized societies for various purposes, such as the supply of Christian literature and the relief of the poor. In this way, although the whole movement was very much under his control, the Christians of Tirunelvelli were saved from the tendency to become parasites on the mission, as had happened at Vepery and Tanjore.

As the Church in Tirunelvelli grew, the question of ordaining some of Rhenius's senior catechists arose, and he asked leave to bestow Lutheran orders on them. C.M.S. replied that they were an Anglican Society, and that now that there was an Anglican bishop in India able and willing to ordain his candidates, he should present them for Anglican orders; but when Bishop Turner visited South India towards the end of 1830, the six candidates for ordination all withdrew their names, giving reasons which were the traditional Puritan objections to Anglican Church polity. As their only source of theological knowledge had been Rhenius himself and his colleagues, it was clear where the responsibility for the refusal lay. Yet the objections were not characteristically Lutheran. Rhenius had been influenced by a new sect, commonly called the Plymouth Brethren, with which he seems to have come in contact through some of the officers in the Palamcottah garrison. This sect had arisen among the Protestant Irish landed gentry and in circles connected with Trinity College, Dublin, and like the Methodists, their relations with the Anglican Church were for some time invidious, though eventual separation was made inevitable by their supposed discovery, as a result of Bible reading, that in the early Church any baptized Christian could preside at the Eucharist. C.M.S. was anxious not to deal too severely with so devoted and successful a missionary as Rhenius, so for the present they let the question of ordination drop, and accepted his suggestion that he should return to Europe for consultation. But in 1833, after he had been visited by Anthony Norris Groves, a leader in the new sect, he decided that it was his duty to remain in his mission. About the same time he distributed widely a pamphlet he had written in which episcopacy was strongly attacked; and the Home Committee, finding this entirely unacceptable, disconnected him, an action of which he was informed on May 18th. 1833. With his three colleagues, all Germans, he set out to found a new mission at Arcot, whilst the Secretary, Tucker, accompanied by George Pettitt, who since his arrival in India had been teaching in the C.M.S. seminary at Madras, and Edward Sargent, the son of an English soldier, then a catechist, hurried to Palamcottah to take over charge. Here they found John Devasagayam, who had been ordained deacon by Turner but had been persuaded by Rhenius to refuse to appear to be priested at Wilson's later visitation. They detected David Pillai, Rhenius's senior catechist, in serious misapplication of funds; and David Pillai at once wrote off to Rhenius begging him to return. Rhenius allowed himself to be persuaded and a most unfortunate schism followed. Corrie, on visitation shortly after his enthronement as Bishop of Madras, was able to do little to effect a reconciliation; but he priested John Devasagayam—the first, and for a long time the Tamil Anglican priest to work in Tamilnadu John Devasagayam, a Sudra Christian of the third generation, had, with his wife, renounced caste when he was made a deacon, a step which exposed them both to much petty persecution; and he now began a long, useful and distinguished career as a C. M. S. missionary in Tirunelvelli. Rhenius died suddenly on June 5th 1838 at the age of fortyseven, and his death put an end to the schism, which had been largely personal to himself. The mission went on under the leadership of George Pettitt, who was joined by several able missionaries, including Edward Sargent. The most remarkable of the others was John Thomas, a Welshman. On Christmas Day 1837 Thomas preached his first Tamil sermon in the little Christian village of Megnanapuram, where he spent the rest of his life. The destruction of the village by a terrible storm in 1845 gave him the opportunity of rebuilding it more to his mind, with wide airy, streets bordered by fruit trees and neat houses in gardens and a church—St. Paul's—which was a wonder for miles round. The reconstructed mission carried on some of the methods which had been devised by Rhenius, and the training given to catechumens was very thorough indeed. There was morning and evening prayer in the church or prayer room, at which attendance was marked, when there was catechetical instruction and a record was kept of the exact point reached by each pupil. After sometimes as much as two years of this teaching, a class of those being specially prepared for baptism was formed. Families were if possible baptized together and sometimes a point was stretched in favour of some old grandmother who proved incapable of learning. After baptism another careful period of preparation began for the bishop's visit for confirmation, and even after this there was a third period of preparation for becoming communicants. In addition to this, all under thirty were expected to learn to read, and there were schools for the children. It is not much wonder that, after a generation of this, the Christian Shanars or Nadars of Tirunelvelli were a transformed people, producing their own clergy and schoolmasters, as well as men who attained distinguished places in Government and other service.

For a long time S.P.G. were unable to do much for their missions in Tirunelvelli, but in 1841 they gained reinforcements from an unexpected quarter. Robert Caldwell, of a rigidly Presbyterian family, born in Ulster and spending his youth in Glasgow, offered himself as an L.M.S. missionary and, as part of his preparation, took his degree at Glasgow University. He was a natural scholar, with a lively, inquiring mind, which led him to an extensive course of theological reading in order to discover which Church was nearest to Christian truth. This finally led him, after his arrival in Madras, to the conclusion "that the Church of England with all its defects was the best home the seeker after truth could find in this world". Accordingly, he received Anglican orders from Corrie's successor as Bishop of Madras, Spencer, and in 1841 started work as an S.P.G. missionary at Idaiyanguddi in Tirunelvelli, where he spent most of the rest of his life. At Glasgow University he had been fired with enthusiasm for the new science of comparative philology and his great work, A *Comparative Grammar of the Dravidian Languages,* is still an authority on the subject. He was by far the most distinguished S.P.G. missionary of his generation in South India, though four men who followed him into the Anglican Church, two from Methodism and two from Congregationalism, all did excellent service.

At this period the C.M.S. and S.P.G. missionaries in Tirunelvelli were on excellent terms with one another, copied each others' methods and adjusted the boundaries of their missions amicably. They were also on good terms with the L.M.S. missionaries to the south.

When Rhenius first arrived in India, he at once opposed the easy-going policy on caste which had been followed by the old S.P.C.K. missionaries. So did other new arrivals, Haubroe and Schreyvogel of S.P.C.K. and the English C.M.S. missionary, William Sawyer. This led to great resentment among the Sudra Christians, and one of the objects of Heber's visitation in South India was to try to find out the truth about the matter and devise a just solution. He had been inclined to think that perhaps the line taken by the new missionaries was a little extreme, but all he had time to do before his death at Tiruchirapalli was to collect opinions and information on the subject, though the supporters of caste sometimes quoted his name as if he had given a decision in their favour. This was one of the most difficult questions Bishop Wilson and to face when he came to South India on visitation in 1835. As early as 1833 he had declared that the distinctions of caste must be abandoned decidedly, immediately and finally. He defined his requirements in a letter to Schreyvogel at Tiruchirapalli of January 17th 1834:—

(1) The converts all sit together in church.
(2) They come without distinction to the Lord's Table.
(3) The country priest or catechist receives into his house anyone that comes to him on a religious errand, whatever his caste.
(4) The Congregation admit into their houses the Catechists who are duly appointed to instruct them and read with them.
(5) The Country priest does not refuse to remain in the village where he is appointed because there are none but those who were formally of inferior castes.
(6) Godfathers and godmothers are taken indiscriminately from whatever caste, and if of a different caste from the rest, no objection is taken.
(7) When the Congregation is called together about any matter, all that can come are welcome, if only they are baptized.
(8) In the churchyard no separate place is allotted for the interment of the higher castes as they are called.

On his arrival Wilson attempted to enforce this policy vigorously, and at Tanjore on Sunday February Ist 1835, at a communion service at which there were about three hundred and sixty communicants sixteen or twenty who had been among the strongest opponents of the abolition of caste mingled indiscriminately with the Pariahs. But caste was a very sturdy plant in the South Indian Church and Corrie, on visitation at Tanjore in 1836, had to face the same kind of opposition.

Hitherto all the missions working in South India, including the L. M. S., had taken the same strict line on caste; but when the Leipzig Lutheran mission arrived in 1842, they won many

sudra Christians back to Lutheranism by adopting the laxer
attitude of the "old" missionaries to caste. This was not the case
with the Basle Lutheran mission which began to work in 1834,
mainly in the Canarese-speaking area in the west, or the Methodists who began to work in Tiruchirapalli in 1818 and, some
fifteen years later, in Mysore State.

Church Missionary Society in Travancore

From 1810 to 1819 Colonel John Muntro was British Resident in Travancore, whose ruler was a very young princess, Rani
Lakhsmi Bai; and for four and a half years he was Diwan as well.
He was a reformer and a keen Evangelical, and he took a great
interest in the Jacobite Syrian Christians. He called in C.M.S.
missionaries in what he conceived as a mission of help to the
Jacobite Church. The plan was that a college should be founded
and endowed in Kottayam, chiefly for the education of the young
Syrian clergy, and also as a centre for the translation of the scriptures into Malayalam. The Metropolitan was to live in the college
which was placed under him; and at this time he was conscious
of the need for reform in his Church and ready to co-operate in
the scheme. Besides Norton, whom we have already mentioned,
three C. M. S. missionaries arrived, Joseph Fenn, whose work
was mainly teaching in the college, Benjamin Bailey who translated the Bible into Malayalam, cutting type for the first effective
printing of the language, and compiling the first modern dictionary
and grammar; and Henry Baker who was concerned with the
rest of the work of the mission. Fenn left for reasons of health
in 1826, and in 1833 Bailey and Baker were both in England on
leave, and the direction of the mission was in the hands of Joseph
Peet, a rough, breezy, tactless man who was said, once have been
a sailor. The years of attempted co-operation had not appeared
to have much effect on the Syrian Church and the new Metra-
politan, Mar Dionysios IV, was keeping aloof as well. As a sign
of independence, he began ordaining deacons to the priesthood
on the payment of fees from their parents without requiring the
certificate from the missionaries that they had satisfactorily completed their college course, as had been agreed. Wilson visited
Kottayam in November 1835 and tried to insist on what he considered the necessary reforms, offering a large money grant to

the needy Church to enable them to be carried out. Mar Diony-sios, however immediately left after having received Wilson and called a meeting of his clergy at Mavelikara which drew up and signed on Januady 10, 1836 a document called the *Mavelikara Padyola* which effectually brought co-operation to an end. In fact there had been some naive misunderstanding on the part of the Anglicans who had so far had to do with the Jacobite Syrians as to the nature of that Church. An episcopal Church not in com-munion with Rome must, they thought, basically agree on all points with the Church of England; hence they at first attributed to the connection with Rome in the 16th-17th centuries every-thing that appeared to them to be unevangelical. Tucker, who knew something of Eastern Churches, was the first to point out "these errors are not of Rome, they are of Antioch".

After the break with the Jacobites, the C. M. S. mission in Travancore started again on a wholly new basis. The college was given up to the Syrian Church, but a new one was established in its place, and the missionaries turned to non-Christians, men of high caste, the low caste Izhavas or slave people, and the tribal hill Arrians. A certain number of Syrian Christian congregations asked to be received as Anglicans, and most of the Anglican clergy in Travancore came to be drawn from this source. The presence of the Anglican Church continued to have a very strong influence on the Jacobite Syrians.

Church Missionary Society in Bengal and N. India.

The first C. M. S. missionaries in Bengal were not men of any particular distinction. The most remarkable was the first, and for a long time the only woman missionary of the Society, Mary Anne Cooke, afterwards Mrs. Wilson, who started female education in Calcutta in 1820. Later she founded an orphanage for girls at Agarpura outside Calcutta; but in 1841 she joined the Plymouth Brethren and her work came to an end. The chief centre of C. M. S. work in Calcutta was Mirzapore, now Amherst Street, where Holy Trinity Church and St. Paul's College now are. Their greatest success was in the Nadia or Krishnagar dis-trict to the north of Calcutta, where the converts came in about equal numbers from rather low caste Hindus who had belonged to the Karta Bhoja group, and from Mohammedan cultivators.

But no such thorough training was given to the converts as had been done in Tirunelvelli. S. P. G. worked mainly in the Sundarbans to the south of Calcutta.

Many of the German missionaries of C. M. S. came from the Basle missionary seminary which had been founded as a thank-offering for the end of the Napoleonic wars; and after 1819, when an Act of Parliament made it easier for bishops in England to ordain men for missionary service, they generally came to England as laymen to complete their training and received Anglican orders. One of the most outstanding of these to work in Bengal was J. J. Weitbrecht who was in charge of the mission at Burdwan and who had the assistance of a most remarkable English wife. Unfortunately severe malarial inflection later ruined Burdwan as a Christian centre. In upper India as it was then called, a mission was opened at Gorakhpur in 1824 at the instance of Robert Martyns Bird, one of the most distinguished civilians of his day, who had married David Brown's daughter. The first missionary and the real founder of the mission was Michael Wilkinson. In 1831 a large track of waste jungle was granted to C. M. S. by the Governor General, William Bentick, on condition that they should clear and settle it; and on this track the christian village of Basharatpur grew up round its church. Converts came from both Hinduism and Islam, and a number of Roman Catholics from Betwa, which had fallen into some decay, became Anglicans. The Christian settlements at Gorakupur are the largest of their kind in the U. P.

At Benares, C. M. S. work began when Corrie was chaplain there in 1818, when he persuaded Jai Narain Goswami, a wealthy merchant, to place the school he was anxious to found to teach the new western knowledge under C. M. S. missionaries. For some fourty years from 1832 the work at Benares was under the dircetion of William Smith, an Englishman, and Charles Benjamin Leupolt, a German in Anglican orders. William Smith was mainly engaged with work among Hindus, Leupolt with almost every other aspect of the mission. Smith was often deeply distressed at his lack of success, but in 1844 he was visited by a brilliant young Brahmin pandit, Nilkanth Goreh, who in 1848 was baptized by the name of Nehemiah. No Indian Christian of his generation had a keener mind, and he himself was responsible for bringing to Christ several notable converts.

Agra was at this time the centre of government of what were then called the North Western Provinces; and a most remarkable group of civilians worked there, headed by the Lieutenant-Governor, James Thomason, the son of Thomas Thomason. A C. M. S. missionary, Moore, arrived in 1837 to shepherd the Christian flock which had been neglected since the death of Abdul Masih in 1827. In 1837 north India was visited by a very severe famine and Moore with the Chaplain, Chambers, did a great work in collecting and caring for the famine orphans. At first they were housed in unsuitable quarters in the city, but in 1838 the ruined tomb of Mariam-i-Zamai, the reputed Christian wife of Akbar, with other buildings and adjacent land near Akbar's tomb at Sikandra, was granted by the Governor General to C. M. S. for the use of the orphans.

Just at this time C. M. S. accepted the services of four experienced Lutheran missionaries of the Basle Mission. They were C. F. Hoernle, F. S. Schneider, C. G. Pfander and F. A. Kreiss. They had been forced to leave a mission which they had founded on the border between Russia and Persia when the country came under Russian rule, and the new Government laid down the unacceptable condition that all their converts should become members of the Russian Orthodox Church. Pfander, the most distinguished of the four, had already written a book in Persian, Mizanul-Hagg, which was considered the best extant presentation of Christianity to Moslems till the end of the century. These were the last men in Lutheran orders accepted by C. M. S. without the requirement that they should take Anglican orders; and questions about their status were raised by the chaplain at Agra. Bishop Wilson ruled that they should exercise a full ministry, but only to the Christians under their charge, and that they should as far as possible observe Anglican discipline, for example, presenting candidates for confirmation to the bishop instead of performing the rite themselves, according to Lutheran usage. Ultimately they all felt it advisable to take Anglican orders with the excepion of Kreiss who died before he could accomplish his purpose to do so, and so ended Lutheran orders in Anglican missions.

The charge of the orphans at Sikandra was given to Hoernle and his wife, while Schnieder looked after the Christians at the Kattra compound in Agra. The education of the orphans was extremely thorough, and they were carefully guarded from the knowledge of non-Christian religions. They were, however, taught Urdu very thoroughly. Whilst it was hoped that some of the most promising boys might in time become catechists and perhaps clergy, it was clear that the majority of the orphans would be unfit for this; but a very profitable occupation was found for many of them with the development of a printing press which came to do all the Government business. Although the orphanage at Sikandra was the largest and most important, other orphanages were established at Gorakhpur, Benares, Chunar, where William Bowley worked till his death in 1847, and by the S. P. G. missionaries at Kanpur. By these means an Indian Christian community grew up in this part of India which future converts could join.

In Meerut the work of C. M. S. was begun by Captain and Mrs. Sherwood, who had been friends of Martyn and Corrie at Kanpur, and carried on under the direction of an energetic Evangelical Chaplain, Henry Fisher.

S.P.G. had been invited to Kanpur by the Chaplain, Midgeley John Jennings, who was later transferred to Delhi, where there was already a Baptist mission. Here there was a Government College in which Ram Chandra had been first a pupil and then a teacher of mathematics. Like most western-educated Hindus of his day, he took it for granted that religion was something no enlightened man could have any use for, but happening to go one day to the English church he was struck by the devotion of the British officials, whom he knew to be men of integrity and ability. This led to further inquiry and to his baptism by Midgeley John Jennings in 1852, together with his friend, Chaman Lall, a sub-assistant surgeon. Jennings exerted himself to get an S.P.G. mission established in the city, which was accomplished in 1854 with what seemed very favourable prospects.

In Bombay the first C.M.S. missionary, Richard Kenny, arrived in 1820 but only stayed till 1826, though he was followed by others. Bombay proved rather barren soil for all the societies who tried to work there, but C.M.S. had greater success at Nasik, where three missionaries, Farrar and Mitchell with their wives and Dixon arrived in 1832. A Christian village, called Sharanpur, on the outskirts of Nasik, was founded in 1855. Part of the difficulty of the work in Bombay was the cosmopolitan character of the place, including not only Hindus, Moslems and Parsis, but

Jews and even Chinese. One of the most interesting of these groups was the Africans rescued from slaves, who were particularly cared for by Isenberg who, before coming to Bombay, had spent ten years trying to open a C.M.S. mission in Ethiopia. A number of African boys and girls were cared for at Sharanpur, and some of them accompanied David Livingstone on his last journey in Africa.

American Missions in N. India

The American Board of Commissioners for Foreign Missions (mainly Congregationalist) was formed in 1810 and in 1812 their first two missionaries, Judson and Newell, arrived in Calcutta. On their long voyage they had been gradually drawn towards Baptist opinions, and contact with the Baptist missionaries at Serampore completed their conversion. This meant that a new American Mission Union had to be formed for their support. Meanwhile they were receiving the usual opposition from the British authorities, and they finally decided to start work in Burma, then a completely independent state. They had little success with the Burmese people, but very much more with the tribal Karens.

Three other American Missionaries from the same Board, Gordon Hall, Rice and Nott, arrived in Bombay about the same time. They also met with opposition from the authorities, but were finally allowed by the Governor to stay and work there. In common with missionaries of other Societies, they found Bombay itself a rather barren field, but some years later had considerable success with the Mangs at Ahmednagar. In 1834 the same Board began to work in Madurai and its neighbourhood and in 1851 in Madras. In 1855 work was opened at Vellore, which, however, was taken over in 1857 by the Dutch Reformed Church of America and came to be associated with the Scudder family.

American Baptists opened work in the Telugu area at Nellore in 1840, and in 1841 began their Assam mission which eventually became one of the most successful.

American Presbyterians began to work in Ludhiana in 1834, the pioneer Protestant mission to the Punjab, in what was already British territory. After the conquest of the rest of the

16

Punjab in 1849, they started work in Lahore, and finding more
to do than they could manage, the two leading missionaries,
Forman and Newman, invited C.M.S. to their help. C.M.S. sent
two missionaries, one of whom, Robert Clark, was to play a
leading part in the Punjab for the rest of the century. They
opened work in Amritsar in 1850. Shortly afterwards Clark with
two companions visited the frontier regions and Kashmir in order
to assess the prospects for work there. A mission was started
at Peshawar in 1855 by Clark and P. ander, who had been sent
from Agra because the group of officers who had asked for the
mission felt that Clark should be assisted, at least for a time,
by someone more experienced than he yet was.

In the North west Provinces (later U.P.) the American Presbyterians began to work at Allahabad in 1836 and at Fatehgarh,
which became their most important centre, in 1838.

The Gossner Missions

Besides the Lutheran missions which have been already
mentioned, there were the remarkable Gossner missions, directed by
Pastor Gossner from Berlin. Pastor Gossner seemed able to
command the services of devoted men, many of them quite
young, and prepared to live and work under the most austere
conditions. Some of these missions ended in failure, like the
tragic case of the four young men who were sent to open a mission at Karenja among the Gonds, who all died of fever within
a few months of their arrival. If a mission appeared unfruitful,
it would be closed, and the missionaries given the choice of
being transferred to some other field, generally Africa, or joining some other mission. Many of them, unwilling that their
Indian experience should be wasted, preferred the later alternative; and the consequence was that a number of them joined
C.M.S., accepting the requirement of reordination as Anglicans.

The most successful of the Gossner missions was opened
in Chota Nagpur in 1845, when four young men, E. Schutz, F.
Batsch, A Brandt and H. Janke[6], settled in Ranchi. For some
years they had no visible success, and then in 1850 they were

---

6. H. Janke died after a year and was replaced by F. Batsch's brother,
   H. Batsch.

visited by four men of the Oraon tribe who wished to see Jesus. They evidently thought Jesus to be a visible presence, and went away disappointed; but their request was repeated, and after they had been present at the missionaries' worship, they profess- ed themselves satisfied, and now only desired to become Christ- ians. From this time the numbers of converts rapidly increased, till by 1857 there were seven hundred baptized Christians for whom a fine large church had been built. But in 1857 a battalion mutinied near Ranchi and the missionaries and their wives and children had to flee for their lives. During their enforced stay in Calcutta they made an excellent impression on sympathetic Englishmen and German merchants, and they returned to find that the Christian tribesmen had suffered greatly at the hands of Hindu landlords, but none had denied Christ.

Scottish Presbyterians and Educational Pioneers

At the end of the eighteenth century missionary societies *began to be formed in the national Presbyterian Church of Scot- land,* and the first Scottish Presbyterian missionary Donald Mitchell, arrived in Bombay in 1822. But in 1824, at the pro- posal of Bryce who, as a result of the East India Act of 1813, had been appointed Chaplain of the first Church of Scotland in Calcutta, the General Assembly, the ruling body of the Church of Scotland, decided to undertake missionary work itself. The first missionary sent out by the Church was Alexander Duff who arrived in Calcutta in 1830. At this time a great demand for western education had grown up among young Bengalis, which was partly satisfied by the Hindu College, founded in 1816, whose tone was strongly secular. Duff at once conceived the idea of founding a college where the teaching of Christian truth should accompany the study of western learning, and he was encouraged by the Hindu reformer, Ram Mohan Roy. The col- lege was an immediate success, and besides the regular classes, general lectures and debates were held. Duff was on the friend- liest terms with the Anglican chaplains and missionaries, who helped in the courses of general lectures, and was quite satisfied when some of his converts became Anglicans. In the early years of his college the converts were quite numerous, and they and their descendants have provided leaders for all denominations of the Christian Church throughout North India. Similar developments took place in Bombay and Madras, John Wilson in Bombay founding the school which developed into Wilson College, and John Anderson, Madras Christian College.

In 1843, however, disaster threatened the missions of the Church of Scotland. An Evangelical party had grown up within the Church of Scotland, and Dr. Chalmers, the leader of this party, had been the inspiration of the early Church of Scotland missionaries. But in 1843 their differences with the more conservative party came to a head on the question whether the ministers of parishes should be appointed in the correct Presbyterian way, by a call from the congregation, or nominated by a patron, usually the local landowner, as had long been the practice. On this question nearly half the members of the General Assembly, led by Dr. Chalmers, seceded from the National Church to form the Free Church of Scotland, a step which entailed their giving up their livings. The loss was quickly made good by generous lay support, but in the missions, while all the missionaries adhered to the Free Church, their mission property churches, schools and missions bungalows—remained with the Church of Scotland. The three flourishing colleges had all to be refounded in new premises; and only in Calcutta did the Church of Scotland succeed in carrying on the original college with new missionaries.

Duff spent some time in Scotland after the Disruption, organizing mission support in the new circumstances, but he was back in Calcutta in the fifties and took an important part in preparing the Educational Despatch of 1854 and in helping to shape the new system of higher education which led to the establishment of the first universities in 1857. He finally left India in 1863 at the age of fifty-seven, and died in 1878.

Christian colleges, and particularly the three great colleges in Calcutta, Madras and Bombay, were the distinctive contribution of Scottish Presbyterianism to India, but other missions founded colleges on the same lines. In fact, Jai Narayan's College in Benares, which we have already mentioned, had much the same purpose, though its success was only moderate. The Robert Money School in Bombay was founded in 1839 by a group of Evangelical civilians in memory of one of their member, Robert Cotton Money, and placed under C.M.S.; but it never had the success of the almost contemporary Wilson College, perhaps because the general tone of the C.M.S. mission supporters in Bombay was discouraging to higher education as a missionary method. More successful was the college founded by Robert Turlington Noble, one of two C.M.S. missionaries sent to start work in Telangana. He opened his college at Masulipatanam7 on November 20, 1843 where, said he, "our first lesson is to be in the New Testament, our second in the Bhagavidgita"; for whilst in other Christian colleges the religious instruction given was exclusively Christian, Noble believed that the Bible could only gain by the comparison afforded by the teaching of the religious books of other faiths. He was a remarkable teacher, and he made several notable converts from high caste Hindus and Moslems of good family.

Shortly after this time, the civilians of Agra conceived the idea of founding a Christian college connected with C.M.S., and in 1851 there arrived as its first Principal Thomas Valpy French, a young Oxford scholar of some distinction. He devoted some ten years to building up St. John's College, which was destined to become the most distinguished of the Anglican colleges. French spent his spare time in a most rigorous programme of language study which earned him the name of "haft zaban padri" and in evangelistic tours. In 1854 a great debate was held in the Kattra compound between Rahmat Allah, a learned young Maulvi of Delhi and his friend Wazir Ali, subassistant surgeon in Agra on the one hand, and Pfander and French on the other, on the rival claims of Christianity and Islam. Pfander challenged Rahmat Ali to allow passages from the Gospel to be quoted in support of Christian doctrine or to bring forth proofs that it had been altered since the time of Mohammed. This he declined to do, and the meeting broke up with both sides claiming the victory. Wazir Ali took such an active part in the affairs of 1857 that he felt it safer to retire to Afghanistan for the rest of his life; but two younger men, Safdar Ali and Imaduddin, were so much impressed by the arguments of French and Pfander that they later became Christians; and Imaduddin received the Lambeth degree of D.D. from the Archbishop of Canterbury for his writings in support of Christianity against Islam.

1857 *and its effects for the Missions.*

In 1857 the whole of North India was convulsed by the revolt. There was later much controversy about how far the work of the missionaries had contributed to the outbreak, and those English-men who had always opposed missions argued that it had fulfill-ed their worst fears. On the other hand, the missionaries pointed out that nowhere had Christian influence been more carefully excluded than from the Bengal army; and that they would never have been guilty of such a blunder as the greased cartridges. Nevertheless, the spread of Christian influence was among the challenges to traditional ways which formed the background of the Revolt; and such events as the great debate at Agra were widely discussed. Generally Indian Christians were in as much danger as Europeans, and when the mutineers were Moslems, were faced with the choice of apostacy or death.

The outbreak began on a Sunday evening at Meerut, where there were two C. M. S. missionaries, Lamb and Medland. Lamb was away at Mussoorie at the time and Medland and his con-gregation escaped by the chance alteration of the time of the evening service. At Delhi the Chaplain, Midgeley John Jennings died weapon in hand; his daughter and a friend were murdered at the breakfast table. Hubbard, the S. P. G. missionary, the two catechists, Daniel Corrie Sandys, son of Timothy Sandys the veteran C. M. S. misionary at Calcutta, and Koch, Chaman Lall and a leading Baptist convert were also killed. Only Ram Chandra escaped, being hidden by Hindu relations and after many adven-tures reaching the English camp. The Delhi mission was comple-tely wiped out. At Kanpur the S. P. G. missionary, Haycock, was shot down as he was entering Wheeler's encampment; the Chaplain, Moncrieff and the S. P. G. catechist, Cockey, perished in the boats, one or other of them reading the funeral service as their companions died. With them perished four American Presbyterian missionaries with their wives from Fatehgarh, who had taken refuge at Kanpur. At Agra, the Lieutenant Governor, Colvin, and the other officials took refuge in the fort, and with them French and the other C. M. S. missionaries and the Chris-tians from the city. When a day or two later the Christians from Sikandra came in to seek refuge in the Fort, the authorities, in a state of near panic, refused them admission until the firm stand taken by French compelled them to let them in. In Agra there was little loss of life but much destruction of property, as the criminals were released from the gaol; and many pupils of St. John's College busied themselves with collecting and restoring the scattered library books. At Benares, the missionaries took refuge with others in the fort at Chunar except Leupolt, who was able to render good service in securing supplies of grain by the general confidence he inspired. At Lucknow there were as yet no missionaries. At Gorakhpur the Europeans evacuated the station in August, but the Indian Christians were then no longer safe, and went off into the jungle, while their village was completely destroyed. They were found wandering, headed by their catechist, by the naval brigade which had been sent from Calcutta, whose chaplain made himself responsible for them till peace was restored.

The Revolt gave the young Indian Church in North India its sowing of martyrdoms, and the devastated missions were soon more prosperous than before.

Conclusion

Until the end of the eighteenth century, Protestant missions in India comprised only the Lutheran missions in the south; but there was then a rapid and varied development which is very difficult to describe summarily. Yet even by 1857 the only really considerable body of Protestant Christians was in Tirunelvelli with few exceptions, the Protestant missions recognized that the things which united them as Christians were more important than those which divided them, and that the field before them was too extensive for any one of them to cultivate alone; and so, except in the larger cities, they avoided working side by side and practised informally what came to be called comity. This toleration did not extend to Roman Catholics, and here each side attracted converts from the other without scruple. As during this period Roman Catholic missions were weakened by the decline of Portuguese power, it is probable that the Protestants were the gainers from this, though the great majority of their converts came from non-Christian faiths. The next half century was to be a great period of expansion and consolidation for them. Now it has to see the first fruit of Nationalization.

CHAPTER XI

THE CATHOLIC CHURCH IN INDIA SINCE THE MID - NINETEENTH CENTURY

By Achilles Meersman, O.F.M., Bangalore.

The year 1857 stands out prominently both in the annals of the Catholic Church in India and in the political history of the country. It was the year of the so-called Sepoy Mutiny after which the subcontinent was placed directly under the jurisdiction of the British Crown and a new era of Indo-British relations was inaugurated. As far as the Church is concerned, it was the year when a new decree (ratified with additonal clarifications and modifications in 1860) was evolved purporting to regularize the relationship between Propaganda and the Padroado. More important, in Europe whence India would draw the necessary means for her renewal, the Church was showing signs of a Revival. The French Revolution and the Napoleonic Wars, which had swept across Europe destroying most of the Church's institutions, was a thing of the past. The Restoration offered at least a measure of security inspite of its weak policy of neglecting to integrate the new and of seeking renewal by resorting to the old. This of course was bound to lead to complications at a future date. New Religious Congregations and Missionary Institutes were being founded and even those established amidst the turmoil of war and revolution were coming out into the open and spreading. The older Orders with their numbers depleted and their houses confiscated or razed, were groping towards renewal. Already they were in a position to provide the Missions with a number of men and soon this trickle would become a steady stream. The Catholic Church in India too would soon experience the benefits of this revival.

Restoration, Reorganization and Conflicts

As a matter of fact she needed them badly. She was just emerging from what was called the dark century in her history.

Of the Religious Orders which had operated under the Padroado and subsequently had been suppressed, only the Jesuits returned to their ancient Madurai Mission (1836). Of those that had worked almost exclusively under the Propaganda only the Franciscans—Capuchins—in the North, the Carmelites in the South and in the Bombay Vicariate, and the Foreign Missionaries of Paris in their Missions of Tamilnadu and Mysore, had been able to maintain themselves albeit in reduced numbers. Of the newer Congregations only the Missionaries of St. Francis Sales (1845), the Holy Cross Fathers (1852) and the PIME (Foreign Missions of Milan—1855) had put in an appearance. Diocesan priests from abroad, almost exclusively from All Hallows and Maynooth (Ireland) too had volunteered to work in part of India, chiefly in the Vicariates of Madras, Calcutta and Hyderabad. Several of them had even been chosen to head these units as Bishops. For the rest, the Indian diocesan priests had to bear the brunt of the work. In Malabar and in the enclaves still in the possession of the Portuguese (Goa, Diu, Damaun) their number was more than sufficient. Many of these chose to serve in parts of the ancient Padroado dioceses where the mission-work at one time had been more intensive and the number of Catholics large. From such areas too vocations were recruited. It is surprising how far away places these priests at times were assigned to. Thus we find that in 1847 Laurence Menezes of Mahim (Bombay) and in 1851 Anthony d'Cruz of Malabar expired at Hyderabad (Sind). That was only a decade or more after Napier conquered Sind. But their number was never sufficient not even for those areas which could lay special claim on their care, not to speak of expansion.

This shortage of the clergy, however lamentable, did not constitute the main drawback under which the Church laboured. It was due to the lack of unity, chiefly among the leaders. They were sharply divided into two camps, the Propaganda and the Padroado. After the promulgation of the Papal Brief *Multa Praeclare* (1838), both parties held that the other did not possess any jurisdictional powers. In Rome itself they were even of the opinion, rightly or wrongly, that the Padroado or at least certain sections had gone into schism, the so-called "Goan-schism". It was to remedy this situation that Rome agreed to the Concordat of 1857. According to its provisions the jurisdiction of which, according to the *Multa Praeclare*, the Padroado dioceses had been deprived, was restored, but with certain restrictions. The Vicars Apostolic would withdraw from territories where the Padroado was actively engaged and function only outside these areas. Moreover, as soon as the Padroado was in a position to assume the responsibility for the areas under Vicars Apostolic as well, the latter would retire and surrender them to Padroado bishops.

At that time this solution was considered a regression and was severely, though unjustly, criticized. The real reasons why the majority of the Cardinals of the Commission voted in favour of its promulgation were of a pastoral nature. They wanted at all costs to terminate what they considered a schism and were willing to make concessions. Moreover they were aware the Padroado authorities would never be able to implement the provisions of the Concordat and eventually take over the existing Vicariates, not to speak of those still to be established over the whole of India. One has merely to glance at the statistics of 1864, as elaborated by Hull. According to them in the four existing Padroado dioceses there were some 250,000 Catholics in 77 Parishes located in Portuguese territories and a little over 200,000 and 206 churches in the rest of India and Ceylon. In the Vicariates Apostolic 332 Propaganda missionaries and a number of Indian diocesan priests looked after the spiritual needs of 800,000 to 900,000 Catholics.

Notwithstanding the Concordat, conflicts between the two parties occurred, especially during the *interregnum* (1857-63), that is between the date of the first draft and the appointment of a new archbishop for Goa, during which period that *status quo* was to be maintained. This, as it were, guaranteed that the controversy was bound to continue even after the arrival of the archbishop. However, we must not exaggerate as if this was the only issue which was debated and the only problem which occupied the minds of the clergy and the laity. There were large sections and areas which were hardly affected by the decree. In the others there was a great deal of forbearance, even cooperation between the two parties. But like all scandals of a sensational nature, they were widely circulated. Moreover they offered opportunities for the English to interfere when cases were submitted to their Courts with the consequent publicity.

Hierarchy in India

As a matter of course Rome was kept informed of all these happenings. Finally in 1884, Leo XIII extinguished the Padroado jurisdiction in Calcutta, Dacca and Hyderabad in India and in Colombo and Jaffna in Ceylon, something the Padroado authorities refused to acknowledge. However, the initiative on the part of the Pope did lead to a new series of negotiations, which in 1886 culminated in a new Concordat, by which the respective claims of Padroado and Propaganda were regulated and a new Hierarchy, covering the whole of India was established. Goa was reerected as an archdiocese with Cochin, Mylapore and Damaun, simultaneously created, as suffragans. The extent of each one's jurisdiction was determined and they continued to resort under Padroado. The Vicariates were all raised to the rank of dioceses and archdioceses and would continue to depend on the Propaganda. They were the following: —

Archdioces	Suffragan dioceses
Agra (O.F.M. Cap)	Allahabad (OFM. Cap), Lahore (OFM Cap)
Bombay (S.J.)	Poona (S.J.)
Calcutta (S.J.)	Krishnagar (MEP), Dacca (CSC)
Madras (Dioc.)	Hyderaoad (PIME), Vishakapatam (MSFS)
	Mangalore (S.J.), Tiruchirapalli (SJ),
Pondicherry (MEP)	Coimbatore (MEP), Mysore (MEP)
Verapoly (O.C.D.)	Quilon (O.C.D.)

With the establishment of the Hierarchy, the Propaganda— Padroado conflict for all practical purposes had been solved. There were still a number of uncommon situations, which caused an amount of dissatisfaction and friction such as the exercise of jurisdiction on the part of the Padroado over sections of their people who had settled in Propaganda dioceses, or over areas not contiguous to their territories, the rights the Padroado enjoyed in the matter of appointments of bishops to certain Propaganda sees, the disposal of the income from certain ancient endowments meant for the local church but now situated in Propaganda territories; but these were insignificant in comparison with the controversies which had marred the past. All these

were finally settled after Independence and when the Padroado
was restricted to the Portuguese enclaves. The problems to
which the integration of Goa into India gave rise have as yet
not been settled as Portugal has so far not acknowledged the
validity of the take over.

Expansion

We must now retrace our steps and see how the Church
extended itself over the whole of India. By then the British had
almost reached their greatest extent and reigned over the whole
country, which was still to endure for a number of generations.
Everywhere there were administrative centres and military cantonments. The Railways and the Telegraph were expanding, and
the number of commerical firms and plantations increasing.
From abroad many Englishmen, among them Catholics, were
recruited, but they were for the greater part administrators and
technicians. To keep all these instances and bodies moving, it
was necessary to engage personnel locally. Among those who
accepted employment were Christians, chiefly from the former
Portuguese enclaves and from Tamilnadu. These groups, both
those from abroad and from India needed the ministrations of
a priest. To care for these people, priests were assigned to towns
over the length and breadth of the country and they began
erecting churches. It was in this manner that the Church expanded to so many places. In other words it was very much the
period of chaplaincies.

The chaplains did indeed try to make contacts with the
people of the towns where there were stations, generally with
no or only meagre results. They were experiencing the same
the Portuguese had experienced before them. In general they
had found that it was most difficult, not to say impossible, to
make converts outside, in the proximity of their forts and settlements. Moreover, at the military cantonments and railway
colonies and their outstations, they were frequently overwhelm-
ed with work. Even the charitable and educational works they
inaugurated were geared to the needs of those christians who
had come from outside. To be sure, it was possible to perform
some missionary work, but generally it was among the non-
Christians who too had immigrated from elsewhere. They had

been uprooted and no longer bound up with the ancient village-structures and hence were more open to new ideas and values. It was in this manner that the church was present in so many parts of the country, but it was not an indigenous church, made up of local people. It remained something foreign, imported. Even the places where the churches were located indicated this. They were built outside the city proper, in the cantonments, and railway colonies. This was very much the case in the North, where the Church had been slow in taking root.

On the other hand we find that in the southern half of the country, converts were being made, chiefly from the low castes. In certain cases we can even speak of mass-movements. Thus the Jesuits in their Madurai mission, chiefly after 1876, made so many converts that the church membership grew to over 200,000. In the dioceses of Verapoly and Quilon, the Carmelites beginning around 1860 initiated a similar movement, though not with the same success as in Madurai. In the dioceses entrusted to the MEP (Foreign Mission Society of Paris) large numbers asked for baptism especially as a result of large-scale relief-work at the time of the 1873 famine. After the PIME were entrusted with the Hyderabad diocese, they established the Church in several areas. The same can be said about the Mill Hill Fathers, who in 1877 began working in the Madras Archdiocese until 1928 when those portions where they had worked intensely were dismembered and the diocese of Nellore was formed. In the diocese of Vishakapatanam the Missionaries of St. Francis Sales penetrated into the interior and implanted the church in places where the people had never seen a missionary. In a number of areas more to the North, German Jesuits began missions and with a measure of success among the Dhers of Gujerat (from 1895) and the Mahars of Maharashtra (from 1878). However in the North the greatest success accompanied the work of the Capuchins in the diocese of Lahore, chiefly after it was confided to their Belgian Province (1880). At present the Punjabi Catholic community numbers over 200,000, but except for a fair number in the Jullunder Prefecture (dismembered from Lahore after India-Pakistan partition and entrusted to the English Capuchins) and in the diocese of Simla-Chandigarh, they all belong to the Church in Pakistan.

Adivasi Catholics

The most flourishing mission of modern times was established in the Chota-Nagpur district among the adivasis or aboriginals. These people never belonged to the Hindu fold. At the time of the Aryan invasions they had been forced to flee to the jungles and hills, where they cleared forests, drained swamps and developed their own way of life with their own form of government, their own culture and religion. However, in the course of the 17th century, their nominal heads began to act like Rajahs with absolute powers, invited or welcomed outsiders to whom they assigned lands in fief, thus converting many of the adivasis into serfs. There was a danger that these people would not survive this crisis and even cease to exist as a unique ethnic group.

In 1862 the Belgian Jesuits were entrusted with the Calcutta Vicariate, in the territory of which Chota Nagpur was located. In the first decades they were fully occupied with the christians, either remnants of the ancient Augustinian Mission or more recent arrivals from various parts of India living in the more populous towns. It was only in 1882 that a man could be spared to initiate the mission-work in Chota Nagpur where the Protestants had already established centres (1848-50). He was Constant Lievens, a man equal in structure and charismatic gifts to a St. Francis Xavier or a De Nobili. He first studied the situation and soon understood that much of the misery among these people stemmed from the fact that they had been or were in the process of being deprived of their lands and that money-lenders to a large extent controlled their economy. He therefore studied the intricacies of the law pertaining to landtenure and began defending the rights of the people in the Courts. After he had won a number of cases more and more people approached him. Soon it became a veritable stampede. Day and night he was occupied with their problems. For days they would camp near his home, patiently awaiting their turn to explain their plight. But slowly on they began to realise that he had something more to offer than material relief. They began asking for baptism. Soon whole villages had become christian.

Though he always insisted that the people should abide by the law and follow its procedures, there were prejudiced and interested parties who accused him of fomenting a revolt (1889). Even some British officials sided with the accusers. After surmounting this crisis, on the outcome of which depended the future of the community, he continued his activities. Finally after ten years of intense labour he was completely exhausted and was forced to return to his native Belgium where he died in 1895 a lonely and unknown man. Since he and those who had been appointed to aid him, being so few in number, had not been able to instruct all these people thoroughly, some there were, prophets of doom, who predicted that what he had built up would collapse. However, among those who succeeded him there were stalwarts, such as Fr. Grosjean who consolidated and expanded his work so that by 1921, when Chota Nagpur was organised into the diocese of Ranchi, there were 170,000 christians and catechumens with a well developed school system, cooperatives and best of all, seminaries and convents where candidates from among these self same adivasis were being trained for the priesthood and the religious life. The work continued to prosper so much so that the Belgian Jesuits were compelled to appeal to others to come to their aid. Jesuits from other Provinces and Divine Word Fathers responded. In 1951 certain areas were dismembered from Ranchi diocese and constituted into the diocese of Sambalpur and Raigarh Ambikapur. Bishop Severin of Ranchi was transferred to the last named bishopric and Ranchi received its first Adivasi Bishop, Nicolas Kunsur S. J.. At present in the three dioceses, two of which are headed by sons of the soil, the number of catholics and catechumens has exceeded the half-million mark and more and more parishes and institutions are being staffed by priests and religious recruited from among the adivasis.

Work among the aboriginals was also undertaken in other parts of India, the most important being the one initiated in 1889 by German Salvatorians in the Garo and Kasi hills of Assam. Their work was interrupted by World War I when the missionaries were interned. After the war they were replaced by Salesians of Don Bosco, who continued and expanded the work of the pioneers, so that at present the territory has been divided into several dioceses and the number of catholics has increased to between 100,000 and 200,000.

Shortly before World War I another group of adivasis was app-

roached. They were the Santals inhabiting chiefly areas to the
east of Ranchi. It was only some years after the World War I
that any real progress could be made there. The Jesuits from
Malta and from Chicago-Detroit were the first to pursue this work.
In the diocese of Dinajpur however the success among the Santals
was not on the same scale as in Patna. In 1938 the Jesuits invited
Third-Order Franciscans (T. O. R.) to share their labours. Subsequently in 1956 a Prefecture, Bhagalpur, which has since become
a diocese, was erected and entrusted to them. For the other
successful mission to the Santals, a special diocese also was erected, that of Dumka in 1962.

A group which proved to be very difficult to approach was
the Bhils of Rajputana. Beginning in 1892 the French Capuchins, among them great men like Frs. Charles and Bernard, man-
fully set to work and with incredible hardships and perseverance
built up a community numbering a few thousands.

Whatever progress was made or still to be made in the following years was not exclusively due to an increase in personnel. It
was partly due also to a better organization of the Indian Church.
Leo XIII erected an Apostolic Delegation for India and Ceylon
in 1884, and the same year he abolished the Padroado jurisdiction in a number of Vicariates. It was extended to Malacca in
1889, to Burma in 1920, to Goa in 1923. Henceforth there would
be a representative of the Holy See to advise and encourage, to
investigate and to report.

Indianisation

Though the number of missionaries from abroad increased
and would continue to do so during the coming years, as long
as the Indian Church depended on foreign help for her personnel
and resources her own character could not be maintained and
developed. As a matter of fact there were events in the offing,
among them the two world-wars, which would have seriously
compromised the Church if they had not been largely neutraliz-
ed by those who had pressed for a quicker tempo of indianisation
especially among the clergy. Fortunately, a beginning had long
ago been made. In the Syro-Malabar church and in the Portu-

guese enclaves the clergy was almost entirely Indian. In those regions which at one time had belonged to Portugal or to which catholics had migrated, there too the clergy was indigenous. But in vast areas, chiefly in the North, there were no Indian priests at all. Thus the report of the visitation Bishops Bonnard and Carbonneaux held in 1858-62, reveals that in the extensive Vicariates of Vishakapatnam, Hyderabad, Dacca, Calcutta, Patna and Agra there was not a single Indian priests. We therefore find that henceforth more attention was paid to the recruitment and training of an Indian clergy. A number of Seminaries were erected which culminated in the establishment of a Papal Seminary in 1894 by Leo XIII and entrusted to Belgian Jesuits. It was located in Kandy, Ceylon, the same place where the Apostolic Delegation functioned before it was moved to Bangalore. Subsequently, after independence, it was shifted to Poona.

As far as Indian Clerical Orders are concerned only two were founded before 1900, the first the Carmelites of Mary Immaculate of the Syro-Malabar Rite in 1831 and the Society of St. Francis Xavier (Pilar Fathers), Goa in 1887. The first is a religious congregation, but the second was initially an Institute of diocesan priests, which in 1939 was reorganized and converted into a religious society.

It was only in the course of the 19th century that Sisters began taking part in the missionary activities of the Church. The first ones to come to India from abroad were the Religious of Jesus and Mary (RJM—1842, Agra), the Institute of the Blessed Virgin Mary Loretto (IBVM, 1853, Patna) and the Daughters of the Cross (DC) of Liege (1862, Karachi). They were followed by any number of Congregations. All of them soon began accepting candidates from India. However, it is remarkable that the integration of Sisters in the apostolate of the Indian Church as a matter of fact antedated the coming of the first Sisters from abroad. Already in 1750 Fr. Ansaldo S.J. had founded the Congregation of St. Aloysius Gonzaga at Pondicherry. Since then any number of religious institutes were established, the earliest being the Congregation of the Immaculate Heart of Mary (1844, Pondicherry), the Franciscan Presentation Sisters (1853, Coimbatore) the Congregation of Our Lady of Dolours (1854, Trichinapoly), the Franciscan Bon Secours Sisters (1858, Pondi-

17

cherry), the congregation of St. Anne of Madras (1863), the Syro-Malabar Carmelite congregation (1866, Kerala). The earliest Congregations of Adivasi Sisters were the daughters of St. Anne of Ranchi, founded in 1897 by Archbishop Goethals S.J. of Calcutta and the Handmaids of the Lord (Prabhudasi Sisters) founded in 1906 by Bishop Caumont OFM Cap of Ajmer. The first Monastery of contemplative nuns was that of the Carmelites in Pondicherry. The first Poor Clare Convent was founded much later, during World War II.

The first Congregations of Brothers to associate themselves with the work of the Indian Church were the Patrician Brothers (Madras, 1880), the Irish Christian Brothers (Bengal) and the St. Gabriel Brothers (Pondicherry, 1903). The first Congregation to be founded in India was that of the Franciscan Missionary Brothers of Borivli. Originally a group of German Tertiaries, they were organized into a Congregation in 1895. Since then several Institutes or Societies have been founded, but except the Sacred Heart Brothers (Trichinopoly, 1903), their numbers have remained small.

World War I and aftermath

While the Church in India was showing signs of renewed vigour, World War I erupted causing a serious setback. German missionaries such as the Jesuits of Bombay and Poona and the Salvatorians in Assam were interned. A number of missionaries of military age, such as the French, were called up. Few if any priests were able to leave war-torn Europe to take their places. It was difficult to maintain the existing institutions, not to speak of expansion.

After the cessation of hostilities it took some time before normal communications were restorted and it was possible to recruit, train and dispatch a sufficient number of missionaries not only to restore the depleted ranks but also to undertake new assignments. We then witness a phenomenon similar to the one we observed prior to the war: a multiplication of ecclesiastical units, a steady inflow of personnel both from the Missionary Institutes and Religious Orders already in the field and from those venturing for the first time into India. At the same time the number of Seminaries, Novitiates and Scholasticates were increased and more and more Congregations, both in the Latin and Syro-Malabar Churches, were founded.

Due to a greater availability of personnel, it was possible to undertake more activities in the charitable and educational fields. More and more schools and colleges were opened. They were meant in the first place to cater to the needs of the catholics, but slowly they began attracting more and more students from the other communities. Though the imparting of a good education in all its aspects was the direct aim of these centres of learning, it was hoped it would also lead to an acceptance of Christ by at least a number of students. But this was not realized and a controversy ensued whether it was wise to continue them, especially the Colleges, where the number of Catholics was minimal. At present their continued existence is not questioned so much, as whether they should not be entrusted to efficient and capable laymen and laywomen.

As far as charitable institutions, such as Orphanages, Homes for the Aged and Refugees, Dispensaries and what not, are concerned, their number increased rapidly. On the other hand very few Hospitals were being operated. In 1935 there were hardly half a dozen. In this field the other Christians held the lead. However, a change occurred after Dr. Anna Dangel appeared on the scene. Born in Tyrol, she was one of the first ladies to take up medicine as a career. After finishing Medical School, she came to Rawalpindi to serve in the hospital the Franciscan Missionaries of Mary maintained in that city. It was there she learned from experience how great the need for more medical facilities really was. She therefore left India and found her own Congregation of Sisters, the Catholic Medical Missionaries. Having thus been assured of a steady flow of nurses and doctors, she returned to Rawalpindi, took over the hospital where she had once worked and founded others. She was also instrumental in modifying the then Church-legislation forbidding Sisters to work in Maternity Homes or Wards. Since then the number of Hospitals run by Sisters has steadily grown. All this activity in the medical field on the part of the Church culminated in the founding of St. John's Medical College, Bangalore. But this occurred in 1966, some years after Indepedence.

Notwithstanding the efforts made on the part of so many dedicated persons, during this period Christianity made little impact on the country as far as the number of catholics is concerned. In 1921 they counted 5,966,000 i. e. 1.77 percentage of the total population.

During the interwar period great changes were taking place in the country which were bound to affect the future of the Church as well. There were demands for greater participation in the matter of government on the part of some, for full independence on the part of others. This movement, however, did not appear like a bolt from the blue. It had been prepared in the recesses of the previous years. One of the most important factors was the revival of Hinduism, which in the days of its weakness and early confrontation with Christianity and scientific advancement had withdrawn into its shell towards the end of the 17th and the beginning of the 18th century. It was inaugurated by Ram Mohan Roy (1772-1833) and his Brahmo Samaj (1826) and carried forward by a group of stalwarts who either joined Roy's Samaj or founded their own. Their combined efforts in the end produced the Neo-Hinduism, which owed a great deal of its inspiration to Christianity. This revival would supply a religious basis for the ensuing struggle, so essential and necessary for any movement to succeed in a land like India, whose traditions are bound up with the search for the divine.

During the latter part of the period which witnessed a revival of Hinduism also witnessed a growing understanding among sections of the population. Clerks and other personnel serving the British were showing signs they were not prepared to remain permanently insubordinate positions. Graduates from the Universities the British had established, when they discovered they were unable to obtain positions commensurate with the effort expended grew restive. These and others began formulating their grievances and their demands for change, for concerted efforts to achieve Swaraj. In 1885 the Indian National Congress was founded. Though in the beginning caution and moderation reigned in its ranks, it was this body, when others took over the leadership, which almost unbidden forged the nation into a single force and with the weapons of non-violence and non-cooperation would wrest independence from the British.

National Cause and Further Indianisation

In the struggle for Independence the catholics did not play an important role. They were not in a position to do so. Politically they were an insignificant minority. All the big issues were decided by the majority communities. Moreover they, like so many of other persuasions, had become enamoured of the peace and security the British Rule had offered the country for so many years. They felt uneasy and uncertain about the future. What would their future be when the giants of the movement would be replaced and men of lesser calibre, especially those who had climbed the bandwagon after the outcome of the struggle was no longer in the balance. Even then there was no doubt where their sympathies lay. Those who lived through those momentous days can still recall with what pride so many catholics spoke of their leaders and the hopes they entertained. Some of them joined the Congress, participated in its activities and on this account suffered. Finally notwithstanding the doubts some entertained, they deliberately those to trust the leaders and refused to press for separate presentation. That their confidence was not misplaced, subsequent events confirmed. Not only were they consulted by the Advisory Committee (1948), but several Catholics were members of the body which drafted the Constitution. By virtue of this fundamental document India proclaimed itself a Secular Democratic State, subsequently Republic. Full freedom of persons and religious persuasions was guaranteed. All citizens, irrespective of caste or creed, would enjoy the same rights and privileges. It can hardly be doubted that the framers of the Constitution drew on a number of Christian principles, thus proving that the influence of Christianity was greater than their number would indicate. The guarantees contained in the Constitution were more than sufficient to allay the doubts and elicit the loyalty of even the most skeptical. Hence it was not surprising that at the first elections a number of Christians were voted into office and that subsequently some were given responsible positions even that of the State Governor. Finally as early as 1948 India and the Vatican exchanged diplomatic representatives.

Before Independence the Indian Hierarchy realized the need for closer contact between its members in order to meet the challenges of the times. There would be misunderstandings, conflicts perhaps with the Government or its representatives, clarifications needed regarding certain customs or convictions.

The church at large needed special guidance chiefly during the first years after Independence. To discover solutions to these and other problems and facilitate communication with the authorities, it was decided in 1944 to institute the Catholic Bishops Conference of India with a number of Committees, each headed by an Archbishop with a staff competent to act in a given field. A few years later, in 1950, a National Synod was convened at Bangalore. It was under the Presidentship of Cardinal Gilroy of Melbourne. A uniform code was drawn up for the Indian Church, taking local conditions, customs and changed circumstances into consideration. It was in this manner the Bishops prepared themselves not only to build up the Church but also to meet the opposition.

Though the majority of Hindus belonged to the Congress, which favoured a secular state, there were some who throughout agitated for the creation of a Hindu State and a nostalgic return to the idealistic days, as described in the ancient Vedas and Upanishads. They opposed the partition of Mother India and disagreed with Gandhiji as far as his non-violent approach was concerned.

In 1954 a Committee was constituted in Madhya Pradesh where the Jana Sangh—a rightist party—is particularly strong, under the Presidentship of ex-Justice Nyogi to investigate the activities of the Church, frame charges so as to justify the introduction of legislation in the hope of preventing further conversions to Christianity. Its publication created a stir. On the whole it was rejected as biased. Notwithstanding in Madhya Pradesh and elsewhere the missionaries or those who approach them are being harassed or warned. In some cases charges are framed against them and they are obliged to appear in Court. Anti-Christian propaganda is circulated, even among the adivasis, whom many Hindus somehow now wish to include in their fold.

But believers in militant Hinduism are not the only ones for whom Christianity is suspect. There are others as well, those who in the period of their formation imbibed a purely secular or positivistic spirit and above all those who have come under communistic influence especially in Bengal, Andhra Pradesh and Kerala, the most Christian State. At present though divided in their allegiance, they wield great influence not only among the poor and disgruntled, but also among believers in idealistic Socialism.

For various reasons, from the year 1953-54, the entry of foreign missionaries was restricted. In fact this legislation has contributed towards the development of the Indian Church. Henceforth she has had to rely on her own resources. Actually the number of vocations to the priesthood and the religious life in India has considerably increased. A glance at the statistics as published in the latest Catholic Directory (1969) suffices to prove the statement.

	Priests	Brothers	Sisters
Indian	7884	1794	28,298
Foreign	796	342	2,007

The hierarchy too is almost completely Indian. All the bishops of the Syro-Malabar Church since 1896 have been Indians. Those of the Syro-Malankara Church from after their reunion (1930), they too are sons of the soil. Though in the 17th century a few Goan Brahmins were elected Bishops and Vicars Apostolic, it was only in 1923 that an Indian was appointed to head a diocese of the Latin Rite. He was Tiburtius Roche, S.J. the first bishop of Tuticorin in Tamilnadu. At present of the 85 members of the Indian hierarchy only some ten are foreigners. India's first Cardinal is H.E. Valerian Cardinal Gracias, Archbishop of Bombay. He was made a Cardinal in 1953, within a decade after Independence. The second is H.E. Joseph Cardinal Parecattil, Archbishop of Ernakulam, the first Indian Oriental Prelate to be called to the Church's highest Council.

Whereas formerly the priests and religious hailed almost exclusively from areas where the missioning on the part of the Padroado had been intensive, at present recruiting is being done in all parts of the country and among all the sections of the catholic population, even among the adivasis. Best of all in recent years there has been a veritable upsurge in the number of vocations in the Syro-Malabar Church.

The personnel of the Church has become rooted in the soil without any great difficulty. A more crucial problem still, but one of equal if not greater urgency, was the indianization of the Church as a whole, including the clergy. The Church, as far as her external manifestations, the formations of her doctrines and the celebration of her mysteries are concerned, hardly blended into the environment or appealed to the religious mentality of the average Indian. Her priests were all trained in Seminaries modelled on the Tridentine pattern and the theology imparted at these institutions was one developed in the West and integrated in the Graeco-Roman culture.

Already before the Independence the question of integration into the local culture had been taken up. On all sides in the footsteps of St. Justin Martyr, the depths of India's ancient religion are being probed to discover the extent of the Word's activity even before the Incarnation or more in the tradition of a St. Gregory of Nazianza, how the sages and sanyasis of yore responded to the urgings of the Spirit and haltingly and darkly described these experiences in writings which constitute some of the richest portions of India's spiritual heritage. Fortunately it is not an uncharted sea upon which the more recent scholars are venturing. As a matter of fact it was in the nineties of the previous century that one of the pioneers flourished. He was Upadhyaya Bramabandav, a Bengali convert, but the manner and extent of his interpretation and adaptation was not accepted by the contemporary Church authorities nor perhaps could they. Imperfections and inaccuracies were to be expected as the theologians of antiquity experienced when they attempted to do the same with the Graeco-Roman culture. But they did not surrender when they discovered the first path they followed led to a dead-end. Hence neither was the Church in India finished with the trend Upadhyaya represented when what he proposed was rejected. Others, undoubtedly inspired, at least partially, by his example took up the challenge. Among the most prominent were the Jesuits Dandoy and Johanns. Unobstrusively they worked with a quiet certainty that what they were doing, would one day be accepted. What they discovered, they published in "The Light of the East" and its series founded by them.

Others were roused to follow in their footsteps, not only in the chosen field of the pioneers, but in other areas as well.

They delved into the history of the country so much of which is bound up with its religion. They examined her art and architecture, listened to her music, watched the performance of her dances, searched for the hidden meaning of her symbolism, investigated the practices of her ascetics. All this they did in a spirit of deep adaptation in order to integrate Christianity into the local culture, to demonstrate that Christ is not so much the unknown as the unnamed.

The problem of adaptation was of such magnitude as to make the claim to exclusive attention on the part of the Church seem justified. Notwithstanding, there were other issues equally important which made similar demands. First and foremost there were the new insights gained in the realm of philosophy, theology and allied sciences which rendered so much of what had been imparted at the traditional Seminaries, obsolete. And after John XXIII opened the windows and convened the Vatican Council II, what was laid down in its documents had to be studied and the directives and directions indicated had to be charted and followed. The relations with other Christians and non-Christians were also affected all this as the bonds which bind all Christians together were stressed and the salvific character of non-Christian religions was brought to the fore.

All these issues had bearing on the missionary-task of the Church. They seemed to threaten the very existence of the missionary as such. At the same time the world at large and the Church in particular were made aware of the needs of the people and some there were who raised the question whether the task of the missionary should not be identified with involvement in development-work and social uplift. Even when there was agreement on the necessity of missionary activity in the strict sense of the word, in the Indian context shouldn't this be more a witnessing by a life of contemplation and asceticism such as was proposed by Monchani and is already being practised in a lonely ashram or in the anonymity of the pilgrim-road, or should it consist of the proclamation of the Gospel as of old. Finally there were the problems to which attempts at identification with the goals of the secular, democratic welfare state like India gave rise.

In the course of the last few years all these problems and issues have been systematically studied and thoroughly discussed at a number of National Seminars. The first was convened on the occasion of the International Eucharistfc Congress in Bombay, 1964, when Paul VI, the first Pope to visit the East, came to India. The following Seminar, called the 'All-India Seminar' on Church in India' was convened in 1969 at Bangalore after three years of intense preparations. The participants—Bishops, priests, religious, laymen, and laywomen, over 600 in number—discussed all the problems affecting the life of the Church in India. The same year a second conference was held in Bangalore, which was attended chiefly by the Rectors and Professors of India's Seminaries and Scholasticates. At the International Theological Conference at Nagpur (1971) the problems of Christian life and expansion, dialogue and evangelization, development and contemplation and relations with other religions were discussed in depth.

The sole aim of all these conferences and seminars was, in as far as it is humanly possible, to prepare the Church to meet the challenge of the changing times and to discover the direction she should follow during the present crisis. In that she depends on the abiding Spirit. It is the Spirit who when the appropriate time has arrived will inspire certain individuals to cooperate with his inspirations and achieve something enduring. Already one such person has appeared on the scene and has made a deep impression on contemporary society. She is that lonely figure, strong only in the conviction that she was doing God's will, who entered that primitive *darmasala* near a kali temple to care for the dying picked up from the streets of a teeming city. She has already inspired hundreds to follow her example to care for the poor and destitute not only in India, but even beyond its borders. She is Mother Teresa of Calcutta.

CHAPTER XII

PROTESTANT CHRISTIANITY IN INDIA SINCE 1858

by T. V. Philip, Bangalore

There is a great variety of denominations and sects within Protestantism with diverse creeds and ecclesiastical politics and practices. This chapter does not attempt to give a detailed history of Protestant Christianity since 1858. What is attempted here is to select courses of events, phases of thoughts, movements here and there, which may serve to give a fair impression of the Christian movement during the last hundred years. It is the magnitude of change in a particular period which makes the historian to make a special study of that period. The period with which we are concerned in this chapter is a memorable one in Indian history. The period saw the creation of the British Empire in India, the growth of cultural renaissance in Indian society, the emergence of Indian nationalism and the final achievement of independence. The church in its varying phases of life and activities has been inevitably affected by what happened in the world both in India and abroad. For the church in India, this was a period of growth and expansion both numerical and otherwise. The growth of the ecumenical movement in the twentieth century found its expression in India in Church union movements. The national movement showed its impact in the various attempts of indigenization, of christianity and in various other national and social development activities.

Expansion of Christianity

It is true to say that Protestant missions in the 19th century, like the Roman catholic missions in the 16th century, largely followed the colonial flag. The growth of the Protestant missionary activities in the second half of the 19th century made it the most vigorous period of Protestant missions in India. For the older missionary societies such as the Church Missionary society, the London Missionary Society and the American Board of commissioners for Foreign Missions (Congregationalists) this was a period of consolidation and expansion into new territories. With the revision of the Charter of the East India Company in 1833, a large number of new missionary societies from America and the continent of Europe started work in different parts of the country. In the year 1851, it was estimated that there were only 91,092 Protestant christians in India and most of them were in South India. Only a very small percentage of protestant christians were found in N. India, and that too mainly in Bengal.[1] It was only after 1850, the protestant church began to grow.

At the beginning of the protestant missionary enterprise, conversion to christianity was slow and the approach was to convert individuals one by one. With the introduction of western education and the starting of christian schools, several educated Indians from the upper classes of Indian society were attracted to christianity and accepted baptism. This movement of educated persons to christianity continued throughout the 19th century and the first part of this century. It provided an intellectual leadership for the Indian church, but the number of such persons who accepted christianity was small. The whole of the 19th century, especially the second half of it, was a period of cultural and religious ferment in India under the influence of western culture, a ferment the first effect of which on Indian intellectuals was a reaction to Hinduism as it existed then. The hope was entertained in christian circles that soon there would be a general movement of the educated class towards christianity. But this soon proved to be wrong. True, the western impact had its results but it was in another direction. Humayun Kabir speaks of the result thus:

> There were Indians who were dazzled by their first acquaintance with western thought. With Macaulay they believed that one shelf of English books was worth the accumulated wisdom of the entire orient. Neither Macaulay nor his contemporaries realized that this was not a simple case of imposition of a European mould on the Indian mind, but a revivification of the Indian spirit which would in time create new forms of thought valid for East and West.[2]

The Western impact did not make the educated class to consider Christianity as a substitute for Hinduism, but rather to take it as a challenge to consider the plight of their religion and society in the light of the new knowledge. The western impact and the resultant awakening had its effect upon Indian politics, art, literature and thought. It created a yearning for enlightenment, the love of the country and a desire for a true and national existence. This positively led to reform movements in Indian society. To such national leaders, several of them educated in christian schools, christianity which was too closely tied up with the British Raj, did not offer an alternative to their ancestoral faith, but rather they saw in christianity an effort on the part of the foreigners to make them subservient to colonial rule. They could find no home for their new aspirations in a church order and system which appeared to them foreign and denationalizing. For these nationalists, the hope expressed by British evangelicals, such as Charles Grant and Wilberforce, that the christian missions would serve the cause of the British Empire, seemed to come true at the time of the Revolt of 1857, when the Indian christians were wholly on the side of the British.[3] Thus the role of the missionaries of this period as apologists for the empire proved to be fatal for the cause of Christianity in India. It was not surprising then, that the Indian educated class turned away from Christianity and in several cases become anti-christian. According to Muhammed Mohar Ali, the evangelizing efforts of the missionaries by the middle of the 19th century aroused considerable opposition in Bengal. The Hindus even utilized the gifts of English education in opposing missionaries. "Thus the rational criticism and historical analysis which the missionaries themselves employed to dislodge Hinduism, were adopted by the Hindus to defend their religion and criticize the doctrine of christianity...Thus in so far the missionaries furthered the cause of western education, they sharpened the weapon of which they themselves were to feel the edge."Mohar Ali continues to state that, "it was also the liberal spirit of the west which led Ram Mohan Roy to advocate the Reform of Hinduism. His followers, however, set out to use a reformed Hinduism as a means of counteracting the influence of Christianity...The expectation of Duff and others that young Bengal would be the forerunner of a generation of educated and influential converts were thus largely belied. Young Bengal was first an encouragement, then a enigma and ultimately a disappointment to the missionaries."[4]

The balt of the numerical growth of protestant christians

in India was thus not due to the conversion of Indian intellectuals from higher castes of Indian Society, but by group or mass
movements from the depressed classes and aboriginal tribes.

Mass movement was not an uncommon feature in the history
of the Church in India. In the 16th century, Francis Xavier
baptized the fishermen of the south western part of India in
large numbers. In the first half of the 19th century, there was a
mass movement to Christianity in the Tinnevelly area. But the
years between 1870 and 1930 was the real period of mass movements. During this period the attention of Christian mission was
turned to the tribal people in W. Bengal, Central India, in the
Nilgiri Hills and in North East India; and to the depressed classes in south Travancore, Tamil Nadu, Andhra Pradesh, United
Province and North Western India. Today the protestant christian community is largely made up of converts from these groups.
In 1930 it was estimated that 80% of protestant christians were
the products of mass movement. Julius Richter points out that
a good four-fifths of the entire success of protestant missionary
work in India was realized among the Panchamas. According to
Richter, in 1871 there were 160,955 protestant christians in India,
by 1900 the figure was 506,019. In 1831 there were only 31
baptized christians among the Kols in Bihar, but in 1881, the
number was 441,000.5 The christian mission was established
among the Nagas in North India in 1886. The growth of the
church was so rapid among the Nagas that by 1950 the christian
population among the Nagas was 50,000.

In the period between 1870-1920, India faced a series of
famines and plagues. Those of 1877 and 1900 were very severe.
In the midst of such calamities, christian churches were active
in organizing relief work. A large number of people were saved
from starvation and death and great mass movements of christianity happened just after the famines or during the famines.
It is commonly assumed that people from depressed classes have
become christians for economic or for motives other than spiritual. It is true that in many cases, mass movements occurred in
times of famine and social deprivations. It is also true that motives for conversion were not always purely religious. Help in times
of famine or epidemic, support against oppression by land lords
and money lenders, hope for better social standards, education

for their children, chances of employment in christian institutions and other such motives might have contributed to their decisions for baptism.6 But it is a mistake to think that such motives alone caused conversions. The work of the christian church among the depressed classes of people is a glorious chapter in the history of Christianity in India. The stigma of untouchability that rested upon them for generations had condemned them to a semi-human existence. They were systematically exploited and kept down for centuries by caste people. For many who joined the church, it represented an escape from the dehumanizing values and conditions of their existence. It was its concern for personal dignity and equality of persons which gave the Gospel relevance and appeal among the outcastes. With the liberation from various social and cultural limitations and with the educational facilities provided by the Church, the converts from outcastes and underprivileged groups made a striking progress in their social and cultural life. This itself was enough justification for the work of the church among these people, and was a contribution which the church made to the national life. The very fact that these people were considered as human beings, with dignity and freedom, and brought to the fellowship of the church was a judgement on the practice of untouchability and a source of tension within the larger Indian society. In the twentieth century, the national movement under the leadership of Mahatma Gandhi took it as its special responsibility to work for the uplift of the outcastes. Moreover the backward class themselves became conscious of their rights and privileges, and got organized under the leadership of people like Ambedkar to demand their right place in society. It was all these which led to the abolition of untouchability by legislation and other measures taken by the Indian government to improve the social conditions of these people.

One ought to speak in the same enthusiastic terms of the work of the christian church among the tribals. The mission of the church has been at work among the tribals of India for roughly between 75 and 125 years. It is estimated that 10-15% of the total christian population in India are tribal christians. The church has rendered three major services to the tribals. The church spread christianity, established centres of education and

promoted medical services among the tribals.7 The church established educational institutions and they were taught reading, writing
and arithmetic. Besides general education, the church gave technical
education to tribal youth. Some churches worked out plans and
programmes for the economic uplift of the tribal people. The
co-operative credit movements in Chotanagpur initiated by the
Gossner Mission as well as the Roman catholic mission are
worth mentioning. In the field of health and hygiene the church
has rendered marvellous service to the tribals.8 Speaking of the
impact of Christianity on the tribal people, the authors of *Tribal
Awakening* point out: 1. the tribals became owners of land and
they were freed from forced labour and other economic injusti-
ces previously done to them; 2. Christianity gave the tribals a
unique social position in relation to their neighbours; 3. They
were freed from inferiority complexes; 4. They got spiritual
freedom. For generations their spirit was under the bondage of
the fear of malevolent spirits. Christianity gave a death blow to
this evil spiritual mechanism that kept the tribal spirit in bondage. Neither education nor contacts with non-tribals could give
them spiritual release. It was only the Gospel of Jesus Christ
that gave a new beginning, a new hope, a new life for the tribals.
In the face of disintegration of tribal society a new hope was
created in and through the fellowship of Christians in the Church.
The liberating force of the Gospel was not limited to the Christian community alone. Even the non-Christian tribals and the
backward communities experienced the social liberation effected
by Christianity.9

A study of the mass movements to christianity reveals the
fact that the real agents in many cases in spreading the Gospel
among the outcastes and the tribals were not the western missionaries or the paid evangelists, but a large number of ordinary
christian men and women who refused to leave their village or
tribe to escape to the security of the 'mission compound', but
chose to stay with their people and witnessed among them to
the new life they had received in Jesus Christ. It has been reported about the Chotanagpur area that "the success of mission
in Chotanagpur did not depend upon the foreign missionaries
alone. Christianity spread like wild fire through the efforts of
the tribal christians themselves."10

Protestant churches and social activities

The period since 1857 was not only a period of great missionary expansion, it was also a period of expansion in the social activities of the church. In the first half of the 19th century, the social activities of christian missions were directed towards bringing about a moral reform in Indian society and to emancipate individuals from the age old superstitions and the tyrannical power exercised by Hindu religion. In this effort the missionaries had the support of the western liberals. For both the western liberals and the evangelicals, the traditional, social and religious institutions were responsible for poverty and social stagnation in Indian society. They demanded open government patronage for their vigorous warfare upon the abuses associated with Hindu religion such as *sati*, infanticide, plight of the Hindu widow. With the support of the liberals and the missionaries, William Bentick initiated several measures of social and moral reforms. But the revolt of 1857 made the government to revise its policy. There was a general feeling among the British administrators in India and a section of the people in England that among the causes for the revolt of 1857 were the social reforms initiated by the government in 1840 and the attack made by the missionaries on Hindu religion and society. Since 1857 it became more or less the accepted policy of the government not to tamper with the religious and social institutions of the people of India. And by the middle of the 19th century, British liberalism had lost much of its self-confidence and reforming zeal. The loss of popular as well as official support curtailed very much the political power of the missionaries and their reforming activities. Moreover, with the rise of Indian national movement in the second half of the century, the leadership for reform of Indian religions and society went into the hands of the Indian nationalists and intellectuals. This led to a shift of emphasis, after 1857, in protestant social activities. The social activities in the second half of the 19th century, though they increased in number, were mainly confined to philanthropic activities, such as establishing and maintaining schools, orphanages, hospitals, leper asylums and agricultural and industrial training institutions. The great increase in the membership of the Church due to mass movements during this period turned the attention of the church and christian agencies from the society at large to the Church. The pastoral responsibility for the new converts compelled the church to be concerned with their total life including economic and social aspects. Thus the building up of a christian church with a strong economic, social and educational basis became their chief concern after 1857 and all social activities were primarily directed to this end.

Education was part of the protestant missionary activity from the very beginning. In the period prior to 1833, establishing and maintaining elementary schools, teaching through the medium of Indian languages formed the bulk of christian educational enterprise. In the period between 1833-1857 the emphasis was on secondary schools and colleges teaching through the medium of English. This change was dictated by two reasons. In the first place English education was seen as a means to evangelize the youth for the upper classes of Indian society. It was believed that a study of western science and literature would undermine the faith of the students in Hinduism and thus would prepare the way for them to accept Christianity. In the second place, financial assistance was available from the government for private English schools. This was made possible by Wood's Educational Despatch of 1854. At a time when private agencies other than the christian agencies hardly existed and the grant-in-aid system mainly benefited christian educational enterprise. Thus the period between 1833-1857 was the age of christian schools and it was during this period that some of the outstanding Christian colleges of our century such as the Madras Christian College, Noble College at Masulipatanam, Hislop College at Nagpur, and St. John's College at Agra, were founded. These Christian colleges and schools exerted a dominant influence on Indian education and Indian thought.

After 1858 the government was reluctant to give a free hand to missions in the educational field and new restrictions were placed on private schools which discouraged many of the educational agencies. Moreover, christians began to feel disappointed with the small number of converts made through their schools. This led to a rethinking on the part of missions as to the place of educational institutions, especially that of English schools in the whole missionary work of the Church and after 1870 several missions directed their attention to establishing more village schools rather than English schools. By the end of the 19th

century, government and other private agencies began to domi-
nate the field of higher education and christian educational enterprise lost its preeminent place except in the area of womens'
education.

The pioneers in the field of womens' education were the
christian agencies. Since 1870, a large number of schools and
colleges were established for women by the protestant churches
throughout India. Womens' christian College in Madras, Iza-
bella Thoburn College in Lucknow, Sarah Tucker College in
Palamcottah and Lady Deak College in Madurai are some of
them. The fact that some of the first women graduates of Indian
universities were christians as well as products of christian colleges is a testimony to the pioneering effort of christians in this
field. The christian educational work for girls provided an impulse both for the government and other agencies to found
schools for girls. Reformers like Gokhale began to impress upon
the Hindu mind the need for better educational facilities for
women. By 1900, the Arya Samaj, Theosophical Society, Rama-
krishna Mission and other agencies began to take interest in
womens' education.

After 1920, the protestant educational enterprise expanded
very little, though the number of Roman catholic schools and
colleges increased considerably. The emphasis in this century
among the protestant educationalists was on quality rather than
on quantity. It is very hard to say whether they have succeeded
in this aim, or not. In 1932, a central board of Christian higher
education was established under the National Christian Council
of India to coordinate the work of the various protestant colleges.
In 1966, at a consultation of Principals of Roman catholic and
protestant colleges held at Tambaram, Madras, a National Board
of Christian Higher Education was formed in order to bring about
cooperation between protestant and Roman catholic efforts in
higher education. The Madras consultation defined the aim of
Christian educational activity as helping in the nation-building
activity in a developing nation; this was definitely a departure
from the earlier view held on the aim of christian schools as a
preparation for the Gospel and training leadership for the
church.

Medical work came to occupy an outstanding position in

the church's activity after 1870 and continues to be so even now. The terrible inadequacy of medical facilities in India induced christian agencies to start hospitals and Dispensaries both in cities and villages. In 1898 it was estimated that there was only one doctor for 300,000 people. Since 1880, the Zenana medical mission was founded to bring medical aid to the women and children of India. Since medical work required trained doctors and nurses, christian medical colleges and Nurses' Training Institutes were started throughout the country during the last hundred years. Today some of the hospitals and medical schools in the country are run by protestant agencies. Vellore Medical College (and hospital) is considered as the biggest single medical college in Asia. The medical College at Ludhiana also had a fine record of pioneering in medical education for women. In the training of nurses and in the department of nursing generally christians have made a distinctive contribution to the national life. For many years Anglo-Indians and Indian christians were almost the only candidates for the nursing profession. In 1940 it was estimated that about 90% of all the nurses in the country were christians and about 80% of these had been trained in christian hospitals. The protestant medical work also included establishing and maintaining several Tuberculosis sanatoria, leprosy, asylums, mental hospitals and more recently psychiatric clinics: In 1926, the Christian medical association of India was founded under the auspices of the National Christian Council of India. It sponsors various forms of medical service and is the central consultative body for protestant medical work in India. At the beginning, medical work was seen as only a part and aid to the evangelistic activity of the church. It is now more and more recognized that the ministry of healing is not simply an aid to convert others to christianity but that it in itself is a valid form of Christian service.

Besides schools and hospitals, the social activities of the church included a large number of other philanthropic and social activities. Every great famine left behind a large number of orphans and widows. Several orphanages and widows' homes were established by the christians. During this period of which the most famous one was the widows' home started by Pandit Rama-Bai near Poona. Since most of the protestant christians came from the economically and socially backward classes, several industrial and agricultural projects were established in order to improve their condition. The Basel mission on the west coast of south India became well known for its tile making and textile industries. Carpentry, furniture making and other crafts were taught to poor christians in Sholapur, Nazareth in Tamilnadu, Tumkur and in several other places. After 1920, there was a great emphasis on rural education and reconstruction programmes in the protestant social activity. The Y. M. C. A., the S. C. M. and the National Missionary Society were in the forefront of rural reconstruction work. Many of those who took part in the rural work were greatly influenced by Mahatma Gandhi's call for the uplift of India's rural population.

Protestant christian Community and the national movement

The period of fifty years following the rebellion of 1857 was characterized by the rapid growth of national consciousness among the Indians which resulted in the struggle for political freedom and the achievement of it in 1947.

The destruction of Indian economy by the British and the attack upon social organization and culture, reducing India to an economic and cultural colony of the west aroused a protest among the Indians which gathered momentum as the time went on. Political subjugation and the resulting misery and humiliation led the educated Indians to search for 'self-identity' in India's past history. Ancient literature, philosophy, science, law, art and monuments which had been buried in oblivion for years were raised to life. In this effort they were greatly helped by the oriental scholars from the west. The rediscovery of India's past cultural heritage gave them a sense of pride in their own nation which provided a powerful incentive to the growth of nationalism. Thus the ground was prepared for political agitation against the colonial rule.

The Indian National Congress was organized in 1885. In the beginning, the congress leadership was in the hands of the educated middle class who were liberals in their political creed. They were not fighting for political independence from the British rule, but only for more Indian participation in the government, and for social and economic improvement. But as the leadership of the Congress went into the hands of Mahatma Gandhi con-

gress became a mass based militant organization, with complete
political independence as its goal. The rising national consciousness and the struggle for political freedom have formed the background for the Church's life and mission since the latter part of
the 19th century.

In the early days of the Indian national congress a number
of Indian christians actively supported it.[11]   At the Madras
meeting of the Congress in 1887, out of 607 delegates, 35 were
christians. The Indian christian community was also represented
at the next four sessions of the Congress. The proportion of
Indian christian delegates to the Congress sessions was very
much higher than their proportion in the population. Some of
the prominent christian leaders in the Congress in this period
were R. S N. Subramania, a prominent barrister from Madras,
Kali Charan Banerji from Bengal, G.G. Nath a barrister from
Lahore, Peter Paul Pillai of Madras and a Madusudan das, a
lawyer from Orissa. Among the women special mention must be
made of Pandit Rambbai the well known christian social reformer. She attended the Bombay meeting of the Congress in 1888,
along with two other christian women. Kali Charan Banerji was
the leader of the Bengal christian community and he was
an eminent scholar, brilliant orator and for many years the most
respected and influential Indian christian in congress circles.

But by the turn of the century, the Christian participation in
the Congress sessions declined considerably and it continued to be
so in the first decades of the century. There were reasons for this
decline. At the beginning of the Congress, the British authorities
in India did not see in it any real danger to the British administration. All that they anticipated was that the Congress would
provide a forum of Indian intellectuals to vent their feelings. Moreover, during the early period of the Congress, the demands of the
Congress were very moderate and there was no revolutionary fer-
vour in the speeches made and the resolutions passed at the
Congress sessions. The presidential addresses at the Congress
sessions "recounted the benefits of India's loyalty to the Crown
and reiterated India's desire to remain within the British empire.[12]
As the Congress began to agitate for political freedom, especially with the appearance of Bal Gangadhar Tilak and Ara-
vind Gosh, the British began to take a suspicious and even hostile

attitude to the Congress activities. The congress was attacked by officials in India and was strongly criticized in the British Parliament. Consequently the western missionaries in India and the Indian christians who were under the influence of missionaries began to leave the congress with apprehension. They began to fear being regarded as disloyal to the government if they participated in the Congress and were anxious about the future of the christian community in case India became an Independent democracy dominated by Hindu majority.

In 1890 W. Harper a missionary claimed that Muslims and Parsis had already parted company with the Congress and that it had virtually become an organization of the Hindus and Christians. He warned Christians that "this alone should be a matter for reflection to the christian community". They are so few that they can hardly be spoken of as a minority, and they are completely at the mercy of the Hindu associates."[13] By 1900 this fear of Hindu domination was generally shared by the christian community. In 1908 Joseph J. Ghose writing on Indian Christians and the national movement, expressed the view that participation in the national movement would be detrimental to the christian community. He said :

"We do not know in what way it will of any advantage to the Indian christians if they joined the non-christians in political agitation. If further political rights and privileges are granted to the people of this country, our poor and small community will not have the remotest chance to be profited by them. On the other hand greater powers in the hands of non-christians may prove dangerous to the very life of our community. We know by experience that wherever the non-christians are in power the poor Indian christians labour under a great disadvantage and have to suffer humiliation, indignities and even persecution."[14]

By the beginning of this century, the opposition of the British administration and the missionaries and apprehension about Hindu domination and fear of losing the favour and support of the British government led the Christian community to be estranged from the national movement. K.M. Panikkar observes :

"Christianity directly contributed but little to the growth
of nationalist feeling. The earlier of high caste converts,
Kalipad Mukkerji, Michael Madusudan Dutt and Raja
Harnam Singh remained nationally minded Indians even
after their acceptance of christianity; but with the growing estrangement between the British government to which
christians as a community looked for encouragement and the
nationalist movement whose avowed object was to recover
India's freedom, the christian community found itself
placed in a very difficult dilemma."15

This alienation of Christians from the national movement
continued into the 20th century. The National Christian Council
which is the coordinating body of the protestant churches at the
national level was not able to take a definite stand on the nation's struggle for political freedom. With regard to this, Khaj
Bhago's comment is important. He says, "Prayer for peace was
the repeated answer of the N.C.C. Review to the pressing political problems, and one cannot hold back the remark that the
frequent calls to that issued from the NCC in the years seem
to have been just about the only contribution the council found
possible to give to the nation's struggle for freedom."16

According to Bhago, the main reason for the inability of the
NCC to give a lead to the protestant christian community in
the responsibility to the nation was the missionary influence
and domination in the NCC. Most British missionaries found
it difficult to stand against the government of their country and
so far as the non-British missionaries were concerned, they were
bound after 1920 by rather strict rules. They were required to
abstain from participation in political affairs but were rather to
work in friendly cooperation with the Government. The educationalists among them had to take a pledge that they would
promote loyalty to the government and make pupils good citizens
of the British empire. What is interesting was that the missionaries demanded the same loyalty to the government from Indian
christians in the service of missions.

In spite of all these, even in the first decade of this century
there were several far sighted and courageous christians who,
in the tradition laid down by Kali Chandran Banerji and others,
wanted the christian community to be part of the national move-

ment. Susil Rudra, S.K. Dutta, C.F. Andrews, K.T. Paul and V.S. Azaria were some of such leaders. While the majority of the western missionaries and Indian christian leaders saw the providence of God in the establishment of the British in India, and in the opportunity this provided for the christian missionary activity, C.F. Andrews saw the providence of God in Indian national awakening and actively supported the Indian national struggle. While Andrews acknowledged that Indian nationalism has the fruit of western political impacts made possible by the British rule he saw a continuity between British rule and the Indian nationalism and interpreted the whole of that history, including nationalism, within the framework of divine providence.17 By his writings and speeches he tried to awaken the Indian christians to their responsibility in the national movement. In 1908 he wrote:

> "As christians we should rather ask: Is the wakening which is now taking place all over Asia real and genuine, and has it elements which make for a higher humanity? Is the movement itself in a measure, due to the leaven of christian thought and literature, which has been working silently beneath the surface for over a century? Are the ideals, which are now gaining ground, in part at least, the outcome of the christian teaching?.............."
>
> I cannot help but feel that it should be the most serious blow to Indian christianity if the impression gained ground that Indian christians were opposed altogether to the national movement and were merely occupied in the interests of their own community.18

In a speech delivered at the World's Christian Endeavour Convention in Agra, he challenged the youth to work for the national cause thus: "Love your country with the love of Christ".19 Such a passionate involvement as that of Andrews, in the cause of Indian nationalism was not seen in any of the other western missionaries.

On the Indian christians, the name of K.T. Paul need special mention. As the secretary of the national missionary society, and later as the general secretary of the YMCA, it was he more than anybody else who prevented the christian community from becoming a communal group. He saw a 'designed place of necessity' for nationalism in the purpose of God for mankind. Speaking of the great opportunity provided by the national movement of christian heroism: "What greater opportunity can arise than the crisis of today?...To be born at this hour in India and to have the opportunity to take share in the shaping of our national destinies is perhaps the most critical point of its history, if that is not an opportunity, What is? It would not only be a lamentable missapprehension of the spirit of Christ but also a grievous neglect of a great God-given opportunity, if it is not realized that Indian christians have a tremendous duty in regard to the secular crisis in India".20 K.T. Paul knew that Indian christians could not always rely on British protection. He kept reminding the christian community again and again of the danger of policy of isolationism. He saw very clearly that the interests of the christian community were closely bound up with those of other communities. K.M. Panikkar's evaluation of K.T. Paul's contribution to the national movement is worth stating:

> Kanakarjan Paul's famous article, 'Watchman, what of the night,' may be considered the first call to christian community to realize the strength and weight of the new forces. Paul, a devout christian, was also an ardent champion of the cultural traditions of India. The alienation of the christian community from the rich inheritance of India's past was a matter of great concern for him. As the secretary General of the YMCA, in India, he was instrumental in publishing, under christian auspices, a series of valuable general studies, entitled. 'The Heritage of India', written by christian scholars but with deep understanding and general sympathy this series of books, which dealt with every aspect of India's cultural traditions, helped the Indian christians to break away from the influence of the narrow missionary attitude of looking down upon everything which was Indian.21

It took time for the Indian christians to break away from their narrow communal interest. During the first non-cooperation movement of Gandhi (1920-23), there was hardly any christian participation. "But the change had come, and in the latter phases of the struggle an increasing number of christians began to identify with the national movement."22 In the period between 1900 and 1930, K.T. Paul, S.K. Datta and V.S. Azariah formed a trio, as it were, who are to be credited with instilling nationalism in the christian community, in the face of series opposition from western missionaries as well as Indian christians. Their efforts were not in vain. In the 1930s and 40s, christians were mainly on the side of the Indian national congress in its struggle for independence. Several christian organizations such as Christian Patriot Group of Madras, Indian Christian Association, were organized to express Christian views on political matters. Realizing the need of communal harmony Indian christian leaders made several attempts to bring about reconciliation between the Muslim League and the National Congress.23

In 1945 a suggestion was made in certain quarters to create a league of minorities to safeguard the political interests of minority communities.24 It was the far-sightedness of christian leaders that made them to resist such temptations. The political maturity of the christian leaders was seen at the time of the drawing up of a constitution for independent India when they rejected the suggestion of a separate electorate for the christians. It was the result of a general realization among christians that they do not have a separate destiny different from that of other Indians and of a conviction that the task of the Church is not to fight for its own advantage, but to dedicate itself for the common good.

Growth of Indigenous Movements

The impact of the national movement on the life of the Church was seen in the rapid growth of several indigenous movements within the church. The history of protestant christianity in India in this period is in one sense the history of indigenization in church government, in worship, in theology and in several other aspects of the Church's life.

At the beginning of the protestant missionary movement, the aim was not to establish an indigenous church, but to save souls from heathenism. At the heart of the missionary theology of the 19th century there was a separation of church and mission. It focused attention on conversion but often neglected the doctrine of the Church.

In 1904 Gustav Warneck, the missionary historian, pointed out that to nearly the whole of the older missionary generation, the task of mission was "to make believers of the individual heathen, that they might be saved through faith" and "to gather those heathen who had become believers into ecclesiolae which were formed entirely after the Pietist or Methodist fashion.25 The great reality for the western missionaries was the missionary society which sent them to India and the converts in India were considered as belonging to missions and not to an Indian Church. The Indian christians themselves did not have a consciousness of belonging to an Indian church. Such a situation could hardly help the growth of an indigenous church. The christian community was controlled and supervised by the missionaries and depended upon the missionary societies in the west for everything. The missionary paternalism in the Indian Church is proverbial.26

There was hardly any effort to develop an indigenous ministry. Several of the missionary societies waited for a long time to ordain Indians as pastors. The Indian teachers and catechists were considered only as 'native agents' of missions. Too much dependence on the missionary societies made the christian community to remain as a potted plant alienated from the general soil of Indian society. Institutions and organizations were built up to commensurate with the financial ability of the western missionary societies without any relation to the economic resources of the Indian church. It is true that the majority of the christians came from the socially backward classes in India. The western missionaries were only too ready to help them in their economic difficulties. But this became a vicious circle. Long continued help made the christian community to depend more and more on aid from outside. A church which has long been dependent upon outside aid cannot be conceived as a normal healthy church. It has been deprived of the discipline and exercise needed to develop its strength and initiative to walk by itself. It can now walk only by the use of crutches, but it will not know the real freedom and joy of walking until the crutches are thrown away. The Protestant Christian community in India faces its greatest challenge at this point.

Even in the 19th century, there were some efforts to build up an indigenous church independent of missionary control. The

Indian pastor and author, Lal Behari Day, in the fifties started a
movement against the excessive missionary control of the church,
advocating that Indian ordained ministers should be put on an
equal footing with the missionaries and have membership in
the Scottish Church Council. However, the movement was quickly suppressed by Alexander Duff.27 At the Allahabad Missionary
Conference in 1872, James Baughan expressed serious concern
over the growing restlessness among the Indian Christians in Calcutta with respect to missionary power. Many or most of "educated native christians" are showing feelings of bitterness, suspicion
or dislike towards European missionaries, he said, and "hard
knocks are from time to time administered to the Missionaries, and
to their policy." He warned these radicals that as long as the "native
church" was economically dependent upon European funds, it
would be more proper to them to display patience with regard
to independence.28 In the 19th century there were also some
efforts on the part of certain missionary societies to build up a
"self-supporting, self-governing and self-propagating" Church in
India. The general feeling among the missionaries was that as
long as the Indian church was dependent on the missions for
help, it could not be treated as separate entity by itself. This view
was expressed even as late as 1910 at the Edinburgh Conference.
Edinburgh's definition of a church in the mission field is interesting. Speaking of the two features which are common to the
church in the mission field, the report says:

> On the one hand it is surrounded by a non-christian com-
> munity whom it is its function to subdue for the Kingdom;
> and on the other hand, it is in close relation with an
> older christian community from which it at first received
> the truth, which stands to it in a parental relation, and
> still offers to it such help, leadership and even control,
> as may seem appropriate to the present stage of its de-
> velopment...In some smaller fields the whole population
> has been so completely gathered into the christian fellow-
> ship that no non-christian community remains outside,
> and in some the early relation to mother and daughter
> church has practically merged into that of sisterhood, the
> younger church now being no longer dependent for the main-
> tenance of its activities on the older. This stage may not
> be capable of precise definition but when it is fully reach-

ed the younger may be regarded as passing out of the domain of "Missions" and its future course lies in the region of General Church History.29

The Edinburgh statement reflected the general thinking of the missionary societies, and for the missionaries in India, the Christian community in India belonged only to the 'domain' of missions and not in the region of church history. Such a theology was not helpful to recognize the Indian church as an entity by itself. It was only after the growth of national movement in the twentieth century the process of recognizing the independence of the churches in India was speeded up. The national movement gave Indian Christian leaders a certain amount of self-confidence and they began to voice the demand for freedom to manage their own affairs. J. N. Farquhar wrote in 1906 that "the rise of national feeling through out India and the desire to prove the capacity of the Indians as such is one of the most remarkable features of public life today. The passions and convictions are quite strong within the Church as outside.30 There were also other factors which contributed to such a development. The ecumenical movement in this century brought to the forefront the importance of the church in the Christian message. There was a slow and steady recognition in the missionary circles that mission belongs to the church. At the Madras meeting of the International Missionary Council in 1938, the main theme was, 'The World Mission of the Church'. And also by 1950, it seemed fairly certian that the period of western domination over peoples of Asia and Africa was coming to an end. In the words of the Indian historan, K. M. Panikar, the 'Vasco da Gama era' has come to an end. The organization, methods and outlook of western missions were subjected to intense criticism not only in India but also in other countries of former colonial rule. The criticisms levelled against the christian missions in China, not only by the Communists, but also by the many Chinese Christians as well, were aimed at their connection with western civilization and western imperialism in particular and at their inability to foster a really dynamic and independent Chinese church. The awareness of such a changed world situation hastened the missionary societies to hand over their responsibilities to younger churches. In India the period between 1940 and 1960 was a period of 'devolution' in missions, and considerable progress has been made since then towards the autonomy of the Indian church, though it has not yet been fully achieved.

One aspect of indigenization that has received attention since the end of the 19th century was the effort to discover the cultural identity of the christian community with the Indian society as a whole. In the 19th century, the western Church structure and the ways of life were imposed upon the Indian Christian Community conversion to Christianity meant a break with the cultural and social traditions of the community, to which the convert previously belonged and accepting a western way of life. This was specially so in the case of individual converts from the caste Hindus. In the mass movement area, such radical social dislocation did not happen but still a western form of church structure in terms of worship, polity and theology was imposed upon them. It was among the educated caste Hindu converts that the question of 'indigenization' was seriously raised. They asked themselves: whether conversion to christianity should mean ceasing to be a member of one social group and joining another; and what aspects of his culture a convert should preserve to make them the media of the expression of his christian faith? While being loyal to its Lord they felt that the Church in India should be truly Indian, should be recognized as such, expressing and organizing the religious aspirations of the Christians in India. The growing spirit of indigenization showed itself in a gradual introduction of Indian music and Indian lyrics in worship and indigenous style in church architecture, and indigenous methods of proclaiming Christ. Some have found in the *bhakti* movement in Hinduism a means to express their devotion to Christ. Among these the most noteworthy is Narayan Vaman Tilak, a Brahmin convert to Christianity from the Maratha country. He is stated as one of the major Marathi poets. Some others have used *Kirthan* and *Kalakshepam* to sing the glories of Christ in the traditional ways of the country. There were also attempts made by certain individuals in the early part of this century to live the life of a Christian sanyasi. Narayan Vaman Tilak, B.C. Sircar and Sadhu Sunder Singh were three of them. B.C Sircar practised yoga and set up a christian shrine at Puri. The most famous among the Christian sanyasis was Sunder Singh.

Two institutional expressions of indigenization which made a very notable contribution to the life of the church in this century are the National Missionary Society of India and the Christ-ian Ashram Movement. The N.M.S. was organized in 1905 by some Indian christians, out of their concern that Indian christ-ians should have a share in the evangelization of the country. It was staffed by Indians, financed from Indian sources, and organized on inter-denominational basis. This evoked a certain amount of loyalty and devotion to it, especially among the edu-cated Indian christians. They saw in the N.M.S. the beginning of a movement that might break the 'mission compound' menta-lity of the Indian Christians and help to reorganize the Indian christian community along indigenous lines. The N.M.S. is still functioning but only in a limited way. The ashram is a very ancient institution in Indian religious tradition. Meditation and silence form the main features of an ashram. Modern Hindu Ashrams, still following the main features of the ancient ashrams, have adapted themselves to modern needs and conditions of life, and include social service as one of their objectives. Rabi-ndranath Tagor and Mahatma Gandhi gave a new impetus to the Ashram Movement in the present century. The Christian Ashram movement is of fairly recent origin and there are several christian ashrams that exist today in different parts of the coun-try. Some are interdenominational, and others belong to different churches. In the first decade of this century, the Indian christ-ians who were looking for ways of christian witness and service in keeping with the tradition of Indian spirituality found an answer in the ashram way of life and work.

A concern for indigenization of ways of life was only a part of a new attitude to Indian culture and religions that has emerged among the christians since the end of the 19th century. At the beginning of the protestant missionary movement, the missionary conception of the people, culture and religions of India was decidedly unfavourable. They shared the Western 'imperial sentiment' and cultural superiority, and agreed with Charles Grant, the spokesman of the Evangelicals in British, when he insisted that it was not any inborn weakness that made the Hindu degenerate, but the nature of their religion. For the evangelicals, India was in darkness and would need the light present in the western world. Claudius Buchanan, another spokes-man of the evangelicals, who had been in India, returned to England with a graphic description of the darkness that enveloped India. Moreover the early Protestant missionaries were children of the evangelical awakening which took place in Europe and America in the 18th and the beginning of the 19th century. They came to India with a gloomy pietistic theology which divided mankind into two parts; the converted and the unconverted, the saved and the lost. The main object of christian work was understood as saving souls of the heathen from damnation and hell. Alexander Duff, whose ideas can be considered representative of the majority of the missionaries in the 19th century, thought that though Hinduism possessed very lofty terms in its religious vocabulary, what they conveyed were only "vain and foolish, and wicked conceptions". According to Duff Hinduism spread out before us like a dark universe "where all life dies and death lives".31 The christian task for him was to do everything possible "to demolish so gigantic a fabric of idolatry and superstition".32 Such an attitude prevented any positive encounter or dialogue between Christianity and Hinduism, or the development of an Indian Christian Theology. This negative attitude was shared not only by the missionaries but also by Indian christians in general.

By the end of the 19th century there was in evidence a gradual change in this attitude. The rediscovery of India's past by oriental scholars and the growing pride in Indian cultural heritage among the Indian intellectuals and the nationalists helped the christians to develop a positive attitude to indigenous culture and religions. William Miller and A.G. Hogg of the Madras Christian College, J.N. Farquhar, S.K. Datta and K.T. Paul of the Indian Y.M.C.A., Susil Rudra and C.F. Andrews of the St. Stephen College, the members of the Madras Rethinking Group and P.D. Devanandan of the Christian Institute for the study of religion and society were some of them. J.N. Farquhar in his book, The *Crown of Hinduism* developed the idea that christianity is the fulfilment of hinduism. His thesis was that Jesus Christ and his teaching in the New Testament fulfils the true glory and genuine aspirations of Hindu religions and society. According to K.T. Paul India has been under the guidance of the Eternal Father of Mankind and has been disciplined in private ways for his purposes of love. Therefore, he said, "there are embodied in India personalities and treasures

19

in Indian culture which are waiting to be tipped by the seeker after better things.33 Such an attitude led K.T. Paul not only to make a distinction between christianity and western culture, but also to make a distinction between Christ and Christianity. Miller, Lucas and Andrews also shared this view. Bernard Lucas recognized the work of Christ and His Spirit in Hinduism, and he insisted on the necessity to consider evangelism as furthering the movement of God within Hinduism rather than to win converts to churchly christianity. In his thinking it was not necessary for the acknowledgement of Christ by a Hindu to result in a change of religious affiliation from Hinduism to Christianity. Since baptism was understood as a mark of such a change of religious affiliation, Lucas said that baptism should not have a place in the propagation of Christianity in India.34

In the present decade Indian christian thinking on the relation between christian faith and other faiths has been greatly influenced by the studies and publications of the Christian Institute for the Study of Religion and Society, at Bangalore of which P.D. Devanandan was the founder-director. According to Devanandan, the uniqueness of christian faith consists in the fact of the new creation in Christ which radically affects human relations in society. In Jesus Christ, both the Jew and gentile are brought together into one new man. The distinction between the christian and non-christian breaks down at this point. The quest of modern India for a new humanity is answered in Jesus Christ. So Devanandan called for the presence of christians at the points where questions about new humanity are being asked, and he saw the christian task within the context of christian and non-christian dialogue on common human goals and its spiritual foundation, and cooperation with all men in nation building activities. Today, though the churches still to a large extent tend to be ghetto churches, there is among many a greater awareness of the need for inter-religious dialogue and cooperation. This attitude is strengthened by the knowledge, born out of the experience of the recent past, that religion can be a disastrous source of division within a nation.

Along with the development of a positive attitude to Indian culture and religions in India, there were also attempts to develop an Indian christian theology. In the 19th century, the christian Gospel was dangerously confused with the western formulations of it. Even when the need for an Indian christian theology was recognized, it was mostly thought of in terms of translation or restating western doctrine into Indian languages or categories. "Doctrine remained unquestioned and to use a metaphor from a study by Gurukul Research Group the legitimate function of theologians in India was at the most to shape an Indian container for the milk of established doctrine and not change the milk itself...But any challenge of the doctrines themselves was to be dealt with as a heresy."35 Efforts of such people were mainly directed towards communicating the Gospel in the languages of India or using Indian philosophical categories and there was little recognition that Hinduism itself would help a new understanding of the Gospel. The missionary theologians, J. N. Farquhar, Nicol Manicol and A. G. Hogg belonged to this group.

But there were several Indian christian theologians who conceived the theological task in India not in terms of translation, but as a truly creative act in the Indian situation. While some tried to build up a christian theology on the basis of Vedanta philosophy, several others used Hindu *bhakti* tradition as a basis. For Brahmabandha Upadhyaya (1861-1907), who had become a Roman Catholic, christianity came to India as a western religion with its purity hidden under a series of unfamiliar terms and structures. But these western terms were not the only possible ones, nor were they final. The Vedanta must be made to do the same service to catholic faith in India as was done by the Greek philosophy in Europe.36 In the 20th century, indigenization of theology was attempted in a variety of ways. Special mention must be made of the work of the 'Madras Rethinking Group' in the 30's and 40's of this century. The group consisted of Indian christian thinkers largely outside the ecclesiastical polity of missions and churches and eager to develop a christian theology which could express the truth and meaning of the Gospel, christian life and experience against the background of indigenous thought and life, independent of western formulations of doctrine. They were a group representing different approaches to theology. But their concern for an indigenous church and theology united them.

P. Chenchiah, a lawyer and judge, V. Chakkarai, a pioneer
in organizing trade unions in South India, A. J. Appaswamy, a
pastor and later bishop of the church of South India, J. Jesuoasan,
the pioneer of Indian christian ashrams in India, A. N. Sunder-
sanam, editor of the *Guardian*, G. V. Job and others of the
group were all committed to Christ and at the same time were
deeply influenced by the currents of thought inspired by nationalism in the Gandhian era. Chakkarai and Chenchiah were the
leading radical thinkers among them.37   With regard to their
appearance in the Indian theological scene, D. A. Thangaswamy
says, "And then, without being heralded by portents and out of
the blue as it were, a group erupted in Madras...And 'erupted'
is the word to describe the manner in which the thinking of the
group burst upon the hitherto placid theological scene in
Madras."38 Religion was not a hobby to them, they were dead
serious about it and about its implication for daily living and
the affairs of the world. They were concerned not only with the
form of expression of christian faith but also with the content.
Chenchiah wrote: "The courage to think through the challenges
to christianity without doctrines and dogmas... may be the new
gift of the Spirit of the time to Indian christians." Theology was
an experience to them and they turned experience into theology.39

In their own time they were regarded as heretics both by the
missionaries and their fellow christians in India. The theological
seminaries did not take notice of them. Only in recent years, attempts are being made, especially by the Christian Institute for
the Study of Religion and Society (CISRS) to popularise their
writings and at present there is a renewed interest in the theology
of the Re-thinking group. In recent years, D.G. Moses has done
considerable work in developing indigenous theological thinking. There are also efforts made to the development of an indigenous theological thinking. There are also efforts made
towards developing a theology of society relevant to our time.
Both Chakkarai and Chenchiah were concerned about this question. They deplored the narrowness of the traditional conception
of christian salvation, which "leaves untouched society in its
own unchristian and anti-christian ways, with the result that the
saved man, while repenting for certain sins like sexual immorality
and a few glaring transgressions, accepts the sins of the social
order as legitimate and even participates in them for his own

advantage.40 In our day, the work of the C.I.S.R.S. and the writings of M.M. Thomas, J.B. Chandran, E.V. Matthew, S.L. Parmar and other associated with the Institute are directed towards relating the christian Gospel to contemporary political and social conditions in India and towards building up an Indian christian theology of social witness. They stress the need for the Church to be open to the world with a concern for genuine humanism in its mission to society.

Inter-Church Cooperation and Church Union Movements

At the beginning of the modern missionary movement, there was a certain amount of cooperation among the various Protestant missionary societies. But by the middle of the 19th century, as the missionary grew in strength and the missionary work expanded, the early cooperation disappeared and there began competition and even 'sheep stealing'. Such an unhappy situation led missionaries to feel the need for some kind of mutual consultations and cooperation. Even as early as 1806, William Carey of Serampore had proposed to his Board Secretary the desirability of a World Conference of missionaries to bring about some understanding among them. It was characteristic of the ecumenical situation of the time that Carey's proposal was rejected. But since 1825, there were several missionary conferences in India—local, regional and national—where the missionaries from different societies met to consider co-operation in mission. Theirs was a pragmatic approach to christian co-operation for the sake of evangelistic efficiency.

There was no questioning of denominational ecclesiology as such, but they felt that there was sufficient spiritual unity among them to cooperate in missions. But in grappling with missions and cooperation, it began to dawn on many of them that disunity is a source of weakness for the spread of the Gospel and some expressed the need for church unity. One result of such discussion was the establishment of several union institutions such as colleges and hospitals. The real impetus for Christian unity, however, came from Indian christians.

In fact it was the protest of the Indian christians against western denominationalism that led to the discussion of church unity at some of the missionary conferences. It was not surprising that initiative for church union came from Bengal where the national stirrings were felt more strongly than in other places. There a group of christians under the leadership of Kali Charan Banerjee left their churches and formed the Calcutta Christo Samaj in 1887. The purpose of Christo Samaj was the propagation of christian truth and promotion of christian union; and they hoped to gather all Indian christians within it, thereby eliminating denominationalism. They accepted only the Apostles' creed as a doctrinal basis, which to the mind of the organizers provided the broadest basis possible. They were critical of the western missions for transplanting the theological and ecclesiastical difference of the west to India, thereby dividing the Indian christians into numerous denominations. At the Bombay Missionary Conference in 1892, K. C. Banerjee said that the Indian church should be "one, not divided, native, not foreign". He made a distinction between the 'substantive' and the adjective christianity. The 'substantive' christianity consisted of the essentials of christian faith as expressed in the Apostles' creed. These essentials should and could never be changed. The 'adjective' christianity was all that had developed in the course of time with the purpose of protecting and conserving the basic truths, such as confessional statements and organizational forms. It could change from place to place. Not only in Bengal, but also in other places there were protests against Western denominationalism. A Western India Native Christian Alliance was formed in Bombay in 1871, having the same objects in view as the Christo Samaj. In 1886, a group of Indian Christians in Madras under the leadership of Parani Andy formed a National Church in India. Their intention was to build up a National Church comprising all denominations and sects. For them, it was unreasonable for Indian Christians to adhere to different western denominations which were the products of political revolutions and dissensions in Europe, particularly since Christianity was Asiatic in origin. How intensely the tragedy of denominationalism occupied the minds of Indian christians was shown in 1879, when the synods of the C. M. S. and of the American Presbyterians met in Amritsar and Lahore respectively. At these synods, the Indian clergy frankly expressed the opinion that the difficulties which stood in the way of the establishment of a National Church were caused solely by the missionaries, "Substantive christianity and not adjective christianity should alone be cultivated amongst us."41

Both the Christo Samaj of Calcutta and the National Church in Madras were started to work for a united church in India. But their efforts did not succeed. Among the reasons for the failure of such attempts in 19th century were: 1. It met with opposition from the missionaries who were unable to give up their denominational loyalty; 2. the majority of the Indian Christians, particularly the evangelists, teachers and also the poorer sections of the Christian community, found it impossible to support a fight against denominationalism for the simple reason that they were economically dependent upon the missionaries and thus tied to the denominational pattern of the Church. Thus the general opposition from the missionaries, coupled with their financial influence over a section of the Indian christian community hindered the success of the Church union movement in the 19th century. It is interesting to note that both the Christo Samaj and the National Church found their members among the educated christians who were financially independent of missions and consequently could afford to disagree with the missionaries.42 Though they did not achieve any immediate results, these attempts of the 19th century for church union are of great significance for a historian.

It has often been pointed out that it was first and foremost the situation in the 'mission fields' in Asia and Africa which gave rise to the ecumenical movement, also in the West. Transplanted to another soil outside Europe, the denominational differences suddenly seemed not only absurd, but harmful. Generally the missionaries in the end of the 19th century have been given credit for seeing this and having started the discussion which led to the Ecumenical Movement. It is a question, however, whether the credit should not go to the Indian, Chinese and Japanese christians who started the protest movements against Western denominationalism. Seen in that perspective, the Christo Samaj in Calcutta and the National Church in Madras are not without historical significance.43

The efforts made in the 19th century began to bear fruit in the 20th century. During the early years of this century some

limited church unions took place among churches of the same
confessional family. In 1901 there was a union in South India
of the Presbyterian churches related to the American and Scottish missions. In 1904 this body joined with several presbyterian
groups in North India to form a Presbyterian Church of India.
A more important step was the inter-denominational union of
Congregational and Presbyterian churches in South India and
Ceylon in 1908 to form the South India United Church. (The
Presbyterian churches in the South withdrew from the union with
the North Indian Presbyterians to join the S.I.U.C.) In 1919 the
Churches related to the Basel Mission in Malabar joined the
union.

A parallel movement in North India led to the United
Church in North India in 1924, again a union of Presbyterians
and Congregationalists. In 1926 nine Lutheran churches joined
together in a loose federal union known as the Federation of
Evangelical Lutheran Churches in India. This is a federation of
autonomous bodies and not an organic union. The more significant unions that took place were those which brought into existence the Church of South India in 1947 and the Church of
North India in 1970. In the C.S.I., the parties to the union were
the South Indian United church, the Anglican dioceses in S.
India, and the south Indian districts of the Methodist Church
(British). The church of north India is a union of the Council
of Baptist churches in North India. The Church of the Brethren,
The Disciples of Christ, the Anglican dioceses in North India,
the Methodist church under the British and Australian conferences and the United church of North India. The Methodist church
in Southern Asia (American origin) which was involved in
union negotiations did not finally join the union.

These two unions are of great historical significance. The
impact of the church union movement in India on church
union movements throughout the world has been substantial.
The union movement has broken the rigidities of denominationalism in an unprecedented manner and has led to new developments in the idea of historical episcopacy, in liturgy and in the
structure of the church. While recognizing these positive gains
it is also necessary to observe that the hope of the Indian christian pioneers for an indigenous united church has not been fully

realized in these unions. The basic approach in these unions was not to create an indigenous church taking into account the realities in the Indian situation, but rather to reconcile and unite western denominational polities and confessions. During the period of the negotiations for the C.S.I., this question has been radically raised by the Madras Re-thinking Group. They said, "The problem of the union should be treated as subsidiary to the problem of the evolution of the Indian church or Indian christianity, which is the main concern of the Indian Christian thinkers. The Indian church should not be treated as a pliable material for conducting experiments for the solution of the denominational problems of the western christendom.[44] M.M. Thomas pointed out a new dimension to our approach to unity when he wrote: "While the C.S.I. recognizes itself as a church seeking to express the truth of the universal church in the thought and life form of India, one cannot say that such has been done theologically to realize the goal of indigenization. Sometimes the C.S.I. gives the impression of having stuck as a hotchpotch of denominational bodies, never growing into totally new unity which was expected of it. The non-theological factors of unity and disunity, like caste, ethos and language peculiar to India, never came up for consideration during the union negotiations, and they are the main hindrance toward a fuller unity."[45]

The same criticism could be equally applied to union negotiations, in North India also. The denominational questions are not unimportant. But so far, this was the primary consideration in church union movements. The questions raised by the Re-thinking Group and people like M.M. Thomas point to a different approach. The Church union movements in India should consider the question not only from a denominational point of view but also from the perspective of common mission and from the necessity to evolve an Indian church. This is not simply a matter of expediency but a question of great theological importance. This question is whether or not union negotiations are attempts to grapple with the question of an ecclesiology for the Indian church or not.

At present there are conversations between Lutheran churches and the church of South India and the Mar Thoma church and the

C.S.I. for a wider union in South India. There is also a move in North East India for uniting the churches in that area.

The ecumenical scene in India is not limited to Church union movements. The modern ecumenical movement has made its impact at various levels of the Church's life. There are various interdenominational agencies each expressing a particular concern of the whole church. The National Christian Council of India which had its origin in 1914 coordinates the ecumenical concern of the churches and christian institutions. It is an organ of common consultation and action on matters of importance in the life of the churches. It represents the majority of the non-Roman churches in dealing with the Government of India. It also serves as a connecting link between the churches in India and international ecumenical organizations such as the World Council of Churches and the East Asia Christian Conference recently renamed Asian Christian Conference. The Y.M.C.A., the Y.W.C.A., the S.C.M. are organizations concerned with work among young people. As we have noted before the Y.M.C.A., in the part of the early century, under the leadership of S.K. Datta and K.T. Paul made a significant contribution in awakening the churches to their responsibility in the life of the nation. The S.C.M. as a movement among the university community has done and is doing more than any other organization in training young men and women for Leadership in Church and Nation. The contribution of the India Sunday School Union has been significant in the field of christian education of the young.

The Christian Institute for the Study of Religion and Society is one of the most creative and dynamic christian organizations in India. With its Sunday programmes, publications, consultations and conferences it is helping the church to understand its mission in a nation of rapid social change and renascent religions. The Institute promotes scholarly study and research in the fields of religions and society and tries to establish vital contact and initiates conversation with those of other religions on living issues. It is pointed out that "C.I.S.R.S. literature represents the most significant and substantial body of Indian christian writing in the history of the Church in India so far." Since 1947 influenced by the World Council of Churches thinking of the role of the laity in the life and witness of the Church, several lay training institutes have been started. Of these, the Christian Retreat and the Study Centre at Rajpur and the Ecumenical Christian Centre at Whitefield, Bangalore, deserve special mention. The latter under the leadership of its director M.A. Thomas is performing a much needed work of training laymen for Christian witness in their secular occupations. It is important to note that the centre receives cooperation in its programme not only from the Protestant churches but also from the Roman Catholic and Syrian Orthodox churches. The christian Literature Society with its headquarters at Madras is the main organ of the christian literature programme of the churches. In recent years under the direction of its General Secretary, A. D. Manuel, the C. L. S. has shown a new vigour in its activities and a greater concern for publishing and circulating indigenous theological literature. The translation of the Bible into regional languages and its distribution have had an important place in the protestant missionary enterprise from the very beginning. The Bible Society of India is now engaged in the difficult task of translating the Bible into a number of languages and dialects as well as revising the older translations. Through a number of Bible houses scattered throughout India, the Society distributes millions of Bibles or Bible portions every year. Interdenominational cooperation is also seen in theological education. Major theological schools and seminaries in the country are affiliated to the Senate of Serampore College. This helps to keep up the standard of theological teaching and training throughout the country. Recently several discussions and consultations were held and various steps were taken to make theological training relevant to the Indian situation.

After Vatican II, a new climate has been created for cooperation and dialogue between the Roman Catholics and Protestants in the country.

The number of protestant christians in India is only about five million. It is not the number that matters most, but the openness of the church to renewal for mission both within and outside, which is going to be decisive for the future development of church in this country.

CONCLUSION

Till recently the Church in India has been understood in terms of Western missionary expansion. The church historians are only beginning to recognize the fact that while foreign missions have played an important role in its life and growth, the history of the Indian church is best understood as an independent story. Whether we accept the St. Thomas traditions concerning the apostolic foundation of the Indian church or not, there is no doubt that the history of the church goes back to an early period. This history from an early period of Christian era up to the present is the common possession of all Christians in India. The history of christianity in any part of India is an integral part of history of the church anywhere in the country . Western missions which came at different periods are only different streams which have flowed in to form one main stream of christianity in India, and they should be seen within the common tradition and not as separate traditions. It is very unfortunate that what has been written so far is only denominational histories. The denominational approach to history is essentially a communalistic approach, and not a catholic one. If we isolate events or segments from the whole, we miss the common identity that comes from the study of the whole. The history of the Church in India is much larger and richer than our denominational histories, whether Roman Catholic, Protestant or Orthodox. The Indian church has a history and a tradition of its own. This understanding of the unity of history is essential to maintain the integrity and wholeness of the Indian Church.

Church History is not simply a study of the church as a religious institution isolated from its world around. It is the history of a people's corporate response to the challenges of the Gospel and their living and growing in constant dialogue with the religious and cultural situations in India. As this book illustrates, several of the creative and dynamic movements within the Church arose, renewing its life and mission, whenever the church lived its life in dialogue with its environment. The openness to the world helped the Church not only to influence the world around, but also to be influenced by the creative movements in the world.

There were periods of 'lights' and 'shades' in the history of the Indian Church. However, the work of the church among the 'outcastes' and the tribal peoples and the efforts made for their upliftment were of great importance. The social activities of the Church helped to create a social ferment within Indian society itself. The impact of the West on Indian life and thought was an important element in the shaping of modern India.

Western Missionary work in India corresponded with the period of cultural penetration of the West; and the christian missions were at the beginning, the main agency for western education. The resultant national awakening confronted the church with a new situation, with implications for religion, society and politics. Thus arose new movements within the Church forcing the church to rethink its relation to the nation, and to restate its beliefs and practices in the context of the Indian situation. In facing the challenges in the new situations, the churches found themselves moving closer to one another. The movements for cooperation and church unions in India have made a significant contribution to the ecumenical movement throughout the world. The church has also produced a number of able leaders who are making significant contribution to the ecumenical movement in general.

India is passing through a period of great social change and reconstruction. It is by our active involvement in the divine movement in the life of the people in India to create conditions for better human life, that we will understand what means to participate in the history of the Church in India.

THE ARMENIAN CHRISTIANS IN INDIA

by E. R. Hamby, S.J.

There were Armenian Christians in India from the 16th century. In 1517 it was an Armenian merchant who led a small group of Portuguese pilgrims from Pulicat to the shrine of St. Thomas at Mylapore.

From the 16th century onwards the Armenians, very much favoured by Emperor Akbar, were found in increasing numbers in the main commercial centres of the Mogul empire, Agra, Delhi, Surat, Benares, Patna, Murshidabad and Dacca. Occasionally they were also found in Portuguese settlements, and later on in those under Dutch control. The Armenian chapel in the Old Cemetery of Agra dates back to 1562. The Armenians were nearly all merchants with trade relations extending as far as Aleppo in the West and Indonesia in the Far East. They belonged mostly to the Armenian communities of Iran. After 1605, when Shah Abbas of Persia deported 12,000 Armenian families from Julfa to Isfahan in order to bolster up the importance of his capital many more Armenians either left Iran for India, or later on came from their Isfahan settlement, called New Julfa, to trade in this country.

They were already found in Bengal, Chinsurah near Calcutta in 1630, then in Sultanati in today's Calcutta in 1645, at Syebad, a quarter of Murshidabad, in 1665; and in Madras in 1666. They were also at Surat where they had two churches, by 1740. Besides the Agra chapel the oldest extant Armenian church is that of Chinsurah (1695). The present Armenian church of Nazareth in Calcutta was built in 1724 and considerably improved in 1790, nine years after the foundation of their church in Dacca. The Armenian church in Madras was completed in 1792. It replaced the older one of 1712 which was pulled down for military reasons. The last church of the 18th century was built in Bombay in 1796; it was entirely rebuilt in recent years.

The quick developments and commercial success of the East India Company were not missed by the Armenians. Actually they had preceded it in Calcutta. They moved in larger numbers there and wherever the John's Company was trading. In the newly established Calcutta the Armenians obtained from the Company favourable conditions for their mercantile activities. Henceforward they remained among the most faithful commercial allies of the British traders. This however did not prevent them from occasional drawbacks; for instance, in 1781, they were obliged to leave Madras with only a few Armenians remaining there, and to settle down for a while in such far-away places as Seringapatanam, Negapatanam, and Masulipatanam.

Their attachment to business transactions did not prevent Armenians from taking up other professions. Khojah Gregory Arraturn who was murdered in 1763 became Chief Minister and Commander of all the forces of Mir Kasim, the English protege and Subadar of Bengal. With his master he bravely fought against the British in several battles. Later on we find an Armenian Colonel, Jacob Petrus, in the Scindia army; he built a church of his own at Gwalior c.1830. During the 19th century quite many an Armenian joined the legal professions. In 1895 the Advocate General in Calcutta was the Armenian Sir Gregory Charles Paul. Other Armenians became medical doctors, e.g., Dr. J.M. Joseph, Deputy Surgeon General in Madras 1880-85. Some entered also the Indian Civil Service of the time.

The Armenians are all Christians since the memorable years of their apostle, St Gregory, the Illuminator (end of the 3rd century). Their attachment to their religion, language and culture has remained untarnished until today, in spite of terrible persecution (one million massacred in 1915-20) and the complete loss of national independence between 1375 and 1918. Their dispersal all over the world was above all due to such circumstances.

In India, especially since the 18th century, they enjoyed complete freedom in fostering their own religious and cultural renaissance. It was shown first and foremost by the many endowments and benefactions sent to their churches and monasteries in Iran and elsewhere. The first Armenian press in India was set up in Madras in 1772, followed by the one of Calcutta in 1797. The first ever published Armenian journal came out in Madras in 1794-96. In 1798 the Calcutta community opened a school for their children, but it was only firmly founded in 1821 as the Armenian Philantropic Academy, better known today as the Armenian College. They had also a school in Madras for sometime. In 1845 a cultural association called the Araratean Society was established in Calcutta. In the beginning of the 19th century a wealthy Armenian merchant of Madras, Agah Samuel Murad, bequeathed a sum of Rs. 640,000 to the Armenian Mekhitarist Order, Catholic religious congregation of great cultural influence (in Venice since 1715), for establishing a school for the Armenian youth in Europe. It still exists in Venice.

During the 16th-19th centuries, many Armenian Christians endeared themselves to various missionary agencies by their generous support. They should be thankfully remembered still today for this reason. The Jesuit mission of the Great Mogul (Lahore, Agra, Delhi) enjoyed many a time the financial help of the Armenians, their active religious sympathy, and their confidence. One of them, Mirzazul-Qarnain, became governor in the Mogul empire in 1619. Thanks to his constant generosity and protection he deserved to be called 'Father of the Christians of Mogul'. He made a substantial endowment for the Agra Jesuit College. In Madras, Khojah Petrus Woskan (d.1751), one of the Armenian merchant-kings of the 18th century, is still remembered for having built the Adyar bridge in 1725, and for having paid in 1726 for the making of the 160 steps leading to the top of St. Thomas' Mount. In the church there, there are preserved fourteen paintings of Christ and the Apostles, a gift, if not a work, of an 18th century Armenian. A similar set of eight paintings is preserved at the Luz church also.

In Calcutta the Armenian community, which reached 800 strong in 1895, was always ready to help any Christian work of education and charity. This was particularly the case of the famed Apcar Firm, founded in 1830 by Arratun Apcar (d.1863). In 1824-31 Mesrob David Thaliatin (1803-58), one of the luminaries of the Armenian renaissance, studied at Bishop's College as the favoured friend of Bishop Heber. Under Thaliatin's own supervision the first Armenian book was printed in 1829 in the College's press, followed until 1846 by several others.

The majority of the Armenian Christians belongs to the Orthodox Apostolic Armenian Church, the supreme patriarch of which resides at Echmiadzin in Soviet Armenia. The Armenians in India always depended on Echmiadzin through the archbishop of Isfahan. Today their very diminished communities are found mostly in Calcutta, with a few families in Bombay and in Madras. Since the 50's they have a bishop residing in Calcutta. Their clergy in reduced numbers live in Calcutta, and occasionally in Bombay and in Madras. It is to be noted that the Armenians are in communion with the Syrian Orthodox Church of India.

The Armenian Christians living in India never tried to spread their faith, except through rare intermarriages. Only when they became Catholic, Anglican or Protestant, could they more directly participate in the expansion of the Church. However many Armenian tombs and inscriptions are found in ancient Catholic churches at Agra, Calcutta, Madras, etc. This fact does not necessarily indicate that they had either joined the Catholic Church or had been Catholics by origin. Each case is to be carefully studied. For on the one hand most of the Orthodox Armenians showed in those days a remarkable 'ecumenical' outlook by accepting practical intercommunion; on the other hand, since the Middle Ages (12th-15th centuries), and still more steadly since the 17th century a Catholic Armenian patriarchate has flourished, and still exists today with its see in Beirut. Hence Catholic Armenians were also found in India together with their Orthodox brethren. Moreover it is certain that quite a number of Armenian families became Indianized thanks to intermarriages with local Catholics, as indicated by such names still kept today by Latin-rite families as Satur and Carapiet.

There were also Armenians who joined either the Anglican Church or various Protestant Churches. Some of them have rendered valuable service, e.g., in Surat, in the early spread of the Christian faith in remote areas.

CHRONOLOGICAL EVENTS

St Thomas the Apostle lands at Maliankara, Kerala	?52
St Thomas dies as a martyr at Mylapore	?72
Bishop David leaves Basrah for India	c. 295
The Indian Church is already linked with Seleucia-Ctesiphon	c. 450
Cosmas Indicopleustes describes the Eastern Church in India	c. 535
Theodore, a Frankish monk, visits Mylapore?	c. 590
Metropolitan see of India	7th/8th cc.
Bishop Thomas with Middle East emigrants comes to Kerala	774/95
Bishops Proth & Sabor with merchant Sabrisho and Middle East emigrants land in Quilon	? 813/24
Franciscan John de Montecorvino visits India	1293
Mar Jacob, Metropolitan of India, at Cranganore	1301
Martyrdom of four Franciscan Friars at Thana, near Bombay	1321
Franciscan Oderico de Pordenone visits Thana and Kerala	1324-5
Dominican Jordan Catalani of Severac appointed the first Latin bishop of Quilon	1329
Papal envoy, the Franciscan John de Marignolli, stays at Quilon	1348-49
Two East-Syrian bishops, Thomas and John, arrive in Kerala	c. 1496
First Portuguese missionaries at Cochin	1498-1500
Three East-Syrian bishops, Yahballaha, Denha and Jacob, arrive in Kerala	1501
Vasco de Gama's first official meeting with Thomas Christians	1503
First Portuguese Franciscans in India	1510
First Padroado diocese for India, Funchal (Madeira)	1514
Duarte Nunes o.p., first Padroado roving bishop	1519-24
Discovery of St Thomas' tomb at Mylapore	?1523
Diocese of Goa. Christianisation of the Fishery Coast	1534
Franciscan Seminary at Cranganore	1540
College of Holy Faith, or St Paul, in Goa	1541
St Francis Xavier in India and the first Jesuits	1542-51
Persian cross discovered at Mylapore	1547
First Dominicans settled in India	1548
Jesuit College at Cochin	1552
Christianisation of Goa begins	1555
First Printing Press in India	1556

Goa becomes an archdiocese with Cochin as its suffragan dio-
cese   1557
Two East-Syrian bishops, Joseph and Elias, arrive in Kerala 1558
King of Cochin's edict of tolerance in favour of new Christ-
ians; Inquisition in Goa   1560
East-Syrian Bishop, Abraham, arrives in Kerala   1563
East-Syrian Bishop, Joseph, is sent back for good to Rome   1565
First provincial council of Goa   1567
Mesa de Conciencia in Goa   1571
First Augustinian friars in Goa   1572
Second provincial council of Goa   1575
Jesuit seminary at Vaipicotta, Kerala   c. 1577/1584
First Jesuit Mogul Mission   1579
First synod of Angamali, Kerala   1583
Third provincial council of Goa   1585
Second Jesuit Mogul Mission   1590
Fourth provincial council of Goa   1592
Third and lasting Jesuit Mogul Mission   1594
Death of the last recognized East-Syrian metropolitan of
India, Abraham   1597
Archbishop Alexis de Menezes of Goa and the synod of
Udayamperur (Diamper), Kerala   1599
Arrival of the Augustinian friars at Bandel, Bengal   1599
Francis Ros, S.J. first Latin bishop of the Thomas Christ-
ians   1601
Second synod of Angamali. Fifth and last provincial council
of Goa. Padroado diocese of S. Tome-Mylapore   1606
Padroado see of Cranganore for Thomas Christians becomes
archbishopric   1608
Robert de Nobili, S.J. arrives at Madurai. First discalced
Carmelites in Goa   1614
First Indian Anglican Christian, a Bengali   1616
Discalced Carmelites in Sind   1618
Augustinian Friars in Sind   1624
First vicariate apostolic in India, of Idalcan   1637
Theatines arrive in Goa, then in Golconda. Capuchins open a
house at Surat   1639
Beginning of organized Anglican chaplaincies   1640
Capuchins come to Madras   1642
Mysore Mission by the Jesuits from Goa   1648
Koonan Croos oath, revolt of Thomas Christians   1653
Robert de Nobili, S.J. dies at Mylapore   1656
Matthew de Castro, vicar apostolic of Bijapur, first Indian
Latin Bishop. First Discalced Carmelites' mission to
Kerala   1657
First Sanskrit grammar composed by H. Roth, S.J. (Agra) 1660

Bishop Sebastiani o.c.d. and second Carmelite mission to
   Kerala   1661
Alexander (Chandi) Parambil becomes the first local bishop
   of the Catholic Thomas Christians, as vicar apostolic 1663
Gregorios. Syrian Orthodox (Jacobite) metropolitan of Jeru-
   salem, comes to Kerala   1665
Spread of Catholic Christianity in Bengal. Thomas de Castro,
   second Indian Latin bishop and vicar apostolic of Kanara
                                                               1666
Carmelite Seminary at Verapoli, Kerala   1675/82
Second Syrian Orthodox mission to Kerala   1685
Venerable Father Joseph Vaz (d1711) to Ceylon. First Paris
   missionary at Pondicherry   1687
First Catholic chapel at Calcutta   1690
St John de Britto, S.J. martyred at Oriur (Tamilnadu)   1693
French Jesuits open Carnatic mission   1695
S.P.C.K. founded in England. East India Company charter
   renewed with an Anglican chaplaincy for each centre 1698
A Chaldean bishop, Simon of Ada, reaches Kerala, and
   gives episcopal order to Angelus Francis of St Theresa,
   vicar apostolic of Malabar, first residing Carmelite bi-
   shop in Kerala   1700-01
S.P.G.F.P. founded in England   1701
'Malabar Rites' controversy begins   1702/07
First Protestant (Lutheran) mission at Tranquebar   1706
First Capuchins at Lhasa, Tibet   1708
Servent of God Fr Joseph Vaz, death of   1711
Tranquebar New Testament in Tamil. C.J.E. Beschi, S.J.
   at Madurai   1711
Bombay under vicar apostolic   1720
Tranquebar missionaries in Madras   1726
Ordination of the first Lutheran pastor of Tamilnadu   1733
End of the 'Malabar Rites' controversy   1744
Capuchins leave Lhasa and Tibet for good   1745
Mar Thomas V, head of the Syrian Orthodox in Kerala,
   seeks union with Rome   1748
First religious congregation for women in Tamilnadu   1750
Third Syrian Orthodox mission to Kerala   1751
Davasagayam Nilakanda Pillai, a Tamil Catholic officer of
   Travancore, is martyred   1752
Expulsion of the Jesuits from Portuguese India   1759-60
Mar Dionysios I, metropolitan of the Syrian Orthodox, In-
   dependent Syrian Church of Anjur-Thozhiur   1772
Foreign Missions of Paris, with vicar apostolic at Pondicherry,
   succeeds to the Jesuits in Tamilnadu & Andhra   1776
Seminary by Paris Missionaries at Pondicherry   1778

Begum Joanna Samru of Sardhana becomes Christian 1781
Joseph Kariatil first Thomas Christian archbishop of Cran-
    ganore (d.1786 in Goa) 1782
Vicariate apostolic of the Great Mogul (Bombay) 1784
Padroado-Propaganda conflicts in Bombay 1789-91
First Anglican Missionary arrives at Calcutta 1790
W. Carey, first missionary of the Baptist Missionary society,
    reaches Calcutta 1793
Fabricius' whole Bible in Tamil 1796
C. F. Schartz dies at Tanjore 1798
Efforts at reunion between Catholic and Syrian Orthodox
    Thomas Christians 1799
Baptist centre at Serampore founded 1800
Bengali New Testament from Serampore 1801
First L.M.S. missionaries in Andhra 1804
Henry Martyn in India. Beginning of C.M.S. activities 1807
First L.M.S. work in S. Kerala and Nagercoil 1809
British and Foreign Bible Society 1811
First American Board missionaries in Bombay. Anglican
    bishopric of Calcutta with three archdiaconates. First
    C.M.S. missionaries in Calcutta 1812/13
C.M.S. missionaries in Madras 1814
C.M.S. missionaries at Kottayam 1816
Serampore College & Baptist Mission press, Bishop's
    College, Calcutta; Tract and Book Society, Madras;
    C.M.S. missionaries in Bombay 1818
Vicariate apostolic of Agra 1820
Arrival of S.P.G. missionaries 1821
Alexander Duff, a Scotch presbyterian, reaches Calcutta 1830
Thomas Christian Carmelite (Tertiaries) at Mannanam 1831
Bombay first Protestant educational institution 1832
Vicariates apostolic for Bengal, Madras and Pondicherry 1832-36
Freedom obtained for Christian agencies by the new East
    India Company Charter 1833
Death of W. Carey, Serampore, Basle Mission in Kanara
American Presbyterians at Ludhiana. American Board
    mission in Madurai 1834
Anglican dioceses of Bombay & Madras. American Baptists
    in Andhra 1835
Suppression by the state of religious orders in Portuguese
    territories. Syrian Orthodox synod of Mavelikara 1836
First Protestant educational institution in Madras 1837
Jesuits from France come back to Madurai, Papal Brief
    Multa Praeclare. and beginning of conflicts between
    Padroado and Propaganda jurisdictions 1838
Gossner Lutheran Mission 1839

American Baptists in Assam, followed by British Baptists and Wesleyan Methodists 1841

Lutheran Leipzig Society in Tamilnadu (Tranquebar).

American Lutherans in Andhra 1842

Mission Synod of Pondicherry. Beginning of Nagpur's Hislop College 1844

Missionaries of St Francis of Sales (Annecy) in Vizagapatanam and Nagpur 1845

Vicariates apostolic of Hyderabad, Mysore, Patna, Tiruchira-palli and Vizagapatanam 1845-47

Gossner Lutheran Mission in Chota Nagpur. Venerable Anastasius Hartmann, o.f.m. cap., first Vicar Apostolic of Patna 1846

Vicariates apostolic of Coimbatore and W. Bengal 1850

American Board with the Scudders in Arcot 1851

Vicariate Apostolic of Mangalore and Quilon. Anglican St John's College, Agra. Holy Cross Fathers and Brothers in E. Bengal 1853

Vicariate apostolic of Poona. German and Swiss Jesuits in Poona, then Bombay 1854

First conference of Protestant missionaries in Calcutta. Milan Society missionaries at Krishnagar 1855

Arrival of W. Butler, first representative of the American Methodist Episcopal Church 1856

Concordat between Portugal and Rome about the Padroado First English Day school for girls by A. Duff in Calcutta 1857

Death of Daniel Wilson, second Anglican bishop of Calcutta. Beginning of Christian Literature Society in Madras 1858

Apostolic visitation of the 18 vicariates apostolic 1859-61

American Episcopalian Methodist J.M. Thoburn (d.1922) arrives in India. Belgian Jesuits in Bengal 1859

United Presbyterian Mission in Rajasthan 1860

New agreements on the Padroado between Portugal and Rome 1860-61

The Chaldaean Bishop Rokkos in Kerala 1861-62

First decennial Protestant All-India missionary conference 1862

Society of St Vincent de Paul in Bombay 1863

C. M. S. Medical mission at Srinagar, Kashmir 1864

Death of Bishop Anastasius Hartmann, o.f.m.cap. 1866

Santal mission of the Northern Churches 1867

S P.G. mission in Chota Nagpur 1869

Y.M.C.A. begins. Anglican Society of St John the Evangelist (Cowley Fathers) in Poona. Isabella Thoburn in Lucknow 1870

Servant of God, Cyriac Elias Chavara death of 1871
First Protestant Women's hospital at Bareilly (U.P.) 1874
Irish Presbyterian mission to the lepers 1874
A second Chaldaean Bishop, Mellus, in Kerala 1874-82
Syrian Orthodox Patriarch Peter VII in Kerala 1875-76
The Mar Thoma Church. Mill-Hill Society in Andhra
    Syrian Orthodox synod of Mulanthuruthi 1876
T.V. French becomes the First Anglican bishop of Lahore
    1878
Italian Jesuits at Mangalore—Calicut 1879
Vicariate apostolic of the Punjab 1880
Zenana Bible & Medical Mission. Anglican Zenana Mission-
    ary Society. Anglican Oxford Brotherhood in Calcutta.
    United Presbyterian Mission starts at Agra the Medical
    Mission Training Institute. First Christian Brothers
    (St Patrick F.S.P.) in India 1881
Pandita Rama Bai (d.1922) accepts Christianity 1883
Creation of a Delegation Apostolic in India 1884
Arrival of the Jesuit C. Lievens to Ranchi 1885
Catholic hierarchy in India (6 provinces). End of Padroado-
    Propaganda conflicts. Arrival of Salesians of Don Bosco
    in Madras. Central Seminary of Puthenpalli in Kerala.
    Padroado diocese of Damaun 1886
Madras Christian College becomes a jointed undertaking
    Vicariates apostolic of Kottayam and Trichur for the
    Catholic Thomas Christians 1887
J.M. Thoburn, first Methodist bishop in India. Mar Thoma
    Church completely independent 1888
American Presbyterian medical mission at Miraj 1889
French Capuchins in Rajasthan 1890
Six provincial synods. Prefecture apostolic of Bettiah-Nepal.
    Papal Seminary of Kandy (Ceylon) 1893
N. India School of Medicine for Christian women, Ludhiana
    1894
St Mary's Tope for Brahmin Catholics, Tiruchirapalli 1895
Anglican diocese of Tirunelvelli. Vicariates apostolic of
    Changanacherry, Ernakulam and Trichur, with local
    bishops, for the Catholic Thomas Christians. Dohnavur
    Fellowship for unwanted girls by A. B. Carmichael
    (d. 1952) 1896
Catholic Indian Association 1899
Sadhu Sunder Singh becomes Christian 1903-04
C.F. Andrews (d. 1940) arrives in Delhi 1904
First General Assembly of the United Churches of S. India
    National Missionary Society founded 1905
British Methodist hospitals for women at Mysore & Hassan 1906

Church of the East at Trichur. E. S. Jones comes to India 1907
South India United Church created. First Lutheran con-
      ference   1908
United Theological College in Bangalore. Serampore College
      re-organized   1910
Division among the Syrian Orthodox. Vicariate apostolic of
      Kottayam for the Catholic Thomas Christians   1911
V.Z. Azariah (d. 1945), first Indian Anglican bishop   1912
National Missionary Council
Prefecture apostolic of Rajasthan   1913
Senata of Serampore College, which becomes interdenomina-
      tional. Medical School for girls at Vellore   1918
Death of Tilak, the Mahratti Christian poet. United Tamil
      Eganglical Lutheran Church   1919
Order of the Imitation of Christ (Bethany) founded by Syrian
      Orthodox   1919-20
First Indian Latin bishop at Tuticorin. Salesians of Don
      Bosco in Assam. Union Christian College, Alwaye   1921
Spanish Congregation of the Mission (Vincentians) at
      Cuttack   1922
Ecclesiastical province of Ernakulam for the Catholic
      Thomas Christians. National Christian Council of India.
      Leonard College, Jabalpur   1923
United Church of N. India. Syrian Orthodox Servants of the
      Cross. Maltese Jesuits in the Santal Parganas   1924
Christian Medical Association   1926
Andhra Lutheran Church   1927
Servant of God, Fr. Agnelo D'Souza, death of   1927
Agreement between Portugal and Rome, suppressing almost
      all double jurisdiction. Second Indian Latin bishop at
      Mangalore. Salesians of Don Bosco arrive at Krish-
      nagar and Madras. Federation of the Evangelical Luthe-
      ran Churches   1928
Scheme of Union of the Church of S. India. Maltese Capuch-
      ins come to Jhansi   1929
Anglican Church separated from the state. J. R. Chitambar,
      first Indian Methodist bishop. Union with Rome of the
      Syrian Orthodox bishops, Ivanios and Theophilos, with
      followers   1930
Death of Kanakarayam Tiruselvan Paul, outstanding Y.M.
      C.A. leader Syrian Orthodox Patriarch Elias III in
      Kerala   1931
Ecclesiastical province for the Syro-Malankara Catholics   1932
Central Puthenpalli Seminary transferred to Alwaye   1933
World Conference of the International Missionary Council,
      Tambaram   1938

First plan of union for the Church of North India   1939
Catholic Bishops Conference of India established. Bible
     Society of India and Ceylon   1944
Catholic Union of India. Catholic Indian Missionary
     Society, Benares. Full-fledged Christian Medical College,
     Vellore   1945
Servant of God Sr. Alfonsa-death of   1946
Inauguration of the Church of South India   1947
All-India Catholic University Federation, Catholic Students
     Union   1948
First local Anglican bishop of Nicober Islands. Catholic
     Plenary Council of India, Bangalore. Missionary Sisters
     of Charity, Calcutta. New agreement with the Padroado
     1950
Negotiating Committee for the Church of N. India. Indian
     Social Institute   1951
Madras archdiocese (Propaganda) and Mylapore diocese
     (Padroado) merged and re-organized. Padroado left only
     in Goa territory. V.Gracias, Archbishop of Bombay,
     becomes the first Indian Cardinal. First Benedictine
     monastery in India   1952
Catholic Thomas Christian dioceses extended to all Kerala
     and to neighbouring districts of Tamilnadu and Mysore
     States. First Catholic Thomas Christian Monastery
     (Kurisumala)   1955
Yuhannon Mar Thoma, metropolitan of the Mar Thoma
     Church, becomes one of the presidents of the World
     Council of Churches   1956
End of the division among the Syrian Orthodox   1958
First Indian Lutheran Bishop of Tranquebar, R.B. Manickam
     1962
New Catholicos of the Syrian Orthodox Church, Basilios
     Augen I installed by the Syrian Orthodox Patriarch of
     Antioch. International Eucharistic Congress in Bombay
     attended by Pope Paul VI   1964
Ecumenical National Board of Christian Higher Education
     1966
Dr M.M. Thomas elected Chairman of the Central Com-
     mittee of the World Council of Churches   1967
Second Indian Cardinal, J.Parecattil, Thomas Christian Arch-
     bishop of Ernakulam. Catholic National Seminar in Ban-
     galore   1969
Inauguration of the Church of North India in Nagpur   1970
Ecumenical Celebrations of the 1900th year since the tradi-
     tional date of St Thomas' martyrdom. All-India
     Ecumenical conference on Faith & Order   1972

BIBLIOGRAPHY AND NOTES

GENERAL

BIBLIOTHECA Missionum (Streit—Dindiger), Aachen, v.4, 1928; v.5, 1929; v.6, 1931.

Coutinho F., *Le regime paroissiale des dioceses de rite latin de l'Inde des origines (VIe s.) a nos jours*, Louvain, 1958.

D'Sa M., *History of the Catholic Church in India*, Bombay' 1910-24 2 vols.

Firth C. B., *An Introduction to Indian Church History*, Madras, 1961.

Garbe R., *Indien unds das Christentums*, Tubingenm 1914.

Latourette K. S., *A History of the Expansion of Christianity*, London, v.3 (1940), p. 247-84; v.6 (1944), p. 165-214; v.7, (1945), p. 274-315.

Meersman A., *The Friars Minor, or Franciscans, in India*, Karachi, 1943.

Melo C. M. de, *The Recruitment and Formation of the Native Clergy in India* (XVI th—XIXcc.), Lisbon, 1955.

Moraes G. M., *A History of Christianity in India from early times to St. Francis Xavier A. D. 52-1542*, Bombay, 1964.

Mullbauer M., *Geschichte der Katholischem Missionen in Ostindien*, Freiburg i. B., 1852

Neill St., *The Story of the Christian Churches in India and Pakistan*, Grand Repids, 1970.

Plattner F. A., *Indien*, Mainz, 1963 (English transl.; Allahabad, 1964)

Richter J., *Indische Missionsgeschichte*, Gutersloh, 1924 (English transl. of the first German edition, Edinburgh and London 1908).

Sherring M.B., *The History of the Protestant Missions in India*, London, 1884.

Soares A., *The Catholic Church in India, A historical sketch*, Bombay, 1964.

Thomas P., *Christians and Christianity in India and Pakistan*, London, 1954.

NOTES

1. The Syriac text is published by P. Bedjan in *Acta Martyrum et Sanctorum* Vol.III Paris-Leipzing, 1892, P.1.175.

   W. Wright, *Apocryphal Acts of the Apostles*, London, 1871, Vol.I: Syriac text; Vol.II. English translation.

   A. E. Medlycott, *India and the Apostle St. Thomas*, London, 1905, p. 221-25, indicates different versions and editions of the *Acts,* and p. 213-97 makes a critical analysis of the same. A. F. J. Klijn, *The Acts of Thomas,* Leiden, 1962, gives an English text, based on Wright's version, with a very good introduction and copious comments; a critical history of the various versions can be found in the introduction.

2. The early references to St. Thomas in India are chronologically: Syriac Acts of Thomas (c.200); 3rd century: Clement of Alexandria; Syriac Doctrine of the Apostles, Origin (c.231, quoted in Eusebius); 4th century: Arnobius (305), Eusebius of Caesarea (d.340), Ephrem (d.373), Gregory of Nazianzus (d.389), Cyrillonas (396), Ambrose (d.397), "De Transitu Mariae"; 5th century: Gaudentius of Brescia (d.after 406), Jerome (d.420), Theodoret of Cyrus (427), Paulinus of Nola (d.431), "Martyrologium Hieronymianum" (mid—5th cent.), Balai (d.c.460); 6th century: Jacob of Sarug (d.521), "Passio Thomae" (c.550), Gregory of Tours (d.594); 7th century: John of Saba (c.630), Isidore of Seville (d.636), etc. Distribution of the testimonies according to Churches: to the Syrian Church belong Acts, St. Ephrem, Syriac Doctrine of the Apostles passages in breviaries; to the Western Crurch, Ambrose, Jerome, Gaudentius, Paulinus, Gregory of Tours, Calendars, Sacramentaries, Martyrologies, esp. "Martyrologium Hieronymianum"; to the Greek Church, Origen, Gregory of Nazianz, Eusebius, St. John Chrysostom, Liturgical Books; to the Assyrian Church, the Ethiopian Calendar of the 12th century.

The books of A. C. Perumalil, *The Apostles in India,* Patna, 1971 (this is a second revised and enlarged edition of his book: *The Apostles in India, Fact or Fiction?,* Patna, 1952), and Medlycott, op. cit. cite many of the texts.

Another important work is the one by A. Vaeth, S.J., *Der Hl. Thomas der Apostel Indiens* ···Aachen, 1925. A good idea of bibliography on the question also may be had from these books. An article by E. R. Hambye, S.J., "Saint Thomas iⁿ India, *The Clergy Monthly,* 16 (1952) p. 363-375, also gives a fairly good idea of the studies, and a personal appreciation of the sources.

3. See Hambye, op. cit.

4. See Perumalil, op. cit. p.5-54.

5. See J. N. Farquhar, "The Apostle Thomas in North India", *Bulletin of John Revlands Library* 10 (1926), p80-111 "The Apostle Thomas in South India", ibid. 11 (1927), p. 20-50; T. K. Joseph, many articles and booklets, particularly, *Six St. Thomases of South India,* Chengannur, 1955; Perumalil, op. cit. and two articles by the same author: The Apostle Thomas in India", *Indian Ecclesiastical Studies,*

10 (1971), p.189-203; "St. Thomas and Gudnaphar", *The New Leader,* July 25, 1971, p.3 and August 1, 1971, p.3; cf. also P. J. Podipara, *The Thomas Christians,* London-Bombay, 1970, p.15-29.

6. Farquhar, op. cit. Hambye, op. cit., Cardinal Eugene Tisserant, *Eastern Christianity in India,* Bombay etc., 1957, p.3 f.

7. See A. M. Mundadan, *Sixteenth Century Traditions of St. Thomas Christians,* Bangalore, 1970, p.60-67.

8. Ibid; p.23-26

9. Ibid., p.38-67.

10. Ibid., p.19-37; 68-80.

11. L. W. Brown, *The Indian Christians of St. Thomas,* Cambridge, 1956, p.35 and p.57, n.2; T. K. Joseph; Heras; in *Journal of Bombay Historical Society,* 2 (1929), p.284-89; cf. Mundadan, op. cit. p.13 f; 82-84.

12. Mundadan, ibid., p.14-18; cf. also p.23.

13. Eusebius, "Ecclesiastical History", 5, 10, *The Fathers of the Church,* Vol.XIX, ed. by Roy J. Deferrari, New York, 1953, p.303; Jerome, "Lives of Illustrious Men", *A Select Library of Nicene and Post-Nicene Fathers of the Christian Church,* second series, ed. by Philip Schaff and Henry Wace, vol.III, Michigan, 1892, p.370; Jerome, "Letters", ibid.; vol.VI; p.150.

14. Other pertaining texts are: "Martyrologium Hieronymianum", ML 30, 436; the Greek "Menology", 2 for February 17, MG 117, 317; Pseudo Sophronius, "De Vitis Apostolorum", 4, ML 23, 722; "Passio Bartholmei" or "The Martyrdom of the Holy and Glorious Apostle Bartholomew", *Ante-Nicene Christian Library,* vol. 16; See texts in Perumalil op. cit. p.108-132.

15. Authors who support the Indian apostolate of St. Bartholomew are: Stillingus (1703-62), Neander (1853), Hunter (1886), Rae (1892), Zaleski (1915). Those who deny it are among others; Sollerius (1669-1740), Carpentier (1822-68), Harnack (1903), Medlycott (1905), Mingana (1926), Thurston (1933), Attwater (1935), Cf. Perumalil, op. cit., p.105-107.

16. Perumalil, op. cit., G. M. Moraes, *A History of Christianity in India...A.D. 52-1542* Bombay, 1964 p.43-45.

17. E. O. Windstedt, ed., *The Christian Topography of Cosmas Indicopleustes,* Cambridge, 1909, p.119.

18. Tisserant, op. cit., p.7 f. 19.

19. Bernard of St. Thomas, *The St. Thomas Christians* (in Malayalam) vol.I, Palai, 1913; Brown, op. cit.; Tisserant, op. cit.

20. Mundadan, op. cit., part II.

21. Ibid., p.88-92.

22. The best study on the Chaldaean Church is the one by Tisserant: "Nestorienne (l'Eglise)", *Dictionnaire de Theologie Catholique,* Vol.XI, Paris, 1931, c.157-323. There are several other studies, and collections of sources, in French, German, Latin, and Italian of which the best known perhaps is: J. S. Assemani, *Bibliotheca Orientalis...,* vol.III, parts 1 and 2, Rome, 1725 and 1728. The following are some of the English works: A Grant, *The Nestorians, or, the lost tribes,* London, 1841; G. P. Badger, *The Nestorians and their Rituals,* London, 1852; W. A. Wigram, *An Introduction to the History of the Assyrian Church,* London, 1910; A. Mingana, *The Early Spread of Christianity in Central Asia and the Far East.* Manchester, 1925; John Stewart, *Nestorian Missionary Enterprise...,* Edinburgh and Madras, 1928; V. R. Aubrey, *The Nestorian Churches,* London, 1937. For a sketch of the history of the Church, cf. A. M. Mundadan, *The Arrival of the Portuguese in India and the Thomas Christians under Mar Jacob, 1498-1552,* p.17-28.

23. Mundadan, Sixteenth Century Traditions, p.92-97; 100-103.

24. Ibid., p.97-100.

25. On the relation of the Church of India with the Church of Persia, besides the general works, see also the following: Tisserant, "Nestorienne (l'Eglise)", c.195-99; Mingana A., *The Early Spread of Christianity in India,* Manchester, 1926, E. R. Hambye, S.J. "The Syrian Church in India", *The Clergy Monthly,* vd.16 (1952), p.376-89; "Some Eastern Evidence concerning Early and Mediaeval Christianity in India" *Indian Ecclesiastical Studies,* vol.9 (1970), p.185-193; "Some Fresh Documents on Mediaeval Christianity in India", *Indian Church History Review,* 3 (1969), p.97-101; W. G. Young, "The Church of the East in 650 A.D., Patriarch Isho' —Yahb III and India" ibid 2 (1968), p.55-71; T. K. Joseph, *The Malabar Christians and Their Ancient Documents,* Trivandrum, 1929; and his "Malabar Miscellany", *Indian Antiquary,* 52 (1923), p.355-57; 53 (1924). p.93-97; G. Schurhammer, S.J., *The Malabar Church and Rome During the Early Portuguese Period and Before,* Trichinopoly, 1934 Some source material will be found in: "Histoire Nestorienne" (Chronique de Seert), ed. by A. Scher in *Patrologia Orientalis,* vol.4, 7 and 13, Paris. 1908, 1910 and 1919; Ishoyahb Patr. III: Liber Epistolarum" ed. by R. Duval, in *Corpus Scriptorum Christianorum Orientalium* (CSCO), vol. 11 and 12, Louvain-Washington, 1905; "Timothei Patr. 1 Epistolae" ed B. Oscar, ibid., vol. 74 and 75, Louvain,

1952; Ibn-At-Tayib, "Fiq-An-Nasaranya" ("Das Recht der Christenheit") ed. by W. Hoenerbach, and O. Spies, ibid., vol. 167 and 168, Louvain, 1957.

26. Gelazii Cysicensis, "Concilium Nicaenum" *PG.*, 85, 1314; cf. Mingana. *The Early Spread...in India,* p. 395; Tisserant, *Eastern Christianity....* p. 7.

27. "Histoire Nestorienne", IV, p. 236 and 292; VII, p. 117; VII, p. 117; XIII, p. 497; cf. Tisserant, ibid., p. 7-9; and "Nestorienne (1'Eglise)" c. 196; Hambye, "The Syrian..." and "some Eastern Evidence....".

28. Assemani, op. cit., p. 219-22; cf. Hambye, "Some Eastern...", p. 187.

29. Cosmos, *loc. cit.;* Tisserant, *Eastern Christianity,* p. 11-13.

CHAPTER II

PART I

1. J.S. Assemani, *Bibliotheca Orientalis* (abbrev. *B.O.*), Rome, 1719-28, III-1 p. 219-22; W. Wright, *A short History of Syriac Literature,* London, 1894, pp. 123-24.

2. As already pointed out by A.M. Mundadan, above p. 14.

3. 'Chronique de Seert', Patrologia Orientalis, XIII, p. 497 (117).

4. A century-and-a-half later, Catholicos Timothy I mentions that many monks travelled to India and China, 'Epistolae Timothei I, *Corpus Scriptorum Christianorum Orientalium* (abbrev. *CSCO* text v. 74, p. 107; translat. v. 75, p. 70.

5. Rewardasir had the title of Metropolitan of Persia and the Islands of the Sea, 'Ishoyahb Patr. III Liber Epistolarum, *CSOC* text 11, p. 251-52; translat. 12, p. 182.

6. Perhaps already under Catholicos 'Ishoyahb III (650-57) or Saliba-Sacha (714-28), but certainly since Catholicos Timothy I E. Tisserant 'L'Eglise Nestorienne', *Dictionaire de Theologie Catholique* (abbrev. *DTC*) XI, 197; Timothee I ibid XV (A) 1121-39.

7. *BO*, III-2, p. 444-45.

8. The spelling of both names is uncertain. Whereas Sabor certainly corresponds to Sapur, a Persian name, Proth may cover either Pheroz or even Aphraat, Pheroz being Persian and Aphraat rather Semitic. A.M. Mundadan, *Traditions of the St. Thomas Christians,* Bangalore, 1970, p. 100-03. In the official list of the Persian dioceses there was a bishop of Pheroz and

Sapur, holding the fourth rank in the East-Syrian hierarchy, *B.O.*, II, p. 459.

9. Some local authors maintain that this immigration is connected with the foundation, or new expansion, of Quilon, for its era' still used today in Kerala, began on August 25th, 825. H. Hosten, 'Thomas Cana and his Copper-Plate Grant', *Indian Antiquary* (abbrev. IA), 56 (1927), p, 25. *Travancore State* Manual, v. II; p. 144.

10. T. K. Joseph, *The Malabar Christians and their Ancient Documents.* Trivandrum, 1929, p. 32-37; A.M. Mundadan, *Traditions,* p. 135-36. The third copper-plate of a collection of originally four such documents comes from Cranganore and is dated by some 1320.

11. Besides the immigrations already mentioned there seems to have been sometimes intermarriages accross the seas, between India and Mesopotamia, J. Labourt, *De Timotheo I Nestorianorum Patriarcha...,* Paris, 1904, p. 63ff. Did the Thomas' Christians have contacts with other Eastern Churches? Only one text has come up to us recently about relations with the Coptic Church of Egypt Coptic Patriarch Simon (700-07) is said to have received a priest coming from India and asking for a bishop, E. Renaudot. *Historia Patriarchorum Alexandrinorum Jacobitarum,* Paris, 1713, p. 184 & 188.

12. G. Levi della vida *Ricerche sulla formazione del piu antico fondo di manoscritti orientali della Biblioteca Vaticana* Citta del Vaticano, 1939. p. 176, 187-89.

13. G.M. Moraes, A History of Christianity in India, Bombay, 1964, p. 89-105.

14. There was also a church near Cape Comorin, called appropriately *Thomaypalli* i.e. Thomas' church. In 1301 the church in Cranganore was called after St. Kuriakose the child-martyr but by 1516 there were two churches, one of St. Thomas, the other of our Lady, Mary. At Quilon, in the 14th cent., there were also two churches, one of St. Thomas, likely that founded or rebuilt by the two bishops Proth and Sabor, and the other of St. George, known to have been built by Jordan Catalani. Though originally built for the Latin use it was taken over later on by the Syrian Christians themselves. Abu-Salih, *Description of Churches and Monasteries of Egypt and some neighbouring Countries,* Ed. B. T. A. Evetts, Oxford, 1894-95, p. 300.

15. Oderic de Pordenone, who was in India in 1324-25, mentions that there were next to the Mylapore church fifteen houses of Christians. *Sinica Franciscana,* Quaracchi-Florence, 1929, I, p. 442.

16. H. Hosten, o.p., p. 23.

17. Hellmut de Terra. 'On the Worlds Highest Plateaus', *National Geographic Magazine* 59 (1931), p. 331-32, J. Dauvillier Temoignages nouveaux sur le Christianisme nestorian ches les Tifetains', *Bulletin de la Societe Achologique du Midi de la France*, 3e serie, 4 (1961), p. 4.

18. Devos P. s.j. 'Le miracle posthume de S. Thomas l'Apotre' *Analecta Bollandiana*, 66 (1948) pp. 231-75. At the end of the 12th cent. 'Ishoyahb of Nisibis (bishop c. 1190-c.1230) mentions that the 'corpse' of St. Thomas was in India, *BO* III-1, p. 306.

19. *BO*. II p. 460. III 2: p. 438-39.

20. Under Catholicos Elias III Abu-Halim (1149-75). W. A Wright, *Catalogue of the Syriac Manuscripts in the library of the University of Cambridge*, London, 1901; I; p. 339.

21. Chabot, *Synodicon Orientale*, Paris; 1902; p. 619-20.

22. *BO;* III-1, p. 346. Under Catholicos Theodosios (852-53), it was preceded by Fars and still followed by China, *BO,* III-2; p. 338-39.

23. J. Dauvillier 'Les Provinces Chaldeennes de l'Exterieur *Melanges F. Cavalera,* Toulouse, 1948; p. 313; BO; III-2,p. 458.

24. Since the time of the same Theodosios those metropolitans of the exterior had to send every sixth year a letter of communion and inform the Catholicos about matters of common interest, *BO,* III-2; p. 438-39. See also Ishoyahb III Liber Epistolarum', *CSCO* text 11, p.257-58; translat. 12, p. 186.

25. Apparently thus since Timothy I, Ibn At-Tayib, Fiqh-An-Nasraniya (Das Recht der Christenheit), *CSCO,* text 167; p. 118; translat. 168, p. 120.

26. J. Dauvillier, o.c., p. 270-72.

27. R. T. Bidawid, *Les Lettres du Patriarche Nestrorien Timothee I*, Citta del Vaticano, 1956; p. 49.

28. Ibn At-Tayib, o. c., p. 119   p. 121. P. J. Podipara; *The Thomas Christians*, London—Bombay, 1970; p. 71-72.

29. Placidus a S. Joseph TOCD, *Fontes Iuris Canonici Syro-Malankarensium*, Citta del Vaticano, 1937-40; p. 73-74.

30. Podipara, op cit, p. 96-97.

31. Placidus TOCD 'Hindu in Culture, Christian in Religion, Oriental in Worship', Ostkirchliche Studien, 5 (1960); p. 89-104.

32. Already in Timothy I's letter to the Indian Christians a king was mentioned as having something to do with the metropolitan's election, Ibn At-Tayib, op cit; p. 167&168.

33. H. Hosten, Unpublished Works (Vidyajyoti Library, Delhi);

v. xvi, pp 46080. In spite of assertions to the contrary (eg. T. K. Joseph' 'A Christian Dynasty in Malabar', *IA* 52 (1923) p. 157-59) this Udayamperur dynasty was never a Christian one, see A. M. Mundadan, Traditions; p. 125-29.

34. H. Hosten, *Antiquities from San Thome and Mylapore,* Calcutta-Mylapore, 1136, p. 463.

35. *Traditions,* p. 130 ff.

36. This has also left many traces in Malayalam, when Syriac religious terms are used, such as qurbana, mamoditha; etc. They are always pronounced in the East Syriac way, never in the western manner.

37. A. M. Mundadan, op. cit, p. 165-66.

38. St. Jerome had already spoken of monks coming from India, *M. L.* 22, 870. To some Indian monks John metropolitan of Karpathos (Island situated between Creta and Rhodes in the Eastern Mediterranean) sent at the end of the 8th cent. an exhortation on the merit of monastic life. *M. G.* 85 791-812; 1837-60; *DHGE* 11, 1111-121; *LTHK* 5(1960); 1049.

39. Last mentioned about 1340 by 'Amr, A. E. Medlycott; *India and the Apostle St. Thomas,* London 1905; p. 96-100.

40. H. Hosten, Antiquities; p. 295-99; in A. D. 780 a 'Nestorian' missionary from India received an award from the Chinese Superior; J. Kennedy, 'The Child Krishna; Christianity and the Gujass, *JRAS;* 1907; p. 457' n. 3.

41. H. Hosten, The Mackensie Manuscripts; Madras; 1926; p. 2&4.

42. Do. 'Thomas Cana and his Copper-Plate Grant', *IA* 56 (1927), p. 122.

Part II

1. B. Descamps, Historie Generale Comparee des Missions; Paris, 1232. pp. 274-75.

2. G. M. Moraes, A History of Christianity in India (A.D. 52-1542) Bombay, 1964; pp. 84.

3. M. Huc Le Christianissme en Chine en Tertetie et au Tibet. 2 vols. Paris, 1957; pp. 367-72.

4. H. Yule, Cathey and the Way Thither (London; 1866) vol. I. pp. 217-18.

5. Ibid, p. 214.

6. Ibid, p. 208.

7. Ibid, p. cXXXII

8. Ibid, p. 208.

9. Fontana, Monumenta Dominicana; Vol. annum 1316, cited in A. Brou, "L' Evangelisation de L' Indian Moyen Age", Etudes, 87 (1901), p. 589.

10. Moraes, op, cit; p. 89.

11. Ibid. p. 91.

12. Yule, op. cit, p. 58, 60; Brou, art. cit, p. 590.

13. Wadding, Annales Minozum, Rome, 1733, 2nd Ed., vol VII

14. Brou, art. cit, p. 591.

15. A.C. Moule, "A Brother Jordan of Severac, Journal of the Royal Asiatic Society, 1928., p. 363.

16. Ibid., p. 364-65.

17. Yule, op. cit. p. 62-64.

18. Ibid. pp. 67-68.

19. Quetif-Echard, S. Scriptores Ordinis Predicatorum. Paris 1719, Vol. I, p. 551, Wadding, op. cit., p. 357.

21. Wadding op. cit., p. 358.

22. Yule, op. cit. p. 70.

23. Ibid, pp. 226-27.

24. Ibid, p. 227.

25. Ibid, p. 229, Wadding, op. cit., Ann. 1321.

26. Wadding 1 p.c. cit.

27. Jordanus, Mirabilia Descripta, London, 1863, p. 56.

28. Paris Bible. Nat. Suare. Oriens, MSS 8934, Vol. XXIII, p. 41, cited by F. Balme, 'Un Missionaire Dominicain au XIVe Siecle', L' Annee Dominicaine 25 (1886), p. 299.

29. Wadding, annal. 1325, no. 14.

30. Andreˢ =Marie, Missions Dominicaines Dans L'Extreme Orient, pp. 41-43.

31. Yule, op. cit, p. 230.

32. Brou, art. cit, pp. 603-04.

33. Yule, op. cit. Vol. III, p. 217, Vol. II p. 321.

34. Ibid, Vol. II, pp. 381-82.

CHAPTER III

BULLARIUM Patronatus Portugalliae Regum, Ed. L.M. Jordao, Lisbon, 1868-79, 3 Vols & 2 Appendices.

EPISTOLAE S. Francisci Xaverii aliaque eius Scripta, Ed. G. Schurhammer & J. Wicki, Rome, 1944-45, 2 Vols.

MEMORIA Ecclesiastica de Archdiocese de Goa, Nova Goa, 1933.

MONUMENTA *Goana Ecclesiastica,* Nova Goa, 1925.

Nazareth C.C. de, *Mitras Lusitanas no Oriente,* Lisbon, 1913; Nova Goa 1924; Vol. 2.

Schurhammer G., *Die zeitgenössichen Quellen zur Geschichte Portugiesisch Asiens und seinen Nachbarländer zur Zeit des Hl. Franz Xavers,* Leipzig, 1932.

Silva Rego A. da, *Documentacao para a Historia do Padroado Portugues no Oriente, India,* Lisbon, 1947-58, 12 vols.

Braganza Pereira, A.B. de, *Historia Religiosa de Goa,* Bastora, 1937.

De Witte Ch., 'Les bulles pontificales et l'expansion portugaise au XVIe siecle'. *Revue d'Histoire Ecclesiastique* 48 (1953) p. 683-718; 49 (1954) p. 438. 61; 51 (1956) p. 413-53, 809-35; 53 (1958) p. 5-46, 443-71.

Meersman A., 'Origin of the Latin Hierarchy in India', *Clergy Monthly Supplement* 5 (1969) p. 67-78.

Saldanha M.J.G., *Historia de Goa,* Nova Goa, 1925-26, 2 Vols.

Schurhammer G., *Franz Xaver, sein Leben und seine Zeit,* Freiburg i.B., 1955-73, 3 Vols.

Silva Rego, A. da, *Historia das Missoes do Padroado Portugues do Oriente I. India,* Lisbon 1949, Vol. 1.

Id.   *Le Patronage Portugais dans l'Inde. Apercu historique,* Lisbon. 1957.

NOTES

1. There exists an abundant literature concerning the *Padroado.* The following works should be especially noted: L.M. Jordão Bullarium Patronatus Portugalliae Regum in Ecclesiis Africae, *Asiae atque Oceaniae* (Olisipone), Vol. I, 1171-1600 (abbrev *BP*); Ch. M. de Witte, "Les Bulles pontificales et l'expansion portugaise au XVe siécle, *"Revue d'Histoire Ecclesiastique",* 48 (1953), 49 (1954), 53 (1958); A. Jann, O.M. Cap., *Missionen in Indien, China und Japan, Ihre Organisation und das portugiesische Patronat vom 18. bis ins 18, Jahrhundert,* Paderborn, 1915; A. da Silva Rego, *Historia das Missoes do Padroado Potruguese do Oriente, India* Vol. 1 (1500-1542) Lisboa, 1949; A. da Silva Rego, *Le patronage Portugais de l'Orient, Apercu historique,* Lisboa, 1947; B.J. Wenzel, *Portugal und der Heilige Stuhl,* Lisboa, 1958.

2. G. Schurhammer, *Die Bekehrung der Paraver* (1535-1537), in *Gesammel te Studien,* II, Orientalia, Roma, 1963, pp. 215-262.

3. *Epistolae S. Francisci Xaverii aliaque eius Scripta,* edited by G. Schurhammer and J. Wicki, (Rome), 1944, I. p. 273.

4. *See* J. Wicki, Problems morais no Oriente portugues do seculo

XVI, *O Centro de Estudos Historicos Ultramarinos e as Comemoracoes Henriquinas,* Lisboa, 1961, p. 259.

5. B. P. I, p. 33.

6. B. P. I, p. 59.

7. Ibid I, pp. 98-99; Jann. pp. 65-66.

8. B. P. I, pp. 100-102; Jann. p. 68-69.

9. See M. Biermann, O. P. *"Der erste Bischof in Ost-Indien, Fray Durate Nunes, O. P."* in Neue Zeitschrift für Missionswissenschaft (a) brev. NZMB 9 (1953) pp. 81-90

10. Schurhammer, *Franz Xaver,* Freiburg, 1963 II/1, p. 144.

11. Ibid.

12. Ibid; also pp. 154-159.

13. B. P. I, pp. 159-163.

14. Schurhammer, *Franz Xaver,* II/1, pp. 152-154, 830.

15. About him see: D. Gaspar de Leão, *Desengano de perdidos,* edited by E. Asensio, (Coimbra, 1958), VII-CIX; J. Wicki, *Documenta Indica* IV-X (abbrev. *D. I*) (Roma, 1956-1968).

16. B. P. I, pp. 232-233.

17. D. I. X, pp. 729-730; XI, p. 46, p. 244.

18. D. I., XI, p. 246, p. 509.

19. J. Wicki, *D. Henrique de Tavora, O. P., Bishof von Cochin 1567-78, Erzbishof von Goa 1578-81, NZM,* 24 (1968), pp. 111-121.

20. Schurhammer, *Franz Xaver,* II/1, p. 152.

21. S. S. Pissurlencar, *Regimentos das fortalezas da India,* (Goa, 1951), pp. 17-52.

22. Ibid., pp. 398-401.

23. B. P., I, pp. 193-195.

24. Pissurlencar, *Regimentos,* pp. 220-225.

25. D. I., XI, p. 755[10]

26. B. P., App. I, pp. 32-34.

27. D. I., VIII, pp. 443-444.

28. See Wicki, *"Die unmittelbaren Auswirkungen des Konzils von Trient auf Indien (ca. 1565-1584)",* Archivum Historiae Pontificiae, 1, (Rome, 1963), pp. 241-61.

29. D. I. XI. pp. 680-692.

30. Wicki *"Liste der Jesuiten-Indienfahrer 1541-1758, Aufsatze zur portugiesischen Kulturgeschichte,* Vol. VII, Münster, 1969, pp. 269-276 (216 names for 1541-1580); Silva Rego, *Documentacao Para .historia das missoes do Padroado Portugues, India,* XI, (Lisboa, 1955), pp. 229-235 (those sent out in 1572 and 1579).

B.P. Bullarium Patronatus
D.I. Documenta Indica

31. Seraphim Leite, S.J., *Monumenta Brasiliae*, V, (Rome, 1968), pp. 95-99.
32. *See* F. Lopes, O.F.M., *"Os Fransiscanos no 'Oriente Portugues de 1584 a 1590,"* in *Studia* 9, (Lisbon, 1962), pp. 65-70.
33. See D. I. VII, pp. 440-442; VIII, pp. 142-143.
34. Wicki, *"Zum Humanismus in Portugiesisch-Indien des 16, Jahrhunderts,"* in *Analecta Gregoriana*, 70, (Roma, 1954), pp. 193-246.
35. *See* Silva Rego, *Historia das missoesdo Padroado, India, 1*, pp. 491-494 (Cartinha de Calcadilha); *Epistolae S. Francisci Xaverii*, I, pp. 105-116.
36. *Ethiopia Oriental*, II, (Lisboa, 1891), pp. 281-294. Santos had his work printed in 1608.
37. *Primeir a parte da Historia dos Religiosos da Companhia de Jesus (.....) nos reynos e provincias da India Oriental*, vols. I-III, (Coimbra, 1957-1962), especially III, p. 453 (Joao III) and p. 485 (Sebastiao).
38. *Conquista Espiritual do Oriente*, I, (Lisboa s.a.), pp. 361-365.
39. Ibid., pp. 33-36.
40. Ibid,, pp. 312-319.
41. D. I., V, pp. 554-555, pp. 657-658.
42. Ib'd, IV, p. 9.7
43. *See* Wicki, *O Livro do "Pai dos Cristaos"*, Lisboa, 1969.
44. B. P., I, pp. 131-133.
45. Schurhammer, *Die zeitgenossischen Quellen zur Geschichte Portugiesisch-Asiens und seiner Nachbarlander zur Zeit des hl. Franz Xaver*, (Rome, 1962), No. 450.
46. B. P. I. pp. 180-185; Jann, pp. 104-106.
47. see, for example D. I. VII, p. 441.
48. Ibid., I, pp. 72-73.
49. Ibid, II, p. 127.
50. Ibid., VI, pp. 711-712.
51. Ibid., VII, pp. 182-183; 440-442.
52. Wicki, *O Livro do "Pai dos Cristaos"*, pp. 55-56.
53. Ibid., pp. 57-62.
54. D. I., X, pp. 328-329
55. This is mostly based on the works of the late Fr. G. Schurhammer, S.J., especially his monumental biography in German of the Saint, *Franz Xaver*, Freiburgh. 1963-71, 3 vols.

CHAPTER IV

N B. Much of the bibliography listed under the previous chapter still holds good for this one.
DOCUMETA Indica, Ed. J. Wicki, Rome, 1948-72, 12 vols.

Documentacao   Ultramarina, Lisbon, 1963, 3rd vol.

Baiao A., *A Inquisicao de Goa*, Coimbra-Lisbon, 1939-49, 2 vols.

Beztrand J., *La Mission du Madure*, Paris, 1847-54, 4 vols.

Correia-Afonso J., *Jesuit Letters and Indian History*, Bombay, 1945[1], 1970[2].

Cronin V., *A Pearl to India, The Life of Roberto de Nobili*, London, 1959.

D. Costa A., *The Christianisation of the Goa Islands 1510-64*, Bombay, 1965.

Ferroli D., *The Jesuits in Malabar*, Bangalore, 1939-51, 2 vols.

Id. *The Jesuits in Mysore*, Kozhikode, 1955.

Heras H., *The Conversion Policy of the Jesuits in India*, Bombay, 1933.

Houpert J., *A South Indian Mission. The Madura Catholic Mission* 1535-1936, Trichinopoli, 1937.

Jarric P. du, *Histoire des choses les plus memorables*, Bordeaux-Paris, 1608-14, 3 vols.

Maclagan E., *The Jesuits and the Great Mogul*, London, 1932.

Meersman A., *The Ancient Franciscan Provinces in India 1500-1835* Bangalore, 1971.

Id. 'Catholic Beginnings in Canara Coast', *Indian Ecclesiastical Studies* (Abbrev. *IES*) 1 1962, p. 290-310.

Paulo da Trindade, *Conquista Espiritual do Oriente* (Ed. F. Lopes), Lisbon, 1962-67, 3 vols.

Sousa Fr. de, *Oriente Conquistado*, Lisbon, 1710; Bombay, 1881, 2 vols.

Wicki J., 'Die aetere Katholische Mission in der Begegnung mit Indien', *Saeculum* 6 (1955), p. 345-69.

CHAPTER V

1. Mundadan, A, M., *Sixteenth Century Traditions: Bangalore* 1970, Part II and T. Puthiakunnel, *Syro-Malabar Clergy, Pachalam* (Cochin), 1964.

2. This precisely is the topic studied in my book: *The Arrival of the Portuguese in India and the Thomas Christians under Mar Jacob, 1498-1552*, Bangalore, 1967.

3. No particular book has been published on this period. There is a doctoral thesis on Mar Abraham by C. Thevarmannil submitted to the Gregorian University of Rome in 1965. A good deal of material will also be found in the following books. J. Thaliath *The Synod of Diamper*, Rome, 1958; D. Ferroli, S.J., *The Jesuits in Malabar*, vol. I Bangalore, 1939; G. Beltrami, *La Chiesa Caldea nel secolo dell Unione*, Roma, 1933.

4. Eugene Cardinal Tisserant, *Eastern Christianity in India*, Bombay-Calcutta, 1957, p. 41.

5. Two recent and important studies are: J. Thaliath, op. cit,; G. M. Antao, *De Synodi Diamperitanae Natura atque Decretis*, Goa, 1952. See also my article: 'The Invalidity of the Synod of Diamper', *Indian Church History Review*, vol. I, 1967, p. 9-28.

6. D. Ferroli, op. cit., vol. I and vol. II, Bangalore, 1939 and 1951; There is a doctoral thesis on Stephen Britto, Archbishop of St. Thomas Christians in Malabar by George Vithayathil submitted to the Pontifical Institute of Oriental Studies, Rome, 1971. The books mentioned in the next note are also pertinent to this section.

7. K. P. Werth, s.m., *Das Schisma der Thomas Christen unter Erzbischof Franciskus Garzia*, Limburg, a.d.L., 1937. There is besides a doctoral thesis: *The Troubled Days of Francis Garzia s.j.* submitted to the Gregorian University of Rome by J. Thekkedath s.d.b. in 1970. This is a very important study on this subject. Cf. also E. R. Hambye s.j., 'An Eastern Prelate in India, Mar Aithallah, 1652-53', *Indian Church History Review*, vol. II, 1968, p. 1-5.

CHAPTER VI

Ambrosius a S. Theresa, 'Hierarchia Carmelitana', Analecta *Ordinis Carmelitarum Discalceatorum* 1934, p. 137-56, 272-88; 1935, p. 105-15, 137-53; 1936, p. 74-82, 145-54; 188-205; 1937. p. 12-32, 217-31; 1938, p. 17-37, 142-68; 209-47 1947, p. 86-100.

Cerri U., *Etat present de l'Eglise Romaine*...Amsterdam, 1716.

Clemente da Terzorio, *Le Missione dei Minori Cappucini. VIII, Indie Orientali*, Rome, 1932.

Dubois J.A., *Letters on the State of Christianity in India*, London, 1823.

Ghesquiere Th., *Mathieu de Castro, premier Vicaire apostolique aux Indes*. Lophem (Bruges), 1937.

Jann P.A., *Die katholischen Missionen in Indien. China umd Japan. Ihre Organisation and das portugiesische Patronat von 15 bis ins 18 Jahrhundert*, Paderborn, 1915.

Kowalski N., 'Stand der katholischen Missionen aus der Jahr 1765....'. *Neue Zeitschrift fur Missionswissenschaft* (Abbrev. NZM) 11 (1955). p. 92-104, 179-90; 12 (1956) p. 20-34.

Paulinus a S. Bartholomaeo, *India Orientalis Christiana*, Rome, 1794.

CHAPTER VII

N. B. Some of the items found under Chapters III&IV have been used for writing this one also.

Annuario da Arquidiocese de Goa e das Dioceses suffragenas, 1890, 1893, 1897, 1907, 1933, Nova Goa.

Bertrand J., *Memoires historiques...,* Paris, 18622.

Besse L., *Father Beschi: His Times and His Writings.* Trichinopoly, 1918. Id. *La Mission du Madure,* Trichinopoly; 1914.

Brou A. 'La disparition des Jesuites dans l'Inde apres les decrets de Pombal *'Revue d'Histoire des Missions* 10 (1913 p. 69-78.

Chandler S. S., *The History of the Jesuit Mission of Madura in the 17th and 18h centuries,* Madras, 1909.

D'Sa M. (Ed.), Documents respecting the Concordat of 1886, Bombay, 1908.

Id. *The History of the Diocese of Damaun,* Bombay, 1924.

Dos Santos E., *L'Etat portugais et le probleme missionnaire,* Lisbon, 1964.

Godinho J. *The Padroado of Portugal in the Orient* (1454-1860). Bombay, 1924.

Lourenco A., *Utrum fuerit Schism a Goanum post Breve "Multa Praeclare" usque ad annum 1849,* Goa, 1947.

Seminario Patriarcal de Rachol. Monografia publicada per occasiao do centenario.... Margao, 1935.

Silva S., *History of Christianity in Canara,* Bombay. 1957; 2 vols

Silva Rego A. da, *Les missions portugaises. Apercu general.* Lisbon, 1958.

NOTES

1. Antonio da Silva Rego Le Patronage Portugais de L'Oriet (Lisboa, 1957), p. 243; *The Examiner,* 25 November; 1933.

2. Jose Pires Antunes 'Primeiro Patriarcha das Indias Orientaes' in J.J. Theodore Martin's *Colleccao de Decretos Diocesanos da Archdiocese da Goa* (Nova Goa, 1912), p. xx.

3. John Wilson, Autobiography.

4. Cottineau de Klogen An Historical Skecth of Goa (Bombay, 1922), p. 2 as cited in Amaro Pinto Lobo (ed) *Memoria Historico-eclesiastica da Arquidiocese de Goa* (Nova Goa, 1933), p. 207.

5. Antunes, art. cit., p. xix.

6. Pinto Lobo, op. cit., 207-231.

7. Ibid.

8. Ibid., pp. 244-248.

9. Antunes, art. cit., p. xx.

10. Ibid., pp. xxi-xxx.

11. *The Examiner,* 3 November 1945. This includes progress under Bishop Texcis also.
12. *A Voz de S. Francis Xavier, Obituary* (Special Number).
13. *BEAG,* vol. xii (1953), pp. 64,66,80,81 (Boletim Eclesiastico da Arquidiocese de Goa). This article is on Cardinal Costa Nunes by D. Jose Viera Alvernae, the Patriarch.
14. Ibid., p. 82.
15. Ibid., pp. 96; 1000.
16. Ibid., pp. 65;93.
17. Ibid., p. 65.
18. Ibid., p. 67.
19. Ibid., p. 61.
20 The leading article in the *Goa Times newspaper* in Konkanim of 17 July 1943 confirms this.
21. J.H. Gense *The Church at the Gateway of India* (Bombay, St. Xavier's College, 1960), p. 448ff; Bento de Souza *India's First Cardinal* (Bombay, 1971) as also D.A. Hurn. This is as good as to say that India got her independence from Churchil. It should not be forgotten that Indianisation of the Archdiocese of Bombay is the direct result of the agitation carried on in the *Goa Times* against the administration of Archbishop Roberts. In contradistinction to the struggle for home rule, the Indian Catholic was indifferent to colonialism in the Church, since the prelates were good men as a rule. An impartial historian writing on the history of this period cannot do without consulting the volumes for the years 1943 to 1946 of this newspaper. Another most valuable book, based on the documents from the Bombay Curia, indispensible for the administration of Archbishop Goodier, is *Pelo Clero de Goa* by Fr Niceno de Figueredo. Fr. Gense, who has not consulted this material, vents his venom on Fr H.R. Hull, apparently because, apart from damage done by him inadvertently to the records, this truthful Jesuit tried to give a dispassionate account of the Padroado in his Bombay Mission History starting as Gense does with abusing this great man. there is no need for the present writer to describe the nature of Gense's book. But it does contain some useful information.
22. From the archives of the Archdiocese of Goa through the kind courtesy of Mgr. Rebello, the Apostolic Administrator who, however, is in way concerned with the views expressed by the present writer. The letter is written in Italian and dated from Wellington, Nilgiris.
23. Pinto Lobo, op. cit., p. 233-241.

24. *BEAG*, vol. XII.
25. *The Examiner*, 20 October 1945.
26. Anastasio Gomes, 'O Cardial Costa Nunes e a Missoes da India,' *A Vida*, 21 August 1961.
27. Pinto lobo, op. cit., pp. 233-241.
28. *BEAG*, vol. XII, the speech of the Papal Legate.
29. *The Examiner*, 25 November 1933, Rev. Fr. Roper; S.J.

CHAPTER VII—PART II

1. Antonio da Silva Rego *LePatronage Portugais de L' orient* Lisboa Agencia Geral 1957, pp. 17-18.
2. Ibid., pp. 18-22.
3. Ibid., pp. 26-29.
4. Theodore Ghasquire *Mathieu de Castro* Abbaye Saint Andre 1937, p. 8.
5. L. de Menezes Braganca, 'A educacão e ensino na India Portuguesa' *A India Portuguesa* vol. ii, pp. 18-70. The treatment of monastic education is unfavourable and even unjust. The history of education in Goa under the Portuguese which is a showpiece has to be written again by a scholar with better equipment and a mind unclogged by prejudices. A reaction of this study by Dr. Panduranga S. Varde who has reproduced the prejudices of Menezes Braganza has appeared in instalments in *GOA TODAY*, a monthly periodical published at Panjim, in the course of 1971. For instance Dr. Varde needlessly repeats the charge of Menezes that during the period of educational domination by the Religious Orders of two hundred years (1540-1759) the Goan intellect lay paralysed. In these educational institutions the subjects taught were, admittedly, the same as those taught in similar institutions in Europe and the present writer puts it to Dr. Varde what difference it could have made, e.g. when a theorem was taught by a Jesuit father and by Dr. Varde himself. No system can keep thought cribbed cabined and confined. It must not be forgotten that Voltaire (1694-1778) who has duly acknowledged his debt to his teachers was a Jesuit product just as Menezes Braganca after whom Instituto Vasco da Gama, Panjim, is now known, speaking subject to correction was that of the excellent teaching in the Seminary of Rachol.
6. Ghasquiere, op. cit., p. 9.
7. Ibid., p. 9.
8. Ibid ., p. 34.
9. Ibid., p. 64.

10. Ibid., p. 68.
11. Ibid., pp. 77-79.
12. Ibid., pp. 80-81.
13. Ibid., p. 88.
14. Ibid., p. 90.
15. Ibid., pp. 93-97.
16. Ibid., p. 107.
17. Ibid., p. 108-9.
18. Ibid., p. 114.
19. Silva Rego, op. cit ., pp. 121-22.
20. Ibid., p. 123.
21. Ibid., p. 124.
22. Ibid., pp. 125-42.
23. Ibid., pp. 151-67.
24. Ibid., pp. 174-75.
25. E. R. Hull *Bombay Mission History* Bombay Examiner Press 1927, vol. i, pp. 58-128.
26. Ibid., p. 164.
27. Ibid., pp. 415-20; Silva Rego, op. cit.; pp. 189-90.
28. Ibid., pp. 190-91.
29. Ibid., p. 192.
30. Ibid., p. 192-95.
31. Ibid., p. 195.
32. Ibid., p. 196-98.
33. *Jeevadhara* July-August 1972, p. 369.
34. Silva Rego, op. cit. pp. 201-7.
35. Ibid., pp. 207-8.
36. Silva Rego *Missionologia* (The present writer regrets that he is not able to supply the bibliographical details of this important treatise, having misplaced the bibliographical card. The book is not available in our libraries in Bombay).
37. Silva Rego *Le Patronage Portugais de L'Orient*, pp. 212-17.
38. Ibid., pp. 232-34.
39. Ibid., pp. 243-47.
40. Ibid., pp. 255-59.
41. Ibid., pp. 260-64.
42. J. H. Gense *The Church at the Gateway of India* Bombay St. Xavier's College 1960, pp. 422-24.
43. Ibid., p. 450; David Abner Hurn *Archbishop Roberts* London Darton, Longmann & Todd 1966, p. 46.
44. Ibid., It is clear from Hurn that Roberts did not agree with the vicar general. Did he stop there? The Jesuit rule, above referred to, could be lifted, as Hurn says; 'when there is no effective alternative'. The objection to hand over the archdiocese to the diocesan clergy was, to the

mind of the archbishop, overwhelming. As Hurn puts it, 'he saw the danger of two big changes being made simultaneously. He felt that it should be done in two stages: first an Indian priest should be appointed, a Jesuit; next a secular priest. 'The present writer does not accept *next* etc. the book having been written long after the successes attending the administration of Cardinal Gracias without parallel in the earlier European administrations, thus justifying the challenge of the first Secretary of the propaganda, Francisco Ingoli (1625), that one good Indian could, when given the opportunity, produce better results than a hundred Europeans put together, and also showing the contempt of the archbishop for his clergy at what it is worth. C. M. de Melo *The Recruitment and Formation of the Native Clergy in India.* Lisboa Agencia Geral 1955, pp. 223&226. The archbishop and his biographer were wise after the event. The Indian Jesuit interlude would be fairly long, but the suggestion proved abortive. See Carmo Azevedo, 'Valeriano Gracias, primeiro Bispo Indiano do Bombaim e o primeiro Cardeal da India', *O Heraldo*, 14 April 1971.

45. Bento S. de Souza *India's First Cardinal* Bombay Examiner Press 1971, p. 59. But when, in addition; it is urged that the appointment of Dyer was a further step in Indianisation, it is clear that a condition had been reached akin to a slave kissing his chains.

46 Silva Rego, op. cit., pp. 265-67.

47. Ibid., pp. 267-68.

CHAPTER VIII

Bibliography—*See* the bibliography attached to chapter I, particularly the works of P. Podipara, L. W. Brown and E. Tisserant-Hambye. To these there must be added: Ambrosius a S. Theresia, *Hierarchica Carmelitana, Series IV, De Prassulibus Missionis Malabaricae,* Rome s. a., pp. 183-367.

Giamil S. *Documenta relationum inter S. Sedem Apostolicam et Assyriorum Orientalium vel Chaldaeorum Ecclesiam,* Rome, 1902.

Dominguo de S. Teresa, *Perspectivas Misionales. Los Carmelitas en Malabar* 1656-1956, Victoria, 1959.

Ferroli D., *The Jesuits in Malabar,* vol. 2, Bangalore, 1951.

Pannikar K.M., *Malabar and the Dutch,* Bombay-London. 1932.

Werth K.P., *Das Schisma der Thomaschristen unter Erzbischof Franciskus Gargia,* Limburg a.d.1., 1937.

NOTES

1. There must have then about 200,000 faithful with some 300 priests.

2. J. Kollaparampil, 'Mar Ahatallah in the light of research' (in Malayalam). *Apna Desh* (Kottayam), March-April 1967 (off print p. 17); E.R. Hambye s.j. 'An Eastern Prelate in India—Mar Aithallah 1652-53, *Indian Church History Review* 2 (1968) ρ. 1-6; K. G. Kuriakose Thomas, 'The Koonen Cross' *Bulletin of the Church History Association of India*, Nov. 1966, p. 9-16.

3. According to witnesses interviewed some years later by Sebastiani the Thomas Christians reproached the Archbishop and the Jesuits with disregarding their customs, etc. Archivum Propaganda Fide (abbrev. *A.P.F.*) Scritture Riferite nei Congreg. Gen. v. 232, fol. 105-15.

4. The other Suddist centres were then Kottayam, Kaduthuruthi, Udayamperur and Thuravur.

5. Archbishop Garzia's letter to Pope Alexander VII, 3 Jan. 1659, *A.P.F.*, ibidem, fol. 297 ff.

6. Some 15 priests with the churches of Muttom, Kaduthuruthy, Palai and very few other. According to the same sources not more than, 1,000 people stayed outside the conflict.

7. Papal documents to be found in *Bullarium Patronatus Portugalliae Regum* (abbrev. *B.P.P.R.*) Lisbon, 1868-79, v. II, p. 79-100.

8. BPPR, II, p. 262, in Alexander's letter of 3 March 1674.

9. They were known among the Malayalees under such names as *Paulstakkar, Sampaluppathirmar, Yesuvittanmar*.

10. In 1676 a new group of Carmelites managed to reach Kerala, two of them accompanied by the Maronite priest, Bartholomew Hanna, who was to teach Syriac in the forthcoming seminary; three years later, another two came also.

11. It seems that Matthew was the last archdeacon of Malabar on the Catholic side, P. Podipara, The Thomas Christians, p. 166.

12. *BPPR*. III, 3, 266.

13. On the political and military field, the last years of the 18th cent. were not always happy for the Thomas Christians. The invasion of N. Kerala by Tippu Sultan brought in its wake destructions of villages and churches; no less than 28 Syrian Catholic churches were thus destroyed. Moreover quite a number of Christians including some clergy were either killed or forced to undergo circumcision.

14. He would have been asked by Mar Thomas IV, and his success was due in part to the tensions then existing between the Vicar Apostolic and the Archbishop of Cranganore.

15. Another Chaldean bishop, Yohannan, seems to have come to Kerala in 1747, but the Carmelites managed to send him away, Anquetil du Perron, *Zend-Avesta*, Paris, 1771, p. 162.

16. The number of churches coming under the Vicariate fluctuated, e.g. in 1769: 62; 1773: 72; 1790: 64; 1808: 40,1827 39. It is interesting to note that in 1780 there were in all 77 Syrian Catholic churches, 29 Orthodox, and 4 used by both.

17. He has taken his D.D. there on April 2, 1786.

18. J. Habbi 'L'Unification de la Hierarchie Chaldeenne...' *Parole d'Orient* 2 (1971), p. 131-2.

19. Though written from the Roman viewpoint, the article 'AUDO (Joseph)', of C. Korolevskij in *Dictionaire d'Histoire et de Geographie Ecclestique* (Paris), vol 5 (1931), 317-56. gives much information and insight about 'Audo's policy towards the Malabar question.

20. On this remarkable character of the period, see A.N. Nidhiry, *Father Nidhiry: A History of His Times, Kottayam*, 1971.

21. Msgr. L. Meurin s.j. Vicar Apostolic of Bombay in 1876-77, and Msgr. Ignatius Persico o.f.m. Cap. in 1877 also.

22. Already by a group of seminarians in 1872, then on a more important scale in 1875, and then the momentous petition of Nov. 11, 1885 handed over to the newly appointed Delegate Apostolic, Mgr. Agliardi, during his first visit to Kerala.

23. There had then some 200,000 faithful with about 360 priests.

24. Lavigne was hardly prepared at all to take up a job which was meant to 'preside over the liquidation of the Latin rule'. Hence he did not always see eye to eye with his Indian collaborators, particularly. E. Nidhiri. Having no knowledge of Malayalam he could not enjoy direct relations with his flock. But he had a certain approach to his responsibilities, which often proved to be prophetic, e.g. he strongly favoured the quick development of modern education, the spread of religious life, the uplift of out-castes, etc. He held a synod at Changanacherry in December 1888.

25. Medlycott endeared himself to his flock; not only because ne fought tooth and nail against the Mellusians, but also for the interest he took in the progress of education, and for his historical investigations on the tradition of St. Thomas. He was however almost as unprepared for his task as Lavigne himself.

26. As early as 1659, Propaganda had recommended to Sebasti-

ani to use the teaching of Latin for the Thomas Christian clerics so as to deflect them from their 'rite' and to lead them into the Latin one, *APF? Scritture Riserite nei Congressi Particolari*, v. 213, ff. 29-36.

27. Placidus à S. Joseph, TOCD., *Ritus et Libri Liturgici Syro-Malabarici*, Thevara, 1933.

28. G. Vavanikunnel—J. Madey 'The "Reform" of the Restored Syro Malabar Qurbana', *in the Malabar Church*, Rome, 1970, p. 87-97.
South India', *Unitas* (Rome), 1953, off print p. 17.

29. Placid TOCD., 'The Efforts for Reunion in Malankara,

30. On this remarkable personality *see* J. Kollaparampil, "Mar Dionysios the Great of Malabar for the One True Fold", *Orientalia Christiana Analecta* 30 (1964), p. 148-92.

31. On the personality and role of this priest, who became well-known under his episcopal name, Mar Ivanios, *see*: M. Gibbons, *Mar Ivanios 1882-1953, Archbishop of Trivandrum*, Dublin, 1962; A. Ayrookuzhiel 'The Motives of Mar Ivanios for his reunion with the Catholic Church', *Unitas* 18 (1966), p. 196-211.

32. Mother Edith OMS., "An Ancient Church and new venture of faith in it", *The Christian East* 9 (1928), p. 103-109.

33. T. Chakungal, 'The St. Thomas Christian Denominations of Malabar and the II Vatican Council', *Euntes Docete* 22 (1969) p. 349-74; S. Buckley, 'Ecumenism and its Influence in Kerala', *Eucharist and Priest* (Alwaye) 10 (1964), p. 5-15.

CHAPTER IX

Brown L.W., *The Indian Christians of St. Thomas*, Cambridge, 1956.

Cheriyan P., *The Malabar Christians and the Church Missionary Society 1816-40*, Kottayam, 1935.

Daniel K.N., *A Brief Sketch of the Church of St. Thomas in Malabar*, Kottayam, 1933.

Germann W. *Die Kirche des Thomaschritens, Ein Beitrag zur Geschichte der orientalichen Kirchen*, Gutersloh, 1877.

Ittoop, *The History of the Syrian Church of Malabar* (in Malayalam).

Keay F.E., *A History of the Syrian Church in India*, Madras, 1953.

Mackensie G.T., *Christianity in Travancore*, Trivandrum, 1901.

Mathew C.P. and Thomas M.M., *The Indian Churches of St. Thomas* Delhi, 1967.

Panicker K.M., *Malabar and the Portuguese 1500-1663*, Bombay 1929.

Paret Z.M., *Malankara Nazranikal*, Kottyam, 1965. 3 vols.
   Id.   *Mulanthuruthy Sunnahados.*
Placid of St. Joseph, *The Syrian Church of Malabar, Changana-cherry*, 1938. Rae G.M., *The Syrian Church in India*, London, 1912.
Tisserant Cardinal E., *Eastern Christianity in India*, Calcutta-Bombay, 1957.
Zernov N., *The Christian East*, Madras, 1956.
Manorama Year Book, Kottyam, 1957-61.

NOTES

1. K.M. Panicker, *op. cit.*
2. E. Cardinal Tisserant, *op. cit*, p. 79.
3. G.M. Rae, *op. cit*, p. 270.
4. Ittoop, *op. cit.* p. 123, F.E. Keay, *op. cit.*, p, 49.
5. E.M. Philip, *The Indian Church of St. Thomas*, p. 165.
6. F.E. Keay, *ibid.*, p. 49. He believes that Mar Thomas III lived and ruled for ten years more. There seems to be some confusion in the reckoning of the early number of Mar Thomas prelates. It is not quite sure either that Mar Thomas III and IV were consecrated by Mar Ivanios.
7. Z.M. Paret, *Malankara....* v. 3, p. 10.
8. Some historians are of opinion that Mar Thomas V was consecrated by the surviving foreign prelates. But there are no reliable proofs for such a view.
9. E. Tisserant, *op. cit*, p. 152.
10. P.C. Mathew and M.M. Thomas, *op. cit.*, p. 7.
11. Z.M. Paret, *Mulanthuruthi....*, p. 151.
12. H.R.T. Brandeth, *Episcopi Vagantes and the Anglican Church*, London. 1961, p. 49-52; P. Anson, *Bishops at Large*, London 1964, p. 105-08.
13. The name of the second Catholicos was Givarghese. Hence he was titled 'Basilos Givarghese I', and not Philoxenos Basilios, though as a bishop his name was Philoxenos.

N.B. The author has relied heavily on his own German book entitled: *Die Syrisch-Orthodox Kirche der sud-indischen Thomas Christen*, Wurzburg, 1967.

CHAPTER X

James Hough, *History of Christianity in India*, London, v. 4, 1845 v. 5, 1860.
Sir John Kay, *Christianity in India*, London, 1859.
S.P.G. Two Hundred Years of S.P.G., London, 1901.

Eugene Stock, *History of C.M.S.*, London, 1899, 3 vols.

Julius Richter (Translated by Sydney H. Moore) *A History of Missions in India*, London, 1908.

E.G.E. Hewat, *Vision and Achievement. History of the Foreign Missions of the Churches united in the Church of Scotland*, Edinburgh, 1960.

J. Ferd. Fenger, *History of the Tranquebar Mission.* 2nd. (Bicentenary edition, Madras, 1896. (1st edition c. 1842).

F. Penny, *The Church in Madras*, London, 1904-22, 3 vols.

W.S. Hunt, *The Anglican Church in Travancore and Cochin*, Kottayam, 1920, vol. I,

George Pettitt, *The Tinnevelly Mission of the C.M.S.*, London, 1851.

F.J. McBride, *Sikandra, 1840-1940*, Agra, 1940.

Henry Morris, *Life of Charles Grant*, London, 1804.

S. Pearce Carey, *William Carey, D.D. Fellow of the Linaean Society.* London, 1923.

C.W.Le Bas, *Life of Bishop Middleton*, London, 1831, 2 vols.

John Sargent, *Life and Letters of Henry Martyn*, London, 1862.

Reginald Heber, *Journals* (Edited by his widow) London, 1828, 3 vols.

Memories of the Rt. Rev. Daniel Corrie, compiled by his brothers, London, 1847.

J. Bateman, *Life of the Rt. Rev. Daniel Wilson*, London, 1860, 2 vols.

George Smith, *Life of Alexander Duff., D.D., L.L.D.*, London, 1900.

Mrs. Weitbrecht, *Memoir of John James Weitbrecht*, London 1854.

CHAPTER XI

Monumenta Anastasiana, Ed. A.P. Jann, Lucerne, 1939 pp, 5 vols.

Catholic Directory of India, Madras etc.

Amalorpavadass D.A., *Destinee de l' Englise dans l'Inde d'aujourd'hui*, Paris, 1967.

Id. *L'Inde a la rencontre du Seigneur*, Paris, 1964.

Banerji B., *Begum Samru*, Calcutta, 1925.

Clemente da Terzorio, *Le Missioni dei Minori Cappuccini*, v. 9, Indie Orientali, Rome, 1935.

D. Sa. F., 'The Crisis in the Mission of Chota Nagpur' *IES* 8 (1969), p. 188 ff.

Fulgentius, *Bishop Hartmann*, Allahabad, 1966.2

Houpert J., The Madhura Catholic Mission 1535-1936, Trichinopoli, 1937.

Hull E.R., *Bombay Mission History*, Bombay, 1927-30, 2 vols.
India and its Missions, London, 1923.

Josson H., *Histoire de la Mission du Bengale Occidentale*, Gruges, 1921, 2 vols.

Kierkels L., *The 60th Anniversary of the Catholic Hierarchy in India and Ceylon*, Bangalore, 1941.

Lafrenz J., *Precis d'histoire de la Mission de Pondicherry*, Paris. 1953.

Launay A., *Histoire generale de la Societe de Missions Etrangeres*, Paris, 1894 ff., 3 vols.

Id.   *Histoire des Missions de l'Inde*, Paris, 1898, 5 vols.

Mathias L., Quarant'anni di Missione in India, Turin, 1965, 1 vol.

Meersman A., 'The Franciscans in India from the suppression in 1835 to the present day', *NZM*, 13 (1956), p. 208-16.

Philip, *A Man of God, Archbishop A.M. Benziger*, Trivandrum, 1956.

Plattner F.A. Christian India, London; 1957.

Pothacamury Th., *The Church in Independent India*, Bombay 1961.

Rayanna P., *The Indigenous Religious Congregations of India and Ceylon*. Madura, 1948.

Schmidlin J., *Das gegenwartige Heidenapostolat in fernen Osten, Die Indische Mission*, Munster i.w., 1930.

Rossillon P., *Sous les Palmiers de Coromandel*, Paris, 1926.

Tragella G.B., *Le Missione Estere di Milan* Milan, 1930-62, 3 vols.

Vath A., Die Deutsche Jesuiten in Indien, Regeesburg, 1920.

Waigand J., *Missiones Indiarum Orientalium Sacrae Congregationi de Propaganda Fide Concreditae juxta Visitationem Apostolicam 1859-62*, Budapest, 1940.

CHAPTER XII

1. Julius Richter, *A History of Missions in India*, Edinburgh and London, 1908., p. 201.

2. Humayun Kabir, *The Indian Heritage*, Bombay, 1955. p. 99.

3. Richter, op. cit. p. 207.

4. Muhammed Mohar Ali, *The Bengali reaction to Christian Missionary Activities* 1833-1857, Chittagong, 1965. pp. 201-202.

5. Richter, *op. cit.* p. 233.

6. S. Estborn. *The Church among the Tamils and Telugus*, Nagpur, 1961, pp. 32-33.

7. M.M. Thomas and Richard taylor (eds), Trbial Awakening, Bangalore, 1965, p. 161.

8. *Ibid.* p. 172-173.

9. *Ibid.*

10. *Ibid.* p. 171.

11. G.A. Oddie, 'Indian Christians and the National Congress', 2 (1968) p. 45. *Indian Church History Review.*

12. Tara Chand, *History of the Freedom Movement in India,* New Delhi, 1967, Vol. 2, p. 551.

13. *Harvest Field,* Madras, Third Series, vol. I, March 1890. p. 343.

14. *The Young Men of India,* Calcutta, 19 (1908) p. 190.

15. K.M. Panickar, *The Foundations of New India,* London 1963, p. 52.

16. K. Baago, *A History of the National Christian Council of India 1914-1964,* Nagpur, 1965. p. 38.

17. M.M. Thomas, *Acknowledged Christ of the Indian Renaissance,* Madras, 1970. p. 247.

18. *The Young men of India. Ibid,* pp. 148 ff.

19. *Ibid* 21 (1910) pp. 1-5-

20. *Ibid* 20 (1911) pp. 3-4.

21. K.M. Panikkar, *op. cit.* p. 52.

22. *Ibid.* p. 53.

23. *The Guardian,* Madras, January 11, 1945, p. 12.

24. *Ibid, January* 4, 1945, p. 8.

25. G. Warneck, *Outline of a History of Protestant Missions,* New York, 1906, pp. 11, 284.

26. See Michael Hollis, *Paternalism and the Church,* London, 1962.

27. Macpherson, *Lal Behari Day* Edinburgh, 1900., p. 70 f.

28. K. Baago, 'The First Independence Movement among Indian Christian's *Indian Church History Review,* 1 (1967) p. 66.

29. *The Church in the Mission Field,* Report of the Commission II, World Missionary Conference, 1910, Edinburgh and London, 1910 p. 5.

30. *Harvest Field,* (New Series) 17(1906), p. 59.

31. Alexander Duff, *India and Indian Missions, Edinburgh,* 1839 p. 191.

32. *Ibid* p. 192.

33. K. T. Paul, *Christian Nationalism,* Papers on India, No.3, London 1921, p. 7.

34. Bernard Lucas, The Empire of Christ, London, 1908, p. 114.

35. D. A. Thangasamy, 'Some Trends in Recent Theological Thinking in Madras City', Indian Church History Review 3 (1969), p. 57.

36. Robin Boyd *An Introduction to Indian Christian Theology,* Madras, 1969, p. 67.
37. M.M. Thomas, "Current Theloogy in India," *Religion in Life,* (Nashville 37 1958), No. 2. p. 211.
38. D.A. Thangasamy, *op. cit.* p. 57. 113.
39. *Ibid.*
40. P. T. Thomas, *The Theology of Chakkarai,* Madras, 1968, p. 113.
41. Julius Richter, *op. cit.* p. 434.
42. K. Baago, "The First Independence Movements" *Indian Church History Review,* 1 (1967) p. 78.
43. *Ibid.*
44. D.M. Devasahayam (ed) *Rethinking Christianity in India,* Madras, 1938, p. 157.
45. M.M. Thomas, *Religion in Life,* p. 217.

APPENDIX

KALOUSTIAN S. 'The Armenian Colony in India', Eastern Churches Quarterly, 7 (1947), p. 252-58.

SANJIAN A.K., The Armenian Communities in Syria under Ottoman Domination, Cambridge (Mass.), 1965.

SETH Mesrovb J., Armenians in India from the earliest times to the present day, Calcutta, 1937.

SETIAN N.M., 'Armenia', New Catholic Encyclopedia (New York), v. 1. (1967), p. 825-30.

Tournebize F., 'Armenie', D.H.G.E. (Paris) v. 4 (1930), 290-391.

INDEX OF PERSONS AND PLACES